D1453844

FRANK | RALPH
LLOYD & WALDO
WRIGHT | EMERSON

FRANK | RALPH
LLOYD & WALDO
WRIGHT | EMERSON

TRANSFORMING
THE AMERICAN MIND

AYAD RAHMANI

LOUISIANA STATE UNIVERSITY PRESS | BATON ROUGE

Published with the assistance of the V. Ray Cardozier Fund

Published by Louisiana State University Press
lsupress.org

Manufactured in the United States of America
First printing

DESIGNER: Michelle A. Neustrom
TYPEFACES: Whitman, text; Mostra Nuova, display
PRINTER AND BINDER: Sheridan Books, Inc.

Jacket photograph by Meriç Dağlı on Unsplash.

LIBRARY OF CONGRESS CATALOGING-IN-PUBLICATION DATA

Names: Rahmani, Ayad B., author.
Title: Frank Lloyd Wright and Ralph Waldo Emerson : transforming the American
    mind / Ayad Rahmani.
Description: Baton Rouge : Louisiana State University Press, [2023] | Includes
    bibliographical references and index.
Identifiers: LCCN 2023012363 (print) | LCCN 2023012364 (ebook) |
    ISBN 978-0-8071-7980-2 (cloth) | ISBN 978-0-8071-8094-5 (pdf) | ISBN
    978-0-8071-8093-8 (epub)
Subjects: LCSH: Wright, Frank Lloyd, 1867–1959—Criticism and interpretation.
    | Emerson, Ralph Waldo, 1803–1882—Influence. | Architecture and society—
    United States—History—20th century.
Classification: LCC NA737.W7 R25 2023 (print) | LCC NA737.W7 (ebook) |
    DDC 720.92—dc23/eng/20230411
LC record available at https://lccn.loc.gov/2023012363
LC ebook record available at https://lccn.loc.gov/2023012364

To Rachel, who was with me all along

CONTENTS

ILLUSTRATIONS

PREFACE

For those familiar with the life and work of Frank Lloyd Wright it should come as no surprise that he was prone to tweaking the truth to suit his own version of it. Just as he took great pains to compose the perfect balance between horizontal and vertical lines, mass and void, so he did with the story of his life. It, too, had to reflect a man who was great precisely because he could weather the storm and land upright. What did not fit he either eliminated or modified, in some cases far enough from the truth to appear like total fiction, in others close enough to resemble the actual events. None of this happened without the advice of Ralph Waldo Emerson, the Concord essayist and father of American Unitarianism. More on him and why he is paired with Wright later in the book, but for now it should suffice to say that the sage played a big role in giving the architect license to play cat and mouse with the truth. Life for him was about self-determination and not fate, shaped less by birth and more by the actions we take to create ourselves. In a nation premised on freedom this much should have been possible, including building on moments of genius when they come, and when they do, we owe it to ourselves to abandon family and friends, and indeed the truth, to make sure they see the light of day.

Truth, what is truth? Emerson scoffed. It must conform to Man, not the other way around. "No truth [is] so sublime" that it can outlast the day, he said in "Circles," "but . . . may be trivial tomorrow in the light of new thoughts."[1] Wright took heed, revising the truth when life demanded that he move in reverse and correct the events of yesterday when deemed false by the events of tomorrow. He may have been born with an average mind and a modest physical stature, but that did not matter. Should his later years prove otherwise, and they did, he was going to tell a different story, of a man who was in command of his destiny and capable of great imaginative powers. The future informs the past and not the other way around, determined by will power and perseverance. Genetic composition is inevitable and inescapable, but what is not and what shapes man's character are the choices that man makes moving forward, sometimes so at odds with the beginning it demands a revised biography.

Historians disagreed and insisted on putting Wright straight, often taking special glee in pointing out the architect's manner of playing fast and loose with the truth. There isn't a page in Ada Louise Huxtable's book *Frank Lloyd Wright: A Life* that doesn't cast doubt on Wright's account of his life. Regarding the events leading up to the building of Taliesin, the architect's home and studio in Spring Green, Wisconsin, for instance, she is not sure about Wright's version of the story. The tale is long, but the short of it starts with Wright's mother buying the land on which the masterpiece will eventually sit. Wright had told the story in placid terms, as if his mother had merely bought land in "up country" and hired her son "to build a small house for her." The reality was not that simple but involved dodging society in light of his famous moral transgression back in Chicago, leaving a wife and six children and starting a new life with a different partner. Buying property and building a house on it under his name, far away from the city where he had been practicing and living, would have immediately drawn scrutiny. He needed a sympathetic replacement, and his mother was of course more than happy to be that. "What makes Wright's story suspect," Huxtable writes, "is that the extravagantly sentimental and expensive gesture of buying land at that moment was wholly out of character for this penurious and careful woman" (Wright's mother). Something was off, and Huxtable goes on to square the story by telling us the more likely truth.

Which is no doubt important. But that is not the approach this book takes. It does not condone lies or even half-baked truths, of course, but it does treat them as signs of a mind suspended between two levels of reality. What the first could not supply, the other had to do, and vice versa, making it clear that to understand the architect, the interpreter must study him in that liminal space. It does not matter that Wright often lied about his age, to mention one trivial but well-known example; the fact that he did should give us insight into his need to, say, appear more accomplished than he really was at a certain age. What might that mean and to what extent did the lie shape, say, the scale and speed with which the architect pursued work? We may ask other questions of the man's many other half-truths, which this book will do implicitly, and in so doing insist that in his transgressions lies not the embodiment of a weak soul but a human yearning for a more perfect life.

But to get there this book will have to adopt a special method of analysis, based less on the retrieval of data and more on drawing connections between the various parts of it. In that we may say it is psychoanalytic, carefully peeling away one layer of truth or untruth to get to the next, or, more likely, the conscious to get to unconscious. The first "misrepresents us," the second "represents" us, according to Emerson in the "The Over-Soul": "What we commonly call man, the eating, drinking, planting, counting man, does not, as we know him, represent himself but misrepresent himself."[2] To reverse course and to see matters for what they are, the psychoanalytic critic must dig and go back in time, all the while seeking to reconstruct realities long lost to the march of time. In so doing he or she must connect dots and draw pictures that best resemble the truth being sought. Be the results what they may, what matters is not that they should look like a monkey or a giraffe, but only that they speak to repressed or forgotten desires. Dig deep into Wright's Unity Temple in Chicago, and what we may find is less a place of worship and more a tomb with which to bury, once and for all, all religious dogma. Not only is the steeple gone but so is the direct route to the altar. What had traditionally been clad with either brick or stone, or even wood siding in the case of churches located next to residential neighborhoods, is now dressed in concrete, placing the temple on par with works of engineering such as roads and sidewalks, and less suggestive of divine intervention.

Other forms of deception that deserve psychoanalytic attention include Wright's refusal to credit anyone or anything but himself. Where did this refusal come from, and how did he sustain it? He did credit Emerson, of course, the subject of this book, and Whitman, and of course Louis Sullivan, his Lieber-Meister, but not others who had clearly played a role. Why? The answer is complex, and it will be the aim of this book to unpack it, but for now it might be worthwhile to look for clues in Wright's curious comment about how designs just fell from his sleeve, which may strike us as silly and even arrogant, but stay with it a little and it could yield material critical to better understanding the aim of the architect. Unlike his peers, Wright did not receive a formal education, or at least not for too long, and in the studies he did undertake, he earned little more than average grades. Was he embarrassed by that, indeed ashamed that he couldn't muster the will to stay the course and earn a degree? Was his rejection of precedent a product of his inability to gather and hold within formal grasp the meaning of precedent? There is more than a hint that the answers are "yes" and "yes." Wright repeatedly lambasted higher education even when there was no need to do so, to Princeton students no less, who probably couldn't have cared less that the master architect disdained university life. Even his dear uncle, Jenkin Lloyd Jones, thought him affected and weak-minded, too prone to the sentimental over the rational. And yet there was nothing to be ashamed about; Wright simply had a different approach to learning than the rest, based less on rote memory and codified laws and more on something like meditation, namely years of observing nature, books, and art and letting the accumulated layers lap over him. Indeed, there was nothing to recoil from, and yet still Wright felt the need to drive home the idea that his brilliance was no product of MIT or the École des Beaux-Arts but a place unknown, totally mysterious. "Here it is, John," he would once say to his son in Chicago, as he was working on the Midway Gardens, an indoor-outdoor winter garden of sorts designed to accommodate the city's German community. "Watch it come out of this clean white sheet." Not from his head but from the "clean white sheet," suggesting that the creativity he conjured wasn't premised on academic knowledge but some other invisible source altogether. As his son would recount the event, it took only an hour for Wright to finish the design, at least conceptually: "Within an hour there it was! Low masonry terraces enclosed by promenades, loggias, galleries, orchestra shell and winter garden popped right out of the clean white paper."[3] What a miracle, and one not unlike that which the ancient prophets had exercised to impress upon their audience the magnificence of a higher power. The story was no joke but showcases the consequences of a mind grappling with an inborn incapacity to sit still and learn. Wright simply had no capacity to match in behavior the demands that industrial society leveled on him and others. He had to cope and find an alternative and in doing so ended up building a fiction just to compensate. That this fiction was powerful should not surprise us, not least because it was based on a commitment to triumph over difficult inherent obstacles. It would fuel the creation of such masterpieces as Fallingwater and the Johnson Wax Headquarters, and later the Guggenheim, all analyzed in this book. Indeed, even as we may find in Wright's rejection of influences something unkind, and we should, we may also realize that by doing so he was merely seeking a creative method by which to stand on his own feet.

We may further apply the psychoanalytic method to unpack Wright's subversive relation to Americans and American culture. What were his narrow corridors, low ceilings, and leaky roofs about? Were they merely the consequence of a compositional law Wright imposed on his work, to keep the relation between part and whole intact? As an Emersonian steeped in the principles of unity, it is likely that that was, in part, the case. Which means that when the visual weight of, say, a roof demanded that the windows below be of a certain height, and the doors below that still be of a specific width, he was going to do what it took to achieve that, often stretching the limitation of construction to do so. And yet, as this book will argue and show, there had to be more, not just aesthetic delight, or even spiritual honesty, but downright mental coercion. Americans were not going to change their minds unless pushed and pulled, spatially, in certain directions.

For too long Americans had been told what to do, what style to follow, and what house to buy, denuding their capacity to think for themselves. It was time to change course, and this Wright would induce by setting up an obstacle course of sorts against which Americans must knock to get ahead and ultimately become more self-aware. As one woman described it, the process involved two steps, the first "an anger at any dwelling-place that presumes to dictate how its occupants live," and the second, "a kind of religious submission."[4] She had lived in two of Wright's houses and could speak from a position of experiential authority, adding at one point that "because a Wright house does not allow for many extraneous possessions, it enforces humility." Indeed, "the stripping of accoutrements resulted in a stripping of self or self-hood." Similar comments litter the Wrightian oeuvre, making it clear that despite Wright's authoritarian hand, his work did cause the American public to pay greater attention to the need for a more disciplined approach to consumption.

———

Finally, a word about the integration of Emerson in the book. He does not appear everywhere, at times even disappearing from the narrative completely, seemingly becoming irrelevant to the book and its overarching message. Nothing could be further from the truth. Indeed, not a single sentence was jotted down or imagined without the sage driving its intellectual locomotion. If he does disappear at times, it is only because the book was never meant to be a mirror between the architect and the sage, only a synthesis. Like salt in water, once dissolved, Emerson's words became part of the architect's intellectual and spiritual DNA, hard to trace back to an original source. We may quibble about which Emerson essay contributed most to, say, Wright's Johnson Wax counterintuitive "Lily Pad" columns: was it *Nature* or "The American Scholar"? The answer is, who knows? All of Emerson's work contributed to that design. Wright famously heeded Emerson's advice to read and then forget what you've read and let the intellectual marbles fall where they may.

ACKNOWLEDGMENTS

To embark on a book project is to quickly encounter an ecosystem of scholars, enthusiasts, societies, geographies, and more. In my case this was no different, for no sooner did I write my first email asking for access to information than the network took off and proved itself vast and as far as the eye can see. My first message was to Avery's Manuscript and Special Collection at Columbia University, the custodians of the Wright Archives since 2012–13, seeking access to the collection. On the other end of the email was Jennifer Gray, then the curator of Drawings and Archives at Avery Architectural & Fine Arts Library, who graciously welcomed and processed my request. I wouldn't meet Jennifer in person for almost another year, well after I had finished my research at Columbia, and by accident. I was by then spending a month at Taliesin West in Scottsdale, Arizona, Wright's second home and studio and so many other things. It was February 2020, and I was walking the glorious paths of the campus. The short of the long story is that there she was, talking to two gentlemen from the Wright Foundation. I couldn't help but barge in, introduce myself, and strike a conversation, one that later led to a wonderful friendship and professional relation, including a collaboration that resulted in a contribution to the *Frank Lloyd Wright Quarterly*. It was because of her recommendation that today I sit, along with her and many esteemed individuals, on the Frank Lloyd Wright Conservancy Board. Many thanks to her for getting me started.

I wouldn't have met Gray and other critical contributors to my project without the gracious welcome of the good people at the Wright Foundation, most notably Stuart Graff, the CEO of the Foundation, who upon hearing about my project opened his doors to my scholarship. For a total of two months

I walked, talked, and generally advanced my work at both Taliesins, first East and then West, both glorious and deeply spiritual. Every day I learned and accomplished something new. It was at Taliesin that I started chapter 2 of the book and at Taliesin West where I started and finished the first draft of chapter 4. To Graff and his elegant team of assistants, many thanks.

But I cannot leave the Taliesins without also mentioning few other individuals, equally critical and gracious. First there was Ryan Hewson, the preservationist at Taliesin and a wealth of knowledge on all matters Wright but specifically the history of buildings at Taliesin. What a generous intellect. He was the one who first met me and showed me around, introducing me to the people on-site, including Keiran Murphy, the Wright historian stationed nearby from whom I learned a great deal about Wright and specifically a letter from Wright to his mother that would later prove critical to one key argument in this book.

It was at Taliesin West where I met Indira Berndston and Margo Stipe, two incredible women steeped in the story of Wright and who head the archival department there. During my monthlong residency, I spent a good chunk of it with them, in a room right next to theirs, reading the literature they supplied me with in response to my request for information. To this or that inquiry, they pointed out books, authors, papers, and photographs—always mixed with personal stories about so many experiences with Wright and those who came to play a role in the architect's success. Indira's mother was an apprentice at the Scottsdale site, at one point publishing a book about her experience, which Indira shared and discussed with me. It was in that book that I learned that Wright, as late as the late 1950s, was still asking students to read Emerson well before embarking on putting pencil to paper. What doubt I may have had regarding the longevity of Emerson in Wright's life, as teacher and architect, now nicely dissipated. As we will see in the chapters ahead, Emerson entered Wright's life early on, but the question is, did he stay? Reading the account by Berndston's mother gives us at least a glimpse at the answer.

Stipe needs no introduction. Known to Wright scholars the world over for her own scholarship on the architect and more, she was the voice of confidence, always available to direct my analytical misdirection if necessary. Through her I learned more about Bruce Pfeiffer, the esteemed Wright scholar and onetime student at the Taliesin Fellowship, specifically the way he so beautifully and naturally wrote about his mentor, no doubt fueled by his passion and respect for the older man. I had read Pfeiffer many times before, but Stipe's admiration compelled me to go back and take another look. The man was indeed prolific and poetic in his many reflections about the architect.

Special thanks must go to the Bogliasco Foundation and Fellowship in Italy, about a twenty-minute train ride south of Genoa, where I spent a little more than a month working on the book and, perhaps even more importantly, meeting and sharing notes with eight other incredibly gifted Fellows. The experience was surreal, made all the more so by a confluence of forces: geographic, human, architectural, and so many more. The villa alone in which the Fellowship is housed was magical, simple in plan but exquisitely placed to command gorgeous views of the Ligurian Sea, just underneath and across from the villa. Every day one looked out and saw a different drama being played out, out at sea, between sky and ruffled sea, each day a different combination of whites and blues and sometimes pinks. It was enough to make one want to do nothing but gawk. And if that weren't enough, the villa's garden was a paradise in its own right, filled with exquisite exotic plants. Everything at the villa was meticulously cared for and organized, including food and the manner in which it was prepared and served. But beyond the amazing physical context of the Foundation, it was the community of people, both Fellows and those who managed the Foundation, all intellectually gifted, who made the time there most memorable. I learned from all and will remember all. It was there that I started and finished the first draft of chapter 3.

None of my travels during my one-year sabbatical, 2019–20, would have been possible without the generous financial support of the Center of Arts and Humanities at Washington State University, where I work. A special thank-you must go to Becky James from the Center, who helped me navigate the requirements of the grant, including finding a reader to evaluate my submission and improve my chances. Her vigilance kept me on pace and turned what might have been an anxiety-producing process into one of calm and pleasure.

Writing a book is a nervous endeavor. You write and you write, and you never know if any of it is adding up. Frequently you feel the weight of self-doubt and, with that, the pressure to give up or at least modify the expectations ahead. All of which happened. But the care of a partner kept me going, and even though we are no longer together, she was instrumental in helping me believe in the project and stay the course. She went where I went and read almost everything I wrote in lockstep, always honest and clear about what made sense and what didn't and how to improve. She did her own research around the arguments I was making and took nothing for granted, checking my assertions and holding me accountable for what I said. Regarding the point about slavery in the introduction she was dogged, insisting that I need to say more, dig deeper, and make more sound connections. She was critical but instructive, and because of her, that part of the book, but others as well, are today stronger than they were initially. To her, in fact, I am dedicating this book.

As the book neared completion, I needed a new set of academic eyes. For that I turned to several good colleagues, first and foremost Vikram Prakash, whose friendship and keen intellect helped shepherd the project from the get-go. Even before I had written much, he invited me to share my thoughts about Wright and Emerson on his excellent podcast called *Architecture Talk*. He read my introduction and offered sound and penetrating feedback, steeped in the history and literature of modernism. He insisted that I tell a compelling story and excite the reader to stay on. I cannot thank him enough.

Others like Vikram included Michael Desmond, professor of architecture at Louisiana State University, inarguably the greatest authority on the union between Wright and Emerson. His hunger for a broader conversation on Wright is insatiable, often involving Transcendentalism and Pragmatism. There is very little about Wright that he does not know, and spending even an hour with him is a gift that keeps on giving. Drop a subject and watch it ripple out to touch many others. The book practically doubled in length and complexity after he read my introduction. Many thanks to him for his gracious contributions to my scholarship.

Other brilliant contributors to the book include Katherine Smith, David Hertz, Phil Gruen, Matthew Sutton, and my good friend and former student Amal Kissoondyal, to whom I frequently return for fresh ideas and stimulating conversations.

FRANK | RALPH
LLOYD & WALDO
WRIGHT | EMERSON

INTRODUCTION

Truly speaking, it is not instruction, but provocation, that I can receive
from another soul.

—RALPH WALDO EMERSON, "Address"

Ask Wright scholars about the architect's link to Emerson and all will
recognize it. But ask them to go further and most will hesitate, likely
citing lack of any evidence beyond the anecdotal that the two had
much to do with each other. All will admit to the architect's reading of the
sage, but most will also stop at seeing in that a lasting and meaningful impact. The link is worthy of a footnote, they may say, but a whole book, not
so much. This book argues otherwise, namely that Emerson was more than
a passing interest but a critical contributor to the architect's intellectual maturity. Without him, any understanding of Wright will remain incomplete.

In pairing the two, a different side of Wright emerges, less the architect
of beautiful buildings and more the nationalist daring his fellow Americans
to change. The country had not fared well in the nineteenth century, slowly
but surely sliding from bad to worse. Steinbeck, in *East of Eden*, called it "a
banged-up century," defined by "cheating" and killing and a wealth of other
injustices. It was "a murderous century of riot and secret death, of scrabbling
over public land." For Emerson, the degradation started early, as early as the
presidency of Andrew Jackson, when politics took an ugly turn and became
violent. Things had started well, with Jackson championing the common
man against the corruption of the political aristocracy, famously purging
the government of bad actors. But then came the debacle over the closure of
the Second Bank of the United States, because it favored the wealthy over the
little man and later used deposits to advance electoral politics. The history

is long and complex, but it boils down to a divided nation, including a Whig party formed to curb the policies of the president. Riots occurred, some violent, as in the New York elections of 1834, causing Emerson to take note and train his attention on the American public. As Randall Fuller writes in *Emerson's Ghosts,* the "events especially as they were manifested in two disruptive New York electoral contests avidly followed by Emerson, allowed him to conceive of politics for the first time as a dynamic contest not so much over ideas as over the *verbal representation* of ideas."[1] But even more than electoral politics, what pushed Emerson over the edge was the continued practice of slavery. Here was a nation otherwise proud of its declaration "that all men are created equal" hypocritically demonstrating exactly the opposite as late as the 1830s. Emerson called slavery a "calamity" that must be stamped out, lest it bring the whole nation down. More on Emerson's struggle with slavery later in the introduction.

Wright was equally aghast, not by Black slavery per se but by a nation that by his time had degenerated into a general condition of slave mentality. Particularly troubling was the way Americans seemed resigned to various forms of domination—political and economic—and unable to think and create for themselves, leaving them, as Louis Sullivan pointed out, "devoid of elasticity and cohesion."[2] Slavery was the only title Wright could give to this view of life that not everyone had the same access to freedom as the next, and that indeed some were doomed to follow and suffer the authority of others.

He was not alone. Many lamented similar abuses, including Henry George, the journalist turned economic activist, and Jenkin Lloyd Jones, one of Wright's five maternal uncles. For George, whom Wright read extensively, the danger lay in the final and utter demise of society along economic lines. The two sides were not talking but in combat. "It is as though an immense wedge [had been] forced not underneath society but through society," he said in his classic *Progress and Poverty.* The problem was the meaning and purpose of "progress," less a matter of incremental improvements and more one about advancement at the expense of the economically disenfranchised. "This association of poverty with progress is the great enigma of our times."[3]

Jenkin Lloyd Jones had put matters only slightly differently, warning at one point in one of his sermons that "the sky of our horizon is darkened with portentous clouds." Of which two were particularly troubling, the first as precipitated by "the strife for office," the other as formed by "the great duel between capitalists and laborers, employers and employees." Of the two "clouds," the latter is the "fuller of forked; lightning," its "thunder . . . more startling."[4] Indeed, by the time Wright had come of age in the 1880s, things were pretty badly off, requiring a special corrective to reverse course. Talk alone did not suffice, and something more assertive was needed, something along the lines of assuming the role of a prophet who issues commands but receives none, or asks for none. So far so good, but elevated wisdom alone soon proved insufficient as well, it, too, requiring an aid to make it catch traction. Which Wright would provide by designing an architecture of obstacle courses, so to speak, against which Americans must bang to awaken to certain critical realizations. Be it through his narrow corridors, low ceilings, or incredibly tiny doors, Wright shrink-wrapped architecture around the individual to keep connected the relation between body and mind, movement and consciousness. In a recent tour of one of Wright's homes in central Pennsylvania, one mother of a newborn said in half jest that only a few months ago she couldn't have fit inside this opening, pointing at a bathroom door.[5] Was Wright saying something there, knowing full well that those who would come to live in the house would likely soon have a family? I can't presume to know, but how could he not have, the limitations being quite clear? Left to their devices, Americans weren't likely to remember key cultural principles, often allowing themselves to be swept away by the demands of the day, and rightfully so. They had to be nudged and elbowed. This is in many ways the arc of this book, first, to tell the story of how Wright elevated himself to the level of the prophet and, second, to explain the way his architecture worked as a physical and coercive program with which to change the American mind.

Of the more inflammatory tactics Wright used to draw attention to the crisis of American self-determination, the one that drew a straight line between Black slavery and that experienced by wage earners was probably the most explosive. To be sure, he never drew that line explicitly, but he certainly did implicitly, his rhetoric making that more than clear. Labor freedom, for instance, was a matter of "emancipation," and attachment to employer a form of "bondage," work unfairly compensated an aspect of "slavery," and so on until the two blurred into a singular critique of American culture. What good was the Emancipation Proclamation, in his mind, if in ending Black slavery it also gave way, and indeed license, to new forms of slavery, not a return to racial subordination but to slavery nonetheless in terms of labor right abuses and so on? Did Wright go too far? Many would say yes, and rightfully so, but his sentiments were not without context, including a corporate culture that used civil rights laws against themselves to subvert labor freedoms in favor of economic gain. More on that in chapter 4, where I discuss the implications of work in Broadacre City, one of Wright's more complete experiments in social reform.

Wright's manner of conflating two forms of slavery may have emerged from a lifelong reading of Emerson. The sage, of course, never said one equals the other, but his critiques addressed both, especially in the 1850s, first lambasting the practice of Black slavery and then quickly switching gears and directing the same ire against American intellectual laziness. In the end, Emerson came to view both as evidence of a singular corrupt national mind. It did not take long for Emerson and all those half-awake to realize that between the mind that subjugated the industrial worker and that of those who fed and protected Black slavery there was little or no difference; both were drunk on political and economic gain at the expense of human life and "the pursuit of happiness."

Wright's National Bent

It didn't take long for Wright to fully grasp the promise of America. As a teenager he had experienced it firsthand, returning to land settled by his maternal grandparents and learning life's more central lessons. If it hadn't been for the generous Homestead Act of 1862, which granted those who wished to settle 160 acres for free "provided that they . . . live on and 'improve' their plot by cultivating the land," neither he nor his grandparents would have been able to enjoy the freedom and self-reliance they would eventually cultivate. All was well for a while, but then, and by the late nineteenth century, Wright seemed to happen upon a different realization. The awakening probably matured throughout his teenage years but came to a crescendo somewhere between Spring Green, Wisconsin, and Chicago, in the one year, between 1886 and 1887, when he moved between home, university, and, later, city. This is when he would later lament that despite the fact that "the country was founded upon a more just freedom for the individual than any known before in all the world," it had also squandered that greatness when it "senselessly adopted" the methods of the "feudal money-getting and property holding" despots of capitalism. If it had made possible "a Thomas Jefferson crossing an Alexander Hamilton . . . a John Brown, Emerson, Whitman, Thoreau, a Henry George, Louis Sullivan," it also fostered "indiscriminate private wealth."[6] To the list of great men Wright might have added a list of great women, the likes of Margaret Fuller and Louisa May Alcott, active and persuasive during Emerson's time, and Jane Addams, Aline Barnsdall, and Marion Mahoney during Wright's, the latter contributing a great deal to the maturity and success of the architect's practice. "In them the original ideal was held still clear," Wright added.

Indeed, Wright's awakening to the degradation of the nation matured unusually early, well before he sat down to write his books on the industrial city in the 1930s and 1940s, complaining about its unfortunate social and political practices. And well before he started working for Louis Sullivan, from whom he adopted the rhetorical invective and manner with which to attack the American cultural lag. The two, according to Elaine Hedges in her introduction to Sullivan's *Democracy*, "show striking similarities of thought and style."[7] For no sooner did Wright land in Chicago in 1887, only twenty years old, than he began to lament a world "stewed in terms of money."[8] Sister Carrie had done the same in Theodore Dreiser's novel by that name, also arriving in Chicago from a small town in Wisconsin, at first finding the city fascinating but then overwhelming and unjust. Looking through her eyes, the narrator tells us that she found "the entire metropolitan center possess[ing] a high and mighty air calculated to overawe and abash the common applicant and to make the gulf between poverty and success seem both wide and deep."[9] Carrie lets the city and the nation lap over her, in a way, defeat her. Not so with Wright. He would fight back, and though he would eventually leave Chicago and head back to Spring Green, his rural hometown back in Wisconsin, he would not do so before leaving an indelible critical mark on the city. He may have not been, in his words, a "master of the orchestra," but he was bright-eyed enough to know that he had "to conquer a hardboiled industrial world stewed in terms of money, and persuade and or please idiosyncratic, sometimes aristocratic clients." No change was likely to happen unless people like him had the probing awareness and the tenacity to do something about the matter.

Where and how did Wright acquire the precociousness to tackle cultural and national rumblings at such an early age? His grades out of the University of Wisconsin, where he enrolled for only one year just prior to embarking to Chicago, did not suggest a natural genius but an average kid, no better or worse than the next one. And yet here he was arriving in Chicago at the age of twenty ready to do cultural battle with people twice, three times his age. He does not explicitly tell us about the origins of his anguish but leaves it up to us to connect the dots, of which this book will argue Emerson represents a critical one. In fact, if it weren't for Emerson, it is not certain that Wright would have gathered the zeal to become the national reformer that he did. He may have still become an architect, as good as many others, but an active resister of the status quo, not so sure. The sage's rhetoric had an effect, again and again insisting that he rise and fight the good fight. It may not have added up cognitively, but physically certainly, in a way knocking him down before picking him up and seeing him soar. Between one sentence and the next there is much beauty in Emerson's literature but not necessarily continuity, at times even great contradiction, packing a revelatory punch precisely because the two were a world and a force all unto themselves. Indeed, Emerson often assembled words less to create meaning and more to deliver a blow to the soul of the person reading them. Compare passages from Emerson's journals with those that were published later on, and the exercise will show "just how carefully [Emerson] altered sentences to create a rhythmic pulse designed to compel the reader onward."[10]

Wright's propensity for Emerson was likely triggered by an early exposure to nature, a topic central to the author's philosophical trajectory and the title of one of his first and formative essays. Working on his uncle's farm at the age of eleven back in Spring Green, Wisconsin, Wright had fallen victim to the reverie of the field, often daydreaming of flowers, trees, and anthills. What lessons he needed to learn and grow intellectually were all there, in the underlying patterns of natural form, better than any book or library could supply. "He was soon happy in such knowledge," Wright later tells us of himself in the third person in his *Autobiography:* "As a listening ear, a seeing eye and sensitive touch had been given naturally to him, his spirit was now becoming familiar with this marvelous book of books."[11]

No doubt, then, that by the time his mother and her siblings, all staunch

Unitarians, first handed him Emerson at the age of thirteen or fourteen, if not much earlier, he was already ready to be a devout believer. Add to that the fact that the sage was repeatedly mentioned and discussed in the house, Wright's own but certainly the Lloyd Joneses, and what you get is a kind of worship. Maginel, Wright's sister, confirms this, saying in her book *The Valley of the God-Almighty Joneses* that Emerson was revered and consulted at every step of the way, a man who wrote "books that one's mother, father and uncles were always quoting."[12] Wright seemed particularly enamored by Emerson's "American Scholar," an essay Emerson read to the Phi Beta Kappa Society at Harvard in 1837 and that, among other things, urged the American to emerge "from under . . . the iron lids" of Europe. Years later, in 1951, and now in the company of students at his Fellowship, Wright would use this same remarkable piece of literature to remind his audience of Emerson's importance, saying of the sage that he was "probably one of the greatest minds, if not the greatest mind we have ever had as a people."[13] Wright liked the piece for a number of reasons but more than anything for its tone of rebellion. It reminded him of how far the country had strayed and the degree to which it was the likes of him that had to shoulder the responsibility of bringing it back to order. The country may have started with a meaningful and sincere contribution to freedom, but it has since been "turned over to the military, to the bureaucrat, [and] to the very thing that [people like Emerson] came here to get away from."[14]

The Problem of Imitation

Emerson did not write to simply please or satiate but to call upon his fellow Americans to rise and fight for social and economic justice, for creativity. His concern would start early, at the age of twenty-six, shortly after he had been hired to serve as the junior pastor to the Second Church of Boston. But finding the ministry limiting and yet his talent and voice expansive, he decided to step down from the pulpit. Society was just too broken to reserve his message to the few. "I have sometimes thought that in order to be a good minister," he confessed to his journal in June 1832, "it was necessary to leave the ministry."[15] In his book *Writing beyond Prophecy*, Martin Kevorkian takes a deep dive into Emerson's decision to change course and talk to the American

---

public directly, tracing it to the sermons he gave just prior to his stepping down. In them we see a figure who had become uneasy operating under the powers of established authority, not least Jesus, who, while full of prophetic council, had left him shackled and limited in his capacity to cast an effective net across the American community. Emerson would fess up in a lecture to the Harvard divinity students. "Emerson's 1838 address," Kevorkian tells us, "had emphasized the preacher's station . . . at the distinct expense of Christ, the Scripture and the Church."[16] He goes on to quote Emerson on this note, saying that "men have come to speak of the revelation as somewhat long ago given and done, as if God were dead." So much so that "the injury to faith throttles the preacher." Emerson, it seems, wanted to be his own Jesus, bringing light to an otherwise troubled land, just as the ancient prophet had done almost two thousand years before.

The first to issue from Emerson's pen subsequent to leaving the ministry was the essay mentioned earlier, which to this day remains the first station at which intellectuals stop to parse the cultural importance of nature. And yet *Nature*, published in 1836, is not what it seems, not strictly a celebration of natural bounty—be it bird, river, or meadow—but something far more empirical than that. Nor was it necessarily an indictment of the city as Morton and Lucia White had suggested in their otherwise excellent essay "Intellectual vs the City."[17] Rather, it was a plea to Americans to shed foreign influences in favor of ideas and cultural productions that were and remain indigenous to American culture, "grown out of the daily circumstances of our life," as Wright would add.[18] For too long, America had relied on Europe for solutions, lifting old ready-made motifs and inserting them where needed to satisfy a cultural void. Some expression of taste was better than no expression at all, the thought went, or, worse yet, a clunky one. Wright fumed, calling this cut-and-paste technique a "mask that [had] thus covered and concealed [the nation's] true nature."[19] What a shame and what a squandered opportunity. Why was the nation so quick to surrender creative control to other countries, despite its open invitation to do otherwise? And if imitation was necessary, why not do so using more indigenous themes, such as those by the ancient "Basketmakers" or the "Cliff Dwellers" in the American Southwest, or so John Lloyd Wright suggested, one of Wright's sons. "It is true," he said, "that we are neither Basketmakers nor Cliff Dwellers. But neither are we les

Louis nor the Caesars. If we must use forms of another day, why not those which embodied the solid integrity of America rather than a conglomeration of forms gathered from every other spot on the face of the globe?"[20]

Either way, everyone seemed confused about America's lack of drive for innovation, including Emerson, who added in agreement that "Our hooks and fine arts are imitations." What is sad is that "there is a fatal in-curiosity and disinclination in our educated men to new studies and the interrogation of Nature. We have taste, critical talent, good professors, good commentators, but lack of male energy. What more serious calamity can befall a people than a constitutional dullness and limitation. The moral influence of the intellect is wanting."[21]

The Europeans concurred and often ridiculed the Americans for trying to imitate them. One visitor to the 1876 Philadelphia Centennial Exposition found himself speechless trying to describe the mélange of architectural styles before him. "It would be very difficult," he said, "to describe some of the bizarre effects produced in many of the attempts to decorate certain of the most modern buildings."[22] According to James Gorman, three stylistic imitations seemed to win out: the first emanating from England, the second from France, and the third from Germany. From England, American architects borrowed "the polychromatic picturesque," commonly associated with the work of John Ruskin; from France, "academic classicism of the neo-Grecera" and the Second Empire metallic building by Viollet-le-Duc; and from Germany "Romanesque-inspired arcuated blocks."[23]

Most telling and damning of the surrender to European expressions, however, was the 1893 Columbian World Exposition. In it, the architects made no qualms of the degree to which they had given up on the American promise; not only was it not available, but whatever was there had to be erased in favor of a full look back to Europe, specifically France. The image was unmistakable, a full-on draping of a classical idiom on top of a basic rickety structure underneath, harking to political hierarchies of the past. The effect was theatrical, intended to impress upon an audience, in a short span of time, much like a stage set, the need to cut to the chase and assume a story inverted and different from the one unfolding elsewhere in the American city.

The show worked, evidenced by the way cities across the nation adopted the look of the exposition to fashion their own federal grounds and buildings.

But Wright hated it, not so much on aesthetic merit as on the premise that it threw away three hundred years of American political and cultural development. This was no mere pose but an honest-to-goodness revulsion at giving up the gift of freedom in favor of a facile return to a style that was not only false but flew in the face of basic American checks against political power. The classical was not just another style but one championed, especially in its resurrected mode from the Renaissance onward, by autocrats and royalists, banks and other national institutions.

Nowhere did Wright show his distaste for it more clearly than in his outright rejection of an offer, by Daniel Burnham, the primary author of the 1893 exposition, to send Wright to Paris, all expenses paid, to attend the École des Beaux-Arts and return steeped in its lessons of academic architecture. Burnham had learned of Wright's talents and was confident that he would become the next American architectural star, even more successful than Richardson and Sullivan. In a conversation with Wright, Burnham tells him that while they, Richardson and Sullivan, "are well enough in their way," "architecture is going the other way." You mean the "uncreative way," Wright would famously retort, grateful but clearly unimpressed. "I felt the weight of the occasion," he would later remember. And who wouldn't? Here was one of the giants of modern architecture and urban planning giving Wright a free ride to one of the premier schools of architecture in the world, and yet the latter was hedging. Not easy, and yet Wright persists: "No Mr. Burnham, I can't run away," and finally bringing the gauntlet down: "You see [I can't] run away from what I see as mine, I mean what I see as ours in our country." His decision was final; Wright would stay put.

As kitschy as the Columbian World Exposition was, the plaster and the classicism on display there emerged in an American context. Wright was not the only one who noticed the shallow derivativeness of American architecture; many of his architectural cohorts did as well. And yet, what could be done? The educational choices in the United States were limited, and what was available was based on technical education and more or less advanced in the spirit of apprenticeship. The only alternative to this was the École des Beaux-Arts in Paris, a famously classicistic school steeped in the method of proper proportions and spatial hierarchy. In contrast to "the American situation," tells us Bernard Michael Boyle in an essay on the topic, "where instruction was paltry and standards non-existent," the École des Beaux-Arts "was a model of order, discipline and excellence."[24] More than anything, what the American architectural scene lacked was consistency and historical stability. Everywhere one looked, including just a mile or two from the Chicago's World Exposition, buildings were random and base, each a world unto itself. Seen together, the city looked chaotic and crass. Classicism was the remedy for many, at least temporarily, including for Mario Manieri-Elia, who stipulated in his essay on the "Imperial City" that "classicism meant consistency of building types and thus economy of design and efficiency of production." What may have seemed like cultural capitulation to Wright and Sullivan "was thus an extremely coherent choice and perhaps even a necessary one."[25]

And yet still, why did it have to be that way? Emerson puzzled. "Why should not we have a poetry and a philosophy of insight and not of tradition, and religion by revelation to us and not the history of theirs?" Indeed, "why should we not enjoy an original relation to the universe?"[26] Emerson is wistful but also firm in the belief that not all is lost and that Americans still had the capacity to build an edifice of their own making. It was not so much that America did not have brilliant minds but that those minds were too busy trying to keep up. In giving up agrarian principles in favor of industrial capitalism, the country inevitably became polarized, between rich and poor, owner and owned, and a minority, on the one hand, who had the time to enjoy leisure activities, and a majority, on the other, who did not, and who did everything in their power just to cope. The country was run by "a certain maniacal activity," Emerson posits, "an immense apparatus of cunning machinery which turns out, at last, some Nuremberg toys." And why not, good for the country, but "[did] it also generate, as great interests do, any intellectual power?" What happened? "Where [were] the works of the imagination—the surest test of a national genius?" The sad truth is that they were absent, and what did appear in the market showed "sterility and no genius."[27]

That Emerson was troubled by market forces should probably come as no surprise. Of the "emerging capitalist economy," Cornel West, in his book *The American Evasion of Philosophy*, quotes him as saying that it is "a system of selfishness, . . . of distrust, of concealment of superior keenness, not of giving but of taking advantage."[28] So repulsed by the market, Emerson went so far as to say that "there is nothing more important in the culture of man than to resist the dangers of commerce."[29] Where virtue in the past may have been calibrated in relation to contribution to community, now it was being calculated against a backdrop of monetary accumulation. How much one earned had a greater register than what one thought or cultivated in character. The concern was widespread, shared by, among other groups, an active and angry clergy in the nineteenth century, who argued that "greed and love of material gain [were] threats to public virtue." So was "worldliness," as expressed in terms of "profanity, boastfulness, avarice, pride, declining respect for authority or the Sabbath, loss of public-spiritedness, intemperance, badly behaved children, [and] gambling."[30] God himself seemed to have disappeared from the scene, replaced, as it were, by a wayward secular world. "In our prosperity," said Henry Boardman, a prominent preacher of the time, "we have forgotten our dependence [upon God]."[31]

Slavery

Indeed, big problems persisted but none more pressing and offensive than the practice of slavery. It had been a problem from the outset, before and after the American Revolution, troubling more than a few concerned citizens, including the esteemed and high-minded forefathers of the country. And yet no one seemed able to consummate its end, not until, that is, the Civil War and the Emancipation Proclamation, signed into law by President Abraham Lincoln. George Washington decried it and sounded a sympathetic tone, claiming that "there is not a man living who wishes more sincerely than I do to see a plan adopted for the abolition, of slavery."[32] Jefferson and Madison said something similar, the latter instructing his fellow Americans to care for the "Negroes" and treat them "with all the humanity and kindness consistent with their necessary subordination and work."[33] And yet none legislated against it, all proceeding with the best of intentions but in a way that was spineless and, in the final picture, hypocritical. All enslaved humans, and however humane they may have attempted to be in their treatment of the enslaved, the enslavers nonetheless proved unable to fully emancipate them as people. The majority of the enslaved, of course, never accepted the narrative of the "humane" enslaver but insisted that even when the white enslaver had seen religion, his cruelty continued unabated. "In August, 1832, my master attended a Methodist camp-meeting, held in the Bay-side, Talbot county, and there experienced religion," recounted Frederick Douglass, the most prolific African American writer and intellectual of the nineteenth century. He continued: "I indulged a faint hope that his conversion would lead him to emancipate his slaves, and that, if he did not do this, it would, at any rate, make him more kind and humane. I was disappointed in both these respects. It neither made him to be humane to his slaves, nor to emancipate them."[34]

How could this be, this state of affair surrounding slavery? Emerson wondered. What kind of a country grants freedom to one group of people but denies it to another? Human freedom should be self-evident; if granted to one, it should be granted to all. And if denied, it should be done so on the basis of legal infraction and a society whose functions rest on shared agreements. In the words of the Fourteenth Amendment: "No State shall make or enforce any law which shall abridge the privileges or immunities of citizens of the United States; nor shall any state deprive any person of life, liberty or property, without due process of law; nor deny any to any person within its jurisdiction the equal protection of the laws."

There was no way to describe slavery other than by its true name: a "calamity." "England" may have its problems with "Ireland," Emerson laments in his essay "The Fugitive Slave Law." "Germany [has] its hatred of classes, France its love of gunpowder; Italy its pope; [but] America, the most prosperous country in the Universe, has the greatest calamity in the Universe, negro slavery."[35] "For Emerson," writes Eduardo Cadava in his *Climates of History,* "America's unredeemed sin is the persistence of slavery in a nation that was to be founded on the virtues of freedom, liberty and equality."[36] By the mid-nineteenth century, even slavery's onetime proponents were themselves describing the problem as "a moral cancer that is eating at the vitals of our piety."[37] Henry Adams was even more damning, saying in his *Education of Henry Adams,* that "slavery struck him in the face," that "it was a nightmare; a horror; a crime; the sum of all wickedness."[38]

Of all the missteps by the country, slavery for Emerson was the most egregious, revealing an ugly underbelly which, unless dispelled, could emerge as the country's true colors. Emerson himself did not know where the truth really lay: Was it in a country that despite all the lofty rhetoric to the contrary was at bottom one with high tolerance for hypocrisy and, indeed, evil? Or was the nation actually benevolent but simply had to shake off this one nasty defect? If there was one aspect of slavery that Emerson found important, it was this: it exposed the fact that despite the country's great achievements, America remained a work in progress, indeed problematic. Changing course was necessary, requiring active and visible participation, a liberal conversation about where matters stood. Otherwise, the remedy will likely remain skin deep and a mere patchwork, likely to fizzle out at the next uprising. For too long Americans had lived under the fog of one impression when another was the reality: it was time to draw a mirror and ask new questions. Did old impressions and belief systems regarding American exceptionalism hold water or were they part of a scheme to manipulate American sentiment? The stakes were high and deserved an equally high act of self-understanding. Did Americans even understand the role and purpose of citizenship, namely that it depended on active participation and not merely standing on the sidelines and cheering? "In times like these," Emerson wrote in September 1862, in response to the preliminary version of the Emancipation Proclamation, not only does "the ruler" have "duties" but so does "the citizen": "When a nation is imperiled, what man can, without shame, receive good news from day to day without giving good news of himself? What right has any one to read in the journals tidings of victories, if he has not bought them by his own valor, treasure, personal sacrifice, or by service as good in his own department?"[39]

By the time Wright arrived in Chicago in 1887, slavery had technically ended, the Emancipation Proclamation declaring as much in 1863. Namely that "all persons held as slaves within any State or designated part of a State, the people whereof shall then be in rebellion against the United States, shall be then, thenceforward, and forever free." Emerson was satisfied, if skeptical that he would live long enough to see Lincoln's words survive the test of time. Wright, too, seemed happy, or at least his parents were, given that they gave him "Lincoln" for his second name, which he would later change to "Lloyd," shifting allegiance from father to mother, "Lloyd" being the name that belongs to her Welsh clan. But just because Black people were freed did not mean that slavery actually ended in his mind. It merely morphed and resurrected itself in a different form. Indeed, the slave never went away, according to Wright, but simply took a dip and reemerged in the guise of a different person, now a cog lost in the machinery of the modern industrial complex.

Where before, in a previous agrarian age, Americans may have been full of life and energy, now they were drained of agency, their freedoms usurped by the owners of industry. These were the "overworked women at their stitching," tells us Jenkin Lloyd Jones, Wright's uncle, in the sermon "The Cause of the Toiler." But also "the immature shop girls at their poisonous tasks, unformed boys fitting their plastic bones into relentless machinery—the men, women and children in our sweating shops."[40] The critique is not a mere matter of conjecture but the product of a report "published by a committee appointed at a mass meeting held last May in Bricklayers Hall on the west side." The message is grim, reflecting the miserable conditions under which a typical factory worker in Chicago suffered: "552 Canal Street, Sweater Rozenzweig, employed by J. V Farewel & Co.; work, plush cloaks, tenement house; workroom in a villainous condition; atmosphere simply overpowering; sanitary arrangements bad; persons employed, thirteen men; daily work, fourteen hour wages." In their attempt to keep up, these miserable workers had to compete and in doing so assumed roles and habits that were neither good nor their own. "The more manhood a man has," Wright says in *When Democracy Builds*, the more he is "frustrated by rank mass—life only competing with life at every step. Never completing life." Meaningful work is what this man seeks, but he is sucked into the narrative of "employment" instead, which may sound alright on the surface but which in the big picture is "the bribe that enslaves him."[41]

The switch from Black to industrial slavery was perhaps best understood and illustrated by the novelist Upton Sinclair. If in *Manassas* he dwells on "the slave's attempt to escape from his pursuers in the swamps of Mississippi delta," in *The Jungle* he spends time exposing the harsh and alien conditions under which the modern industrial worker was forced to labor. In a forerunner to the publication of *The Jungle*, Sinclair would describe the novel as one which "will set forth the breaking of human hearts by a system which exploits the labor of men and women for profits. It will shape the popular heart and blow the top off of the industrial tea kettle."[42] Sinclair's focus was the meatpacking industry in Chicago, seeking to expose its dehumanizing and indeed unsanitary conditions for both human and animal. In a review of the novel, Jack London called it the "*Uncle Tom's Cabin* of wage slavery."

As we saw earlier, Wright fused Black slavery with that experienced under industrial capitalism. For a corrective, he looked to the farm, the same place where Black slavery had started, be it on the tobacco fields of the early seventeenth century or later the fields of cotton. Just as the farm had been the source of the problem of slavery, so it would be its solution. Scale was key: rather than the expansive plantation that had demanded extra hours and high rates of picking, the small farm had to guide the revisionary plan. Here animals and people are no longer in separate zones but coexist happily and productively. Homes and farm buildings, too, are modest in size, an assembly of "prefabricated units [including a] shelter for cars, a comfortable dwelling, a greenhouse, a packing and distributing house, silo, stable, and diversified animal shed." Indeed, "the whole arrangement not only would be good to look at but would be practical *emancipation.*"[43] Under these circumstances, work is conducted unself-consciously and without pressure, each activity traceable to sources of tangible needs. Buying and selling aren't detached endeavors, forever corrupted by the need to offload that which has been dumped on the market by overproduction but calibrated against the practical dynamics of living a simple but happy life. No salesmen, whose verbal and visual gymnastics had become "the great modern art," would be required anymore, selling people products they don't need, only a plain-talking farmer.

Wright's small-farm ethic may have had its roots in New Deal programs started in 1933 under the new presidency of Franklin Roosevelt, specifically the Agriculture Adjustment Act, which, among other things, sought, in the words of one author, to "balance supply and demand for farm commodities so that prices would support a decent purchasing power for farmers."[44] Wright was sympathetic to Roosevelt's "vain endeavor" to save the capitalist system, even as he may have also criticized it for being little more than handouts for those who otherwise just sat around "waiting for their own government to feed them."[45] In 1940 and under the continued leadership of Roosevelt, the government would go further in its commitment to rural development, at one point sounding an ideal message almost perfectly aligned with Wright's own. "The U.S. Department of Agriculture," it said, "believes that welfare of agriculture and of the Nation will be promoted by an agricultural land tenure pattern characterized by efficient family-size owner-operated farms, and one of the continuing major objectives of the department will be the establishment and maintenance of such farms as the predominating operating farm unit in the United States."[46] In her insightful piece on Broadacre City, Jennifer Gray argued that Wright's agrarian values have their allegiance less with New Deal policies and more with late nineteenth- and early twentieth-century concerns of the likes of Henry George and Thorsten Veblen. She is right, but in this case, in 1940, and after a few years of New Deal developments, the two seem to have merged. Talk of "land tenure" and "family-size owner-operated farms" by the US government in the 1930s is right out of George's book and what Wright adopted as his solution to the excesses of capitalism.

At any rate, and back to Emerson's contribution to Wright's thoughts, we see Wright attach one of Emerson's essays to the end of his *The Living City*, the last of the three books on Broadacre City, again, the subject of chapter 4 of this book. The essay appeared in Emerson's *Society and Solitude*, published late in the author's life, in 1870, only twelve years before his death. Wright could eliminate or edit nothing in that essay but felt it necessary to include it wholesale, including an important mention of slaves and slavery. Emerson's point there had to do with the freedom of the enslaved; by the time Wright reproduced Emerson's essay in his own publication, he was engaged less with the enslavement of African Americans and more with the general subjugation of one group of people by another. If the employer class had wondered which was better, a controlled and repressed wage earner or a free worker, they needed to look no further than the farmer. In his freedom he willingly and pleasurably works extra hours, driving his body to exhaustion, producing not a generic product but a superior one, meant to accommodate the needs of his community. "If it be true that not by votes of political parties," Emerson tells us, "but by the eternal laws of political economy, slaves are driven out of a slave state as fast as it is surrounded by free states, then the true abolitionist is the farmer, who heedless of laws and constitutions, stands all day in the field investing his labor in the land and making a product with which no forced labor can compete."[47]

Free the workers and see what they can do for you, is the basic message. Give them back their hours, their day and month, and see how through their renewed joy they will produce more than what is expected of them, and willingly. Don't hold them to a schedule, but honor their needs to take a break and think, or care for their children, their family, a garden, and a community. Not every minute and hour have to be controlled and policed, suffocated by demands that have no basis in reason but follow some premeditated mechanical schedule. Some tasks may only require an hour when three have been allotted, or better managed if mixed with other tasks or needs of the day. Release the workers, and you'll be surprised by how much they'll be able to yield in return. To that, Sophia Forster adds: indeed, let them go and see how much they'll learn and give back to society. For Emerson, she says, the freeing of the slave was not only a matter of better production but better creative integration, and in a time when that creativity was needed to tackle some of the more complex issues emerging in society. Whereas for others, like William Channing and his book *Slavery*, the free labor doctrine meant the construction of personal resiliency, for Emerson it signified the rise of a more diverse mind. She writes that in Emerson's two 1837 labor lectures, he "downplays the anxiety created by physical necessity, describing instead an interplay between individuals and the natural world that embodies a rather different version of the free labor doctrine—one in which labor *educates* the individual in creative development rather than stern self discipline."[48]

Discipline mattered for Wright, who often invoked it synonymously with organic anything, but he, too, saw in free labor not only inner fortification but, more importantly, a self-fulfilling creative prophecy, allowing the individual to rise and achieve great feets precisely because it liberated his outlook to do so. He would naturally "increase himself," said Wright, "not merely because he is employed but because his own initiative had been set free to employ himself to greater advantage of other men like himself."[49]

Imitation as a Form of Slavery

Among other acts of slavery, Wright includes those that involve capitulating to style, here today, gone tomorrow. Or, worse yet, fads, formed around the cult of personality and a certain herd mentality. Of those Wright accused of such transgressions was Philip Johnson, the connoisseur of modern art and architecture, who in 1932 had famously given the American but a passing nod in favor of the Europeans in his installation of modern architecture at the Museum of Modern Art in New York. The slight was particularly inaccurate given the fact that in good part it was Wright who breathed new life into European architecture, not the other way around. C. R. Ashbee, one of the leaders of the Arts and Crafts movement in England, agreed. Writing originally in the Wasmuth portfolio, 1910, short for *Ausgeführte Bauten und Entwürfe von Frank Lloyd Wright,* he made it clear that Wright's architecture represented a "new spirit" that "has for us in Europe a peculiar charm and piquancy just because we do not see in it that reflection of European forms to which we have been so long accustomed."[50] To Johnson's famous dismissal of Wright as "the greatest architect of the 19th century," Wright responds immediately, accusing Johnson of a kind of slavery, blindly following the likes of "Mies, Le Corbusier, Gropius, Breuer, et al.," themselves slaves to nineteenth-century theories and aesthetics borrowed from the bridge engineer. "Philip," he says in rebuttal, "at best your own 'slavery' is to the 19th century because those you slave for in Architecture are thus dated—completely."[51]

Wright's criticism of borrowed styles started right off the bat, only a few days after he landed in Chicago and started working for Silsbee. Joseph Lyman Silsbee was well known to the Wright family, or more accurately to the Lloyd Joneses. He had done work for them back in Spring Green—again, Wright's maternal hometown—but also for Wright's uncle, Jenkin Lloyd Jones, in Chicago. Clients sought him for his beautiful hand, framing houses against a backdrop of picturesque settings. He was just as skilled producing genteel compositions in the Victorian style as he was in Queen Anne, always happy to please. He neither fought nor rejected client wishes but simply did his best to oblige and give that person the most principled product he could. To Wright this smacked of selling out to a moneyed class that had no interest in cultivating taste but simply in buying it, much like a consumer may buy a shirt, ready-made. How could this otherwise highly respected architect allow himself to surrender aesthetic creativity in favor of popular taste? Wright called the practice "haberdashery," a service not unlike that of the tailor who helps clients don fashionable clothing and in short time assume a role and a character that otherwise would have taken years to develop. "To the real pioneer," like Silsbee, said Wright, "it was an unfortunate but sadly accepted fact that the commercial machine, owing to its deadly facility, in these United States, would have to find such ready-made architectural clothes to wear for some time." Wright understood Silsbee's ethic, but still stood his ground. Indeed, "never for one moment" did he, speaking of himself in the third person, "doubt in [his] mind that the practical expression concealed by such cheap expedients would slowly emerge to eventually render the expedient not only unnecessary but absurd."[52] Could Silsbee have done better? Wright wondered. "But Cecil, is Silsbee doing the best he can?" Wright whispered to his newly adopted friend and confidant at Silsbee's firm. "I mean could he do better if he would?" The two had emerged from a similar background, both having grown up under preacher fathers who pursued life with a sense of meaning and higher purpose.

Cecil listened patiently but soon got back at Wright with a response they both could appreciate, given their spiritual background. The message is from the Bible, highlighting the role respect plays in navigating relations, in this case between architect and client. Even more important than aesthetic authenticity is the matter of recognizing and honoring hard work. Silsbee may have capitulated to popular taste, but he did so as a matter of respect to those who rose through the ranks through personal and physical self-sacrifice. Those clients deserved what they wanted, even though what they wanted may have been alien to Chicago's history and geographic context. Cecil warned against quick judgment and quoted from the Bible: "Go ye not into the way of the Gentiles! And into any city of the Samaritans, enter yet not. And into whatsoever city or town enter inquire who in it is worthy. And there abide till ye go home."[53]

Abide and do not create a fuss, for you are barking up against the wrong tree, Mr. Wright. Silsbee's clients may not be artists and philosophers, but they are earnest individuals and belong to families who deserve to reap the rewards they worked so hard to sow. "Silsbee is right," said Cecil. He "doesn't interfere with [his clients'] beliefs or upset their ideas of themselves." He simply gives them what others would have given them but simply "better."[54]

Wright would heed Cecil's advice of keeping low and staying wise until it was time to do otherwise and go home. This wouldn't happen for another twenty years, when in 1909 he did indeed pack his bags and leave for Wisconsin via Europe and a short stint back in Chicago. By 1911 he was already building a house and studio for himself in Spring Green at the urging of his mother. In the meantime, and still in Chicago, he would soon leave Silsbee's office and head to Louis Sullivan's, then one of the leading modern firms in the country. There he would learn the tools of the trade but, more importantly, ways with which to keep fueled the locomotion of cultural criticism.

Sullivan was no ordinary figure but a thinker and a designer who never built anything without also engaging in a high level of philosophical inquiry. Indeed, every line he drew he did in a dogged search for truth and the desire to remove veils of deceptions. He was neither "a romancer, nor rosewater critic," he tells us of himself in the third person, but rather a surgeon of sorts keen on "show[ing] [us] realities in all their ugliness and then . . . other realities in all their beauty." High on his agenda was the intent to "dissolve for us this wretched illusion called American architecture," and to "awaken in [us] the reality of a beautiful, a sane, a logical, a human, living art."[55] In Sullivan, Wright found the perfect mentor for his troubled view of America, indeed the confirmation that what he was seeing and feeling was no product of an impulsive young rebel but a problem entrenched in the modern American nation. Over the course of five years the two would spend hours after work talking and debating the content of the issue, often no doubt bringing up Emerson and the Transcendentalists as a backdrop against which to highlight the tenets of their analysis. Both had been steeped in the author, Wright through an upbringing that involved a mother who read the author on regular basis, and Sullivan through an intellectual appetite that looked far and wide for ideas and cultural understanding.[56] Of their exchange, David Hertz in his book *Angels of Reality* says that Sullivan, "a man of ideas . . . clearly discussed Emerson, Whitman, Wagner, Viollet-le-Duc and many other thinkers with his apprentice."[57] Among the many exchanges, the two must have returned to *Nature* again and again, discussed at the outset of this introduction, no doubt unpacking its manner of seeking in man an honest "correspondence" between inner essence and outer form, or, as John Michael Desmond puts in his dissertation on Wright, "between the immediate and the infinite, . . . matter and mind, which confirmed the development toward a natural theology."[58] Both knew that nature didn't mean "horses and cows, streams and storms only,"[59] as Wright never tired of saying later in life, but something much more psychologically active. How does one lift the barriers of civilized pretensions and make the exterior but a direct expression of one's interior nature?

In part, history played a role in the answer, a great thing in one sense but a dangerous influence, in another. Read it, study it—yes, but never let it overwhelm your sense and capacity for the present. Health is far more important, which if well and good would keep the eye and the mind open to and ready for new and ever more penetrating possibilities. "Give me health and a day and I will make the pomp of emperors ridiculous," Emerson says. "The dawn is my Assyria; the sunset and moonrise my Paphos, and unimaginable realms of faerie; broad noon shall be my England of the senses and the understanding; the night shall be my Germany of mystic philosophy and dreams."[60] Nothing is out of range, and everything is within the capacity of the self to transform the world. In one fell swoop Emerson takes thousands of years and thousands of miles and mangles them like a cheap piece of leftover paper. This is dangerous stuff and if not interpreted could lead to a major personal suicide. Imagine the reader hearing that message and rubbing it in the face of those who took years to build a society, telling them that history doesn't matter, their own biographies are of no consequence, as Wright almost did with Silsbee, until Cecil jumped in and saved the day, and now Sullivan, who in all likelihood was teaching the apprentice how to navigate Emerson's message.

Wright would soon run into trouble with Sullivan and have to leave. He had started moonlighting and potentially becoming a liability to the firm. But if the two had to separate physically, they did not, could not, and would not do so intellectually. Wright remained loyal to and respectful of the older architect, always crediting him for the ideas that would later come to play a critical role in his maturity as an architect. Without the Master, it is not sure that Wright would have come up with his Prairie Style homes, produced right after his departure from Sullivan, especially their unity and the degree to which they reflected American aspirations. These were no ordinary residences but equal part tombs, equal part ships, on the one hand, holes in the ground in which to bury past narratives, and, on the other, vessels on which to resurrect the original journeys along with the promise made on them to God and self.

Ships and Pilgrims

Consider the Heurtley House, for instance, only a few doors down from Wright's own Oak Park home and studio, just outside Chicago (fig. 1). Commissioned by Arthur Heurtley, a respected banker and lover of art, it sits unusually distant from the lot line, a whopping twenty-five feet instead of the more common ten or fifteen. The separation "could easily have been avoided had

---

FIG. 1. The Heurtley House, Oak Park, Illinois, 1902. Note the expansive lawn in front and the prow-shaped low wall at the entrance to the house on the left. Photograph courtesy of Mark Hertzberg.

Wright chosen to do so," tells us Grant Hildebrand in his study of Wright's architecture. But of course he did not. He intended that separation, not for recreational and gardening purposes but, instead, to help him replay the transatlantic journey narrative, setting up Heurtley as the pilgrim on whose shoulders the future of a nation lay. Making that association clear is the "prow-like" low wall at the outset of the house, remarkably like a ship, designed so that those who approach the house must go around before entering it.[61] Inside, and in the belly of the ship as it were, the spaces are dark, dank, and much like a "cave," to use a word Vincent Scully, the late eminent Yale historian, used to describe the interior. They need a fire to warm them up, which Wright promptly provides on the second floor of the house through a magnificent fireplace. Not just any fireplace but one whose design and extent immediately suggest a meaning well beyond warmth. It suggests ritual and a use of fire that speaks to notions of purification, redemption, and renewal. This is not your ordinary opening in the wall but one graced with a brick arch the size of a small temple, reminiscent of the early structures of ancient Rome. The theme had already been popularized by the Transcendentalist giants the likes of Hawthorne, Melville, and Whitman, all protégés of Emerson, who frequently saw in fire the power to induce reverie and transform a deviant mind. Of the fire that burned in the "Old Manse," a house of historic significance that Hawthorne occupied for some time, Hawthorne tells us that it had a "mighty spirit," which, not unlike a human, could "wrap its inmates in [its] terrible embrace, and leave nothing of them save their whitened bones." Fires can destroy, about which Wright knew one or two things, but they can also reveal "domestic kindness the more beautiful and touching," precisely because they extinguish past oppressions in favor of new hope.

In ships Wright saw the basis of American architecture, accommodating the functional needs of an emerging industrial society but more importantly serving as the reminder to Americans of the journeys that brought them here in the first place and through which they were able to find and enjoy freedom. More than symbol and form, these vessels also signified islands of independence, detached from either past or future and on which passengers could cultivate whatever identity they wished to chart. To be on them was to possess the license to forget and assemble one's own truths, indeed, to re-invent reality. This is what Emerson imparted, and this is what Wright will wish on himself and others, breaking almost every rule in the book to do so, at times inverting gravity and playing games with common perceptions of physics and the universe.

In effect, Emerson was asking Wright to be a poet and to see in every object the possibility of a new age, regardless of the degree to which it was poetic or not. Wright struggled with the machine but ultimately heeded Emerson's words, penning an essay that would reconcile to it beauty and agency. "The Arts and Crafts of the Machine" was only in one sense a matter of accepting technology; more so it was a call to insist that, through poetry, the machine can be the source of creative visions. First officially presented to the public at the Hull House in Chicago in 1901, Jane Addams's hub for social and cultural reform,[62] the essay does not mention Emerson but, rather, others who swirled around the sage, before and after, most notably the English poet Percy Bysshe Shelley. Of him, Emerson wrote that while he may lack the imagination of a bard, he is "a good English scholar with ear, taste and memory; much more, he is a character full of noble and prophetic traits."[63] Wright uses him to advocate for an approach to the machine not unlike Michelangelo's approach to the mallet and the chisel, namely "to free" the human figure from inside the marble block. Let the machine liberate us, not stifle us. Let us sit behind it as poets creating useful and practical tools for sure, but also objects whose practical and aesthetic prospects we hardly knew until we sat and began exploring. The poet doesn't create by planning ahead but by maintaining a pulse with the world. He cannot say, "I will compose poetry," Wright quotes Shelley saying about him, "for the mind in creation is as a fading coal which some invisible influence, like an inconstant wind awakens to transitory brightness."[64] Even as the machine may demand that we respond in kind, like machines, the poet will insist on a response through dream and imagination, shuffling established orders to inspire new realities. For Emerson the problem lay in the way we had come to understand the world in siloed terms, the flower as flower, the mill as mill, but never one as the other. Things were either left or right but not a blend of the two. "Readers of poetry see the factory-village and the railway, and fancy that the poetry of the landscape is broken up by these," he laments in "The Poet." Why should that be? Wouldn't we be better off to "see them fall within the great order not less than the beehive or the spider's geometrical web"?[65] Of course we would. Only that way would we be able to consume the world creatively and every day invent a new one out of the old. No reality is too stubborn for the poet to transform into one more beneficial than the one previous, so long we are able to transcend limiting boundaries.

Emerson, for Wright, was not a source of intellectual advertisement. He did not drop his name to show off or in any way push literature on colleagues and clients. He, in fact, talked more about Walt Whitman than he did about Emerson, often using the poet's words to give an event a reflective mood. More so, he recalled Emerson much like a devout person may recall a prayer, to imbue an occasion with spiritual meaning and protect it from falling victim to commercial valuations. Nowhere was this more the case than in the first decade of the twentieth century, when Wright seemed unsure about his own work and life, both potentially succumbing to market pressures. He was still in Chicago and already the author of a few masterpieces such as the Heurtley House, already mentioned, but also the Robie House and Unity Temple. "This absorbing, consuming phase of my experience as an architect ended about 1909," he said in his autobiography. "Weary, I was losing grip on my work and even my interest in it."[66] He needed guidance, and Emerson would come to his rescue, counseling him to "insist on yourself and never imitate." To do otherwise would be to give in to "society everywhere . . . in conspiracy against the manhood of every one of its members." Better to be a "nonconformist" who "can and must detach [him]self." Don't be afraid of trying new ideas, Emerson insisted, or developing new encounters. And certainly don't succumb to a singular professional path in life. Pursue multiple paths and see what happens: "A lad from New Hampshire or Vermont, who in turn tries all the professions, who *teams it, farms it,* peddles, keeps school, preaches, edits a newspaper, goes to Congress, buys a township, and so forth, in successive years, and always like a cat falls on his feet, is worth a hundred of these city dolls."[67] Throughout "Self-Reliance," Emerson urged Wright to do what was in his heart, even if that meant doing so at the expense of others. Which may sound cold but which belonged to a philosophy that stipulated caring for oneself first before one can genuinely care for others. If done authentically, this seemingly selfish pursuit will yield good results later on. Indeed, if done with purity of heart, "your genuine action will explain itself and will explain your other genuine actions."[68]

Wright had fallen in love with a client's wife by then, Mamah Cheney, and wanted nothing more than to pursue a new life with her. His marriage had happened way too early, and through it six children had been born, overwhelming for any parent, let alone one whose eyes and hand and every other thing about the man were always in ten different places at the same time. He wanted out in the worse way possible, and heeding Emerson's words, he abandoned family, friends, and colleagues. He would head to Europe for about two years, spending part of that time with his newfound partner, away from the prying, moralistic eyes back in Chicago.

Whether he knew he would return to Spring Green when he left Chicago is unsure, but that is where he ended up in 1911, at the urging of his mother. Much as his parents, Anna and William Wright, had made their own U-turn back to Wisconsin from Boston more than twenty years earlier, so, too, would he do the same after his trip to Europe. And just as his parents had been called back by the likes of Emerson, to return to the country so they could nurture and develop an independent identity, he, too, would make the same trek based on the same premise. They, the parents, had come "back to the ancestral Valley from the East, by way of Sister Anna and her 'preacher,' the 'Unitarianism' worked out in the transcendentalism of the sentimental group at Concord: Whittier, Lowell, Longfellow, yes, and Emerson too."[69] Wright's mother had grown weary of her husband's vocation as a preacher and of a congregation that was difficult to deal with, a "hard-shell godliness of the provincial Baptist and the consequent consecration of meanness," which "probably made every donation party, an argument for going back home— out west."[70] For someone who was "accustomed to the free stride of her life in the country," that kind of stubbornness was probably too much to take.

It was in Spring Green that Wright would build Taliesin, his future iconic home and studio, named after the sixth-century Welsh bard. It was from here that he would pick up where he left off as a kid, returning to Emerson to re-build his vows to man and nation. Some saw the move as an expression of hatred for the city and immediately pounced on the architect and declared him antiurban. Nothing could be further from the truth; as Neil Levine has shown in his work on the topic, Wright remained interested in the city throughout his life.[71] If he retreated from it, it was only to strike a more objective perspective than would otherwise be possible. Much as we may step back from a picture to obtain a more comprehensive understanding of it, he did the same to cut out the noise and see the beast for what it was. Between city and country there was no tension for Wright, only self-reciprocating forces critical to the integrity of the American mind. "It is easy in the world to live after the world's opinion," Emerson had told him in "Self-Reliance," "it is easy in solitude to live after our own; but the great man is he who in the midst of the crowd keeps with perfect sweetness the independence of solitude."[72] Just because Wright migrated three hours north of Chicago, deep into "the heart of the heart of the country," to quote the name of a story by William Gass, did not mean he had left Chicago. In reality, he carried it with him and sought to care for it better that way. Indeed, he would return to it as early as 1914, only five years after he left it, when he was called to design the Midway Gardens. The city needed the perennial return of rural people like Wright who, having been flushed clean of urban conflict, can give back thoughtfully and objectively. Many indeed had committed the architect to the country wrongfully, including Lewis Mumford, the midcentury critic at large and a dear friend of Wright. In one written response to the architect, and perhaps in frustration, he would describe their relation as being characterized by a separation between the love of city and that of the country. The twain shall not meet: "I am a product of the city, who has learned to like and to live in the country, whereas you are a product of the country who has never really found much for himself in the city." But no sooner did Mumford utter those words than he retracted them, realizing that he had made a mistake: "But that is too simple," he said, in effect, to himself.[73]

For many years Wright went back and forth between city and country and in each established a semblance and a memory of the other. In New York and while monitoring work on the Guggenheim, he famously stayed at the Plaza Hotel, arranging and rearranging his room and generally sustaining his independence from the crowd, as Emerson had advised. "He loved the opulent old hotel, even though he had completely altered his suite," Maginel, Wright's sister, writes at the outset of her book *The Valley of the God-Almighty Joneses* and in memory of a visit she paid her brother while at the hotel: "The walls and cornices were golden, the curtains a rich wine color, and the functional furniture which he had designed was covered in shades of maroon and plum and purple."[74] Back in Spring Green, the same held true but in the opposite direction, living out a country life but once in a while carving out the time and space to turn that environment into an urban party. Wright never missed a chance to invite friends and colleagues to come join him and while there enjoy music, theater, literary readings, good food and drink. Some friends, like Mies, showed up, but others, like Mumford, never did. Wright and Mumford had built a deep friendship over the years, and Mumford's refusal to make the trip deeply disappointed the architect. A common farewell to Mumford often ended on a note of hope that the writer would come see him: "I hope you are well as you looked the last time I saw you, and mean to come with your wife and child to us and ours—someday this spring."[75] So high was Wright's respect for Mumford, rare for a man who seldom credited anyone, he paid him the highest compliment he knew. He compared him to Emerson, saying to a mutual friend of theirs that "he is the nearest mind to Emerson that we possess and the mind most likely to interpret to our country its own neglected ideals."[76]

On Education

Of the more influential topics that Emerson imparted to Wright, education is arguably the most profound. It would surface again and again throughout the architect's career, and every time, it seemed, he was talking to a group of college students. As it stood by his time and in Emerson's before, education had mortgaged the mind to a cadre of experts and global voices. Forgotten was local traction and the fact that students could walk, talk, and play—indeed, turn things with their hands and learn as they went. Worse yet was the fact that in accommodating the demands of the industrial complex, education had become its mirror image, matching in lockstep its rhythms, pace, and delivery methods. Like a machine, all it did was record, store, and spit out information. The problem was worthy of protest, and Emerson would speak up. "We are students of words," he laments in his "New England Reformers": "We are shut up in schools and colleges and relations-rooms, for ten or fifteen years, and come out at last with a bag of wind, a memory of words, and do not know a thing. We cannot use our hands, or our legs or our eyes or our arms. We do not know an edible root in the woods, we cannot tell our course by the stars, nor the hour of the day by the sun."[77]

A much better approach to education must start on the farm, tending the fields, animals, and all the operations associated with cultivating, seeding, and harvesting. Learning would be less the product of abstract thought and structured curricula and more one of relevant responses to real and tangible problems. Wright was steeped in this early on when his mother sent him to work on his uncle James's farm, famously "adding tired to tired," milking cows, shucking corn, cleaning the barn, and much more. It was here where he would observe and appreciate the beauty and unity of art and science, not as two disciplines but as one, tightly woven around a web of self-reciprocating endorsements, critically played out in color, proportion, and balance. Flowers were just as important as machinery, helping the young student understand the order and meaning of the universe. Speaking of himself in the third person, Wright said in his autobiography, that it was "in these adventures alone—abroad in the wooded hills fetch[ing] cows . . . that he learned to know the woods, from the trees above to the shrubs below and the grass beneath." But also "the millions of curious lives living hidden in the surface of the ground, among the roots, stems and mold." It was here, too, that he would soon find himself "happy in such knowledge." He was "a listening ear, a seeing eye and a sensitive touch." The farm was his "book of books, experienced as the only true reading, the book of Creation."[78]

Any other lab would do more harm than good, limiting the capacity of the young mind to develop accurate and commensurate cognitive relation with the world. Universities were dangerous and monstrous places, steeped in the art of cultivating in the mind clever and artificial arguments but seldom the acumen to see in the problem the solution itself. Teaching with precedent might seem fine at face value, but upon further scrutiny it can and often does leave the student captive to foreign and inconsequential ideals. "Four, or six, or ten years the pupil is parsing Greek and Latin," said Emerson, "and as soon as he leaves the university, as it is ludicrously styled, he shuts those books for the last time."[79] Even Princeton couldn't foot the right bill. Lecturing there at one point, Wright couldn't help but tell his audience that they would be better off without the university and on their own, not out of lack of respect or appreciation for Princeton but simply out of a deep conviction that beyond a certain level of high school education, institutional education was counterproductive. He starts, "I have the same nostalgic love for Princeton as for the great founders of our republic." And yet, "I believe that were all education above the high school level suspended for ten years, humanity would get a better chance to be what humanitarian Princeton itself could wish it to be."[80]

Wright could afford to speak from confidence, not least because by 1947, the year of his Princeton lecture, he had already started a school back at Taliesin and knew what he was talking about. For fifteen years and since 1932 he had been running an education based on apprenticeship and rural values, mixing the high-minded with the vocational, balancing learning obtained from books with that gained from fixing a toilet and chopping firewood. What was elevated by philosophy and literature was inevitably and unselfconsciously informed by knowledge that any high school kid should know to keep a place functional, warm, and comfortable. The Taliesin Fellowship, the name Wright gave his school, may have started as a reaction to the economic crash of 1929, trying to stay busy and lucrative, but it soon evolved into an indictment and a manifesto against existing education. First and foremost, its aim was to fight rote memory and ideology and develop in the individual a whole human. "Taliesin," said Wright in his first promotional circular, "aims to develop a well-correlated human being, [currently] lacking in modern education."[81] Nothing was too low or too high for him—all work was honorable if it served the betterment of both self and community. To Wright, no "shovel, hoe, or axe" was too menial to carry and use but, rather, the means with which to develop a keen understanding of the relationship between us and the things we rely on to create a world, indeed, to sustain a living. These were also tools with which to build camaraderie and a healthy system of reliabilities. What one student dug with a shovel, the next cut with an axe, until together the good society was formed. Gone are "the drawing board architects," as Wright called the university-educated students of architecture; replaced, as it were, by apprentices whose "daily bread" was not a metaphor for hard work but the result of several daily tasks requiring manual labor. Each was part of a bigger whole, organically lending a hand knowing that another will be lent back in return. Back and forth until a beehive of sorts became the modus operandi of the place. In that, Wright was following a long lineage of educational theories that started with Emerson but carried forth through William James and John Dewey, all espousing a version of learning by doing, or, more accurately, learning by entering into projects whose completion is predicated on good and vital collaboration. "The same Emerson who said that 'society is everywhere in conspiracy against its member,' also said and in the same essay 'accept the place the divine providence has found for you, the society of your contemporaries, the connection of events.'" This was Dewey quoting Emerson making a U-turn and realizing that even as he was warning the individual against a scheming society, he was also letting him or her know that the path to a meaningful life lies in active connections. "Now," Dewey continues, "when events are taken in disconnection and considered apart from the interactions due to the selecting individual they conspire against individuality."[82] As seductive as it is to think that individuality and isolation are synonymous, the truth is otherwise.

Of the tasks expected from the apprentices at Taliesin, the building and maintaining of structures was the hardest. These were serious and arduous endeavors, requiring careful attention to issues of safety and precision. How to lift a beam or erect a wall was more than a matter of creating space but, rather, an important lesson in mutual reliance. Miss a beat and you risk bringing the whole house down, potentially hurting people. You simply couldn't operate selfishly in scenarios like these; instead, you must work in lockstep with others. Nor could you operate without first understanding scale and proportion; namely, for every problem there is an equal and appropriate tool and method. You don't apply the same tool to steel as you do to wood, nor do you ask the same number of men to lift a chair as you would to lift a roof. Each deserves a commensurate response. Each also adds to the making of a better character, including the capacity for sympathy and empathy.

The Primacy of Character

A central aim of Unitarianism is the integrity of character. See the issue through Emerson and Wright and what you get is a particular focus on the American character. Even more important to them than character was the American character, bolstered and stiffened by a good dose of self-reliance, nurtured and developed by a unique access to land, farm, and expansive views. Nothing Wright designed was for the commission or the income alone; more importantly, he worked to awaken in Americans the realization that this was the case. Be it because of a modern world that had pulled them apart or otherwise, Americans by the late nineteenth century had surrendered all attempts at understanding who they were. To his mind, nothing short of the American project was at stake. To save it, major sacrifices were required, and Wright would exhort his audience to do just that, audibly in talks and speeches, on the one hand, and silently through architecture and furniture and the like, on the other. Not unlike the early Puritans whose jeremiads to the pilgrims had made it clear that they must either do or die, obey God or face eternal damnation, so his exhortations were similarly dire. "If ye deale falsely with our god," said one early Puritan, "in this worke wee have undertaken and soe cause him to withdrawe his present help from us, wee shall be made a story and a by-word through the world."[83] Or like George Whitefield in the age of the Great Awakening in the 1740s, whose words were particularly laced with talk about depravity. For Whitefield, man was doomed, and what hope he had resided solely in his ability to restrain himself and live a pious life. Wright didn't necessarily talk about depravity, but he did about discipline and principle, all in one way or another pretexts to living a life of regulated behavior. As the chapters in this book will show, Wright gave and offered the world much in beauty but always with a keen element of restraint, keeping the ceiling low, the chair precarious, the corridors narrow. Grace in living was important, but so was the reminder that man was insignificant in the context of bigger and more universal values. One without the other could not lead to anything but abuse, of privilege, power, and position. The revelations of the early religious leaders throughout the seventeenth and eighteenth centuries were unforgiving, often leaving man no option or middle ground on which to operate. They needed to be tampered with and reintroduced, especially in the wake of an American Revolution that had decidedly transitioned the country from a religious state into a secular one. Religious sentiment remained, of course, but it had to be transformed into a language that could appeal to a more practical and political American than before, now busy trying to reconcile the industrial functions of the day with those needed to keep those functions spiritually upright.

Emerson and his special brand of Unitarianism, blending Christianity and German idealism, answered the call. Trained at the Harvard Divinity School, a strictly Unitarian program, he preached the revelation that God lies in all of us and all we have to do is dig down and retrieve him, through hard work but, more importantly, through an expansive and immersive contemplation of nature. Wright drank deeply of all of it, finding in the sage a voice particularly powerful precisely because it was at once practical and deeply learned. It was high-minded but never ideological. It pointed, analyzed, and urged but always left it to the reader to find his or her own path to enlightenment. Don't take me at my word, Emerson insisted about himself, develop your own, not least because at times he hardly knew where he was going. "But lest I should mislead any when I have my own head and obey my whims, let me remind the reader that I am only an experimenter," he said in one of his more representative essays. "Do not set the least value on what I do, or the least discredit on what I do not, as if I pretended to settle anything as true of false. I unsettle all things. No facts are to me sacred; none are profane."[84] Wright understood and assumed the reins accordingly, perennially circling back to the sage and consulting with him on proper action.

This book is less an examination of a specific link between Wright and Emerson and more a look at Emerson as a tool with which to open a new discourse on Wright. It treats Emerson as a kind of portal Wright often opened to gain insight into the American project, including ways to correct those aspects of it that had been derailed or damaged. It seeks to connect dots between literature and architecture, words said by the sage and designs imagined and conceived by the architect, some finding expressions in real buildings, others remaining on paper. Sometimes the line of influence between the two is clear and self-evident, marked by direct references and statements. Other times not so much, requiring an interpretive journey in and around Wright's intellectual and artistic orbit.

The first chapter looks at the notion of the prophet and Wright's decision at one point to stand back and assume that role. Society had grown unruly, culturally destroyed by a time and a capitalist system that left it either too poor or too rich and in either case unable to calibrate a proper relationship with art. The poor were too saddled with life's basic needs, the rich too arrogant to wait for culture to mature and acquire authenticity specific to place and people. "We have had to have architecture and have it quick," Wright lamented in a piece in which he interviews himself as a prophet.[85] "What was there to do but to take architecture from the books at the plan factory—that is take it ready made." Something like a prophet was needed to get everyone on board again, listen and obey without reproach. It needed a Jesus, whose name and influence Wright mentioned repeatedly, a figure who understood the lay of the land and could command a corrective with authority. Or an Emerson, a Thoreau, or a Whitman, all of whom Wright followed and who, in the words of Richard Chase, "spoke out as prophets, in the most inclusive language, delineating America and its democratic spirit, describing and exhorting the American and Man in general, speaking in the accents of homily and denunciation rather than of systematic argument."[86] We might also include Taliesin, the sixth-century Welsh bard, after whose name Wright titled his home and studio and later the Fellowship in Spring Green, Wisconsin. Taliesin comes from a time in Welsh history when poets were considered seers and prophets imparting wisdom and beauty to those with whom they came in contact, but particularly rulers and other members of the aristocratic class. In the words of Scott Gartner, bards "were panegyric poets and singers, . . . interpreters of omens."[87] In aligning his creation with Taliesin the bard, Wright made it clear that architecture should assume "a visionary, prophetic role."[88] At any rate, the call for change was urgent and needed immediate action. It needed a prophet. "To wait until "time gives a cleaner perspective etc." [is] to wait too long," not least because to do so would allow "each succeeding generation [to drift] further away from the time that gave its project birth." As much as Wright may have wished to trust public discourse, among and between the people, that kind of democratic exchange was too slow and too prone to corrupt acts of sabotage. "Democracy such as ours," Wright uttered again in frustration, "prefers to divide and subdivide individual honor, so that it may be passed around a sufficiently wide circle before it would let it live."[89] Better to work hard and rise, triumph and achieve a place above the fray, one from which Wright could speak without rebuttal. His father was a preacher and so was Emerson's, and both used that station to first talk to a small congregation and then to a much larger crowd, Emerson, as we saw earlier, making a special point of doing so. This was, it seemed, for the architect the only way to save the nation. It was not for nothing that when it came to assigning a leader to his Broadacre City, he chose an architect like himself to guide it, planning and organizing the lay of the land from above, an eye in the sky, much like a prophet.

Prophets need acts of miracle to captivate and awe their audience, to demonstrate that what they bring to the table is not a matter of hard work, or even sincerity, but one associated with inborn capacities to transcend normal reach. They can defy the laws of physics and make objects hover as if in midair. Chapter 2 looks at the sublime as an instrument by which Wright did exactly that, throughout his work but notably in commissions such as Fallingwater, the Johnson Wax Headquarters, and the Mile High, the latter a tower he proposed but never built for Chicago. In these he pushed engineering to the brink of collapse, often engaging in counterintuitive thinking to challenge common wisdom about how things work and stand. "The typical methods of calculations" couldn't apply here, said Jaroslav Polívka of Wright's work, Wright's structural engineer and a professor of engineering at UC Berkley in the 1940s and 1950s.[90] Who can forget Wright's challenge to the engineers of the "Lily Pad" column at the Johnson Wax Headquarters? There the numbers did not support Wright's design, famously putting the column on its head and inverting its logic, wider at the top and narrower at the bottom. The look alone suggested danger, and yet Wright insisted. And sure enough, the on-site demonstration, famously of sand bags being piled up until the column would finally give way, proved him right. As it turned out, the column he designed was capable of supporting five times the weight approved by structural calculations. Elsewhere, Wright sought special engineers, notably Jaroslav Polívka again, whose expertise in photoelastic stress analysis was instrumental in helping the architect achieve daring ends, including the gallery ramp at the Guggenheim. "Another revolutionary design by F. L. Wright," said Polívka of the Guggenheim in awe, "required three models and about 5,000 accurate measurements to determine the real stresses in the future structure."[91] The sublime is at once a special condition and an intellectual instrument, on the one hand, the product of an impasse between the familiar and the strange, and, on the other, a rhetorical tool used to explain life's most inexplicable encounters. It dates back to the second century BC but finds restoration in the eighteenth century under the brilliant minds of the likes of Edmund Burke and Immanuel Kant. This chapter will rely on it to discuss Wright's penchant for structural provocations and, more specifically, his manner of pushing gravity to push the American to triumph over cultural complacency.

Along with sublime transformations of the mind, another is necessary, and it belongs to the eye. Without a new eye there is little hope that the American will imagine again and produce authentic results. Indeed, a new ocular regime is required, made possible through a spatial choreography involving turns and returns and generally a relation with the horizon that releases in the individual a wealth of visual connections, previously held back by restricted environments. Emerson's "transparent eyeball," a term found in his *Nature,* introduces chapter 3, urging us to find places that restore in us the capacity to see reality in the round, unedited and without judgment. Over the years, and through the rational project of the late eighteenth century and the nineteenth, we learned to admit only a limited alchemy of acceptable and not so acceptable realities, to the point where today we do so almost unconsciously. So much is missed in the process, including special relations with place, people, and the environment. Among other things, the issue gave birth to the continuous window but also the corner window in Wright's hands, fewer compositional tools, and more elements with which to admit unedited encounters with the world around.

Windows were critical, but to fully consummate the ocular renovation that Wright had in mind, a different and much bigger portal had to be opened, at the scale of the city and over the span of at least four square miles. Indeed, the old industrial city had become too congested, restricting light and views and with them the American's own access to self-confidence and the capacity for innovation. Tall buildings, train stations, big factories—all had to come down in favor of low-lying buildings, more or less at the scale of the barn and the farmhouse, and run by those same agrarian values. Fields and orchards instead of asphalt roads and concrete plazas describe the lay of the land, including its ethic and schedule. Occasionally, the tall building may rise and be seen from a distance, but never to the extent of blocking air, sun, or view from reaching their natural destination. So passionate was Wright about this openness that he sent his audience up into the sky to see it, in helicopter-like rides, obtaining panoramic views of all that lay below. This was the premise of Broadacre City, to fight the urban jungle and restore to the eye the ability to see far and wide, replenishing much-needed spiritual and creative fuel. Chapter 4 starts there but inevitably soon thereafter enters into discussions about social, economic, and gender equity or lack thereof. In broadening our scope of vision, Wright also brought to light the need to broaden our analysis of cities, inevitably demanding that we see them less as objects of consumption and more as networks of life systems. Instead of lot lines and property values, land here is defined by principles associated with common acreage, shared and cultivated by a community. Parking lots, shopping centers, office buildings, and more—are all cleared in favor of a look and a proposal that prioritizes soil chemistry. "Tillage" is the word that Wright uses to express it, rendering before us a picture of a place healthy and happy precisely because it heaves with the ground on which it sits, not in struggle with it. This was the time of the Great Depression and the Dust Bowl, both spelling out misery for many and requiring immediate reaction. The focus on the soil, for instance, was in large part an attempt by Wright to bring to the attention of the country the bad tilling practices that caused the Dust Bowl problem in the first place, namely recent machinery that had dug up the soil too deep and ruined its capacity to retain water. Interestingly, all of this comes into view in Emerson's essay "Farming," which Wright adds verbatim to the end of his *Living City*, his manifesto on Broadacre, foregrounding his thinking against that of the author and making it clear the degree to which his ideas have their basis in the author's writing. This chapter will use that essay to weave disparate threads spanning subjects as diverse as vision, economic reform, and social and educational equity.

Having zoomed out and seen the remedy to the industrial city through Wright's agrarian lens, the book zooms back in and focuses on his furniture. In engineering a new ocular regime, Wright had in part relied on furniture, using it as an obstacle course and a magnet with which to push and pull at the body and, in effect, steer it in a certain direction. Wright's main concern was not only the creation of an eye that could see new objects but one that has the ability to perennially renew what it sees. The challenge required a special choreography between body and space, interior and exterior, and generally paths that could bring Americans face-to-face with encounters that naturally and unself-consciously flushed out old images in favor of new ones. Left to their devices, Americans would likely flit and randomly ricochet from place to place, unaware of their capacity for poetic invention. Better to guide and remind them of the vistas open to them and through which they could restore their powers of revelation. The path couldn't be easily altered, otherwise Americans would easily do so, given their penchant for cutting corners and striking a more direct link between A and B. It had to be firm and fundamentally rooted to the ground. What furniture was going to help shape this path had to be heavy or, better yet, built-in, immobile, and one with the architecture to which it was attached.

At the Guggenheim, Wright continued his struggle with the American mind, but this time he relied less on obstacle courses and more on physics, or what he called the "science of continuity." Be it because of the age, namely the 1940s and 1950s, and the rise and role of nuclear power, or something else, Wright at this time in life became deeply interested in the capacity of science to solve man's great problems. He hadn't necessarily been so earlier, but given the ending of World War II, he seemed to change his mind. Atomic energy fascinated him particularly, not least because it embodied the poetic capacity for incremental change and exponential power. But also the fact that it was predicated on recent shifts in gravity, famously set into motion by a diverse group of European physicists at the turn of the twentieth century, of whom Einstein is the most representative and better known to us. In all, they added a new chapter to the discourse on gravity, not so much ending the

---

Newtonian version of it as much as discovering a new angle on it. As it turns out, gravity exerts not only a pull between two objects, say, the sun and the earth, keeping things in check, but a push as well. Bring two objects close enough and they will repel, causing energy to excite, indeed, life to happen. This is how Brian Greene explains the origins of the universe, an "entropic two-step" process that involves an overheated attraction followed by a repulsion and massive explosion.[92] In good part, the new gravity was predicated, among other experiments, on taking a rigid disc and rotating it at high speed, pushing the circumference out and causing it to alter in length. For those who have taken the spin ride at an amusement park, the impact is quite well known. The ride is characterized by a cylindrical object into which the thrill seekers step and stand along its outer walls. Underway and spun at high speed, they find themselves plastered against the wall, hung in space independent of leg or body support. The thrill is enormous, predicated in large part on turning gravity 90 degrees and making it push outward.

The change in material deformations between vertical and horizontal gravities is imperceptible and of little or no consequence to most daily activities. But at the molecular level the story is different, yielding critical data about the properties of atoms. This is not the place to examine the dynamics of nuclear physics; only suffice it to say that Wright found in it the fuel he needed to continue his probe into the American character but also the genre of art he was asked to accommodate at the Guggenheim. Both called for a suspension of gravity of sorts, lifting the burdens of reality just so that the inner core of the human can reveal itself. A collection of shapes and lines, each hanging as if in midair and seemingly in a cloud of dust, nonobjective art, the art that Wright was asked to design for and accommodate, sought to diffuse allegiance to either ground or context. Nothing here is recognizable as anything, either animal, flower, or man. Distances too are scrambled, near and far losing their qualitative meaning on the canvas. For no sooner do shapes and lines expand and shrink and suggest spatial hierarchy than an equal provision of the same emerge and cancel what had begun to foment.

For so long and especially since the onset of the modern rational project, man, and in this case, the Americans, had been pressured to live by standards and protocols that, while important to civil discourse, were not theirs and that over time eroded their self-understanding. Americans had by midcentury become a ghost of themselves, hardly familiar with who they were or what they stood for. So radical was the problem that it required an examination and a retrieval tool independent of rational discourse. Reason had proven important but also manipulative and capable of swaying opinion in ways that were deceptive and counterproductive. Better to aim for the inside of the person, independent of intellectual intervention, at the atomic level, revealing in him or her just as their biology and genetic structure may tell us we should. Much like the thrill seekers plastered against the walls of the spin ride, who find pleasure less because they had anything to do with the operation but because they let physics do the work, so is the intended method here. Whatever the Guggenheim was going to be, it had to set Americans aside in favor of a direct and objective view of their core.

It is not for nothing, then, that Wright decided to turn the Guggenheim's final spiral on its head. He had started with it right side up but then turned it the other way around, wider at the top and narrower at the bottom, not so much to defy gravity as to rotate it sideways and, in releasing it, also to release in man his inner truths, independent of his best attempts to explain himself. Man does not represent himself, but misrepresents himself, Emerson had said in "The Over-Soul," and it is here where we see Wright fully embracing the statement and using architecture to correct the misalignment. Through spinning and spiraling down the ramp, Wright would in effect play a version of Einstein's own experiment with the rigid disc, restoring to Americans their capacity to represent themselves all over again.

And so the book ends on this note, the last chapter making clear the extent to which Wright was willing to remain diverse and flexible in his approach to restoring to Americans the promise of the great American project. As opposed to science as he was earlier in life, he would come around to seeing in it the capacity for spiritual and intellectual salvation. As time went by and new ideas and new technologies evolved, so did his method for changing the American mind, with Emerson always by his side to steer him in the right direction.

1

OF PROPHETS, HEROES & POETS

> In the presence and conversation of a true poet, teeming with images
> to express his enlarging thought, his person, his form, grows larger to
> our fascinated eyes. And thus begins that deification which all nations
> have made of their heroes in every kind—saints, poets, lawgivers, and
> warriors.
>
> —R. W. EMERSON, *Poetry and Imagination*

Just as Emerson stepped down from the pulpit to address a nation directly in 1832, so, later in the century, would Wright do the equivalent in architecture to transform the American mind. As a preacher of Sunday sermons, Emerson felt limited in his capacity to reach a wide audience, indeed, shackled in a way that seemed irresponsible. The country was coming apart at the seams, split by the divisive policies of the time, but also, in the words of Richard Hofstadter, "by a nation growing at a speed that defied control, [and] governed by an ineffective leadership, impatient with authority, bedeviled by its internal heterogeneity."[1] It was well and good to invoke the words of Jesus inside the church, but difficult matters elsewhere demanded that a more contemporary prophet rise and march the streets, spreading wisdom far and wide. Emerson felt he could be that person, a Jesus in his own right who could command communities across the board to lead a certain life, believe in themselves, and cultivate original thought. His decision may have been triggered in no small part by an envy of the ancient Christian prophet himself, whose word effortlessly washed over the flock and changed the course of evil forever. Or so does Martin Kevorkian state in *Writing beyond Prophecy*.

He speaks of the "Emersonian envy" as "the hatred of superiority," namely that "Jesus's superiority to other teachers is that his words are effectual: they have power."[2] Why couldn't he, Emerson, possess those same words and that same power? He had, after all, felt the same moral degradation as Jesus had, including the urgency to mobilize the self to effect change. The moment was nigh, and it needed immediate action.

The rest, as they say, was history, with Emerson embarking on a campaign to reform the American cultural landscape. He would travel wide and take every opportunity to write and speak, using revelatory words and driving passion to impress upon his crowd the urgency of their taking personal responsibility and improving the nation. In those moments he soared on high and spoke as if miles aboveground, urging those below to abandon ties to family, history, and all that may hold them down in favor of a free and independent mind. "Why should we assume the faults of our friend, or wife, or father, or child," he asked rhetorically in "Self-Reliance." Is it just "because they sit around our hearth, or are said to have the same blood?" No, "[we] must be by [our]selves."

It was not long after he arrived in Chicago that Wright decided to embark on his own prophetic project, to accomplish more or less through architecture what Emerson had done through literature. He, too, would step down from his own equivalent "pulpit" and seek to address a nation, first when he emerged from under the tutelage of the grand figure of Louis Sullivan, and then again, almost twenty years later, when he left Chicago to return to his maternal land in Spring Green, Wisconsin. As we saw in the introduction to this work, it did not take him long to realize that the city and, indeed, the entire country had been stewed in commercial interests, its people indifferent to their inability to distinguish the fake from the real. The problem seemed too big for piecemeal critical efforts and needed a command of biblical proportion. Luckily, Wright had already been propped up to think along those lines, not least by Emerson himself but also by a mother who was determined to see her son become a great architect, if not the greatest, a prophet in his own right.

The project would demand some clever manipulation of time and space, including when and how to abandon family and friends, city and country, as Emerson had advocated, in favor of ascension that would allow him to speak with authority and without recourse. The effort would bear fruit, and having become a prophet, Wright would go on to act with impunity, designing and insisting on a kind of architecture that would heroically transform the built environment. But architecture alone would soon prove piecemeal in its own right, too distributed to allow for a concentrated and permanent change in the American character. Something different had to happen to enter the blood of the American mainstream. Emerson spoke of consciousness and the need to alter the very apparatus by which the American becomes aware of the world. "Ours," he said "is the Revolutionary age, when man is coming back to consciousness."[3] By which he also meant that to do so, to "come back to consciousness," Americans also needed to flush out the old and prepare the self for new receptions. They needed to become poets whose power and virtue lay in the possession of an eye and a mind capable of perpetually stamping out the old and replacing it with the new. "For a full expression of such an age," F. O. Matthiessen would say of Emerson in his magisterial *American Renaissance,* "what was needed most was a great *reflective* poet."[4] And yet how does one become a poet? More than training, the matter required a place and a built environment with which to bring about a new ocular regime, which would allow individuals to see the world perpetually in a new way. Every time individuals open their eyes, they must do so as if for the first time. As we will see later and by way of an oedipal interpretation, Wright does this by returning to the womb, psychoanalytically speaking, to that place when the eye had yet to open, and birth is at once the birth of a person but more so in this case the birth of an idea. The journey is remarkable and circuitous, defined, as it were, by a mother who, in wanting an architect for a son, had rejected and buried the father well before he had actually died. But first things first; let us start with Wright's manner of heeding Emerson's words and turning himself into a prophet and a hero.

The Construction of the Hero and the Prophet

It took Odysseus twenty years to get back home, the first ten fighting in the Trojan War and another ten returning. The journey was riddled by all sorts of human and nonhuman obstacles—jealousies, petty concerns, and difficult geographic terrains. It involved men but also women, all vying for a piece of the king's body and mind. Odysseus's story is that of a hero who, in becoming so, has to leave, engage in acts of self-sacrifice, and return home. He follows Joseph Campbell's three-step process of heroic construction: separation, initiation, and return. "The standard path of the mythological adventure of the hero," Campbell tells us, "is a magnification of the formula represented in the rites of passage: separation-initiation-return: which might be named the nuclear unit of the monomyth."[5] The separation starts with a call to adventure, which could come in the form of an accident or something a little more dramatic and intentional. In the case of Odysseus, a brush with the gods set it into motion, specifically Poseidon, whose son Polyphemus Odysseus had blinded as he fought against being captured. It didn't matter that Odysseus didn't know that Polyphemus was the son of Poseidon; the deed had already been done when the news got out that the one-eyed monster was badly hurt and would likely die. Interestingly, to get away, Odysseus had used Polyphemus's own physical powers to set sail and do so quickly. Odysseus had so angered Polyphemus that the latter had started hurling big rocks at Odysseus's ship, each one bigger than the next, and each falling short of the ship but sending it farther away from shore.

For the next few years Odysseus bobs between one island and the next, searching for a way to return home to Ithaca, at one point spending seven years on the island of Ogygia captive to the nymph Calypso, who promises him infinite pleasures and the incredible offer of immortality. Each step seems just as needless as the one before, but in reality each is critical to self-improvement and to the king's ultimate resolve to find home. Does he possess the metal to weather the storm, triumph over difficulties? As one fictional description of his mood tells us, the answer is yes, however riddled the journey may be. He may have hit rock bottom at that point, but he knows he will rise again. The words of a mentor help, "heard . . . thirty years before." And they go like this: "If ever you seek Priam's City, the wide waters will swallow you. For the time it takes a baby to become a man, you will know no home. Then, when friends and fortune have departed from you, you will rise again from the dead."[6]

In that period of hardship and downright depression, he will know what he wants from life, his family, friends, community. He knows he loves his wife and wants nothing but a restoration of their relations. He also knows

---

that to regain her and his kingdom he will need to get back home and fight pesky suitors, now accumulating at his door, or more accurately his court-yard, eager to claim his wife's hand in marriage. The suitors want him dead so they can achieve their end. Word of this had reached him, and he is indeed angry. Not unlike an athlete who has to undergo arduous training, including putting body and mind through the wringer just to compete in a race, so Odysseus has to climb mountains just to reclaim his name on the throne. These are all acts of initiation central to his return and demonstration of heroism, the ability to take on powers bigger than himself, build mental and physical muscle, and save humanity or, at least in his case, family.

Heroes are just as much a product of fate as they are of earthly construct. To become a hero, one must come to the table knowing that he or she pos-sesses special gifts, some assigned by the gods and some by earthly beings. Odysseus was well cared for by both mother and Athena, women of formi-dable strength, and Frank Lloyd Wright by Anna Lloyd Wright, a mother endowed with the powers of birth and sustenance. "*Emanations*," Campbell again tells us, "treats of the coming of the forms of the universe out of the void." Indeed, it is the mother who gives form to life, transforming nothing into something. Having experienced the making of a life inside her, it is in her power to endow that miracle with a force of its own. "The Virgin birth," Campbell continues, "is a review of the creative and redemptive roles of the female power, first on a cosmic scale as the mother of the universe, then again on the human plane as the mother of the hero."[7]

Wright's mother did not merely raise and protect the son but nurtured him on the belief that he was possessed with a certain prophetic gift, ar-riving on earth as if blown by wind on a stormy night. At least that's how Wright relayed the image to Olgivanna, his third and final wife. "He told me," she remembers, "that he had made his entrance into the world on a stormy night . . . as though he had witnessed the prophetic initiation."[8] The story, of course, could have only been precipitated in Wright's mind as a result of his mother's telling it to him, as naturally she was the only one able to authenti-cate such a remarkable scene. Fiction or otherwise, what is interesting about it is the fact that the mother believed it and went on to fashion an identity commensurate to it. Whether or not Wright actually arrived already pos-sessed with special gifts, what mattered was the determination on her part to render him as a miracle, even Jesus-like, and, just like Jesus, without a father but only a mother. The mention of Jesus, incidentally, is no matter of hyperbole but real in the sense that it was to that prophet, second only to Laotze, that Wright would go to speak of his devotion to purity and higher ground. "The greatest philosophic inspiration in my life," he once told an audience in 1953, "next to Jesus was Laotze of Tibet."[9]

Wright may have had a father, but given the latter's restless and less than adequate approach to fatherhood, he might as well not have had one. Biographies of Wright render the father as a brilliant musician and minister but also one who neglected his duties as a provider and nurturer. He moved the family from town to town looking for greener pastures and was personable enough that people took to him quickly. He was charismatic and authentic, and his character shone clearly from the outset. "And yet no sooner had he arrived and conquered than he would mysteriously depart, sometimes within the year."[10] At any rate, more on the oedipal relationship between mother and son later, but for now and for all practical purposes, Anna raised her son alone, almost defiantly against all odds, just to make it clear that her son was no ordinary conception but an immaculate one, a "truth against the world."[11] The son went along and drank in the narrative, changing his middle name from Lincoln, a name and a president highly admired by the father, to Lloyd, reflecting his mother's Welsh heritage.

"The virgin birth," it is worth repeating Campbell, "is a review of the creative and redemptive roles of the female power, first on a cosmic scale as the mother of the universe, then again on the human plane as the mother of the hero." With the father removed and out of the way, the mother could now fashion the son according to specifications as deemed suitable and indeed necessary for global and national awakening. As explained in the introduction, by the late nineteenth century, America had grown and matured but in ways that left many confused, if not lost and demoralized. "During the second half of the nineteenth century," the introduction to a book on the Gilded Age starts, "the United States experienced one of the most remarkable periods of economic growth in all history."[12] The bounty was in part the result of vigorous and speedy industrialization, evidenced by the increased production of pig iron. Between 1850 and 1900, its output "rose from 631,000 tons to 15.4 million."[13] The country was humming but unfortunately not for everyone and often at the expense of the little man: "Most ominous of all [worries], to many thoughtful observers, was the threat to democratic institutions posed by a society in which an ever wider economic gap separated rich from poor, capitalist from worker."[14] If there ever was a time and a need for a hero and a savior around whom the world and a nation could rally, this was it.

But the "immaculate conception" narrative needed intellectual and psychological support; otherwise, it could backfire and bury both mother and child under a pile of judgments and ridicule. It would come in three essential forms: first, through feeding the child a steady diet of literature and philosophy; second, through a summer spent working on a farm; and last but not least, through exposure to the Froebel Blocks, better known as the Froebel Gifts, named after their inventor and educator, Friedrich Wilhelm August Fröbel. These were not so much three different forms of educational strategies as three strings in a single braid, and just like a braid, they were strong precisely because they wove a complementary and mutually self-supporting set of values.

From the first, Wright learned about Plato, Shakespeare, and, most critically for our study, Emerson, the latter repeatedly invoked by "mother and father, aunts and uncles" as Maginel, Wright's sister, would tell us, to gain insights into "the plastic power of the human eye," and to see in "the sky, the mountain, the tree, the animal . . . a delight in and for themselves."[15] At fourteen Wright picked up Emerson to get a firsthand picture of the author. "The American Scholar," one of Emerson's more representative essays, caught his attention, matching in fervor and message those of the household in which he grew up, especially his mother's invocations. In the essay Emerson compels the American to be a scholar, to study books, to read history, indeed, to find education but also at one point to turn around and forget all that and create: "Whatever talents may be, if the man creates not, the pure efflux of the Deity is not his—cinders and smoke there may be, but not yet flame."[16] Emerson's aim is to call upon the likes of Wright to train their focus on becoming great by becoming active. Of the "genius," he says that he "looks forward: [his] eyes . . . set in his forehead, not in his hindhead." "Man hopes: genius creates." And then again about the hero, this time talking about the importance of action: "Inaction is cowardice, but there can be no scholar without the heroic mind."[17] Genius, hero and poet—all three amalgamate into a feature, half God half human, ready to uplift that which has descended into cultural chaos.

What Emersonian principles had been introduced to Wright before the age of eleven, he would train on the farm at that age, at his uncle's property, working hard, milking cows, splitting wood, and generally tending the fields, among other backbreaking tasks. The work was hot, smelly, and dirty—but necessary to disciplining a mind still in the throes of understanding how the world works. Add "tired to tired," his uncle would say, coaxing the young boy to stay the course even when his body was on the brink of collapse. This was how he was going to triumph over petty concerns and achieve self-reliance. "The stoicism was much admired among the Lloyd Joneses," says Meryle Secrest in her biography of Wright. "Like all farm children the boys were men by the age of ten or eleven, expected to work long hours, to take on heavy responsibilities, and to deal alone in whatever emergency arose."[18] To see clearly and attain personal integrity, the uncle seemed to suggest, the boy had to establish direct relations with essential sources of sustenance, and not merely consume them secondhand.

Earlier in life still, Wright learned the same lesson through playing with the Froebel Blocks, simple and even simplistic in one sense but quite sophisticated in the way they trained the mind to see in the whole a complex set of parts and vice versa. Wright's mother had discovered them while on a visit to the 1876 Philadelphia Centennial and bought them to develop in the child a disciplined approach to creativity. For it was Fröbel's ("Froebel" in English version) belief, not unlike Wright's uncle, that creativity is not a mere matter of airing out random thoughts but one in which the basic patterns of organic life are understood first. In Wright's words: "Friedrich Froebel taught that children should not be allowed to draw from casual appearances of nature until they had first mastered the basic forms lying hidden behind appearances. Cosmic geometric elements were what should first be made visible to the child's mind."

The teaching of "Principles" underlay the mission of Fröbel's educational method. One of Wright's favorite words—probably second only to "organic" and "unity"—"principles" appears throughout the "fellowship talks" now stored in the Wright archives at the Architectural and Fine Arts Library, at Avery Library, on the campus of Columbia University. The blocks would contribute to Wright's maturity as an architect and a thinker of systems, disciplining his pencil and keeping it sharp and accurate to the job and challenge at hand. But they would also help him develop an eye that could probe well beyond the surface, seeing in things and relations a reality that escaped others. Indeed, a prophet's eye that could diagnose society's problem in a way that society alone could not do.

By the time Wright made it to Chicago in 1887, he was already steeped in the language and aura of the hero. Of the books he remembers reading, besides those by Emerson but which Emerson himself had read and under whose spell he fell, was Carlyle's *Heroes and Hero Worship*, a narrative of incredible lyricism and power, illustrating in clear terms what it takes to be a hero. Not self-consciousness and certainly not high education but sincerity. The prophet "Mohamet," who was neither literate nor a particularly great philosopher, was heroic precisely because he spoke from the heart and was able to get a whole people and ultimately a whole region to believe in his message. "I should say sincerity," Carlyle tells us, "a deep, great, genuine sincerity, is the first characteristic of all men in any way heroic."[19] A few pages later he says something that in all likelihood shaped, in part, Wright's understanding and finally commitment to organic principles: "A hero, as I repeat, has this first distinction, which indeed we may call first and last, the Alpha and the Omega of his whole Heroism, that he looks through the show of things into *things*."[20]

Chicago as Training Ground for the Hero

Indeed, by the time of his landing in the big city, Wright had been trained to stand outside time and attachment, relinquish ties to family and friends, boss or colleague, and fly away to a far-off place, so to speak, to solve a crisis head-on. For what is a hero other than one who is able to respond at a moment's notice and help people, potentially sacrificing one's life for the larger good of the collective? To be bogged down—including by history, which can tether you to a past you want nothing to do with or from which you have moved and developed—is to be able to do none of that. History, among other attributes, is a collection of mistakes resurrected to prevent future mistakes from happening. It is both guide and code meant to help those moving forward move cautiously. To consider it is to slow down and proceed method-ically, suitable for a legal case but not one in which what is at stake is a response to a moment in distress. Emerson hated it, even as he may have relied on an aspect of it to write his sermons, invoking within a single breath the words of Plato, Saadi, and Carlyle. But he hated it nonetheless because it robbed man of the freedom to think imaginatively and adaptively. "Why drag about this corpse of your memory," he tells us in "Self-Reliance," "lest you contradict somewhat you stated in this or that public place?" Why manage a moment based on a previous one; wouldn't that stymie progress and limit the road to invention? "Suppose you should contradict yourself: what then?" Might not a better approach be this: namely that as "a rule of wisdom never to rely on your memory alone, scarcely even in acts of pure memory, but to bring the past for judgement into the thousand-eyed present, and live ever in a new day."[21] And so what if the facts go by the way side in the process?; it is we who bottle and use them to serve our own purpose. All history is "subjec-tive; in other words." In fact, "there is properly no history, only biography."[22]

Chicago for Wright, as it was for Dreiser's fictional Sister Carrie, may have been no more than a timely opportunity to merge and learn from a world undergoing major change and progress. More importantly and in light of this reading, it was also a ready-made platform on which to practice heroic skills. Just as Odysseus left home to practice and indeed test his heroism, so did Wright travel to Chicago to explore the art of resistance. The city was still in the throes of an economic boom, still the result of rebuilding the city after its demise in the fire of 1871, but also because of a happy geographic accident that made it a convenient and logical hub for moving wood, grain, and beef across the country. "While Chicago inflamed the imaginations of aspiring novelists," says the historian Jackson Lears, "it also played a more prosaic, though equally powerful role, as economic hub of the great Midwestern hin-terland." He continues: "Through the 1880s, lumber companies continued to cut white pines in the great north woods of Wisconsin and Michigan and float them by barge down Lake Michigan to Chicago." At about the same time, "cattle and pigs were being shipped in the millions into the feedlots, stockyards, and slaughterhouses of Chicago."[23] But was the city rebuilding and growing correctly, wisely? Not in Wright's mind; to him the whole thing was a cacophonous mess, and what had risen in the name of architecture was little more than a masquerade of styles erected to please a rising industrial class. "And where was the architecture of the great city—the eternal city of the west?" he wondered in a huff. "Where was it? Hiding behind the shameless signs?" He couldn't quite find it to save his life. Instead, he found "an immense gridiron of noisy streets." It was "dirty" and riddled with "heavy traffic crossing both ways at once, managing somehow." It was a city of "torrential noise."[24] Lears concurs when he speaks of Dreiser's return to Chicago after few years of absence and seeing it characterized by "shabby frame houses" and a stench so bad it is enough to turn your stomach, of "sour beer or stale whiskey or uric acid or sewer gas . . . or poisonous vapors from some distant paint factory."[25] Yeah—the city seemed to be trending awfully.

Yes, just as Wright might have arrived in Chicago to develop and fine-tune his architectural skills, he also came to save it and through it the rest of American architecture. He was going to train his heroic gifts and indeed his prophetic duty on a culture that was very much in need of it. But as we saw, for a hero to be one he must appear without ties or lineage, a unit unto himself. He must parachute from nowhere and save the day, because he has a global duty to rescue others, a community in shambles. A dream during those first days in the city tell us as much. "That night," Wright tells us, he dreamt "a weird dream." He was "up in a balloon, mother frantically holding to a rope dragged along the ground, calling Jennie and Maginel to help . . . all dragged along." Jennie and Maginel are, of course, Wright's sisters and together with their mother represent the family that he must relinquish for him to fulfil his duty as a hero. He "shouted down to hitch the end of the rope to something, anything and make it [the balloon] fast." But to no avail, with the result that the balloon "tore out of the helpless hands and I shot up and up and up—until I awoke with a sense of having been lifted miles to the strange ground of another world."[26] No doubt, it was not easy for Wright to admit to the need to let go of familial ties, but he had to do it to carry out the mission he had set for himself and which he felt himself born to do. No break with family is easy, not least because one may need it later on in life. And yet here he was dreaming of it, wishing it exorcised out of his system, to clear his consciousness and move on. The dream did the job, helping Wright mentally consummate his desire to lift himself from family ties and land on a "strange ground of another world." A world, that is, higher up than the usual one and from which he could now point and guide and altogether tell the earthly crowd below what and what not to do.

And so Wright starts accordingly, with all the pretensions of a lone savior. Again, he needs work to develop his professional skills in the city but also to immerse himself in a culture much in need of saving. The one architect of whom he knows and who could quickly help him, he must neither see nor approach to seek employment. He "wasn't going there." He is a friend of the family, who had on two previous occasions helped the family design and build, first a small rural school back in Wisconsin and then a church for uncle Jenkin Lloyd Jones in Chicago. His name is J. L. Silsbee, a fine and well-respected architect in the area but again one who must be kept at arm's-length or at least as a last resort effort lest the critical persona of a detached hero see the light of day and erode the purity and independence of the hero. But alas, that's where Wright would go, having tried and failed at other offices. "He needn't know who I was," he convinced himself on his way there. The cover was almost busted when later that day he would run into his uncle and tell him where he had just found employment. "That was mighty good of him," the uncle would say of Silsbee, assuming that Wright had gotten the position because of his name. "Told him who you were I suppose?" To which Wright would quickly retort: "No—I didn't."[27]

Soon Wright would switch employment, this time finding a place at the by now famous Adler and Sullivan. The firm was in the throes of a major commission and needed help, a specific kind of help that Wright was particularly adept at, namely to draw details of ornaments, in this case specific to Sullivan's intentions. Adler and Sullivan was no ordinary office, though, but one famed for its inventive and "radical" approach to architecture. Which was good but also not so good: good in the sense that it could elevate Wright's knowledge of architecture and yet no so good in that it could override his place and importance as a hero, not to mention neutralize it. A hero requires an adversary, a crisis to unpack, and a setting that needed no unpacking would be anathema to his ethos and purpose. The approach required a fine balance between recognizing and respecting genius in one's midst but also a way to maintain one's superiority over it, in some manner.

And so, with a "poet's message at heart," Wright applied and received employment from the "moderns," "warned," in Wright's words, "by prophecy and equipped, in fact armed, with the Froebel Kindergarten education I received as a child from my mother." The statement is loaded, packing a complex punch of poetry, warning, and prophecy. A drama of a more Greek outline there isn't, telling us in no uncertain terms that while Wright knew the weight of the moment—the fact that he was just about to work for a major modern figure—he had to remind himself of the prophetic trajectory of his place and time, as a hero on a journey to stay an otherwise unbalanced ship. The warning of the prophecy was no light matter but a reminder that no matter how brilliant Sullivan may have been Wright must not let him become his influence. This was difficult, not least because Sullivan would come to genuinely like Wright and favored him over others in the office and vice versa. The two genuinely admired each other's talents and interest in finding meaning in architecture. But a break had to happen, and Wright would find it in the "Lieber Meister's" interpretations of modern ideas, too sentimental for his taste. Especially in his writing, which he, Wright, "never liked." "Here again was this insidious sentimentality showing even in him," he would say, adding that what suspicion may have germinated inside him regarding the master's propensity for soft thinking had by now ripened "into a rebellion against sentimentality in general."[28] Robert Twombly, the great biographer of both Wright and Sullivan, noticed, saying at one point in his biography of Sullivan that "Wright was sometimes gratuitously critical, as if chipping his "Lieber Meister" down in size in order to surpass him."[29] The full break wouldn't take place until 1893, when Sullivan caught Wright moonlighting and breaking office rules. Sullivan was furious and pushed Wright right out the door, not entirely to the latter's chagrin, but quite the opposite and according to plan. Not unlike Odysseus's judo tactic against the Cyclops, using their strength to serve his own, so did Wright manipulate Sullivan's anger to propel his own heroic project toward the future.

So far so good. But what was Wright thinking when he met and married Catherine and then had six children with her? Shouldn't a hero be above that, free to jump and solve problems precisely because he is free of earthly burdens? Indeed, he had no business having children, and Wright would later admit as much, puzzling over the decision in a manner akin to an outer-body experience. "Is it a quality?" he asked about fatherhood, to no one in particular but himself, or the gods who seemed to have led him astray even as they had elevated him on a pedestal. "Fatherhood? If so I seemed born without it."[30] What feelings of fatherhood he did possess he exhibited not toward his children but his buildings, in effect conflating the two and animating architecture with the will and miracle of life. Architecture not as dead brick and stone but as a form of vitality that could influence and shape minds, restore to the nation its original values. He is sure of it: "I have had the father feeling I am sure when coming back after a long time to one of my buildings." A shocking admission to be sure but one also, we must recognize, as commensurate with the prophecy Wright believed was his. Where others were born to save the day through politics or healthcare, he came to awaken a nation through buildings. In one of his Fellowship talks he insists that his architecture, specifically "organic architecture," will save nothing less than civilization itself. "And if civilization even had it [organic architecture] it would be the end of war; it would be the end of all kinds of strife."[31] Even the way he would eventually leave family and Chicago, dropping everything and never returning, suggests that, though he loved his children just fine, he had no qualms leaving them to reclaim and nourish his heroic capacities. A hero, again, is both human and superhuman. By 1909, Wright had lived in Chicago for more than twenty years, weaving in and out of the human and the super-human, starting and nurturing a family and friends, on the one hand; designing and building such masterpieces as the Robie House and Unity Temple, on the other. By that year however, the human had surpassed its counterpart, and it was time to restore to the prophetic mission its original lore. It was time to reverse course, to change perspective.

The Question of Return

The question of return is critical to the integrity and function of heroes. They return to ordinary life after having attacked and solved a crisis. Or, vice versa, returning to battle after having lingered for a while among the mortals. They need the one to protect and fuel the other. Indeed, their capacity for self-sacrifice and superior acts is dependent on their seeming position as ordinary people. Odysseus's return home was certainly marked by those kinds of switches, ordinary one moment, extraordinary the other. His final return to wife and son wouldn't have succeeded without a blend of the two, first masquerading as a humble beggar but then taking off his garb and revealing his superiority. This is how he was able to seep back into his house amid the suitors, who were lying around the courtyard of his house, waiting for Penelope, Odysseus's wife, to come out and feed and entertain them. Had he entered the house as the superhuman figure, he would have been at a disadvantage, too exposed and likely to fall, given the sheer numbers lined up against him.

Wright grew up with stories like these, of heroes "dripping with gang-gore—but cool with bravery in the constant crash of catastrophe." They came in the form of "a daring hero, usually a lad like [himself] triumphant all the time." Who no sooner went down than he "[came] right up through scrambled Indians and half caste cut-throats, carcasses, bowie knives, and cutlasses."[32] And so Wright must make a similar return to restore in himself that which had been defeated or grown stale after so many years in the city. Like Odysseus, he, too, would take twenty years to do so, ready to take down the suitors once and for all in the case of Odysseus and in Wright's a culture that since the mid-nineteenth century had grown divided and alien to its own first mission.

What battles Odysseus took on during the ten-year Trojan War, Wright would parallel in his own struggles with Chicago, taking on the establishment and managing to at least leave an imprint. Neither fight was easy, which Wright would admit but also insist that while he was "no master of the orchestra," he had "to conquer a hard boiled industrial world stewed in terms of money, and persuade and or please idiosyncratic, sometimes aristocratic clients." To do that, to transform society from within, he had to enter its bloodstream, so to speak, and become a biological cell among other cells. Attending the Hull House was one way to do so, the brainchild of Jane Addams, best known for her pioneering work on women's rights. It was there that he met Emma Goldman, the Lithuanian émigré and anarchist notorious for airing out daring issues for the time, regarding sex, art, and revolution, "and not least what it means to be an American."[33] And there, too, is where Wright would meet his future restless and wealthy client, Aline Barnsdall, who with Goldman had cultivated an interest in theater, and for whom he would design a house in Hollywood, California. It was also at the Hull House where Wright in 1901 would give his influential lecture "The Arts and Craft of the Machine," urging his fellow architects and artists to open their minds and study the industrial age. Why don't we siphon its power toward useful and indeed beautiful results rather than blindly rejecting it simply on the ground that it displaced the work of the hand? Don't just stand there and critique the factory from a distance; take "excursions" to it and "study [the] process in place."[34]

Other influential links included those with Arthur Heurtley and Hamlin Garland, both recent arrivals from the East Coast who, once in Chicago, became engaged and effective members of society. Garland, in particular, imbibed the zeal and mission of Henry George's quest to stop poverty, seemed more than casually interested in making sure that the emerging industrial society did not degenerate into a mean and dispirited place to be but remained infused and indeed spiritualized by higher questions of beauty and truth. His "Cliff Dwellers," a club of sorts, was formed precisely for those reasons, namely, to create a venue through which the artists and the financiers and generally the makers of the city could come together and scheme against intellectual and aspirational malaise. Included in its membership, according to Garland, were "leading painters, sculptors, architects, musicians and literary men of the middle west."[35] Wright was among them and on one occasion in 1908 took charge of hosting a symposium on art, inviting the sculptor Lorado Taft and the poet William Guthrie, among others, to lift the spirits of the day and cultivate a reputation for Chicago as a "regional center for the arts." The event's venue was Unity Temple, Wright's recently completed masterpiece, now a UNESCO World Heritage Site, conducive for its capacity to host large groups of people but more so for the way it could imbue earthly matters with higher purpose.

Chicago did indeed prove critical as a battleground on which Wright could fine-tune his heroic acumen. But by 1909 the skill was beginning to wane, Wright becoming too much like an architect working on commissions, "a little fellow," to quote Sullivan, "who has taken up 'architecture' with all its ins and outs as a trade, a convenient-as-any means of turning a dollar."[36] He needed to become a big fellow all over again, a hero and a prophet. Indeed, he refers to that period, between 1893 and 1908, as a kind of a "negation," not in the sense of the negative and the pernicious but in that of the removal of one entity in favor of another; namely to negate the forces that may have dragged him down during that period and replace them with those that can energize and restore his prophetic powers. In Wright's words, "negation" meant "take that away in order that this may come."[37] It was for him an "affirmation" that the old had become too accessible and, much to his distaste, commercial or worse, bastardized by both a local and a modern European architectural intellectual market. Herbert Muschamp, in his book on Wright titled *Man about Town*, agrees, saying that "after all," that is why he "terminated his first career," namely to "dissociate himself from those [the European Moderns] he felt had robbed his ideas."[38] Wright had by 1909 become a brand and, like all brands, a feature of the market, bought and sold to advance a living and less a revolution. What a curse. The last thing Wright wanted to do was quicken the locomotion of bourgeois taste and see his work reduced to terms associated with real estate.

Where other architects would have normally received the success with joy and celebration, Wright did so with trepidation and a feeling he may have lost the fight against the malaise of the America mind. Not only did the country continue to produce third-rate buildings, worse still was the sense on Wright's part that his work was being used to facilitate the slide toward mediocrity. What was it about the national character that resisted a higher ground, a more principled approach to culture and architecture? he wondered. Why, despite the availability of good minds, was there little or no expression of it out in the open? He demanded answers of himself and others. "We need to know," said Sullivan around the same time, "why the intelligent public, the intelligent individuals, the intelligent architect are jointly and severally so lacking in intelligence."[39]

What made matters worse for Wright was the gulf between him and society, and the frustration that he just couldn't close it. The impasse resembled a "closed road" and a feeling that he was "losing grip of [his] work and even [his] interest in it."[40] God, oh God, why give me this superior vision if you can't also allow me to improve humanity with it? you could hear him cry in desperation. "Everything personal or otherwise bore heavily down upon me," he said. Sullivan said something similar, also calling upon his God to answer the same pressing questions: "Why have you caused this well spring to flow, if its waters avail not, if they are never to reach the sea, or even to form a lake or a shady pool, but are to dry up on the sands, to disappear in an arid human waste?" Sullivan felt unwelcomed and so did Wright, "a stranger in this house of many mansions, an outcast from my world, a guest unbidden at the feast, unwelcome in a garden, unwelcome to a flower, unwelcome to a butterfly!"[41] Indeed, the "road "seemed "closed," and it was time to exit and take a different one.

Leaving Chicago

Meeting and falling in love with a client's wife may have been the pretext Wright needed to push him into mandatory exile. Chicago, and perhaps the world as a whole in 1909, was not the kind of place that could accept moral transgressions of this sort, violating the bounds of marriage and family, and seemingly so cavalierly causing another to fissure and dissolve. To do such a thing, Wright, and his new love, Mamah Cheney, had to exit the scene and evade the prying eye of the public. The local papers famously hounded the two, but particularly Wright, and practically trashed their names. And so they eloped, first to Europe and then back to Spring Green, Wright's ancestral land, both serving as enforced places of solitude from which to think and prepare the next plan of attack. This is what prophets do after all, appear but then disappear, to recharge and gain a wider and more comprehensive understanding of the lay of the land. The American erosion of values turned out to be a much greater and more stubborn problem than originally believed. It required a stance and a position almost God-like, invisible and yet powerful precisely because it cannot be seen, only occasionally heard from: God through storms and calamities, bounty and beauty, Wright through lectures, publications, and, of course, buildings. Spring Green was and remains three hours away from Chicago and many more from New York; perfectly distant enough and difficult enough to find, it might as well be in the clouds.

It was through solitude that Emerson found the power and the ability to put matter in perspective and ultimately offer the kind of wisdom and advice America liked and demanded from him. It was there that he could keep his spirit whole and the integrity of his thought one. It may be fine and indeed necessary to gather and cultivate a community of friends and colleagues, but make that the rule and before too long you will be half the person you had been before. "'Tis fine for us to talk," says Emerson; "we sit and muse, and are serene and complete; but the moment we meet with anybody, each becomes a fraction."[42] He goes on: "Neither Archimedes nor Newton would have been possible without solitude. If these had been good fellows, fond of dancing, port, and clubs, we should have had no "theory of the spheres," and no "Principia." Indeed, "nature protects her own work."[43] It keeps it from coming under attack and being prematurely aborted well before it has had time to gestate and prove its worth. Solitude is where Sullivan made his most sober conclusions, "reached not in the racket of cities, nor in the study of garrulous philosophies, nor in libraries, nor in schools, but in the bounteous open air, within the infinite peace of nature, alone in the solitudes, where the soul in contemplation became peaceful as the dawn, and mirrored the infinite in its own clam."[44]

Sullivan's mention of the mirror is interesting. It speaks of notions of duplication and reaffirmation, of seeing in one's creation the creation of one's identity. Solitude, as it turns out, is not merely a place to which one goes to be alone, but more importantly a razor of sorts one applies to divide oneself in two. In it, one is forced to create to make do, to garden, build, invent. Perhaps even learn a language with which to attract and hunt game. How else is one going to survive without the help of modern technology or nearby neighbors? In all, one is forced to fall back on one's mental and physical resources, and before too long put something together that is truly a product of one's own, a record and a biography of one's own character. Work under these circumstances acquires a new connotation, less a matter of building a world and more one with which to create and develop a self. "There is virtue yet," says Emerson, "in the hoe and the spade, for learned as well as for unlearned hands." Critical here is the simple but important act of transformation, namely that in harnessing one's forgotten or dormant skills, to transform raw nature into useful and lasting productions, one also undergoes a process of transformation of oneself. Which means that solitude does not only help the individual develop and record any old identity but one that could peculiarly experience the art of becoming one. Identity, character, and the like are all works in progress, base initially but refined and redeemable in due change. "In its grub state [the initial act] cannot fly, cannot shine, it is a dull grub." But work it and it will "unfurl beautiful wings and is an angel of wisdom."[45]

Thoreau and the Construction of Self

Had it not been for the likes of Thoreau, the long-term personal and national virtues of solitude would have remained unsure. In going out to the woods and spending two years alone, he forced himself to yield, to become resourceful and find out who he really was. In society we often rely on others to plan and consummate projects. Which is good and healthy, not least because it helps us build meaningful relations. But it can also confuse and distort our understanding of who we are, our individuality slowly but surely leaking out and becoming everyone else's business. Some may see in this an important and necessary practice, especially in democracies, knocking the self a few notches down, just so that it can find in others a happy and natural common ground. A self too keen and strong is likely to chart a course of its own, often at the expense of itself and society. Better to dilute it. Or so the thinking by some may go. John Dewey called it "stupidity," arguing that only the stupid "[allege] that all persons are qualitatively alike."[46] More to the point should be the celebration of differences and the search for those unique traits in others that could bring out the best in us. Individuality in that sense means "intrinsic qualities which require unique opportunities and differential manifestations."[47]

Over the course of two years, Thoreau gardened, built a cabin, and chased wildlife, among other things, generating enough fodder to fill a diary and in effect erect a mirror to life and self. Nothing too difficult but complex just the same, a blend of philosophy, accounting, and reportage. He tells us, for instance, that to build his house he needed 28 dollars and 12½ cents, largely to pay a neighbor for wood salvaged from his shed, a rickety structure that was about to go to waste anyway. For farm material, such as soil and manure, he needed 14 dollars and 72½ cents, for clothing, 8 dollars and 40¾ cents, and so on. Boring stuff but occasion enough to lay bare the various threads with which to weave the fabric of existence. Slowly but surely philosophy percolates, never too complicated but always the product of putting two and two together. Such as learning that during the two-year experience "it would cost incredibly little trouble to obtain one's necessary food even in this latitude; that a man may use as simple a diet as the animals and yet retain health and strength."[48] Keen and clean words but hardly layered and nuanced. Indeed, Thoreau is careful not to veer into a litigious interpretation of his time in the woods, lest he may need to depend on the intellectual apparatus of history and precedent to defend his case. To do so would dredge up continental philosophy all over again and before too long rob the individual of self-construction. His concerns were not with "the when and how of the day," tells us Olaf Hansen in *Aesthetic Individualism*, only with "the present." "Living," he adds, "was his only morality and keeping a record of life hence became the only moral duty of the individual."[49]

To be conscious was to be conscious of the moment, alive to its climatic, natural, and human dynamics, always connected to what is going on in front of one's eyes. This is how one writes one's own story. Some may resort to drugs or mechanical operations to remain conscious, or in fact escape it to escape the burdens of life. But not so for Thoreau. For him the hour was rich and charged with potential, but it does require active participation on the individual's part to make it so. In Thoreau's words: "We must learn to re-awaken and keep ourselves awake not by mechanical aids, but by an infinite expectation of the dawn, which does not forsake us in our soundest sleep."[50] Thoreau's recording of bean and corn yields may have been boring to him and may be so to us, but it was an important source of provisional fuel, keeping the engine of consciousness alive and awake to the moment. "I know of no more encouraging fact than the unquestionable ability of man to elevate his life by a conscious endeavor." Did we really need to learn about his search for nails to assemble his shelter, or of his manner of drying wood so that it can cure and become suitable for construction, or still his battle with wood-chucks who kept at his garden and almost destroyed it? Not really, but we did hear him, nonetheless, knowing that what he offered was a critical lesson in the remapping of historical boundaries, drawn now back around the self.

Wright took heed and followed along, leaving for solitude just like Thoreau had left for Walden, to build a home and allow the self to show its face. Just as Thoreau had built a cabin to build a self, setting up the events from which he could harvest words and write his biography, so Wright would retreat to maternal land and build a home to write his own personal narrative. Even before any stone had been quarried and brought to the site of construction, or any lumber cut for erection, Wright would pad his journal with observations about the lay of the land. He had scanned the hills of the region "where the rock came cropping" and where "the red cedars and white birches" stood next to the "rockledge masses." There, he saw in his mind's eye an emerging reality, "a hill crown back of the house, itself a mass of apple trees in bloom, the perfume drifting down the valley; strawberry beds, white scarlet and green; abundant asparagus in rows and a stretch of sumptuous rhubarb; bees humming over all storing up honey; sheep grazing the meadows and hills." And on and on, including cows and horses and peacocks, a bucolic dream of magnetic charm: "Yes Taliesin should be a garden and a farm behind a workshop and a home." Well before any structure had risen, Wright was setting up his biographical mirror.

Soon, however, work on the house began, and here the "record" would become even more full of life, this time based on actual happenings and not merely a dream out in the future. Here we learn of "a stone quarry on another hill a mile away," which "a team of neighboring farmers" would mine to build and beautify the house. Of the more charming and funny stories we are told, the one about Ben Davis is probably the most memorable. He is the tough mason prone to creative cussing: "One day Ben with five of his men was moving a big rock that suddenly got away from its edge and fell over flat, catching Ben's big toe." Ouch. But Wright wasn't worried about Ben; he was more worried about the rock. "I shuddered for the rock, as, hobbling slowly back and forth around it, Ben hissed and glared at it, threatening, eyeing and cussing it."[51]

In his account of building his humble abode, Thoreau made mention of the fact that when the edifice was up, it served as a kind of ocular tool with which to focus and connect with the natural events unfolding outside. The door and the window, besides being access points to light and entry, were frames with which to appreciate and objectify events that would have otherwise remained unnoticed. "As I sit by my window this summer afternoon, hawks are circling about my clearing,"[52] he tells us and then again, about his door, that while "the view from my door was still more contracted," he "did not feel crowded or confined in the least." Indeed, "there was pasture enough for my imagination."[53] Window and the door would give Thoreau the ability to view and enjoy the traipsing of birds and squirrels without himself being seen by them, enlivening his record with the sound and color of animal life. Rain was the source of similar pleasures, the roof of the cabin serving as a drum skin, amplifying the sound of raindrops falling and crashing and generating something like a symphonic melody.

Wright's home served a kindred purpose, giving man and nature a place to play out their interdependencies and Wright the ability to record his experiences. Even Wright's students in the 1930s, and as part of the Fellowship, picked up on that. As one student would later say of his experience: "What matters really is that here at Taliesin where precept and example are living forces, a young life may use the precept as a door and the examples as windows to look out upon a world to which he aspires to belong." Indeed, as Taliesin grew and became more than a home, but a studio, a school, and even a visitor center, it also became the stage on which Wright could use his own biographical notes to teach others how to write their own. Individuality was at the heart of his concern, setting the ground on which it could emerge and find true expression. Poetic observation and hard manual labor were central to it, Thoreau style, both abundantly available and needed at Taliesin. Indeed, that is how "true individuality" is formed, through a kind of surrender to objective forces, to once again quote the student mentioned above: "True individuality, can only truly grow into something great and useful by means of such objective, if not, then subjective surrender."[54]

When all was said and done at Taliesin, the buildings came together in L and U configurations. More than mere organizational tools, they allowed the inhabitant of one side of the house to view and be viewed by the other across the way, always from the corner of one's eyes, diagonally and discretely, inviting voyeurism but not to violate the sanctity of one's privacy but, rather, to allow that person, or thing, to operate and behave under its own auspices. The visual reciprocities resemble a theater of actors and audiences, each awaiting the other to appear and make the next hour or two a catalog of biographical notes. And just in case humans aren't available, there is always the environment, beautiful and objective, here presented and amplified by features Wright would plant specifically for that reason. In Bruce Pfeiffer's words, the longtime custodian of Wright's work and archives: "the living quarters or 'house' faced out over a water garden below made by damming the stream." And farther out still "to the southwest the Wisconsin river could be seen." There "the hill part of the house opened onto enclosed courtyards paved with limestone, with flower gardens and planting areas for wild grapevines and

FIG. 2. Main entrance at Taliesin, Spring Green, Wisconsin, 1911. Note the degree to which Wright erodes the corners in favor of diagonal views and restless walls. Photo by author.

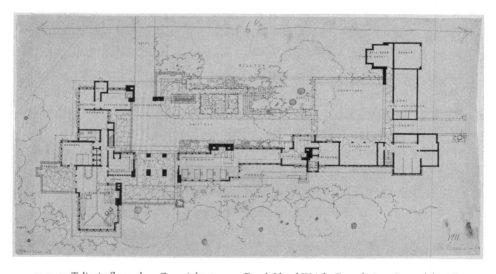

FIG. 3. Taliesin floor plan. Copyright © 2022 Frank Lloyd Wright Foundation, Scottsdale, AZ. All rights reserved. The Frank Lloyd Wright Foundation Archives (The Museum of Modern Art | Avery Architectural & Fine Arts Library, Columbia University, New York)

woodbine vines." Indeed, "Taliesin . . . was its own domain: home, studio, workshop, farm—all connected together around the hill and set under great oak trees." In all, the setting was so designed and assembled that it gave the eye plenty to rummage through and record.[55]

The L and U configuration of the architecture was instrumental in making conscious the play of natural life. But look a little closer, and you'll see that there is something else afoot that makes the exchange between inside and outside even more amplified. It has to do with the restless plan; no sooner does the box of the house assemble than Wright breaks it at the corners, allowing for diagonal views to flow and ricochet in and out (fig. 2).

The whole plan appears as if on liquid ground, slipping and sliding and making possible the play between the natural and the man-made (fig. 3). Or better yet, as if an earthquake had taken place and the walls had come apart, resulting in the rise of such things as planters, doorways, and water features. Nothing is settled here, all in flux. Even the stonework is hardly flush and tidy but, rather, jagged and geologic, reminiscent of an open mountainside, setting up a visual opportunity for weather and shadows to form and give the eye diverse conditions to view and capture. Of such work and arrangements, said Henry Russell Hitchcock in his seminal book *In the Nature of Materials*, Wright had laid the stone "in loosely projecting layers like natural cliffs."[56]

On Ornament in Wright's Work

Wright was just as critical of ornament in architecture as the other modernists—Loos, Le Corbusier and Gropius, to name only three. But he was also different than they, in that he allowed it as an exterior monument with which to pull out an equivalent ornament in man. The modernists had vilified it for being wasteful and superfluous. "What is ornament good for?" Karsten Harries asks on their behalf in his *Ethical Function of Architecture*. "Is it not frightfully wasteful of time and money that would be better spent on education, food and medicine?"[57] For them as for Ruskin, ornament meant a layer applied on the face of a building, to mask and beautify an otherwise brute utilitarian reality. It was compensatory in nature, differentiating between building and architecture. Harries again, speaking of Ruskin, says: "Ruskin lets us understand the rise of the aesthetic approach, and with it the understanding of works of architecture as decorated buildings, as compensatory."[58] Not for Wright. What he found important about ornament was its capacity to draw the monumental inside man, his genius, indeed, his ornament. With the right ornament, namely an object beautiful and original, the best in man can be brought out. Who can deny the effects that great works of art have on us, be they paintings or whole cities, leaving us yearning to return to our own creative corners, to emulate and match in creative power what we have just experienced elsewhere. Superfluous in one sense, ornament seen through this lens becomes the inspiration necessary to fire up the imagination and see the world in a new light.

And yet what was the "right" ornament for Wright? It couldn't be one that compared man to man, or man to God, holding the former captive to the latter and potentially snuffing out his creative and independent potential. No, it had to be otherwise, a feature that was nothing like man but could draw out the best and most original in him. Nature was more like it, following Emerson and Thoreau, not as a photograph one snaps to keep in one's pocket but a lesson about process and change. Namely, nature as performance, ebbing and flowing and putting on display life's natural cycles. And yet to see nature in this way is to bring it close to where one lives, ideally right outside one's home, on ledges and edges and everywhere that it can be within visual and hourly striking distance. It was not for nothing that Wright removed the gutter from the edge of his roofs, to let the icicles form and create a beautiful visual for him to see and record. "I wanted a home where icicles by invitation might beautify the eaves," he said at one point in his *Autobiography*. Nor was it by sheer willful intent that he pushed and pulled at the stone on the face of the house, creating ledges on which to allow snow to accumulate and the eye to see that accumulation, likely changing by the hour and tracing new and delightful patterns. Note the word "invitation" in the previous sentence by Wright, the architect doing what he can to set the stage for nature to arrive, settle, and morph.

You'd have to go back to savagery to find in man the ability for authentic and original expression, translating reality into something uniquely one's own. Everything since has been contaminated by civilization's persistent demand for certain sanctioned behavior. Very little that we do and have done has not also been affected by rules and regulations. Or so Owen Jones main-

---

tained in his book *The Grammar of Ornament*, which Wright read and used to help him assemble a portfolio with which to find employment at Sullivan's office earlier in his career. Even Michelangelo failed, surrounded as he was by great art and a culture that demanded a certain expression from him. "Cimabue and Giotto," Jones says, may "not have the material charm of Raphael or the manly power of Michael Angelo, but [they] surpass them both in grace and earnest truth."[59] Indeed, "when art struggles, it succeeds; when reveling in its own successes, it as signally fails." What Jones saw in the savage is a virgin untainted by foreign and superficial productions, capable of seeing nature for what it is and not a pretext for material and commercial ends. Counter to popular impression, the savage had the best mind as such, capable of processing information and translating it into original contributions. Strange? Maybe, but that is what Jones believed. "It is strange," he says, "but so it is, that this evidence of mind will be more readily found in the rude attempts at ornament of a savage tribe than in the innumerable productions of a highly advanced civilization."[60]

In the *American Renaissance*, Matthiessen describes Thoreau as a kind of craftsman, careful to build a nice and stable structure but also to knit a concrete moment, sturdy and anchored enough to fuel his eye and later his pen and journal. "In his full utilization of his immediate resources, Thoreau was a kind of native craftsman . . . of traditional modes and skills."[61] Indeed, a weaver who, in bringing two planks together, also wove two parts of the self together, inside and out, making identity visible and concrete. It wasn't so much that the joint had to be perfect or perfect looking as assembled to mobilize man's ability to create himself out of whole cloth.

Wright picked up where Jones and Thoreau left off, calling himself a "weaver," he, too, weaving together material and symbolic connections to make visible an ornament of important cultural ties. Did Americans know who they were, including obligation to family, community, and country? The answer, to Wright, seemed unsure at best and at worst a fabrication of artificial threads. Americans had for too long swapped foreign ornaments for native designs, not least because they had no native designs or the knowledge of how to cultivate them. Too focused on wealth, they had neglected the need to invest in institutions whose function is the development of creative capital. They needed a different ornament, and preferably one that is authentic precisely because it spoke to the nation's rural ethos. No more flutes nor volutes, pediments and entablatures, only designs whose beauty and meaning are direct extensions of the land and, more precisely, the materials within it. If stone, then stone; if clay, then clay. Wright homed in on concrete, at first less because of its capacity for authenticity but, later on, very much for that. What other material could achieve such feet and effortlessly? None, really, at once easy to dig up, readily available, and, once mixed, responding with great fidelity to ideas. Just add water and for the most part it is ready to go, namely, pour it into a form and watch it assume the shape of that form.

The results would first find expression in the so-called concrete textile block homes of the 1920s, in Los Angeles, featuring deep voids and patterns that, when aggregated, give the whole the look of a woven fabric (fig. 4). The effect was and remains powerful, but the use of concrete was still less concerned with authenticity than with pushing an otherwise dumb and unattractive material to do more. "Aesthetically concrete has neither song nor any story," Wright said of the material. "Nor is it easy to see in this conglomerate,

FIG. 4. Textile concrete blocks at the Millard House, Los Angeles, California, 1923. Photograph courtesy of Mark Hertzberg.

in this mud pie, a high aesthetic property, because in itself it is amalgam, aggregate, compound. And cement, the binding medium, is characterless."[62]

It would take another twenty years or so before Wright would finally come to an aha moment and realize that in concrete blocks lay buried not only beauty but the great capacity for comprehensive authenticity. The concrete blocks that went into the Usonian Automatic homes of the later 1940s and 1950s were powerful and uniquely, authentically American precisely because they empowered Americans to build independent of a third party, using the very ground on which they sought to build and with their own hands. "Buildings could grow right up out of the ground," Wright said in pride. All Americans had to do was dig up the soil, add aggregates and water, and off they could start. A more authentic picture of America there couldn't be, uniting land, mind and personal labor. When all was said and done, the whole house was an ornament, celebrating not a foreign God, king, or senator but the great American individual. Only seven such houses were built, not least because the effort to do so turned out to be more complicated than first anticipated. But still, that even that many were built remains a testament to Wright's commitment to authenticity.

Wright may or may not have read Gottfried Semper, but the latter's ideas are hard to miss in his work.[63] More than any other modern theorist, Semper placed the heart of human culture in fabrication, tracing it back to human beginnings. In weaving, he saw the expression of an ancient effort to unite and chart a common cause. Carpets, screens, and barriers are in one sense no more than material artifacts we have produced over time to adorn interior space. But in an another they speak to a basic need for shelter, separation, and privacy. Those who created them took their clues from nature, first by observing wildlife weave habitats using branches, leaves, and the like, but later people did the same, putting up fences and hedges for protection against enemies. "The weaving of branches," writes Semper, "led easily to weaving bast into mats and covers and then to weaving with plant fiber and so forth." The oldest form of weaving was a kind of "wickerwork" woven to set "apart one's property," but later to produce "mats and carpets for floor coverings and protection against heat and cold and for subdividing the spaces within a dwelling."[64] Look up any of Wright's interiors and you will see the essence of Semper's words strewn everywhere, in the way the rafters are woven together but also in the way shelves and walls merge. Again and again Wright never let any one aspect of architecture dangle alone, but integrated it with the next piece over, including the seemingly disparate relation between pipes and floors, at one point uniting the two and changing the future of heating and cooling forever. Henry Russell Hitchcock took note of this in his book on Wright, at one point saying of the plaster at Taliesin that it was more "roughly surfaced than on earlier houses, framed above and below by sturdy moulded wooded strings." And of the roofs, that they "no longer form[ed] a simple geometrical cross shape, [but were] varied, with gable elements and penthouses introduced among the predominant hips."[65] Later, Wright would push the notion of the weave even more, this time as related to the integration of steel and concrete and this to achieve more complicated and daring feet. Neither Fallingwater nor the Guggenheim would have been possible without it. But more on that in later chapters.

The Campaign for a New Consciousness

And yet Wright did not return to Wisconsin merely to record reality but, rather, to transform it. If Thoreau was all too content to sit on facts and catalog them in a journal, Wright wanted to go further. More than simply calling forth an identity, his concern was to make sure that that identity was put to good use and mobilized to advance new realities. Besides being unsure of their identity, Americans had lost their creative possibilities, beaten down to such an extent they dared not imagine doing things differently. They had become captive to a narrative and a routine outside their own and by powers too big to control. Architects in particular had lost their signature authority over design and ways to shape a national aesthetic vison. "We do not have architects now," Wright railed. Instead, "we have designers, [and they] are back in the backroom again," producing and reproducing copies of the same plans over and over again.[66] They were like robots responding to orders without knowing why or for whom.

A reverse course was in order and one that could restore in the architect "that quality in life we call creative."[67] The process required nothing short of flushing out the old consciousness and replacing it with another. Emerson proposed a poet's, uniquely equipped with the capacity to forget and to start all over again. For the poet, nothing is sacred and nothing is profane, and all is up for grabs, including language and history. "Ours is the revolutionary age, when man is coming back to consciousness," Emerson had said. "What we need is a reflective poet."[68] And one who could take established facts and shatter them into pieces in favor of new constructs. "The chief value of the new fact," Emerson wrote in "The Poet," "is to enhance the great and constant fact of life, which can dwarf any and every circumstance, and to which the belt of wampum and the commerce of America are alike."[69] No two dissimilar realities are beyond the poet's capacity to fuse. He or she is just as capable of putting chair and table together as chair and ceiling, turning gravity upside down and assembling a new world order. His or her imagination is bound-less, meant "to flow and not to freeze." Here Emerson cautions against giving the notion of the "record" too much credit, lest it might create in its author a heightened sense of self-consciousness, not consciousness. Keeping a record is well and good, but staying within those bounds can defeat the very purpose for which the record was intended in the first place. The distinction for Emerson marked the divide between true and false subjectivity. In Matthiessen's words, Emerson "was occupied with consciousness, not self-consciousness."[70]

The Making of a Poet

And yet, how does a poet form? What does need to happen to allow one the means and the capacity to see things as if for the first time, naturally and shamelessly letting go of the past or other countless forms of moral attach-ments. To the poet, no fact is sacred, none too profane, but all are subject to scrutiny and overhaul. What the ages had built and turned into law, the poet undoes to rebuild new ones. Of his biggest attributes, forgetfulness is the most productive, effortlessly letting go of lessons learned in favor of ones that have yet to form. "By an ulterior intellectual perception," Emerson tells us of the poet, he gives symbols, words, and other established facts "a power which makes their old use forgotten, and puts eyes and a tongue into a every dumb and intimate object."[71] Whatever it takes, the poet seems to thrive on the return to ground zero and see the world through the eyes of an infant or, better yet, an unborn fetus, his or her nerve endings yet to unfold and receive the world. Indeed, a return to the womb seems necessary.

In a recent study on Wright, Kenneth Frampton, the esteemed Columbia University historian, calls Wright's return to maternal land in Spring Green in 1911 "Oedipal." But he does not go on to explain, no doubt because the term and the theory behind it can be contentious and lead to overwrought rhetoric. He relies on the reader's muscle memory and popular understanding of the oedipal complex to put two and two together. Which is fine but misses the opportunity to unpack some of the more interesting possible scenarios behind Wright's imaginative outbursts. Where did they come from?

To call something oedipal is to crisscross ancient and modern territory, on the one hand going back to Sophocles's play *Oedipus Rex*, on the other to Freud's use of the tragedy to unpack the complex process of human development. Oedipus is the son of King Laius and Queen Jocasta of Thebes, prophesied to kill his father and marry his mother. Finding the prophecy repulsive, Oedipus tries everything in his power to thwart it. Unfortunately, he doesn't succeed and ends up blinding himself, unable to bear, or see, the facts anymore. Freud popularized the story in modern times, using it to map out the various sexual stages through which we pass to become functional human beings. "King Oedipus," he says in *The Interpretations of Dreams*, "who slew his father Laius and married his mother Jocasta merely shows us the fulfillment of our own childhood wishes." We all arrive with an inbuilt desire for mothers and a hate for the father. But over time and through stories such as Oedipus Rex we learn how to navigate instincts and taboo desires, slowly but surely "detaching our sexual impulses from our mothers and forgetting the jealousy of our fathers."[72]

As the interpretation goes, the child arrives with a longing for the mother, specifically her breast, understandably to obtain milk and remain alive. Before too long the longing matures into a full-blown obsession and a desire to possess the mother at all cost. Unfortunately, the father stands in the way and bars access to the mother, resulting in a feeling of deep fear, akin to a kind of "castration," to use Freud's term. The father is so strong and powerful he will stop at nothing to make sure the sanctity of the mother is preserved and remains his. Melanie Klein's diagnosis of the same impasse speaks of anxiety, first depressive and second persecutory. The depressive stems from the realization that the object of desire is lost, while the persecutory from the need to exercise aggression to restore access. In Klein's words, "the depressive anxiety is predominantly related to the harm done to internal and external loved objects," whereas the persecutory deals "predominantly with the annihilation of the ego."[73] Interestingly, both—but primarily the depressive anxiety—are "bound up with guilt and with the tendency to make reparation," which, as we will see, plays a critical role in Wright's own restoration project with mother and culture as a whole.

As much as the child may wish to lash out and gain access to the mother by force, he can't, and over the years learns to tamp down or repress feelings of desire in favor of a functional and reliable relationship with the world, not least because of the need to self-preserve. What starts as turbulent soon stabilizes and becomes part of a healthy cycle of growth and emotional development. However punitive the father's presence may seem, he is necessary for emotional control and social interaction. Wright did not have a father, or at least not the complete presence of one. The father he grew up with in his youth was soon removed by the mother in favor of her direct access to the son. She had it in her mind that the son was going to be the greatest architect in the world, and nothing was going to stand in the way. Rather than the son seeing in his mother an object of desire, it is the mother, by then obviously a mature woman in control of the situation, who sees her son as one.

Naturally this strange reverse course had an impact on the son, distorting his sense of power relations with the world. The fear of castration that was necessary for a modest and balanced approach to life was gone, replaced by a direct and unmitigated access to pleasure and fulfilment. The castrator was himself castrated, by the mother on behalf of the son, giving the latter an amplified sense of himself. Not unlike Jesus, who had no father but only a mother, so Wright would journey across the cultural landscape as such, often speaking from a perch well above his station.

But as arrogant as he may have been and presumably thankful to his mother for pumping so much hot air into him, there is enough evidence that he was also resentful of her for subjecting him to an upbringing without a father. For one, he never spoke badly about his father and remembered him fondly in his autobiography. By the time the mother had pushed the father away, the son was old enough to remember the conditions under which he left and as such knew that there was no major reason for him to go, but in fact the opposite, namely, that he was a talented scholar and musician. "The son had sympathy for his talented father," Wright wrote in his *Autobiography*, "as well as admiration."[74] Years later, as a father himself, Wright would play the piano, Beethoven or Bach, in front of his own children, in memory of his father, who had favored the classical artists when Wright was a kid. "One day without previous warning, a Cecilian Piano player was rolled into the house," tells us John Wright in his book about his father, Frank Lloyd Wright. "Papa pushed it up to the keyboard of his Steinway concert grand and pumped Beethoven by the roll. His eyes closed, his head and hands swaying over the throttles, I think he imagined he was a Beethoven."[75]

Wright never openly castigated his mother about his father. But in 1910 he would write a letter to her that may address his thoughts about this, though not explicitly but through some interpretation. He is in Italy, after having left Chicago and spent some time in Germany working on his Wasmuth monograph. By then he had already had his midlife crisis and eloped to Europe with a client's wife, Mamah Cheney. He had created quite a stir back home for breaking society's moral code, and his future was unsure. In the letter he is implicitly asking for forgiveness, presumably for his moral transgressions. Or so the first reading may seem to suggest. But upon the second, something different emerges. The double reading hinges on a critical mention of the "prodigal" son, a reference to the Bible, Luke 15:11–32. "I dread the aspect my return must wear," he says in the letter, "I am the prodigal—whose return is a triumph for the institutions I have outraged." In the Bible the son insults his father by asking for his inheritance well before the father is dead or about to die. The request amounts to a killing of the father while the latter is well and fine, a kind of burying him alive. The father, being wise and at peace with the world, grants the son his wish and gives him the money, only for the son to go on and squander it. So low does the biblical son fall that he has to clean pigpens just to survive, a symbol in the Old World of utmost humiliation and degradation. Long story short, the son, having hit rock bottom, returns to his father and asks for his forgiveness, which again the father grants and allows him to return home. The prodigal son is the story of fathers and sons and the dynamics of atonement, not mothers. And yet here was Wright bringing it up in communication with the mother, assigning her powers she did not possess and hinting at the mess that she had created.

Which means that while the recipient of the letter is the mother, it is also intended to implicate the father in the process of atonement. First and foremost, Wright is writing to ask his father for his forgiveness, knowing full well that it was he, the son, who caused the separation with the mother. Had he not been born the mother and the father may have continued living a happy and fulfilled life. But once he was born, the mother did everything in her capacity to nourish and maintain access to the son. As Meryle Secrest tells us in her biography of Wright: the "mother had successfully pushed his father out and devoted herself to him and his sisters."[76] And not only that but she had also trained her children to think of their father as dead, an awful realization made, in all likelihood, doubly bad when the father actually died in 1904. Of this feeling, Secrest adds that "for a son who had been taught to think of his father as dead, it must still have been a jolt to have him actually die, a reminder that would likely release some long repressed feelings of bitterness along with self reproach, a sense of lost opportunities and host of buried memories."[77]

Just as the biblical son had buried his father before his time, so Wright had done the same despite the fact that he hardly had any say in the matter. The mere fact of his birth had spelled the father's demise, and now it was time to atone for his mistake, in no small part by getting back into the womb of his mother and resurrecting the process of birth all over again. This time around he would do better by his father, correcting the process and perhaps reversing the course of his gender, in effect eliminating the mother's wish for a male architect and keeping the household steady and happy.

If we were to follow the analysis of Karen Horney, the Neo-Freudian who countered Freud's "penis envy" with her own "womb envy," the same mother would come across as a kind of dread, to be feared and controlled at all cost. Between child and mother, the latter guards the gate to pleasure and security. In barring it, she gives rise to a mélange of feelings, a mix of anxiety, fear, and anger, a monster of sorts against whom the child must conduct eternal battle just to be on equal terms with her. "In her paper 'The Dread of Woman,'" Christina Wieland tells us in her book *The Undead Mother*, "Horney explores the many myths and fairytales in which the hero must overcome horrifying female forces, variously portrayed as witches, sirens, medusas, sphinxes, monsters, and dragons of all kinds."[78] One result is "the wish to return to the womb" to control and conquer that which gave rise to the child's anxiety in the first place. With Melanie Klein, the Freudian known for her pioneering work in the 1920s and 1930s on infant anxiety and psychosis, the frustration gives rise to a "strong sense of inferiority, rivalry with mother, and a strong wish to appropriate the inside of her body."[79]

No doubt there is much in the relationship between mother and son in Wright's case to support a campaign of revenge by him against her. But as angry as Wright may have felt, he was also appreciative and indebted to his mother for putting him on a pedestal and pushing him to transcend his meager beginnings. And so just as much as he was returning to her to avenge his father's demise, Hamlet style, he was also doing so to repair their relationship, marginalized in no small part when he married early and in effect replaced the mother with the wife, well before it was time to do so. He was barely twenty-two and his bride two years younger, both bright eyed and happy and sure of their path. But the mother was having none of it and did everything in her power to retain the son and reap the benefit of years of hard work nurturing the boy. She even sent Cecil, whom we encountered in this book's introduction, to drill some sense into him. But to no avail and much to Wright's annoyance: "Mother! Why go around to Cecil about Kitty and me?" And then again: "Why this worry, anxiety, anguish, curiosity and prying, praying and gossip, to make a perfectly natural thing scandalous?"[80] The answer was obvious, but he was too young to know. The mother was not happy and for years remained at odds with her daughter-in-law, Catherine, fighting over how to keep house and raise kids. Things did not get any easier when Wright again displaced her by displacing his first wife, now running away with a client's wife, a smart and independently minded woman. If Catherine had been a threat, Mamah Cheney was even more so.

Indeed, when Wright eloped with Mamah to Germany and the press was after him for salacious news, it was Wright's mother who, in all likelihood, revealed their whereabouts. Or so Meryle Secrest believes. "It is the kind of maneuver Anna [Wright's mother] was capable of," she tells us, "because at least at first she saw Mamah Cheney as more of a threat than Catherine, and took the latter's side."[81] Wright was, among other things, testing out a new relation far away from the prying crowd, and the last thing he wanted was to reveal his address and give the media, which had vilified him back in Chicago, the opportunity to ruin his vacation. At any rate, Wright would survive the moment and eventually return to Spring Green, interestingly not by himself but with his new lover and her two children, throwing yet another wrench into the relationship between mother and son, itself deserving of analysis all its own.

Wright's mother provided the land that she had bought from her brother, paving the way for the son to come and take it. As Wright would put it, she had in fact "prepared the site for [him] and asked [him] to come and take it." Which "[he] did" in 1911,[82] where he would eventually build what amounts to a cathedral of sorts, not unlike those whose images the mother had plastered in his room and right above his bed growing up. "Fascinated by buildings," his mother had taken a full ten "page wood engravings of the old English Cathedrals from 'Old England' [and] had them framed simply in flat oak and hung them upon the walls of the room that was to be her son's."[83] What turrets and ornaments the Middle Ages made visible on the face of cathedrals, Wright would resurrect in natural form, by eliminating gutters (as mentioned earlier in this chapter) and downspouts and letting winter take care of the rest. What better way to express in architecture divine intervention than designing the kind of architecture that would allow divine intervention to appear on its own terms? "I wanted a home where Icicles by invitation might beautify the eaves. So there were no gutters. And when the snow piled deep on the roof and lay drifted in the courts, icicles came to hang staccato from the eaves. Prismatic crystal pendants sometimes six feet long, glittered between the landscape and the eyes inside. Taliesin in winter was a frosted palace roofed and walled with snow, hung with iridescent fringe."[84] More fundamentally, the house itself, Taliesin, was built according to methods and techniques akin to those that went into building cathedrals, retrieving stones from nearby quarries and assembling them with local masons and craftsmen: "Country masons laid all the stone with the stone quarry for a pattern the architect for a teacher." And just like the masons of fore, so the masons of Taliesin are intergenerational, fathers and sons, the sons learning from the fathers and slowly becoming steeped in the art of craftsmanship: "Perhaps old Dad Signola, in his youth a Czech, was the best of them until Philip Volk came." Taliesin may not have looked like a Cathedral per se, but it was a kind of "palace," built on the same spiritual foundations as those which made the magnificent medieval churches possible. In effect, the son

---

had come full circle in giving the mother what she had always wanted, not necessarily a cathedral but a son who could design and build with the same veracity structures on equal par with those who built cathedrals long ago. He in effect had replaced the father, or resurrected him, and in so doing the ability to penetrate the mother and restart the birth and conception process all over again. This is where poets dwell, at that precipice between life before birth and life after, when all that the world has to offer has yet to be seen for the first time. It was only two or three years after Wright built Taliesin that he would design Midway Gardens in Chicago, revolutionizing public space and sculpture, and only few years later, in the 1920s, that he would breathe a new life into the concrete block system, transforming it from a flat and dead entity into one full of life and intricacy. John Lloyd Wright would describe the Midway Gardens, with which he had helped his dad, as "phantom," emerging from his father's hand as if by magic. "Watch it come out of this clean white sheet," he recalled his father saying to him as he was just about to lay pencil on trace paper. And then, indeed, as if by magic he saw his father's hand move, "rapidly, firmly, up, down, right, left, slantwise." Voilà. "Within an hour, there it was."[85] The product of a true poet.

Prophet, hero, and poet—these were the three characters Wright wove in himself to convince Americans to change. When his ordinary voice did not work, he moved heaven and earth to elevate it. The effort required the help of heroic acts of self-sacrifice. Of which there were many, including severing relations, at least temporarily, with Louis Sullivan at a time when Wright still needed the master's help to get ahead. Others involved weathering social judgment, losing professional battles, and rebuilding after devastating fires. Every time he went down, he soon found a way to come back up again, always seeing in the return an opportunity to resurrect in himself the power and function of a poet, and in the nation the promise of creative renewal.

2

ON THE BRINK
OF FEAR
The Sublime in Wright's Work

The *beauty* of nature reforms itself in the mind, and not for barren contemplation, but for new creation.

—R. W. EMERSON, *Nature*

Having turned himself into a prophet, Wright now had to prove that he was indeed worthy of the title. Prophets don't just walk the streets but here and there perform miracles, turning blood into wine, curing the blind, and multiplying loaves of bread. They may look like any other human but when needed can defy gravity and turn the laws of physics upside down. Whatever architecture Wright was going to produce, it had to do the same—transcend conventions and traffic in the inexplicable. It didn't matter if this architecture looked like an apple or banana; it only had to disarm old habits and make Americans believe in their own creative powers again. A nation so "stewed on money" and institutional blueprints had to be rattled—indeed, pushed—to the brink of disaster to reverse course. Determining how to do that was not easy, but Wright would find an answer in the sublime, coercing architecture to do things it did not know how to do, at least as determined by the laws of nature. The risks were high, but they had to be taken, angering more than one client, engineer, and city official.

This is why Wright's architecture often looks weird, intended less to accommodate function and more to move people. The more out of the ordinary it looked, the more it could seem divinely inspired, as if the hand of man had nothing to do with it, as if the whole thing just fell from his sleeve.

Even some of Wright's more straightforward work, such as his residences, has enough quirks that it cannot be fully digested without reflection and a new vocabulary. Indeed, that was the aim, namely, that by simply looking at it, Americans had no other choice but to simply utter new words. Having had no ready-made catalog of ideas, they would have to invent new ones and as such become born-again individuals, now capable of understanding the opportunities they possessed but which they had missed all along. There was no time to waste.

This chapter takes up the sublime as subject and method with which to explain Wright's prophetic productions. It will see in his architecture the intention to trigger in the observer sublime responses, both of the work itself but also the sites unto which the work opens. In that it is at once the object of observation as well as the stage from which to appreciate nature's great offerings. Be it a window or a floor, Wright's architectural elements either challenged common perception of reality or framed views that gave rise to the same. Both drew gasps of disbelief.

The sublime has a long and interesting history. Those who study it usually start with Longinus, a first-century AD Greek figure who invoked it in reference to great oration, "raising" the "soul" and presumably moving a person to do great things. "Sublimity," he said, "is always an eminence and excellence in language." Edmund Burke and Immanuel Kant would modernize the topic many centuries later, now theorizing that it was not limited to the impact of great words but included a kind of cognitive impasse between a thing seen and the ability of the mind to make sense of that scene. Between the two there is a gap, and in trying to close it observers finds themselves triumphing over current cognitive limitations, indeed generating surplus intellectual firepower they did not know they had. Be it a magnificent mountain range or a terrifying car crash, the discrepancy between phenomenon and reason is so vast that even the smallest attempt at closure is bound to get the mind to leapfrog its boundaries. Nothing less than self-doubt is cast aside in favor of personal and creative realizations.

For Edmund Burke, pain was central to the rise of sublimity, not actual pain but the promise and metaphor of it. No one needs to actually jump over a cliff and risk dying, but simply experience the imaginary version of doing so. That's why art is there, to give us a view into the terrible while keeping us at safe distance from it. Film is particularly useful in this realm, reenacting danger but without being dangerous and actually putting us in harm's way. In fact, says Burke, we should be careful not to get too close to actual danger, for that would overwhelm the intellectual benefits intended by inviting fear in the first place: "When danger or pain press too nearly, they are incapable of giving any delight and are simply terrible."[1] Indeed, actual danger is no fun, closing down the channels of insight instead of building them. "Whatever is fitted in any sort," adds Burke, "to excite the ideas of pain, and danger, that is to say, whatever is in any sort terrible, or is conversant about terrible objects, or operates in a manner analogous to terror, is a source of the sublime."[2]

Kant picked up where Burke left off, not only articulating a theory of the sublime but laying out the process by which it matures and translates into a production of creative impact. According to Mary Arensberg writing in the *The American Sublime,* he broke down the makeup of the sublime into three stages, the first being a mere encounter between subject and object, "a smooth correspondence between inside and out." Between the material world outside and the mental one inside there is at first a level plane, an "equilibrium" of sorts.[3] But once matters settle and the scene is realized for the extraordinary phenomenon that it is, the ground shifts and "the relationship between subject and object is destroyed." Anxiety ensues, "resulting in displeasure and unease," which must be satiated in some way. Stage three involves the mind contending with the instability, seeking ways with which to level the ground once again. The struggle inevitably triggers works of mental surplus, in art and science overflowing their cup and turning the ordinary into extraordinary works of poetic production. What had been far-fetched now is inevitable or at least possible.

The sublime can be set off by any number of encounters, some natural, some man-made. Magnitude helps but is not necessary. Thomas Jefferson was awestruck by a rock formation and couldn't contain himself. Unable to describe his feelings at first, all he could do is rattle off numbers: "two hundred and seventy feet deep" and some "forty feet wide at the bottom and ninety feet at the top." What could the poor man do but let the encounter settle down first? He was letting Kant's first stage play itself out, reach an equilibrium. Soon, however, the breech unfolds, and he realizes that between him and the rock there is no chance. Indeed, "it is impossible" to find anything more "sublime" than this. The "rapture of the spectator is really indescribable."[4] Niagara Falls would induce similar feeling, causing one visitor to say in amazement that "when I saw Niagara, I stood dumb, lost in wonder, love and praise."[5] Of the more manufactured sublimes, we can look to the work of the nineteenth-century landscape painter Thomas Cole for ideas. Here, too, the theme is nature, but unlike Jefferson's object of admiration, the view in this case is far from natural; rather, it is a compound of mixed and imaginary landscapes. Its aim is to compete against and replace normative reality, at least temporarily, so that you, as its consumer, can transcend yourself and in effect become a more developed thinker. In the words of Bryan Wolf, it seeks "to defeat the claustrophobic and imploding centers of meaning . . . substituting for past forms of art the narrative of its own peculiar genesis."[6] Through wide terrains and expansive vistas, it invites the mind to entertain new explanations while swallowing whole old ones. "Through the romantic sublime," Wolf adds, "Cole invents his own story, filling the silence of non-narrative vistas with the clamor of self-discovery."

The Emersonian Sublime

The sublime was a popular theme during the Enlightenment, a helpful and convenient tool with which to accelerate critical and objective thinking. Emerson was well aware of it but also critical of his predecessors, not so willing to reduce it to black-and-white terms. Yes, it could be triggered by dramatic changes in scale, but it could also arise out of life's more ordinary encounters. According to him, something as simple as the "crossing [of] a bare common, in snow puddles, at twilight, under a cloudy sky," could be sublime too, the source of "perfect exhilaration."[7] Why divide the world into worthy scenes, on the one hand, and not so worthy ones, on the other? Wouldn't that bifurcate our use of it and as such produce waste in the process? If we adhere only to one side and neglect the other, what would become of the latter? "Not the sun or the summer alone," Emerson insists, "but every hour and season yields its tribute of delight; for every hour and change corresponds to and authorizes a different state of the mind from breathless noon to grimmest midnight." Not a moment deserves to be thrown out, nor season or geography, but all must contribute to life's more essential joys. If he could hold it, the moment, within the palm of his hand, he would. He would become "glad to the brink of fear."[8] Nothing terrifies him more, hyperbolically speaking, than feeling the moment slip by from underneath his grip, uncaptured in some way. Should he retain it, he would be able to retain youth and, through youth, a fidelity to self. Let the moment go, and it will have to answer to the march of time, past and future judgments, and as such become heavy with moral responsibility. No person can remain authentic that way but will soon have to acquire a dual personality, one in and one out, each sailing on a ship of its own seas. Which is no good. Better to align the two at all cost. And yet how to do all that? Where should one go to keep the moment from slipping? Emerson proposes nature: "The lover of nature is he whose inward and outward senses are still truly adjusted to each other; who has retained the spirit of infancy even into the era of manhood." "In the woods is perpetual youth."

Wright couldn't agree more and spent a lifetime returning to the woods, physically and in memory, always reminding his audience that it was because of the work on his uncle's farm, earlier in life, that he ended where he did, a successful and creative architect. It was at that youthful moment when he learned about hard work, natural patterns, community, color, and more. But also about what it means to have one's inward and outward senses "adjusted to each other." He never let go after that, always insisting on a perfect correspondence between interior and exterior expressions in himself and in others. Anything short of that would be imitation, fakery, and a form of slavery.

Years later he would return to the farm all over again, only a mile or so from where he experienced it the first time around, in Spring Green, this time on his own property. Years after that he would pass the baton to his own students at the Taliesin Fellowship, teaching them architecture through the same tools, more or less, that his uncle had used to teach him life's lessons, milking cows, tending to the fields, and fixing things. Some fellows puzzled, asking at one point, politely, about the reason behind linking cows to architectural education. What is the logic of that? How could cows be in any way useful to understanding the conventions of design, floor plans, and the like? To which Wright responded, with perfect Emersonian pitch, that "it is only when your mind is present in what you are doing that you are growing in that thing." Which means that it is not so much that the milking of cows is important to architecture as it is to helping a mind focus and learn from the task at hand.

How else would genius find the light of day? We all have it, but only those who are able to dwell in the moment can retrieve their best inner potential.

The Emersonian Sublime and the Opening of Homes

Underlying Emerson's inward and outward adjustment is the call to lift all unnecessary barriers between inside and out. Indeed, lift them and the two sides will naturally see each other better, and before too long become one and the same. Wright followed suit, shedding as many interior walls as possible, and as early as the earliest Prairie homes in 1890s. He even thinned out the exterior walls and began to think of them as "screen" and less defensive fortresses with which to protect the interior world or privacy from the exterior. "My sense of the wall," he tells us, "was no longer the side of a box. Rather it was "the enclosure of space affording protection against storm or heat only when needed." Yes, only when needed; otherwise the wall did not need to be of brick and stone, only a line of glass doors, which when open give breezeway access between living space and fresh air. And when closed do the same through wide views and plenty of light. As much as possible Wright wants "to bring the outside world into the house and let the inside of the house go outside." Emerson was right; Americans had come to think of the world in binary terms, one side good and worthy of enjoyment, the other the opposite. What a waste, and not until Americans can see how wonderful life is in the round will they ever change. "To the attentive eye," Emerson says, "each moment of the year has its own beauty, and in the same field, it beholds, every hour, a picture which was never seen before, and which shall never be seen again."

Those who came to live in Wright's Prairie homes were all captains of industry. They didn't get where they were by accident or nefarious ways but by a commitment to hard work and ethical values. They wanted to do things the right way, not the cheap way, a fine balance between art and professional success. Wright couldn't help but feel the promise of a better nation in them. Not unlike the first captains who set sail to the new world in the seventeenth century, they, too, triumphed over turbulent seas through vision and determination. And just like them they, too, had to stand high atop a masthead of sorts so they could stay above the fray, see clearly, and plan ahead. The high vantage point interested Wright greatly, as metaphor but also as a tool with which to peer over the city and keep within view nature and the horizon beyond. Only this way would Americans be able to elide the urban crowd and retain the power of personal choice. Look through the perspectives he produced throughout life, but particularly those his apprentices drew of Broadacre City (see chapter 4), and you will see that a great many of them were taken from a place high above the ground, showing vistas as far as the eye can see. Which is why when Wright came to design the Prairie home windows, he located them high and above a certain "water table" line (see the discussion of the Heurtley House in the introduction). To see out, his residents had to stand and, very much like the captains of old, scope and navigate the troubled seas ahead. In that, Wright went a step further than Emerson in his attempt to adjust relations between "inward and outward senses," this time as calibrated next to a much broader national ambition. It wasn't enough that Americans had to find ways to adjust their insides with their outsides; they now also had to do so in relation to a country that needed their stability to gain stability itself.

The Usonian Sublime

There were other forms of openness. Once underway, Wright never stopped opening his architecture to itself and to the world beyond. He continued to agree with Emerson that by opening up space you also open up the mind, inviting it to see solutions where none seemed to exist before. Where two entities may have appeared separate before, now they appear as if with tentacles capable of extending and creating interesting and fruitful connections. Nowhere was this more needed than in the aftermath of the market crash of 1929. Overnight Americans went from riches to rags, a good many soon losing property, home, and, perhaps more importantly, self-confidence. The Hoover administration did not help, urging Americans to be resourceful and tenacious but in so doing destroying morale. Big and creative solutions were needed and quickly, and of the kind that required sidestepping old barriers in favor of new open intellectual terrains. No idea was too out there, impossible, or stupid. Everything had to be on the table. The result was the Usonian home, as opened up as the earlier Prairie homes but now even more so, physically but more importantly creatively.

Gone were the massive brick walls, here replaced with a much more limited version of them. Also gone were second floors, complex roof formations, and, most importantly, the bulk of the house itself. Instead of the squarish footprint of the Prairie homes, the Usonian plan took on a much skinner configuration, specifically two wings that intersected at right angles and formed an L scheme, leaving behind a garden of central importance. So important, in fact, that it may have been more important than the house itself, allowing Americans the stage on which to explore and advance notions of self-reliance. Besides building shelter, Americans needed to build self-worth and this by building things. It didn't really matter what as long as those things helped Americans slowly but surely climb out of the rut they had fallen into. Be it growing food or building a piece of furniture, it did not matter; what did matter was the ability to build and let the results be the source of self-reflection and pride. To that end the garden was "no backyard affair," as Wright put it, but a serious attempt at helping Americans restore confidence. "No kernel of nourishing corn," says Emerson in "Self-Reliance," "can come to him but through his toil bestowed on that plot of ground which is given to him to till."[9]

Indeed, Americans were not going to stand on their feet unless they toiled again, and "on that plot of ground which is given to [them] to till." If so, they could soon reap the benefits they had sowed, gaining more and more hope as they go. The only question was whether they could see the work they had done, or not. Transparency was key, between inside and outside and across the house, allowing the garden and the productions played out on it to play out in real time inside the house. Opacity must give way to total visual access. A window here and another there wouldn't do, only a continuous row of them, and more preferable still, a battery of doors that once open leave little or no doubt as to the work underway outside. "Do your work and you shall reinforce yourself," Emerson insisted. And then again: "[Do] your work and I shall know you." Indeed, do your work and both God and your inner strength shall conspire to lift you out of difficulty and get you to a place where you can help yourself and others get out of difficulty.

Sitting inside the Usonian home and looking out, only five or six French doors stand in the way. Opened they create a near seamless visual connection with the garden, at once void and Eden. As void it calls Americans to action, much like a clearing in the woods, to translate ideas into work and work into a product of some use. As Eden it showcases the progressive movement underway, from a state of distress to one about hope and achievement. All is well, but Wright does not stop there. He brings the logic inside, especially between the kitchen and the living room, transforming both forever. What work takes place there is honored and indeed blessed by the caring eye of the family; a spouse, a sibling, now lounging across the room. No longer is it in fact a kitchen per se, but a "workspace," to use Wright's own word, conflating two or more otherwise disparate environments, home on one side, the factory, say, on the other. Heat, at one point a reminder of awful labor conditions, is here revisited as a source of civilizing and strengthening family relations. Where it had created suffocating environments in one place, inside the Usonian home it becomes the element with which to develop strong human bonds. As Reyner Banham tells us in his *Architecture of the Well-Tempered Environment*, Wright, more than any other modern architect, insisted on a unified approach to heat and architecture, certainly at the Usonian home, where he famously ran hot water pipes through concrete floors, but elsewhere as well. Most notably at the Larkin Building, where the circulation of people up the building and that of air and other environmental conduits were seen as one and the same, stemming from the same call for health and comfort. "In this the Larkin Building is something of a watershed," says Banham. "It must be judged a design whose final form was imposed by the method of environmental management employed, rather than one whose form derived from the exploitation of an environmental method."[10]

Included in the transformation of the Usonian home into an active theater of good work was the elimination of both basement and attic, spaces in which otherwise essential domestic performances can hide and potentially never be seen again. Also gone, technically, was the middleman, in this case the contractor, who in building a home on someone else's behalf acts as a kind of barrier, keeping the American from finding and acting upon his potential. The home as a handover job is no different than any other aspect of the commercial market, an abstract exchange between buyer and seller that leaves both little invested in the product between. Better to hand the rein to the Americans to build their own homes. All they need is a kit of parts and off they can go assembling the pieces. They may not be builders, but given the prearrangement of the parts, including the way they could dovetail and connect, the whole would be possible. What could be more sublime and self-empowering than to build the structure that will allow you to outlive the structure through creativity, family, progeny, and lineage? This was how the Usonian home was billed, as a kit of parts prefabricated off-site and then shipped and assembled on-site by the owner. The reality, however, turned out a little different, perhaps not surprisingly given Wright's obsessive interest in glove-in-hand approach to details and a product that had to be different from the usual mail-order variety of yesteryears. Indeed, the assembly of the Usonian home proved beyond the pale of the layman. Walls were tightly wrought, gaining strength, among other ways, by the way they turned ninety degrees and wove a connection with shelving units attached to the wall. As one author put it, "these were not simple walls to build" but in fact "exposed essential details to showcase the carpenter's craft." Ultimately "they required a carpenter to build up the frames from stock lumber."[11]

Wright would modify the scheme and make the Usonian idea more constructible in the 1950s, when he conceived of the so-called "Do it Yourself Usonian Automatic System" homes. Automatic precisely because they were based on a scalable system of concrete blocks, each designed to dovetail into the next and in effect rise and become a house independent of either expert or contractor. This was a step up in the project of self-reclamation, namely not only simplifying the design but also reducing its modularity to a scale and a weight that could be handled by a diverse spectrum of Americans, across gender, age, and economic class. According to Wright, "this house incorporates innovations which reduce most of the heavier building costs, labor in particular." Indeed "to build a low-cost house you must eliminate, so far as possible, the use of skilled labor now so expensive."[12] Other manual work eliminated includes plastering and painting, now that the material was concrete inside and out. In the words of Bruce Pfeiffer, one of Wright's premier scholars and custodian of the architect's oeuvre, Wright "was eliminating the extra work and features that invariably raised the costs of construction and furnishings."[13] The scope and reach of the project seemed to change and acquire the lexicon of democracy, empowering people at the individual level but also at that of the community. "Indeed," said Matthew Skjonsberg, "through all the building materials he worked with, Wright sought a system that would bridge house and community."[14] This would be a sublime of a slightly different kind, not quite the same as that which matured between Jefferson and the natural outcropping he encountered, as we saw earlier, but not too dissimilar in principle, either. Both are based on an inverse relation in scale between self and the world, small and large, in the case of Jefferson between man and magnificent rock, and in that of the Usonian Automatic between one man and many Americans. "Just as the print press democratized access to knowledge, Wright's self-built system aimed to democratize access to architecture."[15]

It may be interesting to note that just as Wright was publishing his drawings of the "automatic" system (fig. 5), so was the mathematician Norbert Wiener issuing his own reflection on the "automatic" machine. The two share not only a lexicon but the same effect. In both there is the attempt to sidestep human influence in favor of a self-regulatory and indeed automatic system that decides not based on moral judgement but on patterns traced over time. At issue is speed and the degree to which the human is fast enough to react in time before or when disaster hits. Or, if fast, then slowed by its desire to think matters through. Thinking so often leads to overthinking, aborting a process that is otherwise better served by impulse. Much like responding to touching a hot pan does not need thinking but instead a swift and immediate removal of the hand, so certain other encounters in life require a similarly unedited response. Not only could we risk getting the right answer wrong, but so wrong it may spell the end of life here on earth. Climate change is a good example; if left to human debate to correct, we may lose the earth before there is enough time to conserve it. Better leave the corrective to machines, tracing patterns over time and finding a commensurate response to save the day. In his 1954 essay "Men, Machines, and the World About," Wiener differentiated between two industrial revolutions, the first as triggered and symbolized by the steam engine, the second by a new cybernetic machine, "replacing human judgement and discrimination at low levels by the discrimination of the machine." He compared the latter to the body's nervous system, efficient and strong precisely because it does not discriminate but rather reacts in a manner not unlike that in which a nervous system responds to stimuli. "In particular," Wiener said, "it seemed to us a very hopeful thing to make an automatic feedback control apparatus in which the feedback itself

FIG. 5. Toufic H. Kalil House, an example of the Usonian Automatic, Manchester, New Hampshire, 1955. Photograph courtesy of Mark Hertzberg.

was carried out, in large measure by the successive switching operations such as one finds either in the nervous system or in the computing machine."[16]

In this new brave world, the machine now appears "not as a source of power, but as a source of control and a source of communication." What could be more powerful and desirable than a world run by machines, circumventing some of humanity's more destructive indiscretions, including those that had led to its cultural demise in the past? Or so Wright hinted. In "Machinery, Materials, and Men," one of his Princeton lectures in 1930, with a title eerily similar to Wiener's, he forecasts the mathematician's distinction between past and present industrial revolutions. "The difference," he says, "to the architect and his fellow artists, between our era and others, lies simply enough in the substitution of automatic machinery for tools." Which may not sound like much, until we realize that the results spell "the automatic acquiescence of men."[17] Which means that the new machine did not just make things but sublimated the cognitive capacity of the individual to act on his behalf. Under the powers of this new machine the American willingly and unself-consciously surrendered his will-to-power without a fight. Like a docile pet, he lay down and let the operations of the new machine take over. In any other time and circumstance this would have been bad news. But not with Wright at this time in America history. He is not so sure that the news is all that bad in fact, now speaking so many years after he had first given his presentation on the machine at Hull House in 1901. This time around the automatic machine may have something more useful to offer than the first tool machine, which had enabled the architect to produce more precise and refined details. Indeed, "at first blush" the difference between the old capacity of the machine and the new one can be judged "appalling." But upon second thought, "who knows where [that difference] is going?" It might very well solve the country's crippling mediocrity by inserting in society an automatic system that quietly and secretly undermines the country's worst and self-sabotaging democratic practices. Democracy has its attributes, but in America, Wright wagered, it is used as a bludgeon to defeat higher ideals. "The republic" may have succeeded in going "further, faster, and [in being] safer, but in doing so it has also become more "comfortable and egotistic in a more universal mediocrity than ever existed on earth before."[18]

More than a building tool, the Usonian Automatic System was a "communication control apparatus," to use Wiener's words, established to help control a dialogue between Wright and the American public for whom he designed and whom he sought to change. Direct talk didn't quite work anymore, often degenerating into an outright shouting match between architect and client, evidenced by the mountain of angry letters Wright wrote over the years and the client back at him. Better design a system that can operate independently of the author but through whose unfolding his message is not only made clear but starts its own automatic and self-regulatory system of dissemination. The strategy almost worked but later proved too cumbersome and expensive. Only seven Usonian Automatic homes would be built when all was said and done. Had it worked, it would have been a sublime of a different reach, more penetrating than its wooden predecessor, pixilated and reduced in scale to a block just so that it could seep through the cracks, so to speak, and reach interiors well beyond the pale. Not just the interior of homes but that of the mind, working a message of self-reliance, empowerment, and personal pride. In that the Usonian Automatic concrete block was just as much a tool of communication as it was construction, each a word unit unto itself, equipped with the means to interface with others in an effort to create, codify, and deliver a critical message. And just like any other code language, this one, too, forms a self-repeating pattern meant to spread independent of the source that set it in motion.

Hoovervilles and the Usonian Homes

Between the Usonian home and Hoovervilles there may not be a shared biographical note. At least not that this author was able to find. But the two do share a background of economic hardship, both rising in response to the need for quick, efficient, and affordable shelter. Hoovervilles were, of course, the shantytowns that were built during the Great Depression and in response to massive unemployment and subsequent evictions. Named after President Herbert Hoover, whom many had blamed for the Depression, they embodied structures that were assembled out of scrap gathered here and there from junkyards and derelict construction sites. Their walls were "the same inside as outside," in this case out of utter necessity and lack of otherwise more refined and finished products. Commonly, they were found in parks, waterfronts, and urban edge conditions, some as big as little towns (fig. 6). In many cases, those who built them took pride in cleaning them and keeping them tidy, making sure they did not degenerate into petri dishes for the spread of disease. Some had mayors and advisors, addressing concerns regarding garbage pickup, children, education, and job training. Seattle was particularly exemplary on that note, featuring Hoovervilles, according to Donald Francis Roy, that were "an integral part of a highly differentiated urban design," functioning "as a segregated residential area of distinct physical structure."[19]

The Usonian home was not assembled out of discarded material, cardboard or otherwise. Far from it; it was constructed out of architectural-grade plywood, brick, concrete, and so on. But it did pick up on the ethic of shacks, namely thinned-out planes lifted, leaned, and stacked against each other to enclose a space. Prop up any one of those planes, and it will collapse back on itself, but lean it against the next one over, and it will have already gathered enough stability to stand up. Add another and yet one more, and already an enclosure is underway. Top the whole with yet one more, and a shelter

FIG. 6. Homeless man sitting in front of a shack in Hooverville, Seattle, Washington, 1931. University of Washington Libraries, Special Collections, James P. Lee, photographer, Lee10544B.

is formed. Peg the pieces to each other in some way, and what you have is essentially a self-supporting construct that needs little skill to accommodate the basics of living. Wright's Usonian home was naturally much more complicated than that, but it, too, rose out of the simple logic that between wall and wall and wall and roof there need not be a complicated and overbuilt pile of stuff-studs, nails, sills and headers, and so on, but planes which when erected and gathered like cards can do the job just fine, not to mention efficiently and elegantly. To that end Wright says in *The Natural House:* "Although it is getting to be a luxury material, the walls [of the Usonian home] will be wood board-walls the same inside as outside—three thicknesses of boards with paper placed between them, the boards fastened together with screws."[20]

Regardless of the overlap between the Usonian home and the Hooverville shacks, what Wright saw in shack-like architecture, and by extension the economic depression, is an opportunity to interrogate the American home. Over the years it had puffed up and acquired bulk, in construction but also in space that now invited and protected material excess. Walls had doubled in thickness unnecessarily, the same with floors and roofs and so on, and this because of an industry that no longer thought creatively but only expediently. To the problem of thermal protection, it had piled one layer against the next and merely solved the problem by increasing width. Why not integrate the pieces instead and see in walls and roofs at once structure and insulation, opacity and transparency, inside and outside? This was too much for the commercial contractor and so Wright took up the gauntlet himself.

It is to that extent and in the same vein that Wright believed, with Emerson, that ethical living is inextricably linked to a measure of poverty, not actual poverty, but the discipline to know how to live a meaningful life with less. Hoovervilles may have been trashy and ugly, but they were deeply authentic in the way they expressed resourcefulness, modesty, and a capacity to live by needs and not wants. They should not be romanticized but understood, and if Wright did indeed observe them, what he may have been touched by, more than anything, is their poverty of spirit. Nothing short of democracy depended on it, and he would say as much: "poverty of the spirit is thus built into our own free country." Not until Americans can release themselves from excess will they actually be free. Instead, they will always remain beholden to either bank or some other exploitative entity. "The great depend on their heart," said Emerson, "not their purse. Genius and virtue, like diamonds, are best plain set, set in lead, set in poverty."

Hoover had asked the country to rely on self-reliance and neighborly help to get through difficult economic times, going so far as to veto a 1932 public works bill intended to provide thousands of jobs throughout the country. And so here were Americans doing just that, relying on their own internal physical and mental capacities to make do, including Wright, who seemed to have taken the challenge quite seriously, devising a home whose ethic is premised on the idea of cobbling together boards and assembling a roof over one's head. He may not have succeeded in giving Americans full autonomy over the construction of their house, as we saw earlier, but the intent was nonetheless there, providing them with a kit of parts and empowering them to rebuild in the spirit of Hoovervilles, this time with dignity and pride of place. There was a way to do what Hoover had asked for, but whereas the president had simply urged Americans to dig in and be resourceful, Wright also provided them with the tools to do so.

Hoovervilles as an aggregation of objects and spaces had no boundaries or, of course, property lines; they simply sprawled as they needed to, growing as the evicted and homeless populations grew. If they did have boundaries, they were marked by water edges such as shorelines and riverbanks. Some did organize and elect leaders to manage and guide essential activities. But for the most part Hoovervilles were amorphous in scope and destiny. In that, they spoke of common property and the right of people to land and country, harking back to what Henry George had insisted on in *Progress and Poverty*, namely that so long as man shall own property there will always be those who can afford it and those who can't. The result is a society divided between rich and poor, eliminating the potential of the common man to improve. In his words: "What is necessary for the use of land is not its private ownership but the security of its improvements." Indeed "it is not necessary to say to a man, "this is your land," in order to induce him to cultivate or improve it. It is only necessary to say to him "whatever your labor or capital produces on this land shall be yours."[21]

Wright took note by leaving the remaining corner of the Usonian home open, visually and spatially connecting it to the next home over, inviting social and critical skills to travel between the two (fig. 7). "Democratic man demands conscientious liberty for himself no more nor less than he demands liberty for his neighbor"; the two working together to reveal the "uncommon" in each.[22] What one household may discover in, say, methods for better gardening or those that amplify the use of tools, the next could develop and turn into an invention of its own. Wasn't that Hoover's dream, a society whose members can lean on each other so that collectively they can rise together? Wright again answered the call, showing how the built environment can be an important complement to laws and policies whose power would otherwise be limited to print. In his words, if "literature tells about man, architecture presents him."

The Usonian home evolved out of Wright's struggle to democratize access to the great American home but also to the great, or not so great, American city. From the get-go it had been premised on the philosophy of property and

FIG. 7. Herbert Jacobs House, Madison, Wisconsin, 1936, arguably the most iconic Usonian home. Photograph courtesy of Mark Hertzberg.

the distinction that what's mine is mine and what's yours is yours. Anything in between technically belonged, and still does, to the government and is often wasted since the government cannot be there to take care of it all the time. The whole set-up seemed assembled against collective action, and the interest of the people to see in land the means with which to cultivate shared benefit. In response, Wright took the L scheme of the Usonian home and paired it with another, now forming a large garden between the two. What had been a private garden, limited to the concern of a single owner, was now a little more public, or at least inclusive of the next garden over. Between the two Wright proposed no fence, and thus no visual obstruction.[23] What one neighbor did on his or her property was now the purview of the next, back and forth, until over the years a certain crescendo of mutual benefits resulted, lifting the neighborhood out of its rut. Multiply the pattern across the city and what you get is a new dissertation on collective power, not communism and a certain repressive regime against the individual, but the power to see in the inventions of others the seed of your own. Under this political and economic system, copyright laws would become null and void, everything soon becoming the property of everyone else. A more creative sublime there isn't, and Wright agrees: "Why should man own ideas, they can never be his own if they are any good." Except, that is, "to get money out of them."[24]

Once underway the Usonian home never stopped, Wright continuing to reproduce it to push Americans to see more and connect with nature and each other. There, Americans were the sublime. In them lay the great solution to the national problem. All they had to do was catch themselves in the act of work to work again. Today we may record ourselves to do the same, replaying footage to assess the degree to which we have progressed or not. Back then Wright used architecture against itself, taking down barriers to make clear America's great buried potential.

So far so good, but the national problem remained a thorn in Wright's side. Even with the Prairie homes now in place and the Usonian underway, the country remained a cultural blot on the global scene. Even as other modern nations were advancing—Japan, England, France—America was degenerating. "How can you, with reason," he implored his fellow Americans, "expect national prosperity when our nation is dominated by ideas . . . that belong way back in the dark ages?"[25] Capitalism per se wasn't the problem, only the degree to which it failed to manage the relation between excess and meaningless accumulation. Wealth seemed naturally cursed by immediate gratification and the need to quickly match in financial success expressions of beauty, which beauty does not know how to do. Beauty takes time, requiring an iterative process that can take years to turn and transform into authentic productions. Having no patience for that wealth makes a beeline for the ready-made, short-circuiting the natural process of creativity. For Wright the problem came down to a critical distinction between commercialization and civilization: "we have commercialization instead of civilization," he said, which "is itself naturally sterilizing."[26] We may walk the streets and visit theaters, enter museums and engage in discussions, and think we are participating in a civilization. But the reality is otherwise. The whole thing is a sham, leveled on us by a cultural industry constructed specifically to satisfy our needy desire to showcase success. Neither the sidewalk, the play, the painting, nor the art of the debate is there for us to grow a mind; rather, they serve as facades with which to assume a certain pomp we never had. Worse, architects succumbed to this lie, becoming mere "designers" putting up replicas of work from distant lands, causing Wright to issue a warning. "The fate of the architect is largely in doubt," he cautions. "No longer an essential factor in our civilization, he is now a "designing partner" or an employer of "designing partners." To fight back, the architect, and by extension Americans, has to "expand his mind." And quickly if not suddenly. Matters are too far gone for slow change; a jump start is in order.

The Necessity of the Sublime

The expansion of the mind was just as much about unlearning as it was about learning. All the university education that went into raising a generation had to be dumped into the ocean before any real expansion can take place, which meant, among other things, the capacity to now make clear distinctions between X and Y, that while there may seem to be a similarity between the two, they are actually very different. Experiment and experimental may seem alike but are in reality very different, Wright tells us: the first is noble and feeds into man's need for self-improvement; the other is speculative and wasteful. Similarly, between "the curious" and "the beautiful" there may seem to be an overlap, but the two are actually nowhere near one another. The first concerns "sight," the other "vision"; the first is fleeting, the next, introspective and complex. "It is a line that is seldom surely drawn in our time by the educated individual," Wright observes.[27] Indeed, it is the educated individual who is to blame, too locked into a certain frame of knowledge to think clearly or properly. Something urgent was needed to reverse course: a sublime intervention, not in the vein of Emerson anymore but now in that as theorized by Burke and Kant.

The Encounter with the Big Bad Lands

While on a trip to South Dakota, Wright had experienced it, a special nexus between man, nature, and the unbelievable. He is in a car driven by a man named Paul Bellamy, who is from the area and knows the geography very well. Ahead, are the "Big Bad Lands, Black Hills and Spearfish Canyon." Wright is spellbound and right off the bat begins to describe the scene in terms specific to the theory of the sublime as Immanuel Kant describes it in his *Critique of Judgement:* "I've been about the world a lot and pretty much over our own country but was totally unprepared for that revelation called the Dakota Bad Lands." He goes on: "at about four in the afternoon, something came into view that made me sit up straight and look at Bellamy to see if he saw what I saw." In true Kantian rhetoric, Wright speaks of the power of the infinite over him: "Endless trabeations surmounted by or rising into pyramid(obelisk) and temple, ethereal in color and exquisitely chiseled in endless detail, they began to reach to infinity spreading into the sky on every side; an endless supernatural world more spiritual than earth but created out of it."[28] Just as the scene is infinite, so is Wright's narrative of it, sprawling and endless and not sure how to stop. It seems that Wright is so overwhelmed he has lost command of his language. Yes, in fact the view is so riveting it gave him "an indescribable sense of mysterious other where—a distant architecture, ethereal . . ." and on and on. The words are almost identical to those that Jefferson issued upon seeing the natural bridge discussed earlier. The two men, while steeped in language, all of a sudden find themselves unable to articulate. Where did the Bad Lands come from? Wright wonders. Why do we know of the Grand Canyon and not this canyon? he questions his companion. In response to which he is told that South Dakota lies off the beaten path and away from the main east-west highway linking the two ends of the country. Between the two, Wright feels that the Dakota outcroppings are much more powerful precisely because they had not been commercialized. In fact, he finally wagers, the degree to which we receive something as sublime or not depends on the extent to which it has been sold and oversold to us. Frequency of exposure matters.

For Kant the sublime could indeed move people beyond themselves, specifically as generated through encounters with the infinite and the boundless, not unlike those that Wright experienced while being driven toward the Big Bad Lands of South Dakota. Here we see the architect, again, a man otherwise full of words, finding himself speechless, unable to describe what he is seeing. The crisis is one of representation, trying to name that which cannot be named. At a loss, he starts conjuring up likenesses as best as he could: "a distant architecture, ethereal, touched, only touched with a sense of Egyptian, Mayan, drift and silhouette." What Wright has just encountered does not match the catalog of words and images he has in his repertoire. They are "beyond all comparison," to quote Kant. It opens before him a kind of gap between him and those magnificent rocks out in the distance. As much as he'd like to let go, he can't, not least because the scene grabs him back as if by the lapels, its magnificence too magnetic to bypass. There is nothing he can do now but to try to match in thought what nature had worked in scale and color. Indeed, for Kant the matter is intellectual, requiring from Wright brainwork to level a deeply unstable playing field. And yet his current brain is all he has. He must use it to manufacture new thoughts, combine two or more dissimilar ideas into a new line of inquiry. Interpretation, not imitation, is what he needs, "the ability to think and create a mind that "surpass[es] every standard of sense," according to Kant. Naturally a kind of "violence to the imagination" ensues, pushing the mind to think the unthinkable and ultimately transcend itself.

Should he, Wright, be able to place Americans at that same precipice, to think the unthinkable, Wright wagered, he might stand a chance at reforming them, including the educational system from which they emerged. And so he took a chance. Three or four projects are representative, namely Fallingwater in Mill Run, Pennsylvania; the Johnson Wax Headquarters in Racine, Wisconsin; and the Mile High in Chicago. We may add the Guggenheim in New York, although that building will get its due interpretative course in the final chapter of this book. Fallingwater, the Johnson Wax Headquarters, and the Guggenheim belong to a specific kind of client—enlightened men who were both wealthy and principled, perfect tools with which to leverage the kind of architecture that will awaken a nation.

Fallingwater

The son of German immigrants who arrived in western Pennsylvania in the 1860s, Edgar Kaufmann, the client for Fallingwater, was a hardworking and well-known owner of a major store in Pittsburgh. According to his son, also named Edgar, he was "magnetic and unconventional" and "loved to build things," exactly the traits Wright needed in a client. The two men would find their match in each other right from the start, Wright finding in Kaufmann a love for adventure, Kaufmann in Wright a passion for art. Between the two there would arise a great rapport. "Mr. Wright and Mr. Kaufmann," remembered John Howe, one of Wright's more famous apprentices, "had a great rapport from the start, each with a genuine admiration for the other."[29] Central to the success of the relationship was Kaufmann's keen ability to sympathize with Wright's plight as a misunderstood artist. Most clients call on architects to help them design and build structures; Kaufmann called on Wright to do that and more, becoming a patron and at times the cool head to Wright's tempestuous one. Realizing Wright's place in history, he would introduce him to some of his influential friends, at one point taking the effort to let it be known that despite Wright's reputation as a crank, there were still people who appreciated his contributions. He was no doubt one of them. Even though Wright had received the "severest [of] oppositions," he said, from public officials and building regulators, he was nonetheless appreciated by "open minded sincere American businessmen and women who realized from their own experience the value . . . of what he had to give them."[30] Wright couldn't wish for a more sympathetic endorsement, in effect telling Wright he had his back, a sublime moment in its own right, at least for an architect who at that time in history, during the Depression years, had been reeling from lack of work. Where most Americans will harp, and still do, about matters of function and lack of comfort in Wright's structures, Kaufmann was willing to transcend all that and champion the genius in the architect. And soon he would come through as such, as a patron, lending Wright five hundred dollars in support of building a model of Broadacre City (see chapter 4) before he, Wright, had done much in return.

What Wright had felt at the Bad Lands in 1935 he had already experienced at the future site of Fallingwater in 1932. He and Kaufmann had driven down there on one of his trips to Pittsburgh. Only a couple of hours away from the city, in Mill Run, Pennsylvania, it is defined by a magnificent composition of trees, ravines, and a stream. Immediately he was struck by "the falls, the trees, the rock, ledges, the boulder, and rhododendron." Immediately, too, he was at a loss to find a match in human history for what he was seeing before his eyes. Neither train, plane or car nor works of architecture, for that matter, satisfy. Rather, it is the "story" of the rocks that come close and speak to his true "longing." The infinitely expansive feeling he experienced upon the encounter he must find an equivalent for on the other side, in words but then in walls, doors, and windows, transcending human history and becoming one with geologic time. The sight would stay with him, soon morphing into a "vague shape" in his mind, influenced by "the music of the stream."[31]

From beginning to end the house was an expression of sublime manifestations, both in the way Wright conceived of the design, famously "slipping from his sleeve," but more profoundly in that which dared man to question life's basic assumptions, including gravity. Indeed, he would take his beloved ferroconcrete materials, invented and developed in the latter part of the nineteenth century, and push them to the brink of failure. The images are iconic, two balconies jutting out of the main body of the house and hanging seemingly in midair, one from the living room, the other from a bedroom one floor above (fig. 8). The whole thing seemed, and still does, crazy. But Kaufmann loved the design and wanted to see it through. "I have [now] had time to look at the plans," he tells Wright shortly after he received them, "and study them with no end of thrill."[32] Yes, no end of thrill but also no end of fear that the cantilevers may be more fiction than fact, especially as Wright had designed and located the foundations underneath. And so he, Kaufmann, sent the plans to his engineers, separate from those whom Wright had employed, to assess the reality of the proposal. The reply was less than reassuring, making it clear that what Wright had drawn was simply not possible. And this even before they could get to the cantilevers. Wright had drawn the foundations to rest on and in rock outcroppings and at a place where the stream may flood and erode the integrity of the footings. The comments listed various reasons why the design was problematic. The first comment goes like this: "The end of one of the foundation walls is shown to be approximately 15 feet from the crest of the waterfall. There is a possibility of future undercutting sufficient to endanger the foundation at this point." Another comment warns of "heavy driftwood at time of flood," which could batter the foundation and cause it to fail. But the most damning comment didn't come until later, namely that Wright could place the house on top of a waterfall, but "in our opinion there could be no feeling of complete safety" by doing so. "Consequently we recommend that the proposed site be not used for any important structure."[33]

Wright hadn't known at first of Kaufmann's communication with the engineers, Morris Knowles. When he did and learned of their recommendations and what must have appeared to Wright as scare tactics, he issued a warning, reminding Kaufmann that extraordinary buildings require extraor-

FIG. 8. Fallingwater, Mill Run, Pennsylvania, 1936. Photo by Christopher Little, courtesy of the Western Pennsylvania Conservancy.

dinary measures: "You seem to forget all I said about building an extraordinary house in extraordinary circumstances."[34] The work pressed on according to Wright's designs. But then came the actual cantilevers, and the same rancor appeared again. As formwork was being readied for the pouring of the concrete on the first-floor cantilever, Kaufmann worried. Naturally so; the jut was going to go out over midair a whole eighteen feet and with calculations made in Wright's office by two competent engineers but not by an engineering firm. And so again Kaufmann sends the design to his engineers, this time to the Metzger Richardson Company in Pittsburgh. And again they specify a different design than the one Wright had submitted, adding twice as much steel reinforcement to the concrete. Just as the first time so with the second, Wright gets enraged. How could Kaufmann not trust him and why waste effort calculating and drawing the engineering twice? "If we are paying to have the concrete engineering done down there, there is no use whatever in our doing it here. I am willing you should take it over but I am not willing to be insulted."[35]

Kaufmann was willing to endure Wright's invective, always returning to the table to make peace, but he wasn't willing to live with structural insecurity. The cantilevers worried him to no end, especially when cracks began to appear, first at the parapet on the ends of the cantilevers and second in the lower slab itself. So much so that he reached out to the engineers again, asking them to analyze and remedy what deficiencies were occurring in the construction. Which they did, finding that stresses exceeded what was allowed by code and proposing a pier to alleviate the problem. Yet again Kaufmann had gone behind Wright's back to get peace of mind, this time during a period when Wright had fallen seriously ill and wasn't functional. Once again, Wright would become furious and lash out, asking for the pier to be removed or else. Wright would refer to the occasion as a "scare," telling Kaufmann to trust him, indeed, demanding his word that he would not move again without his consent. "The scare over the integrity of the structure is the usual exaggeration where such matters go," he reassured Kaufmann.

Back and forth the story of Fallingwater went, with Wright doing everything in his capacity to advance a sublime that was about not only infinite distances but also the horror of total and final demise, bringing us back full circle to Burke. No great deed and, certainly, no great thought is likely to happen unless we encounter a moment in which what lies before us induces in us a feeling of utter terror. Not in real terms but in the more abstract sense. The greater the pain, the grander the awakening, central to Wright's aim. The cantilevers were only in one sense ledges from which to appreciate nature and the Emersonian sublime; in other, more tangible terms they were real constructs meant to control fear by conquering it. Fear, that is, of the unknown and the product of habitual customs. Fear, in fact, is what caused the end of American creativity, Wright believed, namely the inability to be "children again" and experiment with "child-like innocence." To the question as to why the American mind had remained provincial, he replied, "I say it is [because] of fear."[36] In his daring of the engineers and of even the real appearance of cracks in the concrete, Wright courted danger in concrete and psychological ways. Walking to the edge of the terraces, even today, and after much restorative work done on the house, one cannot help feeling terror well up inside, not least because the parapets were and are notoriously low. Should the observer lose sight of distances and indeed become taken by the sights ahead, he or she may just fall to his or her demise. Just as nature "violated" Wright's "imagination" and pushed him to come up with a moral and aesthetic equivalent, so he places the American here in the same spot, importantly to propel him beyond himself. Kaufmann's terror of collapse never left him, always worrying that deflections in the cantilevers might one day destroy him and his family. But Wright's force in the end proved too much to counter, and Kaufmann became resigned to the architect, uttering one final statement to him in exasperation: "You must take full responsibility for [the] stability of the concrete structure taking into consideration the results of our tests."[37]

Twice did Wright mention suicide as an answer to America's slide into cultural ruin in a talk on man and parasite. Greed and profit had sent American culture down the abyss of aesthetic and spiritual malaise, with no end in sight. What would end this tragedy, he wondered: "suicide?" The "profit-motive," he said, had destroyed the spirit of the nation, "an ultimate revenge when taken as a motive of a civilization." And yet "what would be the inevitable end? . . . Is suicide the only answer?"[38] Maybe, and it is in that liminal response where the true ethic of the cantilevers at Fallingwater lie, platforms that in all likelihood were never really in danger of collapsing but always operated with that promise in mind.

Sublimity at the Johnson Wax Headquarters

At just about the same time that Wright was finishing the commission for Fallingwater in 1936, he received another. This one was from the Johnson Wax company in Racine, Wisconsin, only about 150 miles east of Spring Green, where his studio is located. The company had started with Samuel Johnson in 1888 selling parquet floors, then quite popular among the Victorians of the era. Samuel was a religious man who cared for his flock, donating 10 percent of his wealth to church and other social organizations. By the time representatives from the company arrived at Taliesin in 1936 to meet and hear from

Wright, Johnson Wax was more than a distributor of floors but a producer of chemicals central to a nation and a market, now rich with industrial products. It was also by then in the hands of Herbert Johnson, Samuel's grandson, who, just like his father and grandfather before him, was keen on continuing the company's belief in fair and just treatment of community but specifically of employees. No worker at the company should feel the need to agitate out of frustration, either for lack of a good working environment or fair wages. "Call it enlightened selfishness if you like," he would say, "for when people get proper wages and proper working conditions they don't feel the need to organize to fight for what they want."[39] Again, Wright seems to have found his next ideal client in Johnson Wax.

The Johnson Wax Administration Building, and later lab tower, is arguably Wright's most inventive building, evidenced by the fact that fourteen patents were issued in its wake. He seemed to be reeling from a sublime encounter himself, as if a man possessed and ready to re-create the world in his own image. Whether that was because he had produced only two buildings since 1928 and had pent-up energy for creative work is not sure, but what is certain is the fact that there wasn't a nook nor cranny in that commission that did not present itself as an opportunity for invention, including the office typology itself. But for our purposes here, what matters is the structure of the by now iconic "Lily Pad" columns, measuring nine inches at the bottom and "widening two and a half degrees from the vertical axis," to a height of twenty-one feet (fig. 9). There are shorter and taller versions of the same column. The taller columns are mostly hollow, their walls being only three and a half inches thick. At the top and "capping the stem is a wider hollow, ringed band, which Wright referred to as a calyx," borrowing the term from botany. The whole thing looked nothing like anything the world of architecture and society in general had seen before. Naturally the officials, the Wisconsin Industrial Commission, denied the design, refusing to issue permission to build the columns, even though Wright's engineers, Wes Peters and Mendel Glickman, had done and submitted the necessary structural calculations to prove the design worked.

And so Wright offered a challenge. Let him build a prototype with which he could demonstrate his design, and if all went well, let him proceed with it. Reports have it that between him and the commissioners there ensued

FIG. 9. Lily Pad columns in the Great Workroom at the Johnson Wax Headquarters (S. C. Johnson & Son, Inc.), Racine, Wisconsin, 1936. Courtesy SC Johnson Global Corporate Communication; photograph by Andrew Pielage.

several heated arguments. But finally, the officials acquiesced, not so much because of proof that Wright's ideas were workable but simply out of exhaustion, "a proper capitulation on their part," as Wright would put it. And so the work on the protype would begin, first erecting the column and then adding sandbags to test the column's capacity but also to set the stage on which to play out the dynamics of the sublime. The code had called for twelve tons, but Wright's column would end up supporting five times that much when all was said and done. Wright reveled in the sight, calling for the continuation of sandbags, asking the workmen to keep adding them, which they did until there was no room to add any more (fig. 10). What differentiates the beautiful from the sublime in Kant's calculus are numbers; the greater they are, the more dramatic the effect. If the beautiful is about bounded objects, the sub-

FIG. 10. Wright (*far right*) with city and company officials at the testing of the Lily Pad columns, Johnson Wax site. As shown here, the Lily Pad columns could withstand the weight he said they would and more. Copyright © 2022 Frank Lloyd Wright Foundation, Scottsdale, AZ. All rights reserved. The Frank Lloyd Wright Foundation Archives (The Museum of Modern Art | Avery Architectural & Fine Arts Library, Columbia University, New York)

lime is about boundlessness. And so "therefore," if the "satisfaction in the one case is bound up in the representation of quality, in the other [it is bound up] in that of quantity," he says. Indeed, Wright's call for additional sandbags was not merely to prove a structural point but to mobilize the sublime through sheer visual mathematics.

The number of sandbags on the Lily Pad might as well have been infinite, the pad accommodating only so many of them before they started to spill over. The spectacle was unmistakable, opening before the observer a cognitive gap, between known and unknown, to be filled by reflection and imagination. It is a kind of an assault on the self, or, to use Kant's term, on one's "judgment," not "of senses" or "of logical" determination, but "of reflection." By setting the test to unfold the way it did, out in the open and in front of a gathering crowd, Wright was in effect challenging the town, and eventually all Americans, to reflect. Might they be able to outgrow their provincial limitations and tackle the impossible? Pictures of the opening day show a line of men and women as far as the frame can fit, lining up to capture the miracle of the building and, if Wright could help it, to begin to explore methods by which they could rise to its level of greatness, or better yet transcend it. Whatever numbers were responsible for the first sublime, in the form of sandbags on top of the column, they found their equal in the number of people converging on the site.

Reflections are a form of prayer; they require a protective environment with which to incubate and blossom into works of great wisdom and invention. Contaminated by worldly forces, they are likely to fall apart and become copies of copies, following paths already taken and of no particular consequence anymore. High walls are what they need, and light, not from a hole in the wall but from the heavens, somewhere well above human height. The result is the "Great Workroom" at the Johnson Wax Headquarters, at once forest, pond, and cathedral, and perhaps many other things, altogether conspiring against the ordinary and in favor of the divine. Critical to this surge of feeling are the Lily Pads, of course, but also now a different invention, a set of skylights and Pyrex tubes that, on the one hand, sit right above the forest of columns and, on the other, between the roof and the wall. The idea of the window here is gone, replaced by a very different reference to transparency and void. Where the window and even the clerestory had been about a cut and a portal on the face of a building, the tubes are something else altogether. Yes, they are technically clear and allow light, but they are also double, circling back and creating a hollow space within themselves. What light goes through them naturally gets deflected and diffused, although as it turned out later also focused and laser-concentrated at certain times of the year, creating problems of glare in the workspace below. But be that as it may, what was amazing about the tubes was not so much their shape but their location, forcing a gap between the wall and the roof, precisely at that juncture where no gap must occur, lest the whole box of the building may cave. To separate architectural elements in this manner is to challenge the very definition of constructability, including the conventions by which a building is assembled. But also safety and security. Indeed, by decoupling the vertical from the horizontal, Wright invites the possibility of disaster, a demise of near cataclysmic scope. It is here where a building garners strength and stability, counteracting forces of rack and shear. There is more than a hint that what Wright was after was the message of death and resurrection, of structural failure but also one that was blessed by the light of God, evidenced by the way the Pyrex tubes circled the Great Workroom above and affected a kind of halo. Jonathan Lipman, the author of a book on the building, got it in reverse. "This quality of light, enveloping the columns," he said, "lends a greater reality to the enclosed space." In fact, it lends it the opposite of reality, something more like the divine. If "the columns generate the space; the light makes it tangible."[40]

The Pyrex tubes took more than a year to solve, with Wright and associates working with Corning Glass to address pressing technical issues of length, assembly, and closure, among others. But when all was said and done, the effect was "beyond description," as Edgar Tafel, the famed Wright apprentice, said shortly after assembling the pieces and seeing the results firsthand.[41] Beyond description was also the number of inventions the tubes would generate in their wake, evidenced by the seven patents the US Patent Office would issue Wright for his designs. The sublime does not stop at the first encounter with design but continues on, giving birth to secondary and tertiary set of discoveries. Indeed, its power lies in its capacity to keep going, to remain unbound and expansive. If the beautiful concerns itself with "the form of the object," says Kant in his Critique of Judgement, "which consists in the object being bounded," the sublime is defined by "formless objects," namely thought. "And so it seems that we regard the beautiful as the exhibition of an indeterminate concept of the understanding, and the sublime as the exhibition of an indeterminate concept of reason."[42]

The Mile High: The Technological Sublime

Numbers are what the Mile High is all about, a building Wright proposed in 1956 in response to a call for a telecommunication tower but, more fundamentally, to an inner desire to fire up the American imagination, this time around topics wholly different from those with which he started his career sixty years before. The skyscraper had already become an integrated component of the American urban landscape, invented by William Le Baron Jenny in Chicago but which, by the 1950s, had become an expression of a different kind, of power and hubris. Wright up until then wanted nothing to do with it, taking every opportunity to lambaste its makers for violating a sacred American trust in the ground and an agrarian way of life. This was no product of architecture at all but a "feudal tower" erected to "make money" and "to sell over and over again as many times as there are floors the owner's original loft."[43] And yet by the time he unveiled the Mile High, also known as "The Illinois," he had seen in it a different possibility, not another tactic meant to coerce out of architecture greater economic and spatial yield but something else altogether, a new technological sublime. Indeed, the Mile High had nothing to do with the problem of the tall building as Tafuri laid it out in his "Skyscraper and the City," and which came to a head in 1922 when the *Chicago Tribune* issued a call for a competition to design a new tower to house, in part, its offices. The brief had made it clear that the focus of the challenge was less structure and function and more form and expression. As Tafuri points out, "Significantly the official program of instructions distributed to the entrants was wholly concerned with formal eloquence while structural aspects were completely ignored."[44]

If Wright's previous attempts at the sublime were largely qualitative, at the Mile High they would become quantitative. Indeed, there is no other way to understand the tower than through numbers, piling up without end, seemingly infinitely. It is neither beautiful nor ugly but a calculus of relations set into motion by the very height of the building itself. To travel that high up in the air, 5,280 feet to be specific, is to recalibrate the order of architecture, from art to math, not least to make sure that structural safety is ensured and sustained. Here the square must give way to the "tripod," the four to the number three, the "most stable of all forms of structure." But so do the foundations; they, too, must be revised, from simple piers and pylons to a tree-like "taproot" system thrust "into the ground several hundred feet."[45]

Other impressive numbers follow suit, of facts such as that the tower houses 100,000 people, supports two helicopter pads and 100 helicopters, parks 15,000 cars, encloses 6 million square feet, and demands fifty elevator cabs. But the most generative remains the height and what it means to the person standing inside looking out and the other way around. At approximately six feet high, we are able to see up to three miles out in the open and toward the horizon. Increase that to one hundred feet, and the number stretches to 12.2 miles. At one mile, the scope reaches staggering proportions, covering in effect a whole nation, at 644 miles, maybe not the whole of the United States, but at least Usonia, Wright's mythical version of the country. Indeed, to understand the tower is to draw an arc between it and the national scope in which it sits. Do Americans know that? Do they know that what they do right here and now, in this pinpoint of a building, is a function of their national role in it? It hardly matters what lies in between, not least because standing even ten blocks from the tower it remains impossible to fully visually take it all in. You really have to go out, way out, into the horizon to see it.

Burke found depth far more generative of the sublime than height. "I am apt to imagine," said he, "that height is less grand than depth; and that we are more struck at looking down from a precipice, than looking up at an object of equal height."[46] Wright agreed but also realized that depth needed height for its impact to become part of a national consciousness. It is to that end that we may think of the Mile High as little more than an elevator ride taking Americans to the top and back, to scope out the national expanse from above but then compare it with the limitations imposed on the ground. Between standing at the top and seeing 644 miles across, and on the ground and seeing only three, there is a vast difference, which when internalized inevitably yields great measures in the person absorbing the blow, be it in the form of creativity or some other acts of matching transcendence. The journey up and down must take a lot of time, but to quicken it Wright proposes nuclear

---

power, specifically "approximate[ly] . . . one mile per minute." "By atomic power," he tells us, "56 through-going tandem cab elevators in series of five units high approximately eight feet square are made infallible and independent of ordinary suspension system." Yes, these are no ordinary elevators but shoot up at high speed and at one point become part of the crystalline expression of the building, remaining straight as the tower tapers to a point: "As these elevators rise through the tripod they become graceful features of the exterior."[47] Engineers at Otis elevators come along but naturally change a few numbers. In a letter to Wright, they start with a straight face as if the building was about to go into construction the next day. "Dear Mr. Wright," they begin. "We have checked the sketches which you have turned over to me several days ago and note the following."[48] Of the several bullet points they note, elevator numbers, speed, and turnaround times are key. Here we learn that a total of 600 elevators will be necessary, each accommodating a "3500 pound capacity to serve the building." Speed-wise, the elevators should vary, "with the low rise banks being at 700 feet per minute and the high rise at 2000 feet per minute." For the round-trip time just for the high-rise elevators, they expect it to take "nine minutes." Interestingly they don't throw cold water on the atomic idea but say it is likely: "It is not unlikely that special cars can be designed with the motive power to the car platform as you explained to me. The source of electric or atomic power might be provided with a 'third rail' arrangement."

That Wright knew about the power and impact of atomic energy is a matter of course, but that he was confident enough to make it a central part of his architecture is a different story. The technology had, even before its devastating use in World War II, been the source of many comments on the sublime, specifically by those who witnessed its testing in Nevada and New Mexico. This was no ordinary force but something akin to divine intervention. As one account described it: "the effects could well be called unprecedented, magnificent, beautiful, stupendous and terrifying." Indeed, shortly after the explosion, "the air blast press[ed] hard against the people and things, to be followed almost immediately by the strong, sustained awesome roar, which warned of doomsday and made us feel that we puny things were blasphemous to dare tamper with the forces heretofore reserved to The Almighty." No word could match in beauty and terror what had unfolded then.

"Words are inadequate," the account continued, it had "to be witnessed to be realized."[49]

In America, *Life* magazine had, almost single-handedly, popularized the result, at one point equating the images of the mushroom-looking cloud generated in the wake of the bomb with mushrooms in mushroom soup, daring Americans to think of one in terms of the other, the cataclysmic billowy smoke in terms of something as normal and consumable as mushrooms in soup, and mushrooms as the product of a force as great and indeed as godly as the atomic bomb. The audacity of the conflation was sublime in its own right, urging the simple to come up to the grand and the grand to be brought down to affect human consumption. Needless to say, the Japanese, or for that matter the rest of the world, did not see it this way. To them the mushroom clouds were little else than reminders of holocaust, "horrible pictures of blindness, deafness, pain, disease, loss and death."[50]

Life, the magazine, however, pressed on, continuing to publish images of atomic destruction to play out the dynamics of the sublime and in effect affect national consciousness. As a bestseller of its time, *Life* took as its mission the need to shape American values. "To look at life in this regard," says the author of "Imagining the Atomic Age," "is to discover a complex set of stages in American's accommodation of the atomic bomb, beginning with incomprehension and ending with something beyond dispassion, something closer to acceptance." How might America, and indeed the world, take a work of scientific invention thus far limited to death and destruction and flip it to serve peaceful ends: that was the six-million-dollar question. By 1953 the inquiry was no longer just cultural but political as well, prompting President Dwight D. Eisenhower to urge the United Nations to "establish an international agency which would promote the peaceful uses of atomic energy."

Throughout the 1950s, the question of atomic energy in America slowly but surely morphed into one about space exploration, taking the awesome power of the former to propel satellites into outer space, for scientific reasons but political ones as well, namely surveillance against what the US government perceived as a rising and malevolent Russian power. "In spite of their many spectacular triumphs, both the space age and the nuclear age have very recent beginnings," begins a report titled *Atomic Power in Space*. "They date from the period following World War II when America assumed worldwide responsibilities."[51] And yet not much had been done since the war to carry the union into a new phase of technological and generally cultural greatness. The bomb and the rocket had proved lethal as a force of intellectual and imaginative potential, but civic action on their behalf, translating them into some form of civic purpose, remained lacking. In 1956 Wright got that and sought to do something about the issue. Behind his atomically powered elevators there was more than a circulatory solution to a very tall building; there was also a message about untapped potential. This was the civil version of the rocket meeting the atomic bomb, exploding right before our eyes, not as a force of destruction but one that could propel Americans into a whole new stratosphere of creative outpouring.

Indeed, the elevators were not mere conduits between up and down but a necessary spectacle for all to see. At about one-third of the way up, they go from being completely hidden to completely revealed. "As these elevators rise through the tripod they become graceful features of the exterior," to quote Wright again. Graceful because of their slenderness but also because of their steel-and-glass enclosures, showing their contents and the seemingly weightless and thus elegant glide of their cabs. Up until then nuclear technology had been operating and unfolding behind doors, in secrecy, largely limited to the experts behind the science. Unlike other achievements in the technological sublime, such as the design and construction of the Brooklyn and Eads Bridges, in New York and St. Louis respectively, explorations in nuclear power were largely kept away from the public. "The Atomic bomb," writes David Nye in *American Technological Sublime*, "had come into being not as a result of open debate but as the result of a secret that was never subjected to the normal controls of a democratic political process."[52] By exposing the elevators on the exterior of the Mile High, Wright would in effect seek to reverse that trend, making it clear that embedded in the new atomic age there lies both the symbol and the reality of man's capacity to transcend himself, a notion Americans needed to see in full sight.

Wright isn't known for his love of technology, often blaming it for man's slide toward intellectual laziness. He hated Le Corbusier's "machine for living in," believing no good could come out if it except more machines, humanoids, robots of sorts. And yet with atomic power he seemed to adopt a different stance, a belief that this technology was not only useful but transformative, catapulting man into the imaginative stratosphere. To a group of Unitarians seeking a building from him, he waxes poetic in a letter dated March 12, 1946, about the future of what he calls the "Era of the chemical revolution." It is through this amazing breakthrough that humanity will achieve "universal power." Up to that point, it had been used for destructive ends, but now it was time for change. Americans had to take upon themselves the responsibility to turn the bad into good, use this new chemical power to advance constructive and creative projects, echoing figures from the University of Chicago and Temple. The time was fraught with opportunity, and, depending on what Americans did, that opportunity could be squandered or used to empower new American exceptionalism: "Universal Atomic power looms ahead of all our present day institutions ready to render them all obsolete: looms not so much *a danger as a new expansion of human life on earth.* This great new implement of democratic freedom lies ahead to liberate or destroy as humanity will decide."[53]

Wright did what he could to play his role in shaping this moment in history, his Mile High being in some sense no more than a pretext to air it out. What city after all could have handled such a monstrous height, let alone a single developer to manage and lease the offices inside? Indeed, no one particular city or individual needed this building, only the nation, as Wright wagered, putting forth an example and an idea with which to urge the national character forward, mobilizing its creative and intellectual energy toward positive end.

To be sure, Wright was not the only one advocating for a peaceful use of nuclear energy; many were right off the bat. "There is only one subject," University of Chicago chancellor Robert Hutchins said to his national audience of teachers in 1946, "and that is the atomic bomb," making it clear that no matter what they taught or how they taught it, both method and lesson objectives had to take on the challenge of turning evil into good. A Temple University professor, Merrill Bush, added at that same time that nothing short of global survival depended "more than anything else on the American people."[54] They must "hold meetings," talk "with everyone [they] can persuade, or force to listen to." The scientific community felt equally charged. Shortly after the war ended, in fact, the US government created the Atomic Energy Commission and charged it with the task of finding "peaceful purposes" for this awesome source of energy. Other cultural outlets predicted that soon nuclear energy would be accessible to anyone who wanted it. David Nye mentions one science editor predicting that "people would soon drive cars for a year "on a pellet of atomic energy the size a vitamin pill."[55] All that is true, but what Wright possessed in his hand was the unique ability to put this power on display and mobilize it in a way so that Americans could see its potential and connection to the rest of the country.

In his unveiling of the Mile High, Wright made it a point that America needed to build this building or else the Russians would do so first. And sure thing, within a year, in October 1957, they would do just that, not a Mile High per se but something equivalent, a satellite named *Sputnik* with which they orbited the globe and gathered data. America was embarrassed, prompting one journalist from *Aviation Week* to demand answers: "We believe the people of this country have a right to know the facts about the relative position of the U.S. and the Soviet Union in this technological race which is perhaps the most significant single event of our times. They have the right to find out why a nation with our vastly superior scientific, economic and military potential is being at the very least equaled and perhaps being surpassed by a country that less than two decades ago couldn't even play in the same scientific ball park."[56] *Life* magazine didn't mince words either: "let us not pretend that Sputnik is anything but a defeat."

Chicago didn't build Wright's building, but America did seem to wake up in its wake. In January 1959, President Dwight Eisenhower would reveal in his office the "world's first atomic battery." Two years later the US Navy launched the first "radioisotope thermoelectric generator-powered satellite," and a month after that, President Kennedy committed America to put man on the moon. The rest, as they say, was history.

Unprecedented Structure at the Guggenheim

The last chapter of this book will be devoted to Wright's Guggenheim Museum in New York. There will be more on the story of the iconic building there, including Wright's troubled relation with Hilla Rebay, the baroness who led the charge in hiring Wright for the job. But for now, and in light of the topic of this chapter, I would be remiss to go on without mentioning the role the famous spiral played, and continues to play, in the dynamic of the sublime. Just as with the previous buildings, so here, too, we see Wright proposing an architectural element less because it was functionally necessary and more because it could set into motion the effects of the sublime, in this case as siphoned through vertigo and that terrifying feeling of loss of balance and subsequent fall into the abyss. As before so here, the sublime was not limited to those on the ramp looking down but to the makers of the ramp itself, a sublime mystery in its own right. Should it be solved, it would mean the very expansion of the mind, indeed, the reinvention of reality as we know it, including ways to unlock the question of gravity. Burke referred to this process as "modification," whereby in tackling a conundrum, one also inevitably modifies one's intellectual powers. "Besides these things which directly suggest the idea of danger," he wrote, "and those which produce a similar effect from mechanical cause, I know of nothing sublime which is not some modification of power."[57]

At the helm was Jaroslav Josef Polívka, a structural engineer and recent émigré from Prague, particularly suited for the job by his talent but more importantly by his capacity to welcome and thrive on difficult problems. He had known of Wright back in Europe and treasured the opportunity to work with the great American architect. And yet even he, as smart as he was, had to confess: "Frankly I was not able, and no engineer at that time was, to solve this problem theoretically. This type of shell never has been investigated before and no structural analysis developed and corroborated by tests." To solve the problem, new "experimental" tests and strategies had to be conducted to "secure the absolute safety of such unprecedented structure."[58] Wright swiped at the need for such an in-depth analysis, but Polívka insisted, ultimately generating ninety-seven sheets of drawings to prove the structure could withstand the likely onslaught of "frightening vibrations." The architectural community hated Wright's design, not least because it could not wrap its head around a form that flew in the face of demands normally placed on exhibit spaces. Circular surfaces and flat art just do not go together. What the community did not realize is that Wright did not see the experience of art as an end in itself but rather a pretext for transforming the American mind. Step to the edge of the ramp and lean against the low wall of the parapet, and it is hard not to feel the horrific sublimity of the moment. Luckily the parapet is there, however short it is, to protect against falling over, for, as Burke said, it is not actual demise that is necessary, only the prospect of dying. That version of terror should suffice to cause the visitor to the museum to recoil back from the edge and into the self, reflecting on the moment and ultimately doing what Polívka did, which is to invent a new system by which emerging possibilities can become new realities.

In Summary

Looking back at this chapter, we see that there is more than one side to the sublime but at least two, first as defined by Emerson, the other by his predecessors Burke and Kant. All locate the final reward inside the self, but where Burke and Kant find fuel in the extraordinary scene, Emerson does so in the ordinary. Magnificent mountains are no doubt gripping, but so is the simple moment of sitting in the sun and watching birds land on trees. Wright found need for both types, first to restore to Americans self-worth lost during the years of the Depression in the 1930s, and, second, to reignite in them the love and capacity for expansive imagination.

3

DESIGNING FOR A
NEW OCULAR REGIME

The eye is the first circle, the horizon which it forms is the second; and
throughout nature this primary figure is repeated without end.
—R. W. EMERSON, "Circles"

A t one point in *Nature,* Emerson happens upon an odd but powerful feeling. He is in the woods, in that "Plantation of God" where everything is pure, fresh, and beautiful, uncontaminated by worldly competing forces. No banks, schools, or commercial buildings stand in the way, only trees and the sound of birds chirping away. So pristine is the scene, Emerson is not sure that even he should be there, lest he may contaminate the scene himself. The less of him there is there the better, perhaps no more than a "transparent eyeball," hung in midair to receive everything and edit nothing.[1] "Standing on the bare ground," he says "my head bathed in the blithe air and uplifted into infinite space—all mean egotism vanishes. I become a transparent eyeball; I am nothing; I see all."[2]

Not two transparent eyeballs but one, eliminating perspective and flattening Emerson's reception of the world. Perspective, at least since the Renaissance, had been used as an instrument with which to regulate power relations between subject and object and generally bring under a singular ocular order ruler and ruled. To remove it is to collapse established cultural hierarchies, erected over time to monitor the flow and access of knowledge. In good part, perspective was the product of political systems that sought to compartmentalize and control society, but also of a scientific revolution predicated on reducing information to few key facts central to the experiment at hand. Gone were the "old symbols," says Lewis Mumford in his *Golden Day*, in favor of an approach to the world that "reduced the rich actuality of things to a bare description of matter and motion." Intuition and theorization lost out to empirical data, exacted through advances in medicine, mathematics and optics. "Rule, authority, precedent, general consent—these things all became subordinate in scientific procedure to the methods of observation and mathematical analysis: Weighing, measuring, timing, decomposing, isolating—all operation that led to results."[3] Dissection stood as both metaphor and reality. The body, once sacred and not allowed to be opened, was by the sixteenth century cut and studied close up, including its neurological and musculature infrastructure. The work of Andreas Vesalius is here critical, correcting age-old anatomical pronouncements based on "analogies drawn from animal dissection" but not the human. His *De fabrica* was at once a minute record and a work of art, on the one hand, a product of "descriptive reporting," on the other, a "trained eye of a great anatomist."[4] Vesalius was also a trained "draughtsman and block maker" who used his keen artistic skills to generate detailed drawings that would help future physicians advance their own understanding and approach to the human body.

This chapter will leverage Emerson's transparent eyeball to examine Wright's own manner of pulling the curtain wide open and letting the world lap over the self. Architecture, for too long, had become victim to the same forces of exclusion as science, admitting certain information at the expense of another. And to the detriment of the human. It was time to change course. Of focus will be Wright's windows, covering the gamut of types, from the stained to the colored, casement and corner. In each there is a keen intention by Wright to awaken in the American the realization that in seeing there is more than a passive response to light, views, and the like, but an apparatus critical to the way we understand the world.

Science has saved the world, curing the sick, doubling the day, and easing the burden on those who perform hard and dangerous labor. But it has also limited our response to the world to a narrow and cold collection of data, usually at the expense of information and knowledge central to navigating emotional difficulties. It was time, by the mid-nineteenth century, to open up the scene and let more data in. Or so Emerson believed, calling for a time and a place when man had yet to leverage the mind but remained a mere vegetable of sorts. And what better place to do that than in nature, a place of "the greatest delight." It is here where the "fields and [the] woods minister . . . [to] an occult relation between man and the vegetable." Not man and man but man and vegetable. Competition forces man to speed up, slow down, and generally warp the truth just to keep up, accelerating time and the aging process. We are perpetually twenty going on fifty, older than we really are. Without that, man stays a "Youth" and a "child." "In the woods, too, a Man casts off his years, as the snake his slough, and at what period so ever of life is always a child. In the woods is perpetual youth."[5]

In aiming for a vegetative state, Emerson no doubt hoped that we could at least go back far enough in time to question how and what we see. The science of the eye by his time had been enough formed that we took for granted the relationship between subject and object. We stopped questioning what we saw because what we saw had already been cataloged and recorded. For the religious police, upholding a certain moral code, or the professional bureaucrat keeping an ethical one, the news was not all bad, but indeed welcome, narrowing choice and maintaining control over those on whom they relied to further themselves. Efficiency, not creativity, was what they looked for in men and women, keeping the engines of capitalism alive and well. Over time the eye narrowed and could only see a limited amount, strategically redirected to locate certain realities and not others. How unfortunate and sad, suffocating human potential. Better to open the eye wide and restore to it the capacity to become "transparent," shaping reality just as much as the other way around.

Fire in the Eye

Emerson's call takes us back to the early Greeks, who went back and forth debating the extent to which seeing was a matter of light entering the eye or leaving it. The first is known as "Intromission," the second as "Extramission." Aristotle, for instance, believed that seeing rainbows was in part possible because of "sight passing outward from the eye."[6] Empedocles, before him, believed similarly but went so far as to suggest that seeing is not unlike a lantern whose "fire blaz[es] through the stormy night" and is protected from the elements by "transparent sides which scatter the breadth of the winds."[7]

We are just as central, in other words, to the construction of what we see as the thing seen is responsible for who we are. Over the centuries, "Extramission" lost out to "Intromission," in large part due to a perennial renewal of interest in optical science. The medieval Arab scholar Alhazen had a say in the matter too, and so did Kepler and Newton later on, among others, each adding their own exacting analysis to the one before. Just as the retina registers the world upside down, so did each station in optical studies turn our impressions of received truths on their head. And just as in righting the image the mind reverses perceived but incorrect observations, so did each station afford the same, not least a heliocentric revolution that shocked the world and put Galileo, its promoter, in jail. "If nothing else," says A. Mark Smith in *Sight to Light,* "Galileo's observations constituted definitive evidence against not only Aristotelian cosmology but also Ptolemaic astronomy, and as such, challenged the core assumption of absolute egocentricity."[8]

Still Emerson felt we went too far, biasing the world over Man's capacity to change it. "It is certain," he tells us on this note, "that the power to produce . . . does not reside in nature, but in man, or in a harmony of both."[9] Indeed, what helps us get through the day and the various difficulties that stand in the way is "the heat of [our] own fire." Wright took note and went on to fashion, among other things, an architecture that would glow and emanate light just as much as it would admit it, his Fallingwater perhaps being the most famous example of this, insisting that inside the American mind there lies a passion that must not be burnished. More on that later, but for now perhaps we can begin with Wright's fascination with the eye.

Wright's Eye

Not unlike Emersion, Wright, too, wanted to go back to a time when the subject of sight and seeing was still under study. And this to flush out debris that had accumulated inside the eye, preventing it from seeing accurately and creatively. What caused sight to happen in the first place? How does objective reality turn into intelligible acts of life-changing consequences? Opacity and color played a central role. "At the most fundamental level," says A. Mark Smith again, speaking of Ptolemy's work, the first-century AD Greek mathematician and author of the influential *Almagest,* is that "visibility is a function of the luminosity and physical compactness of a given object." Next comes color: "At the next level of visibility come colors, which are "primarily visible because nothing besides light that does not have color is seen." In short, color "is the sole proper object for sight."[10]

Let's look at each in relation to Wright's work. Sight occupied a central role in Wright's thinking. In one personal essay, he tells us that he is "eye-minded" and that when he opens his eyes, he "gradually becom[es] more universal."[11] Sight was important to Wright because it allowed him not only to visualize and appreciate the world but also to gather the material with which he can respond to it morally, responsibly. This necessarily meant having a critical eye, inevitably made so by an ability to change angles and bring within one view different, even conflicting, worlds. No doubt, changing perspectives on a daily basis comes at the risk of sounding inconsistent and as such untrustworthy, constantly flipping this way and that. How can you trust a person who tells you one thing today and another tomorrow? At best, they may look like buffoons and at worst liars who must be kept at arm's length. But that is not how Emerson saw it. "Suppose you should contradict yourself," he tells us in "Self-Reliance," "what then?" He goes on: "It seems to be a rule of wisdom never to rely on your memory alone, scarcely even in acts of pure memory, but to bring the past to judgment into the thousand-eyed present and live ever in a new day."[12]

The problem lies in the ability of the eye to intercept and scramble familiar sights, never letting them settle into common scenes, consumed without scrutiny. Nothing is more dangerous than that, namely allowing the world to become so standard and common we stop noticing it. One of the characters in the *Age of Innocence*, a novel by Edith Wharton, describes "opening my eyes to things I'd looked at so long that I'd ceased to see them." Seeing clearly is important, but so is seeing in a befogged way, at least temporarily, deflecting and diffracting light rays just as much as admitting them. Here is Wright allowing himself the ocular freedom to admit conflicting visual messages and letting them play out their own course: "mere accidental colored chalk on the sunlit sidewalk . . . will make me pause and 'something' in me will hark back to 'something,' half remembered, half felt, and as though an unseen door had opened and distant music had for an instant come trembling through to my senses."[13]

Letting sights enter the eye unedited does more than allow the eye to see; it also allows the mind to remember and, through that journey backward, "doors" to open, "music" to be heard. Before too long, sight is no longer limited to a narrow relation between object and the image formulated of it but instead involves a comprehensive survey of other senses, including their awakening in us. To properly admit all sights makes us hear more, feel more deeply, smell penetratingly. It opens "doors" and in so doing lets a whole lot in, some compatible but others much less so, contributing to a potpourri of, among other things, visual, auditory, and olfactory effects. The result is a certain cloudiness, necessary to keeping the mind, and in this case specifically the eye, temporarily distracted and unsettled, lest it may engage in premature ocular judgment. Cloudiness is important, to blur and indeed confuse sight so that it can see again, in a more complex way. No meaningful and lasting contribution to the world is otherwise possible.

Nowhere did Wright illustrate the machination of this duet between clarity and cloudiness more forcefully than at the Winslow House, one of his earliest commissions as a young architect just emerging from under the wings of the great master Louis Sullivan. There he adds to the main box of the house a form seldom seen in his oeuvre before or after, a hemicycle extending the interior a little into the exterior. Less for the love of the hemicycle and more for that of teaching the eye how to see (fig. 11). There he was, in his mid-1920s, already set on changing the American mind, and he knows that to do so he

FIG. 11. Hemicycle dining nook at the back of the Winslow House, River Forest, Illinois, 1893. Note the perimeter pattern and the degree to which it clouds vision and sets up a visual counterpart to the clarity of the center of the window. Photograph courtesy of Mark Hertzberg.

has to start with the way Americans, including himself, see. And so he puts both himself and his client back into the eyeball, the hemicycle, inviting each to study all over again the operations of ocular dynamics. How does the eye really work as an apparatus of visual invention?

Interestingly, Wright places the hemicycle not at the front of the house but at the back. At the front he gives us a facade strangely at odds with his disdain for classical orders. Even at this early stage in his career, he was already railing against the restoration of Renaissance architecture across the American urban landscape. And yet here he was doing just that, emulating the Renaissance tradition of breaking the architectural facade into a tripartite hierarchy of parts, namely bottom, middle, and top, but also left, right, center, and so on (fig. 12). Had it not been for the back side of the house and its utter disregard for prim and tidy placement of lines and shapes, the front would have remained a mystery. But the difference explains everything and that is that the front facade was not without a reason, namely to appease a Victorian eye too hooked on classicism to change. For those too lost to the past, the front facade is for them to enjoy but then move on. But for those keen on the American experiment of renewal and innovation, the back is for them.

William Winslow, the client for the house, was no ordinary man but one of those unique Americans industrialists who held within one view an appreciation for art and business. Wright would surprisingly peg a lot of hope on men like him who were capable of navigating a delicate line between practi-

FIG. 12. Front facade of the Winslow House, River Forest, Illinois, 1893. Photograph courtesy of Mark Hertzberg.

cal culture and innovation. Surprisingly, because it seemed not too long ago and in a different place, Wright had questioned their capacity for aesthetic restraint and original taste. Was he speaking out of both sides of his mouth? Likely, but for a good reason. Baudelaire before him, that great French author of *The Painter of Modern Life,* had done the same in Paris around 1846, similarly seemingly disgusted by the bourgeoisie but then at one point praising them for the job they had done in lifting the city out of its rut and modernizing it. In his by now classic book *All That Is Solid Melts into Air,* Marshal Berman quotes him as saying that they, the bourgeoisie, "are the majority—in number and intelligence and therefore they are the power." And not only that, but "together they had formed companies," and they "have raised loans." They hold the key to the future, in "all its diverse forms—political, industrial, artistic."[14] The words are almost too much to take, and one wonders if they weren't said in mockery. But perhaps more in the spirit of an appeal to those who can change the world to do so with care and art. Otherwise they could do a lot of damage. Wright faced the same conundrum, stuck between a rock and hard place, on the one hand repulsed by the cultural degradation that comes with excess money, but on the other wondering what other options he had. Not only was it bad business to bite the hand that feeds you, but if it is the only limb that can effect change, then why not guide it and in so doing allow it to become the force of positive change? And so, not unlike Baudelaire, Wright would prop up the industrial class and put them on a pedestal, in the hope that they, like their French counterparts, might come along and support artists like him and together restore cultural vision to a country that had lost it. These were the ones he called "American men of business with unspoiled instincts and ideals." They were innovative and daring but also cautious of the milieu in which they lived, still stuck by moral distinctions between right and wrong, front and back. The two shall not mix, at least not yet. And thus, in 1893, the Winslow House, too, had to abide by those rules, between a front responsive to a buttoned-up state of mind, and a back expressive of an owner looking all around for new ideas.

Marching around the edge of the hemicycle are windows, half-befogged, half-clear. On the perimeter of each runs a dense "dragonfly-wings pattern" that "shrouds the view" to the garden in the back of the house.[15] At the center of each, however, lies clear glass, allowing a full and unmitigated view to the outside. Between the two, there is a mutual system of support, a back and forth, the befogged relying on the clear, the clear on the befogged, the former blurring just enough view for the other to be clear in a meaningful and authentic way. Too much clear seeing and you stop seeing at all, taking the world for granted. The perimeter vs. center dichotomy is further played out in the very design of the hemicycle bay window itself, it, too, distinguishing between peripheral vs. axial vision, which, much like the eye, also distinguishes between clear and blurred vision. "Visual perception," we are told, "diminishes according to both distance from the vertex of the visual cone to the visual axis within the cone."[16] Sight, in other words, "diminishes" the farther away it moves from the visual axis of the eye. Which of course makes sense, seeing better directly across than to the side and at an angle, prompting us to move our heads and see what our peripheral vision may have conjured in curiosity. In so doing, we affirm the fact that our heads do sit on a swivel, capable of moving around and seeing the world in the round. This is how authentic responses to the world are generated, by collecting as much diverse, and indeed conflicting, data as possible. Being in this intimate and half-circle alcove in the back of the Winslow House is a study in the kind of seeing that is comprehensive and yields complex and accurate analysis of the world.

William Blake

It is hard not to think of William Blake here, whose work Wright often quoted and on at least one occasion, in March 1956, read to his Fellowship. In that session, a couple of sayings catch the architect's eye. He reads them: "We are led to believe a lie when we see not through the eye / Some are born to sweet light." And then again: "He who respects the infant's faith, triumphs over hell and death." To which Wright responds by offering his own interpretation. "In other words," he says, "fresh faith unspoiled is really a seeing eye beyond the seeing of sophistication." He continues: "Here he's saying [about Blake] that education and sophistication and all that you pass through is a conditioning of your mind, rather than enlightenment. But the fresh mind sees with a seeing eye and is likely to see truth. But the more you are educated and the more you are conditioned, the less able you become to see straight."[17]

Wright is fascinated by the idea that we possess two eyes, or have come to do so over the course of civilization, the first as having evolved and been conditioned through education, the second as precisely the opposite, namely one that has maintained the capacity to stay the course and see beyond cultural accumulation. Might the one be a decoy for the true functioning of the other? The Winslow windows seem to suggest that, a persistent flicker between opacity and clarity, straight and periphery. We shall return to Blake in a moment.

Color

No examination of seeing is complete without the study of color. As mentioned earlier, color is one of at least two environmental components responsible for the act of seeing, the other being luminosity. The Winslow windows, or at least those that went around the hemicycle, did not involve color, only clear and patterned glass. For color we'd have to look elsewhere, most fruitfully at the windows in Unity Temple in Oak Park, Illinois, one of Wright's more iconic contributions to religious architecture, and now a UNESCO World Heritage Site. There, color in windows is played out at several locations, most notably in and around the main congregation space, better known as the "sanctuary." Look up toward the exterior walls and you'll see several panes of glass, sitting just inside massive concrete piers, running the length of the room, unbroken by either metal or wood frame, only *cames*, a work of hammered lead that holds the glass together and upright (fig. 13). "They differ from normal windows," says Thomas Heinz, in his book *Frank Lloyd Wright's Stained Glass & Lightscreens*, "in that they have no wood frames and are continuous across the entire length of the hall."[18] They contain an abstract pattern of squares and rectangles designed to resemble veins of rain coursing down slick surfaces. Color is minimal but present, hazy yellow squares staggered back and forth to foreground and blur the impact of concrete pillars on the other side and, indeed, concrete reality in general. Together they serve as precursors to what is about to happen just around the corner.

Yes, come around and sit in the center of the sanctuary and you will be under a grid of skylights, twenty-five in total, each containing a yellowish center and a clear perimeter (fig. 14). The effect is unmistakable, somewhat

FIG. 13. A line of clerestory windows with cames situated in front of the concrete piers on the exterior wall at Unity Temple, Oak Park, Illinois, 1908. Photograph courtesy of James Caulfield.

reminiscent of "heavenly glow." It doesn't matter what the weather is doing outside; inside it is always "a happy cloudless day," according to Wright, "daylight sifting through between the intersecting concrete beams, filtering through amber glass ceiling lights."[19] Rain or shine, the interior always possesses "the warmth of sunlight." What gods the Unitarians worship here are associated with neither image nor icon but simply light, inspiring imagination and reflection. No overt expressions of religiosity exist here, only abstract signs to trigger thought. "Instead of us pointing up to [Him] somewhere," says Alan Taylor, the Temple's current senior minister, His "Holy comes down to us inside this space" and through the "art-glass" above.[20]

Taylor may have been familiar with Wright's own words when he uttered those words. In his presentation to the building committee in charge of hiring the architect who was going to design the Unity Temple, Wright had talked about a man who went up the mountain to see God only to be rebuffed and sent back down. The committee may have been contemplating the addition of a steeple, and this was Wright's way of convincing them otherwise,

FIG. 14. Skylights directly above-head in the sanctuary of the Unity Temple, Oak Park, Illinois, 1908. Photograph courtesy of James Caulfield.

not least because such explicit expressions of religiosity traveled against the "ideals of liberal religion."[21] Among other points, the story amounts to God coming down to us and not us going up to Him, in this case through light which spreads evenly across space, allowing man to "study man" and have "a good time." "Was not the time come now," Wright admonishes, to be more simple, to have more faith in man on this earth?"[22]

The image of light coming down to earth from the heavens to humanize instead of to judge or control recalls Blake's *Urizen* series, depicting a demigod bent over from a position way up in hell, looking down and imposing his rational will on the people of earth. Behind him is a sun, so hot it has burnt everything in its wake, except Urizen of course and his kind (fig. 15). Rain or shine it is present, intensely amber, reflecting Blake's "somber satire of Milton's account of the Creation" and through it the "seven phases of the imprisonment and 'binding' of 'the caverned man.'"[23] This man is now in prison precisely because in the process of creation his appreciation of the world became denuded, reduced to the five senses. As much as he'd like to go wild and see things upside down, he can't but is instead limited to smell,

FIG. 15. *The Ancient Days*, Copy D, by William Blake, 1794. © The Trustees of the British Museum.

touch, and the like. How awful and punitive. Making matters worse was a science revolution from the fifteenth century onward that divided the world in two, on the one hand, as based on physical properties, on the other, sensation. Material things possessed weight, size, height, and length, among other properties, independent from the way we may receive and feel about them through smell, color, and touch. The two belonged to two different worlds, never to mix so long we kept searching for singular answers to links between cause and effect. Further, they had to be measured to be of value and practical worth, first through observation but ultimately through mathematical analysis. It wasn't enough that one could "eyeball" the extent of an object; one had to find an equivalent for it in numbers. No one caught the ire of Blake more than Newton, that "soul shuddering vacuum" who insisted on reducing experiences to finite calculations, turning nature into laws of codified knowledge. It is to that extent that the author of *The Scientific Revolution* can say that "Newton following Galileo formulated his laws of motion as laws of nature having completed applicability within the fabric of mathematical physics."[24]

Another who struggled with Newton's division of the world was Niels Bohr, the early twentieth-century physicist who sought to erase the barrier between observer and observed. According to Karen Barad in her book *Meeting the Universe Halfway,* Bohr "called into question two fundamental assumptions . . . of Newtonian Physics; [first] that the world is composed of individual objects with individually determinate boundaries and properties"; and second, "that measurements involve continuous determinable interactions such that the values of the properties obtained can be properly assigned to the premeasurements properties of objects as separate from the agencies of observation."[25] Which means that between the person watching an object unfold and the object itself there is no relation beyond analysis and calculation. Bohr rejected that in favor of notions of reciprocity and "wholeness." Or even "phenomenon," which Bohr "designates to be a particular instance of "Wholeness."[26] Wright might use "unity" instead, staying closer to Emerson, similarly believing that knowledge is best served when all the information generated to create it remains available, unedited, and open, even if some of it may prove less than relevant at first.

In his pouring over the earth, Blake's Urizen holds a divider, not quite a compass, an instrument of navigation and mathematics. He is ready to divide the world into districts, zones, and the like, limiting their potential for each other. His mission is to "impose order on chaos," according to one scholar. Blake hated nothing more than this, the excess control of ideas by science. For him this meant "the reduction of the infinite to the finite, and therefore the destruction of the imagination."[27] Behind Urizen is a blazing sun, at once a source of light but also intense heat, imagination but also hell. By Blake's time the two were inextricably linked, the satanic mills already turning numbers into heat and a miserable way of life. To contend with one, you had to contend with the other. To get to the imagination you had to go through hell, or better, use hell against itself to access the imagination. Wright understood the calculus between the two and went on to assume the method, using Urizen's instruments of divisiveness to restore imagination to mankind. He may not have used the divider to design the grid that would come to support the skylights above the sanctuary at Unity Temple, but he wasn't far off either, in all likelihood relying on T-squares, rulers, and triangles to finish the job. Either way, what is important is that he too uses precision tools to shape the world but also diffused light to protect against excess regimentation. What light enters the sanctuary does not take the shape of the grid, refusing to be measured and filed under a specific category.

Wright's description of the amber skylights may have been a bit pedestrian, but the reality is otherwise. To fully understand them, we'd have to stay with William Blake a little longer. From him Wright borrowed the idea of the sun as "the natural cycle of life," at once a source of destruction and renewal. "The natural world is based largely on the daily return of the sun and the yearly return of the vegetable life," says Northrop Frye speaking of Blake.[28] Between the sun and the tree lies the symbols of death and resurrection. The perpetual presence of the sun, now hovering right overhead at Unity Temple, is not merely a matter of adding warmth to an otherwise cold room but more one meant as a reminder that to live life, and in this case to think like a Unitarian, is to perennially torch received wisdom, scrutinizing even the most sacred of texts. Nothing must remain of the past, but all must be turned to ashes to be used in the reconstruction of reality, a metaphor turned actuality when Wright used the ashes from the first burning of Taliesin in 1914 as mortar to construct its resurrection. Even joy must be perennially replaced by new forms of happiness, never to settle and pacify mind and soul. Keep your spirit open to the world and "it would be like experiencing a sunrise that never ends," writes Blake.

He who binds to himself a joy
Does the winged life destroy
But he who kisses the joy as it flies
Lives in eternity's sunrise

Unity Temple, built for the Unity Church, a branch of Christianity, is visited by its parishioners on Sunday, once a week. For renewals on a more daily basis, we'd have to look to Wright's use of lightscreens in homes and offices. The Frank Thomas House of 1901, in Oak Park, would be a good candidate and so would the Lawrence Dana House. Both play host to impressive displays of lightscreens, just inside the homes and behind front doors, in cozy vestibules meant as decompression chambers between the incessant world outside and the intimate and indeed spiritual world inside. As thresholds of arrival and departure, front doors naturally speak to notions of beginnings and endings. Attach lightscreens to them, of amber, yellowish glow, designed to emulate the sun, and what you get are references to sunsets and sunrises, awakening and renewal. Everyday Americans must be reminded of their duty to start all over again, erase old habits in favor of new ways of doing things. Every day they must engage in acts that blot, like the sun, established norms in lieu of mind-sets open to innovation. No imagination is likely to happen without them. Indeed, "the first condition of any life of the beautiful is a clearing of the encumbered ground," says Wright in an essay distinguishing between the curious and the beautiful.[29] If the curious is a mere matter of being drawn to the beautiful, the beautiful is a different matter altogether, requiring erasure of reality as found in favor of that which has yet to be constructed. A clean slate every day. In that sense, the lightscreens just inside Wright's homes are expressions of enlightenment but more fundamentally solar fire ready to extinguish all that the Americans had come to rely on to feel comfortable. "He who does not imagine in stronger and better light than his perishing mortal eye can see," tells us Blake, "does not imagine at all."[30]

Nowhere was this imagination more called upon to show its face than in 1893, when Wright had just left Louis Sullivan's office to open his own.

A time also when Chicago and America were reeling from the gilded age of excess wealth and bad taste. The two for Wright seemed to go hand in hand. "I know the real poverty-stricken America today," he says, "is our ultra successful rich citizenry." They may be rich financially, but they are poor culturally. They breathe bad air "because [they are] impressed from birth with fashion and sham." America needed education, not so much in the principles of academic architecture but in the importance of imagination: "An artist is a workman who gives his work the touch of imagination." Which for Wright, interestingly, is not so much a matter of exercising one's capacity for fantasy but more recognizing things for what they are. In his words: "It takes creative imagination to see stone as stone; see steel as steel; see glass as glass and to view traditions as tradition." In the office he shared with Cecil Corwin, from whom we heard in the introduction, there was a drop-down ceiling and in it a light spreading a glow not unlike that of "sunlight."[31] No photo or drawing of the feature has survived, but Wright made a point to mention it in his autobiography: "Cecil and I had a draughting room, each, either side of the common central room for business. Defending this room was an anteroom or vestibule with the ceiling dropped down to the top of the doors. A straight line glass pattern formed this ceiling glass, diffusing artificial light. The effect of this indirect lighting in the small anteroom was like sunlight, no fixtures visible."[32]

Intromission and Extramission: A Fire in the Eye

Even though it had been well understood by the time of Aristotle that sight is the product of light traveling from object to eye and not the other way around, it remained a matter of conceptual intrigue to Emerson and Wright that the theory of extramission could still hold sway. The theory dates back to the fifth and sixth centuries BC, when it was believed that not unlike a lantern whose glass cover protects the fire from going out, the eye, too, embodied a kind of flame that made objective reality visible and true. "Just as when a man thinking to go out through the wintry night makes ready a light, a flame of blazing fire, putting round it a lantern to keep away all manner of winds," said Empedocles in the fifth century BC, "so primeval fire, enclosed in the membranes gave birth to the round pupil in its delicate garments."

Fire inside the eyes was, for the ancients, like a hand shooting out of the eye and grabbing that which held it captive, connecting in a tangible way subject with object. For Emerson and Wright, it signified a necessary fuel with which to restore to the self an aspect of agency, affecting reality just as much as the other way around. Embedded in the self is a will ready to take action, they believed, but which unless ignited was likely to stay ineffective and dormant. The issue fascinated Wright to no end, who found in the open furnace mills in Chicago a suitable expression and metaphor. Perched atop the Auditorium Building during his early years in Chicago while in the employ of Adler and Sullivan, he would spend hours lost in the glow of the Bessemer converter just across the way, south of the city. It resembled that which the ancients had attributed to seeing: a vitality critical to transforming raw ideas into useful things. In his words: "When in the early years I looked south from the massive stone tower in the Auditorium Building, a pencil in the hand of a master, the red glare of the Bessemer steel converters to the south of Chicago would thrill me as pages of *The Arabian Nights* used to do with a sense of terror and romance."[33] What could be more terrifying and yet more beautiful than watching man use intense heat and fire to turn nothing into something, a shapeless world into objects of productive potential. Wright was under a spell, mesmerized by that "incandescent of the kiln," which generated "fabulous heat, baking minerals and chemical treasure on mere clay to issue in all the hues of the rainbow, all the shapes of imagination and never yield to time, subject only to the violence or carelessness of man."

He was envious, not unlike Prometheus before him, of the gods—in this case the gods of industry—and wanted to enjoy what they enjoyed and by extension use the remaining surplus influence to advance an improved and much more innovative American society. The remaking of the world was emerging from right underneath Wright's eyes, and he couldn't help but be pulled by its magical resonance: "These great ovens would cast a spell upon me as I listened to the subdued roar deep within them."[34] Gaston Bachelard, in his book *The Psychoanalysis of Fire*, locates the envy in the child's desire to outdo the father and later the teacher. "The child wishes to do what his father does," he says, "but far away from his father's presence." And so "like a little Prometheus he steals some matches" and soon "heads for the fields where, in the hollow of a little valley, he and his companions build a secret fireplace that will keep them warm on the days when they decide to play truant from school."[35] Isn't that what Wright eventually does, steal matches in Chicago and later use them to outdo Sullivan, his teacher and father figure (even though Sullivan was only few years older than Wright), and beyond that burn down the architectural laws of the land? He, too, would do so by heading for the fields, where in the hollow of the valley of Spring Green he would "build a secret fireplace" through whose warmth he would cook up schemes for a better and more innovative America.

And just as with the Bessemer converter, so too with Aladdin's lamp. It, too, would transform ideas into worlds of magical objects. Aladdin, we may remember, was the kid from *The Arabian Nights* who was tricked by a magician into retrieving a lamp from a cave and ended up getting buried alive. With the help of a ring the magician gives him, though, he would escape and return to life once again. The lamp survives and with it the magical powers of transformation which Aladdin uses to live a happy and eventful life, including marrying the princess of his dreams and building a magnificent palace for the two of them. Along the way he shares his good fortune with the people of the town, spreading his wealth every time he walked the streets and encountered the crowds. The magician does return at one point to again trick Aladdin and retrieve the lamp, but by then Aladdin had become quite clever himself and was able to trick the man back, finally reliving the good and high life.

The lamp that Aladdin was tricked into getting, interestingly, had no light, its fire snuffed out on the order of the magician when directing Aladdin into the cave. "When you are on the terrace," he instructed, "you will see in front of you a niche in which there is a lighted lamp. Take the lamp and put it out and when you have thrown away the wick and poured off the liquid, hold it close to your chest and bring it to me."[36] We may recall that the order was initiated by a fire the magician starts at the outset of his trick. He had gathered some twigs and set them on fire: "He set light to the pile and the moment the twigs caught fire, the magician threw on them some incense that he had ready at hand." Between outside light and inside light there is a binary condition; either one or the other must survive but not the two simultaneously. The magician's ultimate aim is inner light, the power to initiate and re-create the world in one's own image, or at least independent of foreign forces. But to get there he needs the outer light of magical curiosity. He instructs Aladdin to "put out" the light because he wants to relight it himself, conflating fire with fire, the fire of the wick with that of inner will. Which means that the fire of the lamp never really goes away but is merely displaced by another, the fire of the energetic self.

The missing fire of the lamp, in other words, is our fire; the author snuffs it out so that we can reignite it and change the course of civilization. From total darkness to total light, that is the story of the eye seeing reality all over again. In many ways Aladdin's conundrum in the cave is a reenactment of the ancient narrative of sight and seeing, involving darkness, light, color, and final consciousness. We may remember that in his worming his way through the "barrel vaults" of the subterranean world, Aladdin has to go through a beautiful garden of trees bearing what should have been something like citrus fruits but which in actuality bear crystal glass and stones of many colors. The same colors, that is, the ancients had specified were necessary to seeing objective reality. These "trees were laden with the most extraordinary fruit: each tree bore fruits of different colours—some were white; some shining and transparent like crystals; some pale or dark red; some green; some blue or violet; some light yellow; and there were many other colours."[37]

For a while Aladdin appreciates none of these colors as he sits in total darkness, shut out of the world by the evil doings of the magician. The latter had asked Aladdin to hand over the lamp on his way out of the cave, but the kid wouldn't budge. He just didn't want to relinquish his treasure, perhaps sensing already that the magician was up to no good, at which point the magician gets angry and retaliates by shutting the cave and burying the kid alive. Luckily Aladdin had kept the ring the magician had given him and by accidentally rubbing it during a moment of prayer he is finally saved and catapulted out into the open: "For two days, Aladdin remained in this state, eating and drinking nothing." At last, on the third day, believing death to be inevitable, he raised his hands in prayer and, resigning himself completely to God's will, he cried out: "there is no strength nor power save in great and almighty God."

It takes a while before Aladdin recovers fully, needing food and rest to find his energy again. He hadn't eaten or slept in three days, and back home in the company of his mother he is instructed to eat and drink slowly. Between total darkness and total light, the process of translating unconscious light into conscious cognition takes more than few minutes, in this case three or four days. But once there the world opens up as a field of interest and participation. Aladdin becomes that much more aware than ever before, wittier and more caring. He had been something of an idle figure, lazy and good for nothing, but now, having gone through a revival of ocular realization, he becomes active and engaged in the life around him. He even outwits the magician who bamboozled him in the first place.

Fire in Wright's Work

Fire was everywhere in Wright's life, as tragedy but also as a source of warmth, family gathering, and glow. As one author said, it seemed "to follow him everywhere he went." We know of the fire that killed his love and mistress Mamah Cheney and that which almost burned down his entire house and studio in the 1930s. But there were others lit to warm relations between family members and those between Fellows throughout the Fellowship years. "On winter nights," tell us Roger Friedland and Harold Zellman in *The Fellowship,* "when dry snow squeaks beneath one's feet, Wright would build a fire and he and Olgivanna [Wright's third wife] took turns reading stories aloud, starting with fairy tales for Iovanna [their daughter]."At one point in the Fellowship, movies were shown and afterward discussed, not in the theater space where they had been projected but "around the fireplace."[38] Indeed, no education was complete for Wright unless also handled from the proximity of the fireplace, where students and mentors can be seen huddled discussing a central topic. No American architect, Wright seemed to hint, could be anointed as much unless trained and nurtured under the warmth of such energy. "When once Americans are taught at their firesides," he tells us, "in terms of building construction the principles so dear to them, the architect will have arrived."[39]

For warmth as it was for mood, fire seemed here a necessary element with which to cut through inhibition and foster collegiality. Just as the Cakchiquels in Eduardo Galeano's account stole fire from the gods to help them speak again, so Wright steals fire from his own devious gods to thaw away the barriers between students and mentor, husband and wife, friend and host. "The nights were icy," writes Galeano, "because the gods had taken away fire. The cold cut into the flesh and words of men. Shivering they implored with broken voices," but "the gods turned a deaf ear." To give them their fire back, the gods demanded that they "cut open their chests with obsidian daggers and surrender their hearts." The hell with that, said the Cakchiquels and "slipped away on feathered feet through smoke, stole the fire and hid it in their mountain caves."[40] Like fireplaces for caves, Wright seeks them to cultivate an air especially conducive to the open and free exchange of ideas, indeed, like the Cakchiquels, to thaw away the frozen mind and the frozen jaw so that together they can move the human community, and in this case the Fellowship, to probe beyond the common scene and unearth ideas buried by years of having to survive under harsh economic and industrial realities.

Bachelard, in *The Psychoanalysis of Fire*, uses "reverie" to explain the impact and need for fire. "One can hardly conceive of a philosophy of repose that would not include a reverie before a flaming log fire," he said. This is where man looks to shake loose the hardened bonds of reality, not least to perennially assess its value and worth to us. "The fire confined to the fireplace was no doubt for man the object of reverie, the symbol of repose, the invitation to repose."[41] Utility was fine but left unchallenged could leave us unable to charge the world with poetic visions. It would grow mean and uninspiring. Bachelard would carry the analysis to death and destruction and see in both a metaphor for renewal. Fire in this case for him suggested "the desire to change, to speed up the passage of time, to bring all of life to a conclusion." In this "the fascinated individual hears the call of the funeral pyre" and detects "renewal." Wright must have assessed the gruesome death of Mamah Cheney in that way, a call for total change, a moment when "love death and fire are united at the same moment," as Bachelard would eerily put it years later, as if knowing about and describing Wright's specific tragic occasion back in 1914. "Through its sacrifice in the heart of the flames, mayfly gives us a lesson in eternity."

There is a near and a far to every furnace and fireplace, the near as manifested through gatherings with friends and family, but a far in the sense of generating glow and having those in the distant horizon bask in its light. That's what captivated Wright in the Bessemer converter in Chicago, and that's what he will seek to achieve in his work. Of which Fallingwater is the most famous, serving as a retreat from the city and a place with which to enjoy a connection with nature but also as a lantern of sorts through whose windows a glow of yellowish, reddish, vitality would emanate. Words by Franklin Toker in his book *Fallingwater Rising* describe the effect perfectly. They were not about Fallingwater to be sure but about a house by Richard Neutra, a onetime student of Wright who had gone on to make a name for himself in California, building homes whose ethic owes a lot to Wright. That house, also for a Kaufmann, this time the son of the Pittsburgh businessman, was in Palm Springs, California. Not unlike Fallingwater, it too featured a large glass opening, meant to blur the distinction between in and out but also to serve as a beacon at night, when "both the house and its natural setting glow with surrealist energy."[42] To be sure it wasn't the fire that was responsible for the energetic glow but artificial lights, located in strategic locations to obtain the desired results, but the point is the same, namely that besides accommodating basic needs, Fallingwater was conceived to express the fire of self-determination. A fire within is what Wright himself had ample doses of, fueling his originality and his will to survive, sometimes well after the world had declared him and his influence dead in the water. Years later, when Olgivanna came to write about her husband, she described him in those terms as well, as a mind so full of fire and yet so underutilized by his country. This was the time of the Second World War, when not much architectural work was available except what the government had commissioned. "Here is Frank now," she said "like a lion in the cage, pacing the floor of Taliesin. Full of force, full of fire, will to work—and nothing to do."[43]

To the side of the fireplace in Fallingwater, Wright designed a built-in kettle. So built-in, in fact, a special niche in the stone was carved out just so that it could dissolve into the woodwork, so to speak, and then swing over when needed (fig. 16). Of spherical shape and made out of cast iron, it was at once an eyeball and a tribal icon of prehistoric, or at least premodern, significance. Why spherical, it is not clear, but an article titled "Fire as an Agent of Human Culture" speaks of certain stoves from sixteenth-century England, as having "spherical" shapes, "balls of metal with screw caps," which were "used as hand warmers." Wright had a special affinity to native American Indians, and it is entirely possible that the kettle and the fireplace are references to their culture and prior presence on the site of Fallingwater. "What Wright absorbed in his visits to Bear Run," says Toker, "went beyond its waters, its trees,

FIG. 16. Living room at Fallingwater, showing the fireplace and space carved out in the stone wall to accommodate the steel kettle when fully swung over. Photo by Christopher Little, courtesy of the Western Pennsylvania Conservancy.

and its rock outcrops to encompass its animal life, the history and legends of the place, from George Washington to the Indians who supposedly had made campfires on the boulder where Wright would later set his fireplace."[44]

To the Kaufmanns he proposed that they boil wine in the kettle, an ancient Roman practice meant to sweeten and preserve the wine. "To enhance a wine's sweetness," one author tells us, "a portion of the wine *must* was boiled to concentrate the sugars in the process known as *defrutum* and then added to the rest of the fermenting batch." The Kaufmanns tried the practice once and never returned to it, probably boiling just water after that to keep the room humid and warm during winter months. Just as Emerson had sought in the transparent eyeball a scientific look, a flask-like container with which to, in effect, boil chemicals and draw out of their visible nature an essential yield, so too with Wright's kettle, he intended a cauldron of sorts with which to draw out from an inert state an active one. It is not enough to have a fire within, Wright seems to be suggesting here, but also the container and the chemical to which the fire can be applied and which together can turn energy into action. The volcano may have all the fire it needs, but without the minerals inside no lava would issue forth and thus no new life could form ahead.

In Wright's use and fascination with fire, there is something of an Ethan Brand, the man in Nathaniel Hawthorne's short story by the same name.

Brand had traveled the world in search of something he calls the "Unpardonable Sin." What that is no one really knows, only that it does not exist out in the world but in the man's "own breast." He had searched long and hard but, finding little to quench his existential thirst, returns home to confront his old demons and meet his end. The process involves a lime burner and his son, who keep a kiln to turn marble into lime. The two, or three if you count the son, enter into a conversation about the journey Brand takes out and back, all the while keeping a keen eye on the fire blazing nearby. The heat is intense, but Brand is unfazed by it, not least because his experience had trained him well. The man had seen everything, and no small fire was going to affect him: "He stirred the vast coals, thrust in more wood and bent forward to gaze into the hollow prison-house of the fire, regardless of the fierce glow that reddened upon his face." When father and son go to sleep, Brand stays up, says a few words, and finally throws himself into the fire, turning life into dust, form into formlessness. The quest for meaning must go on regardless of the degree to which we can find answers for them. For Brand, as it was for Wright, fire was important precisely because it provided the heat by which thought can be formed and developed, but then pushed aside in favor of a new thought. It blended and thickened but then eviscerated an idea, preventing it from an ever becoming a law.

Matching Inside with Outside

As mentioned already, pre-Socratic philosophers relied on the lexicon of fire to explain the underpinning of sight, namely that perception is the product of fires inside the eye traveling outward and capturing the world outside. But also in the other direction, of fires outside traveling from the sun toward the object of observation and into the eye. Here sight is treated as the meeting point between external light and internal light, of like meeting like. "Empedocles," says Olivier Darrigol in *A History of Optics,* "believed vision to depend on two kinds of fire, from flames (including the sun) and from the eye, according the general principle of action of the like on the like."[45] Plato in the *Timaeus* would follow suit and explain that "whenever this visual current is surrounded by daylight, then it issues forth as like into like, and coalesces with the light to form one uniform body in the direct line of vision, whenever it strikes upon some external object and falls in its way." To see reality accurately, in other words, there would have to be an alignment between the inside world of the eye and the outside world of objects. Anything else would be dishonest, blurred as it were by fogged vision. Yes, we may continue to see things, but those things would likely amount to make-believe. It was not so much for the love of green pasture that Emerson in *Nature* wanted his audience to immerse themselves in nature, but more for the love of pure intentions. The matter involved a degree of cleansing, of decontaminating the medium between inside and outside the eye. What good would it be, after all, going out into the woods and taking it in if the inner soul weren't well adjusted with the outer world to receive it as it really is? Indeed, "the lover of nature," Emerson says, "is he whose inward and outward senses are still truly adjusted to each other." This is what it means to be at peace with oneself, from which all good tidings are likely to spring. No original thinking is likely to occur and no honest dealing with client and culture are likely to go on unless the architect, in Wright's case, is at one with themselves. Repose is not a matter of kicking back and enjoying a sunny afternoon but a feeling in which the part and the whole are "perfectly adjusted" to each other. "Do not imagine that repose means taking it easy for the sake of rest," Wright says, "but rather taking it easily because perfectly adjusted in relation to the whole, in absolute poise, leaving nothing but a feeling of quiet satisfaction with its sense of completeness."[46]

Indeed, the modern world had divided Americans into several identities, each manufactured to tackle a side of reality at odds with the next one over, one meant for the office, the other for the school, the shop, and so on. The results were barriers erected to protect each identity from the influence of the other. The one responding to the demands of the office couldn't allow itself the contamination of the home and vice versa, and so on across the problem. Over time the self becomes a collection of silos, each having nothing to do with the next and more fundamentally convinced that it is a unit unto itself. Nothing good emerges from such a psychological organization except a nation full of confused and indeed dishonest people. Americans must be restored to themselves if they were going to go on to innovate and live happy and connected lives.

The correction must start with eroding barriers in favor of a seamless continuity between inside and out. There are moments in Fallingwater when

---

FIG. 17. Corner window at Fallingwater, showing the degree to which Wright went to eliminate window frames and blur the distinction between wall and glass. Photo by Christopher Little, courtesy of the Western Pennsylvania Conservancy.

it is not quite clear when the one begins and the other ends, the two seeming to flow in and out of each other. Even at the corner windows where glass had traditionally converged and met at steel or wooden corner frames, here Wright takes those vertical elements out in lieu of continuous transparency (fig. 17). In the main living room, something of the same takes place, this time taking transparency to a new dematerialized level, glass and stone not so much meeting as bleeding into each other. The result is such that even the presence and feel of glass as a container of space subsides in favor of complete continuity between self and nature. Richard Neutra, the Austrian émigré mentioned earlier, would years later take this continuity to a whole new level, opening up the frame of architecture and letting the outside enter the house, not so much as view or even nature per se but as environment. Cloud, rain, and mist, all seem to come in, uninterrupted, as it were, by what should have been a complex barrier of walls, columns, and doors but which in this case is only a seamless and barely visible expanse of glass. Corners and walls lose their previous role and definition, becoming less objects of resistance than mere membranes keeping weather out and temperature in. Mountains and meadows, rocks and trees, and whatever else lies outside—all move in as if by the breath of God, filling interiors, including the self, transforming it into a thinking and introspective psychology. Between the godly and massive outcropping beyond and the self there is no comparison but unstable and unequal ground. No way could the self compete under these conditions, but it must shrink back and in effect vanish, removing itself as the conscious and active manipulator of the scene out front, giving way to the supremacy of nature. Indeed, in looking at the photographs that Julius Shulman took of Neutra's homes, say of the Singleton House in Bel Air, California (fig. 18), the human is almost never included, and even when he or she is, as in Neutra's own presence in his own home, the figure is shown as diminutive and in deep thought, less a person and more a bundle of thoughts. Geography had turned the man into an introspective being, contemplating matters of existence and pathology, among others. As walls and windows merge, so do the

FIG. 18. Singleton House, Beverly Hills, California, 1959. The house was restored by Studio Tim Campbell for Ronnie and Vidal Sassoon in 2007. Courtesy Studio Tim Campbell, photo by Andrew Bush.

two sides of the self, inside and outside; they, too, unite in view of seeing the flows of nature travel uninterrupted, becoming equally seamless themselves. "Uniquely in Neutra," say Sylvia Lavin, "the corner and the window merge into an indefinite environment complexly articulated through window walls that offer the inhabitant not just visual opportunities but vectors for bodily and spatial traffic between inside and out."[47]

The Health of the Eye

Necessarily contemplation requires free and uninterrupted vistas, be it inside the mental space of the mind or, as in our case here, looking out and letting the eye settle on a distant scene. Anything else would stymie access to the inner self, such as that put up by the modern capitalist city, restricting the views to singular and narrow corridors of power. Tall buildings may have been important in accommodating the rising need of the business class for office space, and under limited spatial and economic circumstances, but they also created canyons of heavy psychological impact. To walk through them was, and is, to feel the crushing force of scale, bulk, and political influence come down upon you. You are little or nothing by comparison, requiring extreme fortitude to stay relevant. To invert matters and restore individual control, over oneself more than anything, it would be important to helicopter up and high above the buildings. In the next chapter we will see how Wright proposed a new city just to achieve that end, including the machinery with which to gain the critical elevation. But for now, and should the individual reach heights beyond the tall buildings below, it would be the horizon that would come into view, now nicely independent of social and political institutions. Neither obelisk nor steeple stand in the way, or for that matter penthouse or office, only infinity. Ah, it is from this vantage point that the eye can relax and roam around, reclaiming agency all over again. What the street level may have taken away, the horizon now gives back. Emerson agrees, saying at one point that "the health of the eye seems to demand a horizon," and then adds that "we are never tired, so long as we can see far enough." Matters even out from a distance, harmonizing that which up close may have been disparate and contentious. Even beauty, which is normally in the eye of the beholder, seems to acquire equal reception from afar and indeed greater appreciation. "If I could put my hand on the north star would it be as beautiful?" asks Emerson in the same vein. Of course not. The act would despoil the star. Better stay away and while at it realize that by keeping distant the very thing observed loses specificity, indeed function, and becomes merely an impression, perfect for contemplation. What geometry may have distinguished this use from that, now gives itself up to a general blend of lines and forms, ready for the eye to enjoy and the mind to think with. Up to a point, much of this remains in the abstract, but while on a trip to Italy Emerson finds in this otherwise philosophical treatise on aesthetics a practical traction. Between nearby "prodigious churches" and "extended mountain prospect,"[48] there is an important function, the first triggering "exhilaration," the second, "sensation," the first important to the study of science and method, the second to that of art and poetry.

A slightly different view of height can be gleaned from Nathaniel Hawthorne's *Blithedale Romance*. There the matter, among others, was authenticity, a term and a philosophy central to Wright's struggle against the erosion of the American character. At one point, Coverdale, one of the main characters in the novel, climbs a tree in search of objective truths. Underneath, fellow residents walk and talk, work and play, unaware of the fact that one of their comrades is hanging above the fray, eavesdropping. He does not mean to do so but does so anyway, hearing and seeing enough to allow him insights into the hearts and minds of those around. They had converged on this spot for a reason but Coverdale is unsure what that reason is. Is it similar to his or are the two misaligned? He wants an objective answer but wagers that he will be unlikely to get it unless he somehow can lift himself above the fray and remain invisible for a while. The story is long but amounts to Coverdale getting closer to the truth than otherwise. "Ascending into this natural turret, I peeped, in turn, out of several of its small windows," he tells us and goes on: "The pine tree, being ancient, rose high above the rest of the wood, which was of comparatively recent growth. Even where I sat, about midway between the root and the topmost bough, my position was lofty enough to serve as an observatory."

The height that Coverdale covets Wright sought to obtain as well, for the same reasons, maybe not by climbing trees per se, but by pulling back and allowing himself the space with which to gather and sustain the question of authenticity, in himself and others. "I was born an American child," he tells us, "of the ground and of space welcoming spaciousness as a modern human need as well as learning to see it as the natural human opportunity."[49] The statement is mangled, but in it lies the belief that space has in it the natural capacity to multiply itself, first on the outside and across the American landscape but later on the inside and throughout the American mind. Space begets space, namely the desire to move out and encounter the next expansive territory, but also to move in and find a commensurate expression inside the self. All of Wright's architecture embodies this elasticity, in one form or another, of sending the eye out but then reeling the psychological goods back in. We have already seen the effect in summary at the Prairie homes, specifically as made possible through the high "water table" mark windows (see the discussion of the Heurtley House in the introduction). Here and in the next few words we shall turn to Taliesin to explain a slightly more elaborate version of the same, namely the way Wright used architecture to braid a special psycho-spatial reciprocity between outside pastoral landscape and interior mental awareness. We can again start with the window. The previous hole in the wall wouldn't do, limiting views to a singular visual vector out into the open. No, it had to change and reinforce the long stretch of the horizon. No more "holes cut in the walls as holes are cut in a box," Wright would say, "because this was not in keeping with the ideal of plastic."[50] Instead, Wright would offer the "wraparound window," traveling across the face of the building and around the corner. Not only did this maximize the cone of vision, but it activated the swivel of the head, further braiding a link between horizon outside and human biology inside, nature and consciousness. So far so good, but the window alone could only do so much. Without a visor-like feature its good ocular projections may go unnoticed. A roof would help, and especially one whose projection beyond the edge of the building could equal in scope the ocular trajectory of the eye, or at least frame it. The results were Wright's infamous deep eaves, some so far out they required steel and elaborate detailing to make them stand. These were more than features extended out to protect the building from rain, but telescopes of sorts bringing the distant horizon into sharp focus within. Richard Etlin describes them as suggestive of "vectors of energy flying through space but also anchored to the chimney stack."[51] Some went out so far, such as at the Robie House in Chicago, Illinois, and the Boylston House in Rochester, New York, that they boxed out the scene outside, turning it into an architecture of its own, on par with the one at hand. The eaves at Taliesin are not as dramatic, but they do accomplish the intended purpose of directing views and pulling back content for psychology.

Gone is that old cave-like home, awful for the way it forced psychology to feed upon its own stale air, unable to vent and obtain fresh views. Instead, now there is shelter, a mere station at which one stops to restore energy and scope for the next stage of outward movement over. The eye and the mind must keep exploring, metaphorically if not literally too. Wright is clear about this: "I began to see a building primarily not as a cave but as a broad shelter in the open, related to vista; vista without and vista within."[52]

Psychological transformation needs turns and returns, changing minds through a turn back toward the self and a repeating of the process again and again. What effect the horizon may have leveled on the eye must be put to good use, probing the machinations of the self. From exterior to interior the switch must go, from distant view to center of room, here doubling as the center of the self as well. The turn is engineered through a perimeter zone just inside the window, thick and room-like and marked by a substan-

FIG. 19. Built-in furniture in the great living room at Taliesin, redirecting the eye back to the center of the room. Photo by author.

tial built-in piece of furniture, on the one hand, and a soffit just above head height, on the other (fig. 19). Having approached the perimeter and looked out into the distant horizon, the body must sit and in so doing look back and face the center of the room, bringing everything back home, so to speak. Between the center of self and center of room there is overlap, reinforced by a rug but also a ceiling that emphasizes the ridge line of the roof. Color, texture, and materials—all further conspire to reinforce the dynamics of returns between center and edge. In one fell swoop, the simple acts of sitting and standing acquire new potential, no longer the mindless moving around of the body but the consequential translation of exterior environment into interior thought.

Breaking the Box and Diagonal Viewing

Wright railed against the modernist box, for the way it was so square and closed, by walls but more importantly by a rational system that had shut the world of ideas and opportunity out. Even when it was surrounded by glass it had remained little more than a Greek temple of steel and glass: "Old man box merely looks different when classified, that's all. The more the box is glassed, the more it becomes evident as a box."[53] And besides the challenge was never, at least for Wright, to overexpose modern man but to steer ocular orientation in ways that could restore mental strength. Overexposure was just as bad as limited exposure, and the question was how much should the architectural box be broken to allow for just this end. Le Corbusier in his *Towards a New Architecture* had given the engineer the upper hand, one of the most rational of all beings, who with his "calculations derives from natural law . . . harmony." He must lead "the way" for he "holds the truth." From him we learn about the role and importance of "regulating lines," lines whose purpose is to discipline and order the laws of perception. Nothing is random or willful anymore but based on reason and a functionalist ethic. "Modern architecture in the interwar period," says Thomas Mical, "overtly drew upon rationalism in the form of instrumental logic, mono-functionalism to order the inherited world, and objective fact over subjective effect."[54] The project can be traced all the way back to the Enlightenment and its attempt to tighten the link between cause and effect, compartmentalizing reality so that it can be addressed and improved one problem at a time. Knowledge for knowledge's sake may have been well and good at one time, but now it had to be applied to a specific problem, not least to solve some of the world's more pressing emerging needs, such as those associated with urbanization, industrial work, and economic inequity. Science went from being a branch of philosophy to a discipline and a study unto itself, concerned with issues of health, energy, planning, and more. From the beginning, then, the modern project was premised on exclusionary tactics.

It took architecture a while to catch up, but when it did it resulted in a world subdivided along functional and later aesthetic and material lines. In one corner of the emerging urban city there were the factories, in another the housing blocks, and in yet another the schools and the hospitals—all linked through roads and highways and the like. Some compared the results to the human body, each function taking care of its own digestive dynamics and pushing the residue to the next organ over. Roads and highways were like veins and arteries, parks like lungs, schools like brains, and so on. Inevitably this led to a city in which buildings became institutions of unwieldy power, made all the more so by the fact that they were islands unto themselves, ruled and regulated by their own independent laws. For someone like Michel Foucault, who spent a lifetime of scholarship analyzing institutional power, the results amounted to a kind of a prison, attracting and capturing people but also "seeing, observing and spying" on them. As Denis Hollier put it in *Against Architecture,* for Foucault the prison of buildings "is the embodiment of an architecture that sees, observes and spies, a vigilant architecture."[55] Be it school, hospital, or home, modern institutions have their basis in incarceration, isolating functions just so that their keepers can exercise control over those in their power.[56] What is the shopping mall, at least in its latter-day twentieth-century version, but that, a concrete box, high and mighty, distinguished by its capacity to divide the world into two, inside and out, the first interesting and active, the other stark and desolate. Nothing short of gravity begins to pull in opposite directions, one sacred, the other profane. The starker the difference, the stronger the pull, which, in the case of the mall, results in consumers now more than willing to consume precisely because they feel rescued, saved, or delivered from a lost and meaningless world.

In the hands of the early twentieth-century moderns, the bipolarization of life and the built environment meant a similar bipolarization between nature and architecture, ground and building, the first organic, the second abstract. The two were separate and separated by a process of scientific analysis and mathematics. Architecture was the manifestation of nature but not a direct reflection of it. It took several steps before the earth turned into finished walls, windows, and doors. Indeed, by the time nature became architecture, architecture was but a mere distant relative of the earth, an abstraction of the natural elements. And so they had to stand apart, even as they were necessarily interdependent. In shape and color too, they had to look distant, the first shapeless and of reddish-brown tones, the second, geometric and white, the summation of all colors. A famous early example of this would be Le Corbusier's Pavillon de l'Esprit Nouveau, a model home constructed for the 1925 International Exhibition of Modern Decorative and Industrial Arts in Paris, France. In it and through it we see the culmination of a science revolution finding expression in architecture, including a nod to a camera obscura, which since the sixteenth century had translated ocular science into a philosophy specifically tailored to serve useful ends (fig. 20). Le Corbusier focused on standardization, namely that once adopted by industry science soon led to standardization. Which for him meant a positive manifestation, allowing "dwelling[s] to be standardized to meet the needs of men whose lives are standardized."[57] Everything that made and which came to be housed by the Pavillon was standardized, including kitchen equipment and furniture: "The scientific study of chairs and tables has, in turn, led to entirely new conceptions of what their form should be: a form which is no longer decorative but purely functional. The evolution of modern manners has banished the old conventional ritual that used to dictate our sitting posture."[58]

As seen in the picture, the pavilion was little more than a box, designed and constructed in the same guise as that of the camera obscura, thin and cardboard-like, and punctured on one side by a circular hole. Le Corbusier made a point of letting us know of his intention in this light when he made the windows synonymous with the void of the mass of architecture, and in so doing revealing the thinness of the construction. So thin and light, in fact, and by extension the rest of modern architecture, it hardly needed structure to support it but a mere four stubby legs and later "Pilotis." Wright, of course, complained, not necessarily about the Pavillon in particular but about the

FIG. 20. Pavillon de l'Esprit Nouveau Pavilion of the New Spirit, by Le Corbusier, 1924. A model home constructed for the 1925 International Exhibition of Modern Decorative and Industrial Arts in Paris, France. Banque d'Images, ADAGP / Art Resource, New York.

whole modernist obsession with white boxes and rickety architecture, saying that "most new modernistic houses manage to look as though cut from cardboard and scissors," with surfaces "glued together in boxlike forms—in a childish attempt to make buildings resemble steamships flying machines or locomotives."[59] Curious about the hole at the Pavillon is that it appears in the roof of the box and not the side, as it had traditionally appeared on the box of the camera obscura, in effect inverting its purpose for modern times. If the hole in the camera obscura had served the purpose of recording the dynamics of nature so that scientists could metricize it, at the Pavillon, Le Corbusier seems to suggest, its new purpose is to spiritualize the same. Pointing at the sky and with a lone tree piercing through it, there is more than a hint that the hole of the Pavillon is there to inaugurate a new role for architecture in its campaign to synthesize a relation between nature and science.

From Isaac Newton in the sixteenth century onward, the camera obscura was used to explain the transfer of knowledge from the outside world to the inside, how light transcribes an image onto the surface of the eye and from there the brain, turning abstract lines into intelligible ideas. Newton used it to explain the divergence of light into a spectrum of colors. John Locke, the famed English philosopher of the seventeenth century and a major intellectual contributor to the American Declaration of Independence, used it to assess the link between understanding and representation. The world may be all around, but until it is translated into an image of communicable value, it can't be known. "External and internal sensations are the only passages that I can find of knowledge to the understanding," he said and then compared the translation of knowledge into understanding to a light coming into a dark room. The only thing needed is a hole in the wall. "These alone as far as I can discover are the windows by which light is let into the dark room. For methinks the understanding is not much unlike a closet wholly shut from the light, with only some little opening left." Pricked and the wall of the "closet" would admit just enough light to capture a facsimile of the world outside, or at least that portion of it contained by the scope of the light admitted. What had been dark and devoid of understanding is now otherwise, a little brighter and little more aware: "To let in external visible resemblances, or some idea of a thing without; would the picture coming into such dark room but stay there and lie so orderly as to be found upon occasion it would very much resemble the understanding of a man."[60]

Not until the world is registered on some surface, on the interior back of a box, could intelligibility begin to mature. This was the magic box of the camera obscura, giving scholars the ability to visualize "spatially the operations of the intellect," but also to control how and what we know. Note Locke's mention of the "little opening left" signifying the modest size needed to translate random scenes into clear and bound images. That's all it takes, a small hole in the wall, and the intellectual process is underway. Which means that this hole can easily be shifted and manipulated, allowing "the subject to guarantee and police the correspondence between exterior and interior representation, excluding anything disorderly or ugly."[61]

Indeed, the camera obscura and the Enlightenment after which it was modeled operate by privileging certain forms of knowledge over others. In

the words of Jonathan Crary, the aperture corresponds to "a single mathe-
matically definable point, from which the world can be logically deduced by
progressive accumulation and combination of signs."[62] So far so interesting,
but neither Wright nor Emerson would have it. The calculation seemed all
too constricting and deterministic. Fundamentally it was not organic and
did not allow for a symbiotic relation between subject and object, man and
the universe. The modernist box cut a very sharp distinction between what
was in and what was out, right and wrong, left and right. It held man behind
bars and limited him to one function and one profession at a time. A better
approach would be to explode the box and open it up at the corners, letting in
light, views, and more nuanced understanding of the world. Wright's invention of the corner window was not first and foremost an aesthetic decision
but one that introduced and encouraged diagonal vision. Nothing short of
modernity depended on it, namely the notion that knowledge is predicated
on angular, and to use proper terminology, refracted light. Kepler in the sixteenth century had said as much, correcting prior misconceptions by such
optic scholars as Vitellio and Alhazen, and explaining, among other phenomena, "the diminution of the moon's diameter in solar eclipses" and "reflection
and refraction of light of the stars." Light did not simply pierce the lens of
the eye but was refracted by it, calibrating the expanse of the world to the
size and geometry of the eye. To understand the world as such was to understand how we proportionally fit in it, where we stand in the larger complex
systems of the universe. Indeed, there was already enough proof by the time
industrial modernity rolled in to suggest that the truth of reality lies not in
direct light alone but in the manner with which that light was bifurcated into
refracted and diagonal light. We may start with direct light but before too
long must bend it to get to the heart of the matter. Glass, prisms, and other
such instruments of transparency are key to this splitting of light into vectors
of truths. And Wright loves it; it is what distinguishes the ancients from the
moderns. If "shadows," says Wright, "were the "brushwork" of the ancient
architect," the "modern [architect] now work[s] with light, light diffused,
light reflected, light refracted."[63] The prism is his or her diagnostic tool: "The
prism has always fascinated man. We may now live in prismatic buildings,
clean, beautiful, and new." All in all it is "glass" that differentiates modernity
from the past, the "one clear "material" proof of modern advantage."

FIG. 21. Interior perspective of the Robie House, Chicago, Illinois, 1906. Note the way Wright prevents the walls from meeting at the corner by inserting a window in that location, pulling sight in that direction and out to the street beyond. Photo by author.

FIG. 22. Exterior view of the Robie House. Photo courtesy of Mark Hertzberg.

Wright challenged his audience to find a building of his in which he had kept the corner. None existed, according to him. Instead, he had "aimed at an organic building—an integument rather than a box." Now exploded at the corners, his version of the box unleashed an important tension between axial and angular visual forces, and by extension between given facts and the layers of interpretations necessary to turn those facts into lessons of cultural import. One without the other is but half a life. Nowhere is this better illustrated than at the Robie House, where in blowing out the box Wright also blew out the singular hold that the axial had had on Americans (fig. 21). The axial remains, held in place by a massive fireplace in the middle of house, but now checked by diagonal glances dialed in by the corner windows. Back and forth the eye moves, between formal relationships within the house and informal ones without (fig. 22). What classical and moral judgments had been leveled inside may now be informed by refracted values from the outside.

At Fallingwater the tension is at once relaxed and energized, relaxed because the geometries are looser than those at the Robie, and yet energized because the visual and physical notes are more plenty. Windows, doors, and built-ins—all contribute. Consider the master bedroom, for instance. Upon entry, the axial is reinforced through door, fireplace, and bed, but also the balcony just outside, which continues the scope of the room. Each is at right angle to the other, the door and the fireplace, the bed, the balcony, and so on. The effect is unmistakable. And yet no sooner is the axial locked into place than it is dialed sideways, across the room and by way of a corner window and a complementary piece of furniture underneath. One floor below the same is repeated, but this time in a more perpendicular direction, marked by the orientation of the balconies going in the opposite direction. The two work in tandem, upper and lower orientations, back and forth, as if Wright were playing with Froebel Blocks all over again, stacking his boxes at cross pattern to each other. Turn up the speed between the two, and the eye settles somewhere in between, looking diagonally across the way and out unto the open, soliciting the same back from the outside. Indeed, most of the photographs taken of the house are from that direction, the most famous of which is from down by the water looking up, fusing water and house into a singular message about unity and nature. No classicism here, please, not because it is not beautiful but because it puts the horse before the cart and insists on an established reality instead of a discovered and organically grown one. The diagonal, then, is nothing short of a rejection of the artificial, and that "mask," to employ a word Wright liked to use, we place over our heads to control troubled and even volatile divisions—between public and private, rich and poor, and so on. "The classical ideal can allow nothing of the [organic] kind to transpire," Wright insists. It is "more a mask for life to wear than an expression of life itself." How awful. Instead, modern architecture should strive to reject the architecture of "the major axis and the minor axis" and all that stands "in military, fashion, heels together, eyes front, something on the right hand and something on the left hand."[64]

Gone is the little hole of the camera obscura, now expanded and taken around the corner, bringing within a singular view a disparate collection of objects, natural and otherwise. In rejecting the classical, Wright, the true modern, also rejected a singular approach to life, a strict division between outside and inside, form and function, here and there, architect and engineer, the whole collapsing into a unified narrative about openness and creativity. As the eye pans and sees more of the world, so does it accumulate more material, more knowledge, some compatible, others less so, but all necessary to a more complex and indeed complete existence in the world. Why restrain analysis to one theory, never to include others, defining how we navigate and evaluate shared space? Why not match in personal philosophy what the world offers in variety, even at the risk of saying one thing one day and a contradictory one the next? Isn't that the mark of an open mind and a vigorous democracy? "Why should you keep your head over your shoulder?" wonders Emerson. "Why drag about this corpse of your memory, lest you contradict somewhat you have stated in this or that public space?" And "suppose you should contradict yourself; what then?" Memory after all is not what it is cracked up to be, an imperfect instrument with which to document and record the past. Just ask Beyle, the character in W. G. Sebald's *Vertigo* and one based on the real life of Marie-Henri Beyle (1783–1842), "known to the world as Stendhal." In returning to a battle scene and finding it at odds with the memory he had of it, he can't help feeling a kind of dizziness come upon him. The scene is far worse than he ever remembered, his memory no doubt modifying the reality to contend with the trauma caused by the scope and cruelty of the occasion. Sebald writes: "The difference between the images of the battle which he had in his head and what he now saw before him as evidence that the battle had in fact taken place, occasioned in him a vertiginous sense of confusion such as he had never previously experienced."[65]

Truly, memory is unreliable and often transformed by technologies of the day, be they associated with construction, transportation, or instruments of representation, of which film and photography are perhaps the most impactful. They do not merely record the world but transform our psycho-spatial and visual understanding of it, giving rise to desires and ways of wishing to be in the world. Baudelaire was certainly affected by them, shaping his rendition of the flâneur, a person who much like a camera himself observes the world without necessarily being of it himself. As Judit Pieldner says: "The 'visual boom' of the streets," during Baudelaire's time, as "complemented by the emergence of new visual media, i.e. photography and film[,] transformed the city into a new spectacle, which led to an altered state of the individual and the observing gaze."[66] Wright himself was a consumer of such visual technologies, using them to impart on us a reality he worked hard to manipulate, and by which he wished us to remember him. Much has been made, for instance, of his early use of the camera to choreograph a special relation with family and friends and a domestic life, carefully calibrated to show him as a caring father and husband but also one who marches to a beat of a different kind. It was to that end that Wright would carefully compose a picture of him and his family sitting on a Persian carpet on the steps outside his home in Oak Park, just so as to, in the words of Ada Louise Huxtable, "create an appropriate aesthetic background."[67] Persian carpets were never meant to be outside, and yet Wright here drags one out just to impress upon us a memory he'd worked hard to construct.

The Corner Window and American Pragmatism

But at any rate, and back to the corner window, it would dovetail with the lexicon of Pragmatism already underway at least since the 1890s, a uniquely American philosophy shaped in response to a nation now struggling with questions of diversity, as precipitated by sudden and escalating migrations, between nation and nation but also between country and city. How should people converge and share resources, live in close proximity, and generally contribute and make the world a better place as a collective? In the context of the American scene, where migrations meant the confluence of radical differences—in religion, education, race, and more—the answer seemed to require a position of flexibility, adaptability. American Pragmatism was the result. Based on the four basic principles of "interaction, pluralism, community and growth," it espoused a philosophy as "investigation" and less as "view point," a method of understanding the world by engaging it. Where a philosophy based on "view point" may guide through distinctions, setting up criteria by which to live a moral life, one based on "investigation" is different. It is "a process of reflecting on habits, established beliefs and ways of understanding and interacting with the world." William James and John Dewey, along with Charles Pierce, are its authors, insisting on finding ways to come together and release in individuals their best potential. Wright was familiar with them even as he may not have mentioned their names often, largely through aunts who adhered to their philosophy to shape their own progressive educational agenda, but also a Chicago milieu looking to advance new urban strategies. In his *Frank Lloyd Wright and His Manner of Thought*, Jerome Klinkowitz attributes to William James, more than the other two Pragmatists, Wright's passion for a pluralist America, including the architect's attempt to modernize Emerson and resurrect his influence in the American popular imagination. "If one wants a more current model for Wright's intellection," he says, "it is found in the works of William James, especially his religious thought, the manner of which the young architect emulates through his revision of Emerson."[68]

Very true but equally so is the fact that John Dewey was in Chicago at the same that Wright was, between 1894 and 1904, both looking to democratize, along with Dwight Perkins and others, America's relation to space and the modern metropolis, even if in very different ways.[69] Any full analysis of Wright's pluralist corner window must include Dewey in some way, starting with the Robie House and Wright's first inclination to break the box, as institution and dogma.

What had been pried open by the corner window would soon blossom into an even wider opening, this time through the agency of the city. At that scale the freedom wouldn't remain private and limited to one or two households at a time but would be expansive and distributed to effect a national outlook. Looking around and askance wouldn't remain a matter of personal philosophy but one associated with matters related to cultural equity. Here institutions such as banks and insurance companies, city halls and stock markets, would subside in favor of horizons, long and wide, which allow the eye to see as far as the eye can see. This is the story of the next chapter. In it we will encounter the expanse of Broadacre City, a proposal Wright had been thinking about all along but which wouldn't mature into a physical and mental production until the 1930s, when work had subsided and there was time to think about concerns that transcended the individual commission. It is truly an extension of this chapter but with different means. Just as Wright erased a corner piece of structure to design and build his corner window, he would do the same in Broadacre City, but this time at an urban scale, by equally lifting buildings to allow the eye to roam uninterrupted. Buildings of course remain but at a much lower scale and at a much sparser rate, pulling back and making room for the Pragmatists' program of interaction, pluralism, community, and growth.

Broadacre City is no Chicago, but it would come to resemble the big metropolis in some ways, not least through a tall building that was designed for Chicago but now appears in Broadacre. What progressive breakthroughs Chicago had initiated in education, parkways, and urban public space, Wright would siphon to shape the new American city, never explicitly but implicitly. The boundaries the Pragmatists had destroyed in favor of porous institutions meant to encourage and foster interaction belong to a world and a vision that would find expression in Broadacre.

4

THE LOSS OF PERSPECTIVE
IN BROADACRE CITY

Of what use is genius if the organ is too convex or too concave and
cannot find a focal distance within the actual horizon of human life?
— R. W. EMERSON, "Experience"

With his wraparound window, Wright sought to equate seeing with
feeling, eye with psychology. By inviting Americans to look widely,
from sea to shining sea, or more specifically across the meadows,
he hoped for an equally expansive horizon on the interior of self. Nothing was
edited until it was time to do so, letting the diversity of visuals enrich rather
than stifle the production of ideas. Just as the horizon does not discriminate
between various life-forms, or for that matter between the natural and the artificial, so by contemplating it Americans would remain open and diverse in
their approach to solving some of the world's most pressing problems. There
was no need to look back to history or borrow images from the next town over
or, more importantly, from Europe. All Americans needed to do was keep their
gaze perennially fixed on the horizon. The way to close what Wright called
the "cultural lag" was not by copying that against which the lag was formed
but by bridging unlikely scenarios and in that way inventing new forms.

Using the wraparound window to connect Americans to the horizon was
predicated on the fact that there was a horizon already available to look at.
But that was not necessarily the case by the early twentieth century. The
modern city had suffocated it out of view, its canyon of tall buildings replacing it with icons of political and economic power. Obelisks, fountains, and
later large works of urban art marked the scene, beautiful in one sense but

---

also clear in their manner of replacing nature with instruments of cultural control. The horizon Wright sought to resurrect had to be intentionally restored to the American landscape. You could climb to the roofs of the buildings and try to see it, say, in the manner of King Kong in the 1933 movie by that name, but the effort would be futile, not least because it would be temporary and limited to those who could afford to get up there. A better option would be to leave the city altogether and head to the country, start a new and more open version of the old. This was in large part the aim of Broadacre City, a patchwork of sorts between architecture and nature, stitched together in an effort to deformalize the relation between the two. Where one ends the other begins without formal and regulated transitions, often without sidewalks or other expressions of urban civilization. Yes, it was the product of the economic struggles of the 1930s, including federal plans to stabilize otherwise uncertain times, but more critically it was also the result of a deepseated desire to resurrect the horizon after years of passing. Only one or two tall buildings stood in the way; otherwise they were gone.

The Horizon and the Eradication of Time

Nowhere is this made clearer than in the perspective drawings of the city in the 1950s created by Wright and his apprentices, always from vantage points well above the ground (fig. 23). Where perspectives of places are normally drawn from angles closer to the ground and most commonly human height, not least to simulate integration with real life, these insisted on eyes way up in the sky, not so far up to where the ground becomes little more than a series of abstract paintings but far enough to capture a total picture of the city below. Thousands of years vanish in the blink of an eye, eradicated when two empires separated by that many years are rendered side by side. Look at the two buildings in the background in figure 23, the first a tall building and a product of twentieth-century technology, the other a ziggurat or a pagoda, two, three, or four thousand years old. In his *Living City,* the last of three books on Broadacre City, Wright called the former simply a mixed-use tower, mixing apartments and offices, the latter a "nonsectarian cathedral." In any other setting this union would have been deemed weird, incongruent, or downright wrong, but not here. Here, the two buildings are compatible pre-

FIG. 23. Pencil perspective drawing showing the key components of Broadacre City: tilled fields, roads, a sparse scattering of low and high buildings, and so on. Drawn by apprentices of Wright in the 1950s. Copyright © 2022 Frank Lloyd Wright Foundation, Scottsdale, AZ. All rights reserved. The Frank Lloyd Wright Foundation Archives (The Museum of Modern Art | Avery Architectural & Fine Arts Library, Columbia University, New York)

cisely because the horizon has made them so, washing away artificial codes of aesthetic context in favor of natural reflex. Who says you can't place a modern tall building next to an ancient temple? As long as there is a horizon that can override stylistic differences, anything goes. Make nature the backdrop against which architecture and culture appear and all shall be well, canceling or at least relaxing hegemonic and stylistic rules. What had been controlled and restricted by academic laws now gives way to natural flows. Just as nature does not erect boundaries between life-forms, so is the case with Broadacre; it, too, does not prematurely divide styles, favoring one over the other. It accepts all and, in so doing, inverts more than one association, including time.

Look at the two buildings mentioned above, and you'll see that though they are separated by thousands of years stylistically, the first modern, the other ancient, in real life they are only a ten-minute walk away from each other. The matter becomes even more interesting when we include the viewer in the mix, here sitting or standing about a half mile away. It takes less time to go from ancient Ur to a midcentury skyscraper than it does for the viewer, who occupies the here and now, to walk to either one of those buildings. The message is clear, namely, that should one stand far back enough and let the horizon, and not some artificial and punitive legal code, define the law of the land, no two historically and conceptually disparate entities will remain foreign to the eye; indeed, they will become part of a harmonized whole. Without the horizon, it is the role of political institutions to keep the peace, regulating behavior and codifying social and political transactions. Force would be required to make sure the misaligned remain aligned, with each other but also with the instruments of state. As Thomas Lemke said, studying Michel Foucault's theories of power, it is at this point that "general principles" would stop functioning, such as those associated with "divine wisdom, human reason, natural law, and so on." Concrete measures would be necessary. "Instead of being determined in reference to transcendental principles," peace and harmony would be achieved through "immanent relations of force."[1]

Transportation as the New Religion

And yet how might one reach that distance, that far back? The secret lies in the means of modern transportation. In the perspective drawing we see a family of four standing on a sidewalk, not too far from where the viewer of the scene in the drawing is standing, or sitting. Two parents and two kids, a boy and a girl. With hands locked and placed around the area of the navel, the parents seem to be in the middle of a prayer. The posture resembles that adopted by Catholics attending church, devout and silent in their manner of listening to the sermon ahead. The couple is turned slightly sideways, at an angle from the road, looking at what appears to be a hybrid vehicle, half bicycle, half helicopter. The God they are paying their respect to is one with modern circulation, promising them the capacity to move about and regain freedom all over again. Unlike other vehicles, this godly one is of a special nature, allowing not only linear movements but those which soon will mature into many directions and possibilities. It may start as a simple bicycle of sorts but soon transforms, larva-like, into a machine, unique and powerful precisely because it allows for free movement, in all directions and at a moment's notice. Look up and you can see them in their more developed condition, now fully grown in the form of flying saucers, buzzing around in random directions. Which is what the two kids do, look up, the boy pointing to them with excitement and wonder.

Nothing is more evil than the modern city, and the more quickly one gets out of it the better, or so Wright insisted. It is a "whirling vortex built from the top down," says he, by landlords and bankers who have held everyone hostage to their "rent"-minded mentality and control of humanity. Here skyscrapers create canyons of darkness from which it is hard to find one's way. They come down crashing like "haphazard masses upon the bewildered eye," which peers upward in return "from the black shadows down below."[2] Like a "volcanic crater," the city contains "blind, confused, human forces," which push "together and grind upon each other." They are "moved by greed in common exploitation, forcing anxiety upon all of life."[3] Movement is the only way out, en masse and as quickly as possible. No wonder the parents in the perspective are looking at the hybrid vehicle as if it were a source of divine intervention. They are worshipping it on par with the savior Jesus Christ, its wheels reminiscent of the communion wafer discs Catholics ingest while consummating their union with the Lord. Or if not holy communion, then at least the grillwork of the secessionist Viennese architects, whom Wright admired, and who in anointing the rise of modern industry merged ironwork with ornament, often in the image of curls and wheels swirling about each other (fig. 24). So fast can the vehicle go that it can pretty much fly, and, indeed, it may represent the first step in the making of what looks like a bunch of UFOs overhead: "The instinct of the amorphous human herd exploited by the city, swarm with the swarm in the erstwhile village streets, but the swarm is taking wing—or to wheels which is much the same thing because increased facilities of lateral movement are comparative flight."[4] The kids stand slightly apart and independent of the parents, themselves holding hands in seeming agreement about the future that lies ahead. One of them is also pointing up

FIG. 24. A zoomed-in view of the wheel on the car in Broadacre City, "half bicycle, half helicopter."

at the sky, as mentioned, to the strange but compelling flying machines now zipping all over the place, giving the eye free rein over the terrain below. There is no better spot than here from which to see the horizon and the land of milk and honey. If the parents are busy paying tribute to the vehicle on the ground, the kids are giddy about the future. You can almost hear them saying after Wright that a "fond human dream is about to be realized."[5]

We may note while still looking at the foreground that both the hybrid vehicle and the flying saucers overhead are uniquely designed around the individual, as if tailor-made to suit that person, the way they stand, step, sit, and so on. It may accommodate more than one person but certainly not more than two, the whole thing resembling a double-breasted jacket, tightly wrapped around the body. However we attempt to understand Broadacre City, we cannot do so without analyzing the role of the individual. This is a different kind of person than we had known before, one who is less about getting ahead at the expense of others and more about being self-possessed and strong because they are internally reconciled. It is not the individualism that capitalism created, needy and selfish, but one founded on integrity. "The 'rugged individualism' that now captains our enterprises and becomes the capitalist is entirely foreign to this idea of individuality," insists Wright. Rather, this individuality is based on selfhood: "The actual difference between such ism and true individuality is the difference between selfishness and selfhood."[6] This will be in part the aim of this chapter, to investigate how drawing back the curtain and revealing the horizon also lays bare the making, but also the unmaking, of the individual, now psychologically delaminated by capitalism.

Middle Ground

But for now, let us turn to the middle ground in the bird's-eye view of the new Jerusalem. If the background made plastic the relationship between space and time, history and geography, and the foreground gave us the religious conditions under which the new city is blessed, what might the middle ground offer? It is marked by a building halfway inside the picture and halfway out. It seems to have just arrived from somewhere and to be on its way to somewhere else, dragging into the picture a swath of vegetative land behind. What might this building be? It looks like no other and certainly nothing like the commercial "boxes" back in the city. It has no shops on the ground floor or any other human-related function for that matter. Neither doors nor windows exist here, but one large arch serving as what seems like a gateway to some other precious land beyond. Indeed, the first-floor wall is entirely blank, save for few upturned semicircular windows resembling the belly and side of a boat, half-submerged underwater and on its way to the next port. If so, the first floor is little more than a storage compartment or one associated with housing mechanical operations, typically where stokers slaved to feed the engine furnace with coal. One floor up and the iconography begins to morph, slowly changing from marine architecture to locomotive design, the latter evident by the circular forms turned arches marching down alongside the deck, reminiscent of locomotive wheels. More on the latter in a bit. Both, ship and train, have a place in modern twentieth-century America, now reinvented in the image of the automobile and other advanced technologies. Both had interrupted the peace and quiet of the country, the bucolic nature and manner with which a whole American society had stayed close-knit and happy.[7] The ship had done it by allowing immigrants throughout the nineteenth century to come over and mix with local blood, contaminating the cultural and religious code of the country, or so the sentiment back then went, the train by violating natural habitats and the sanctity of the small town.[8] The two are in fact connected, at least in the latter part of the nineteenth century, when the plan to reach the west coast by train required men "willing to dynamite the earth, blast away at the mountains, and lay the tracks to build a network of canals, roads, and railroads."[9] The country was growing and urbanizing by leaps and bounds, and it needed more people.

Wright never explicitly complained about immigrants, but he did have plenty to say about imported ways, lamenting why "culture must come from abroad."[10] Additionally, to succeed, his organic architecture was predicated on keeping pure the biology of the seed, so to speak, namely, that to influence an idea is to corrupt its DNA. And that can't be good, not least because it would erode national identity. In "Wake up America," he argued against sending troops overseas, to fight in World War II, lest they too may get corrupted and lose their American right to choose: "Democracy is a way of life in which the individual and what makes him one—his character—has an open chance to develop under a way of government wherein choice is free to the human soul." Indeed, he added, "to every individual and that within that inner realm of conscience there can be neither invasion nor compulsion." A better approach would be to send the troops in the other direction, to the prairies, the land of "their birthright."[11]

But if ships were invasive culturally, trains were intrusive physically, reaching well into the country and remaking it in the image of the city. No matter what rural residents did or desired to remain independent, their plight now became forever hitched to that of the urban center. Neither distance nor peace of mind could in effect be maintained. Nathaniel Hawthorne lamented the disturbance: "But hark!" he said, "there is the whistle of the locomotive—the long shriek, harsh, above all other harshness, for the space of mile cannot mollify it into harmony."[12]

He had gone out to a nice opening in the landscape to hear nature sing its song and restore his senses. But lo—not for too long. No piece of land by the mid-nineteenth century was out of range of modern industry, its sounds penetrating the meadows and violating man's communion with nature and ultimately his inner constitution. Hawthorne goes on about this invasiveness:

"it tells a story, of busy men, citizen, from the hot street, who have come to spend a day in a country village, men of business; in short of all unquietness; and no wonder that it gives such a startling shriek, since it brings the noisy world into the midst of our slumberous peace."

The locomotive must be halted, stopped in its tracks. Or capsized and made into a relic of past ages. And so, Wright goes to work doing just that, flipping his middle ground building upside down and dragging it well into the earth. With wheels cut off at half circle and up in the air, the old train loses its locomotive capacity and becomes a museum of sorts. "The present cumbrous establishment [of railroad travel]," he tells us in this light, "is already obsolescent as human passenger traffic in America has taken to the air."[13] What this building is we don't know, but what we do know is that whatever it is, it has lost its actual mobility in favor of mobility of a different kind, namely, one as defined by the rhythm of arches marching across the picture and out of the frame. Much like a curtain about to be drawn to the side to let the drama behind begin, so do these arches march sideways; they, too, seem in the process of moving to the left to let the drama of Broadacre City unfold.

The Drama of Broadacre City

Composed of several acts, nine or twelve acts depending on how you see the grid of the city, each illustrated by a different cultivated lot, it tells the story of a community steeped in farming practices and philosophy (fig. 25). Buildings here have been cleared in favor of furrowed fields, all neatly combed and laid out to receive as much sun as possible. On one side an orchard runs the length of a long field, bearing fruit, apples or peaches. The trees are short enough that they can be picked by hand on the ground or with the help of a short ladder. Closer to us in the foreground the fields seem still in the throes of an early spring. Vegetable greens have yet to sprout. It is mid- to late April, and all will soon conspire toward an active and happy "performance." The script is based on Emerson's essay titled "Farming," which the author published in 1872 in a book called *Society and Solitude,* and which Wright tags verbatim at the end of his *Living City,* the last of three books on Broadacre. In it, Emerson starts with a celebration of the farmer, extolling his virtues as a generalist in a world overrun by specialists. In him there is no

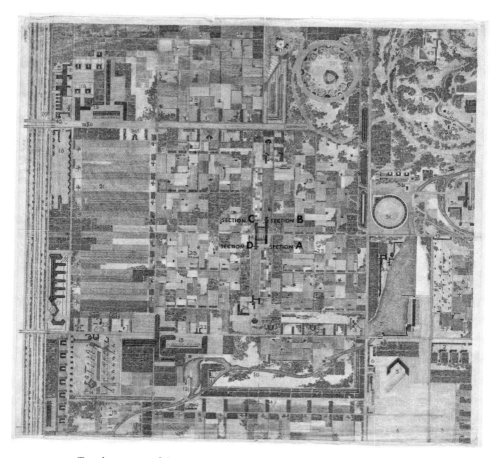

barrier between artist and engineer, architect and builder, but a wholesome figure capable of doing it all, not by choice but by necessity: "The glory of the farmer is that, in the division of labors, it is his part to create." If he does not produce people won't eat, the air won't clean, the soil won't rejuvenate. He levels the ground "poisoned by town life and town vices," reminding us that no matter our worldly aspirations, we remain beholden to basic provisions: food, water, air. "The first farmer was the first man, and all historic nobility rest on possession and use of land."

Industrial production and capitalism back in the city had given the idea of work a bad name, so riddled, as it was, by oppressive hierarchies and dangerous work conditions. Better to correct that reputation and restore work to its rightful place in the world of spiritual and meaningful engagements. What better place on which to do so than the farm? This is where farmers wake up every day and take to the fields, clear and cultivate the land, plow and seed it, their joy and hard work evident in the trace they leave behind. "Tillage" is what Emerson calls it, the look of finely groomed, furrowed soil. One look and it is hard not to feel in one's bones a deep admiration for the effort that went into those lines, or perhaps, more spiritually, the hand of some higher being at work. Indeed "every man has an exceptional respect for tillage," says Emerson and adds that mere sight of a tilled field will trigger in us "the feeling that this is the original calling of [our] race," restoring in us attachment to earth, place, and community. No doubt Emerson was channeling his Transcendentalist German predecessors, specifically Fredrick Henry Jacobi, who more than anyone took stock in the power of the gaze to see "essential truths." One look and man could detect truth from fiction, underpinnings from superficialities. Man possessed a "spiritual eye" capable of giving "evidence [to] things not seen and substance to things hoped for." It is "a faculty of vision," tells us Octavius Frothingham in *Transcendentalism in New England*, "to which truths respecting God, Providence, Immortality, Freedom, the Moral Law, are palpably disclosed."[14] Of all the professions laid out across time, farming is "the nearest to God, the first cause," says Emerson, and all it takes is a keen look at the fields on which that practice is performed. To it we must go to heal and reclaim our individuality. This is where the "injured shall go . . . to be recruited and cured." This "shall be their hospital."[15]

Health is the subject of another book Wright read and on which he premised the planning of Broadacre City. *Erewhon* is its name, "Nowhere" spelled backward, a novel by Samuel Butler telling the story of one journeyman traveling across a terrain and a country of unknown origin. It has all the machinations of a colonizer's quest into a world unlike any other, whose people approach things in ways that are diametrically opposite to those back home. Including healthcare. Here health is of utmost importance, and a lack of it is considered more serious than any other transgression we may consider egregious in the Western world, say, stealing or adultery. Stealing in fact is considered totally fine and, indeed, is a source of pride, making it clear that in the final balance of values, any fuss devoted to money, including economic inequity, is a sign of lack of sophistication. No one cares about rich and poor. Go ahead and rob a bank and see if anyone bats an eye. No one does. But get sick and you will be ostracized. Especially prized is mental strength. Those who live in Erewhon particularly "admire mental health and love it in other people, and take all the pains they can to secure it for themselves."[16] So critical is health in this city that it is considered a kind of crime to let oneself fall ill. Or, if not a crime, at least a source of tremendous shame. No one in his or her right mind would appear in public should they fall sick. Better to stay home and fade away.

Health is everything to Broadacre City, in body, mind, and soul, clear in the way the sun feeds the soil, the soil the plant, air the skies. The image is unmistakable, perhaps only rivaled by the source that gave rise to it in *Erewhon*. The protagonist of the novel had been traveling for some time in search of the land of bliss, Erewhon itself, up and down hills and valleys, mountains and rivers. He is exhausted but nourished by the prospects ahead. At one point he climbs so high he is above the clouds, in that rarefied atmosphere where dreams and heady thoughts are made. There is nowhere else for him to go but down at that point, hoping beyond hope that what lies on the other side matches in reality what he had built up in his dreams. The man is not disappointed, for no sooner does he make it "below the level of the clouds" than "a burst of brilliant evening sunshine" erupts before into his eyes. He is immediately cheered. "Oh how [the] light cheered me." The sight was like no other, "an expanse as was revealed to Moses when he stood upon the summit of Mount Sinai, and beheld that promised land which it was not to be his to enter." Out in front he "could see many a town and city, with buildings that had lofty steeples and rounded domes." Nearer, the scene offered ridge behind ridge, outline behind outline, sunlight behind shadow, and shadow behind sunlight, gully and serrated ravine." Remarkably like Broadacre or the other way around, he "saw large pine forests, and the glitter of a noble river winding its way upon the plains." He is so overwhelmed and tired that the best he can do is lie down and let the valley lap over him, become part of his dream. "I was quite tired out; and presently, feeling warmed by the sun, and quieted, I fell off into a profound sleep."

Waking, he finds four or five goats feeding nearby, happy and without a worry in the world, including fear of humans. Clearly this is not a place where humans are a threat to animals or the other way around, but one in which the two can coexist peacefully, a good place to restore one's sense of peace and well-being. If the city had destabilized the internal balance of Americans, it is to a place like Erewhon or Broadacre that they must return to diagnose and cure their ills. What had been thrown out of sync, between their biological or-gans but also between inner and outer countenance, can here find alignment once again. In adjusting to urban life, Americans had lost connection with natural time, often extending functions well beyond their natural hours, into the night, the weekend, and so on. Summer and winter reversed order. What had been limited by summer heat now became doable through advanced mechanical systems, and the other way around across other seasons. The same went for the speed of life; be it because of telegraphy or automobiles, or other technologies of movement, time and space truncated or at least became more elastic. A corrective was needed, namely a return to farming and a life timed back to "nature and not to city watches." A life, that is, neither too slow nor too fast but just right, adjusted to the needs at hand. Much as "the sails of a ship bend to the wind," so the new Americans-turned-farmers react to "the order of the seasons, the weather, the soils and crops," says Emerson in "Farming." Being well-adjusted to the context and functions underway, their senses would awaken to the world around, registering reality at the pace, smell, and color from which it had evolved in the first place. Natural patterns resurface again after years of burial at the hands of artificial instruments, now vivid and beautiful precisely because they had not been contaminated by layers of cultural transformations. Instead of composition, beauty would be defined by "tranquility and innocence." In "the care of bees, of poultry, of sheep, of cows, the dairy, the care of hay, of fruits, of orchards, and for-est," there would arise an equilibrium between man and nature, "giving him, [man], a strength and plain dignity like the face and manners of nature."

But let there be no mistake about it; nothing about getting to that state of repose is easy. Nor is it a matter of tourism, accomplished on the weekend and part of a packaged plan. "The farmer's office is precise and important, but you must not try to paint him in rose color," Emerson reminds us. Indeed, there is nothing romantic about his work but a commitment to direct dealings with the world, clean and honest. Just like the protagonist of *Erewhon* had to pay his due diligence to be the citizen of the city of his dreams, traveling up and down treacherous terrain, so the return to farming must not be romanticized. Once there the joys and rewards are the product of hard work. No strike of the earth goes to waste here, instead finding equal and opposite strike inside his soul. The more Americans work at it, the more the two intertwine, soil and soul at one point fusing in an unself-conscious struggle against the world of scientific and academic distinctions. Donna Haraway may refer to the process as "Symbiogenesis," or systems "that do not have a self-defined spatial or temporal boundaries," and whose "information and control are distributed among components." In time biology and religion will have become "looped, braided, outreaching, involuted, and sympoietic."[17] Farming "is done by one kind of man," Emerson says, "not by scheming speculators nor by soldiers, nor professors, nor readers of Tennyson; but by men of endurance—deep chested, long winded, tough, slow and sure, and timely."[18] The farmer is great not because he is clever, or even strong and patriotic, or smart and steeped in books, first and foremost, but because he is a model of mental and physical equilibrium, his inside matching his outside. What does it matter if the speculator is efficient, the soldier tough, the professor erudite; none is likely to yield meaningful and lasting results unless that person is at peace with themselves. And if so, not only will they benefit, but others will as well. The individual who possesses a strong inner-outer constitution is one who has no axe to grind but wishes others the best, paving the way for their own success. John Dewey, who had read and admired Emerson's philosophy, agreed, adding that it is precisely this character in the individual which constitutes the true making of democracy. Democracy may be about collective agreement and consensus, voting rights and the like, but more so it is about the way individuals and society in general release in others their inner potential.

Indeed, for Dewey, whom Wright had known through aunts and the progressive education movement of the late nineteenth century, as mentioned in the previous chapter, there is a fine dance between democracy and the individual, at first seemingly at odds with each other but, on deeper analysis, very much in lockstep. For him, individuality does not offer itself at first ready-made but "spontaneous and unshaped," open to "potentiality [and] development." Like a piece of canvas, it is of no consequence unless acted upon with paint and artistic intent. It "is not something complete in itself, like a closet in a house or a secret drawer in a desk, filled with treasures that are waiting to be bestowed on the world." No, it is "a distinctive way of feeling the impacts of the world and of showing a preferential bias in response to these impacts." As such it does not acquire "shape and form" unless it "interacts with actual conditions."[19]

Of Land and Fences

How this may take place in Broadacre City is a matter of curious interest. Look closely at the fields in the perspective we have been using throughout the chapter, and you'll see that there is no one around. What human presence there had been is now gone, having moved elsewhere, perhaps to the home or the factory, among other critical places. In its wake we are left with a silent but telling visual narrative in which the absence of the fence and the boundary is important. Where there had traditionally been a barrier to differentiate one property from the next, here there is none. The fields are without fences, and the only way to differentiate between one and the next is through the way the furrowed patterns turn at ninety degrees from each other, each, interestingly, open to the general lay of the land beyond. As a pedestrian in the city, you could technically leave the road and walk diagonally across the fields to your next destination, taking care, of course, not to damage the plants, something Thoreau would have loved to do and, indeed, did do before the fences finally arrived. "At present, in this vicinity, the best part of the land is not private property," he tells us in his essay "Walking." For now, "the landscape is not owned, and the walker enjoys comparative freedom." But the days are nigh when that landscape "will be partitioned off into so called pleasure grounds, in which a few will take a narrow and exclusive pleasure only, when fences shall be multiplied, and man traps and other engines invented to confine men to the *public* roads, and walking over the surface of God's earth shall be construed to mean trespassing on some gentleman's grounds."[20]

Property is not what it seems here. Unlike its counterpart back in the city, it is defined by neither wall nor fence but runs uninterrupted across the terrain of the entire place. Lot lines and other legal boundaries are noticeably absent. In Wright's words, "The tin can barbed-wire fence[s], once the bulwarks of advancing civilization, are long since gone."[21] Indeed, land in Broadacre City is for everyone, shared by residents of the city under a contract different from the one advanced by the philosophers of the modern state. John Locke, writing in the seventeenth century, had tied individual sovereignty to property, namely, arguing that to exist in a sovereign state, the individual, at some point, must inevitably claim a piece of it, which unless protected will be taken away from him by the more powerful. In his assessment of the balance of power between the state and the individual, the only power he could assign the state is that which must be exercised to protect the life and property of the individual. Otherwise, it should have no power and, in the words of G. D. H. Cole, must be beholden to "the consent of [the] governed."[22]

Free Land

Henry George, the journalist turned fierce social activist in the late nineteenth century, must enter the picture here. Wright mentions him regularly. It is from George that Wright learned about common and free land, and to him Wright returns to grapple with ideas that are at base foreign to a political and economic system based in capitalism. How do you give away land in a country premised on ownership? For both Wright and George, free land is critical to giving everyone a fair start, leveling the terrain of opportunity and self-determination. Without it the privileged will always have a leg up and the unprivileged an uphill battle. Which is terrible, indeed, repressive in every way, keeping the citizen too bogged down to keep up, too preoccupied in daily affairs to step back and know how to contribute to the instruments of democracy. Free land is necessary in alleviating the problem, especially available to those who could prove that they could make the land "pay." In Broadacre City it comes in the form of a one-acre parcel of land, to build a home and raise a garden. The matter is one of human right and not merely economic. Everyone has a God-given right to land, from the outset, namely that even before a child is born "he finds his own acre waiting for him when he is born." Indeed, "society must . . . make available to [each poor man] . . . acreage according to his ability to make good use of the land."[23]

———

And yet again, Wright knows that the sound of free land wouldn't sit well with capitalists averse "to anything free." And so he adds a note, "I am well aware of the academic economist's reaction to . . . free land or anything free." But still he insists that "Henry George showed his people clearly enough the simple basis of human property."[24] And so did Silvio Gesell, the German economist and anarchist from whose book *The Natural Economic Order* Wright borrowed the terms "free-land" and "free-money" and who, according to Lionel March, sought "to establish an equitable distribution of land and medium of exchange."[25] As currency lost value, Gesell's logic went, so did the incentive to hoard money in favor of using it "as soon as possible as a medium of exchange."[26]

Wright's openness to an otherwise socialist and rather un-American twentieth-century approach to land and property no doubt came as a result of having benefited from a nineteenth-century version of it himself, not directly but through maternal grandparents, "the God Almighty Joneses," who in the 1850s had left Wales in search of better economic opportunities, soon finding relief in the Homestead Act of 1862. So long as you were "an adult citizen, or intended citizen," the act stipulated, and one "who had never borne arms against the U.S. government[,] you could claim [up to] 160 acres of surveyed government land." All "claimants were required to do [was to] improve" the plot by building a dwelling and cultivating the land."[27] What good is land unless cultivated to improve human potential, indeed, serving as the "simple basis of human property." Having worked hard, and after only five years, "the original filer was entitled to the property, free and clear."

Land factors big in the story of European settlements in America. Nothing less than the premise of hope and self-determination rides on it. "One comes upon" narratives of the land "in almost every valid piece of early American thought," tells us Lewis Mumford in his *Golden Day*, adding that we may think of "moorland pastures by the sea" in this light, "dark with bayberries and sweet fern, breaking out among the lichened rock," and so on.[28] Walt Whitman had waxed poetic about it:

> All things invite this earth's inhabitants
> To rear their lives to an unheard of height,
> And meet the expectation of the land

Indeed, land may have even contributed to the progressive philosophy of democracy, or so Scott Pratt argues in *Native Pragmatism,* going back to the early discussions between native Indians and the white settlers. In one account, we hear of an encounter between a Quaker and a Delaware leader by the name of Teedyuscung. The two had converged in the mid-eighteenth century to settle a native claim around indigenous land. They enter into an interesting debate about the "Golden Rule," which the Quaker in earnest used to see if he could assimilate Teedyuscung to the manner of his ways. It called for treating others as one might wish to be treated by them, a paying of respect based on a kind of symmetry of emotions. Teedyuscung is not convinced and politely rejects the "Rule," arguing that there is no way that its philosophy could survive the test of human nature, not least because we are all born different. The challenge then, he would go on to argue, is not that we should assume that man is universal but that in fact he is different. Teedyuscung further inferred that it is not the role of the human to see in others a facsimile of oneself but more to pave the way for understanding and appreciating the differences between one and others. As Scott Pratt put it, "Given 'human nature' from the Native prophets' viewpoint, the proper rule is not seeing others as oneself but seeing oneself from the perspective of others as a member of a particular nation, as part of a particular place." Interaction and common space are key to that challenge, both employed to honor and facilitate a "richly diverse humanity." In effect, "Teedyuscung expects standards to emerge from interactions involving shared interests and using established sources as a means to settle present concerns."[29] In his mind, the idea of equal treatment amounts to mumbo jumbo, fostering "ways of life that commodify the land and contribute to human progress." For "if it is human nature to move toward civilization through progress and progress involves leaving traditional homelands or selling parts of it, then The Golden Rule [would amount] to a justification for the Native dispossession."[30]

Land played an important role in the native argument, not because it was particularly aesthetically precious, although it could be, but because it belonged to neither side of the conflicted parties. In fact, the less attractive it is the better for the purpose of debate and conciliation, neither side coveting it for "investment" reasons. A land so rich in minerals and beauty could easily fall victim to biased intentions and pit the two sides against each other all over again. Which of course need not mean that the land has to be ugly or desolate, only that the way we consume it intellectually must not be burdened by questions of beauty.

Emerson in "Farming" mentions fences but does so through a different sense, less as a political device with which to lay claim to a piece of property and more as one to close the emotional gap between us and nature. Left alone, nature may grow just fine, but draw a fence between us and it, and we should see that it will yield special fruit. Much as we may like and even love a child not our own, to birth and raise one of our own allows us a greater ability to ensure that that child contributes to a meaningful and better future. "Plant fruit trees by the roadside and their fruit will never be allowed to ripen," said Emerson. But "draw a pine fence about them and for fifty years they mature for the owner their delicate fruit."[31] The matter is one of space and proximity, not possession. Where Wright and Emerson may have seemed at odds for a while on the subject of the fence, the first rejecting it, the other desiring it, in reality they are aligned, agreeing that at the end of the day what matters are ways to grow a healthy identity. Proximity in this case breeds understanding, and understanding breeds care and attention. Wright would translate this fusion of tree and fence into a tree as fence. Rather than a concrete wall or even a wooden fence, he would look to the row of trees as the formation of such a barrier, or the hint of a barrier, visible but still porous and welcoming. We can see it in the apple or peach orchards, again shown in the perspective, rich and healthy and about to bear fruit.

Other contributors to Wright's fences were Jean-Jacques Rousseau and Thorstein Veblen, whom he credited, to chart his strategy for Broadacre City. Both understood that should walls and fences be built, they will end up isolating those behind them rather than connecting them with the community next door. Worse, they could be weaponized to alienate and limit the freedom of others, making neighbors enemies instead of friends. Fences in this sense do not simply protect but over time grow taller in terms of entitlement. What had been a placid individual now becomes a monstrous member of the community. Rousseau saw through the weakness and proposed a counter-theory in his *Social Contract*, breaking down what John Locke in the seventeenth century had set up in walls and doing away with the idea of property altogether. But with a caveat, of course, that under this new regime the individual understands that their allegiance to state and self must necessarily change; it will not be entirely eradicated, but it will now acquire a new flux. Rather than the state, their ties would now form around the group, smaller in number than that which would otherwise assemble under the state. Instead of a million, it is now a thousand or two. Under this agreement, says Rousseau, what right the individual had "to his own estate is [now] subordinate to the right which the community has over all."[32] What the individual gives up in rights they gain in equality, broadening the meaning of joy and self-worth. Material accumulation and hoarding give way to active membership in the community: "The peculiar fact about this alienation is that, in taking over the goods of individuals, the community so far from despoiling them, only assures them legitimate possession and changes usurpation into a true right and enjoyment into proprietorship."[33]

Veblen couldn't agree more, but to him the call for common ownership of land was urgent less for political reasons than for those that had to do with dealing with conspicuous consumption. The two, politics and excessive waste, of course were in the end one and the same, two sides of the same coin, but what he found offensive and destructive was the unconscionable slide toward the destruction of culture and ultimately earth itself. Under capitalism, or what he calls "pecuniary culture," where success is measured in wealth and not, say, in knowledge, property walls no longer look physical, or at least not limited to actual fences at all. Instead, they find expression in a different kind of construct, in objects and purchases whose purpose is to match in kind and style what the neighbor had put up next door. Material acquisition, in this case, says Veblen, is valued not so much as evidence of successful forays but "rather as evidence of the prepotence of the possessor of these goods over other individuals within the community," with the "invidious comparison now becom[ing] primarily a comparison of the owner with the other members of the group."[34] Indeed, under this scenario fences interestingly could come down but only if the second neighbor could demonstrate that they are willing and able to keep up with the standard of living demonstrated by the first. It did not matter that they were merely "buying" to keep up with the Joneses; so long as it allowed them to keep up the pretenses, the method was fine. Veblen called it "emulation." Wright called it "importation," lamenting not only the acquisition of material things to keep up with the next person over but the manner in which the American did it, importing from various places to claim instant cultural superiority. "General riches," he tells us, "so rapidly outran indigenous culture that our so called 'American culture' became the great low in eclecticism of all time. Culture, this taken over ready-made, became more and more a commodity." The result was the "wasteful, shameful makeshift."[35]

The Seeming Absence of Work

Another stark message of the empty fields back in the perspective drawings is the way they make clear the absence of work. Even as they may consume a good chunk of the drawing and the space of the city, no one is working on them. They are the beneficiary of ample natural light, but no one seems to be sweating or doing any tilling or plowing on them. Yes, work for the day may have stopped and migrated elsewhere, say, indoors, but still the dearth of activity remains curious. Did work really cease or is there a different reality going on behind the scene? Louis Sullivan gives us a clue in his own dissertation on democracy. He tells us that while signs of work may be absent here, other kinds of activity, in some ways more critical, are underway elsewhere. It involves thought, perhaps taken up in the chapel, at home or at the school. It may not be visible but very much there, critical to the machinations and sustenance of a true democracy. For Sullivan no claim on worth can happen without thought. It is just as important as building a home, fixing a car, and tilling the soil. This is how we understand a people: "In order to arrive at a just estimate of the values of our results as a people, in order to trace backward, from these results to their origins in the thought of the people, we shall assume it axiomatic that the thought of a people is to be read in the acts of the people; and that, the acts of the people are its thoughts."[36] The cycle of return between action and thought is clear, namely good action is predicated on good thought. Which in turn is predicated on the ability to refrain from action just as much as taking up action itself. "And further we are to note this special qualification, that *refraining* from action is a definite act, expressing positive thought."[37]

No action is likely to acquire meaning and lasting worth unless invested with introspection and spiritual contemplation. Life back in the city is fast and competitive, every moment burdened by the pressure to be on time, excel, and just keep up. How could the individual in a democracy be expected to make intelligent decisions that way, to enter into meaningful discussions with fellow citizens, and ultimately move community and nation in a positive direction? "Why does the stress of living become daily tenser in a land overflowing, in a land whose resources have not as yet been drawn upon in an intensive way?" Sullivan asks in exasperation. "A land in which famine is unknown: Or should we stop here and say a land in which a widespread spiritual famine prevails, though seemingly unknown and unsuspected?"[38] In the land of plenty, only the few seem to lead a happy and fulfilling life, the rest restless in their back-and-forth trying to make ends meet. Wright agrees. He, too, is troubled by incessant distractions but also insists that we can find a way to reclaim personality through thought. No democracy will survive without it: "But now what do we do with it [personality] when we go to work upon it intelligently ourselves—to provide something by way of our thought and feeling in ourselves. Then only are we fit subject of a democracy."[39]

Among the many things Wright did not like about the city, the reduction of work into mere employment, or "bondage," to use his term, was the most egregious. To pay rent the worker had to slave away their body and mortgage his or her mind to the boss. "Mere employment," says Wright, "has been dangled before his worried artisan eyes to keep him properly citified and poor—long enough?" So terrible and debilitating was the impact that it "dumped him in an early grave."[40] "Slavery" was what work had amounted to, and Wright was not afraid to draw a moral equivalent between the two to sound the alarm: "Officially dangling employment before a man may be after all only the means of keeping him tied to a money-getting and money-distributing system that amounts to international slavery and inevitably means some form of conscription when any showdown comes."[41] No sooner did America free one kind of people than it imprisoned another, Wright seems to suggest. What good and lasting meaning could the Emancipation Proclamation bring if shortly thereafter another class of society found itself beholden to an equally crippling routine and soulless and dangerous work conditions. For the historian and political scientist, including Emerson, these may have been two very different regimes of oppression, the first regarding Black people, the other the poor and the desperate. But not for Wright. He insisted that the two were one and the same, of equal cruelty and equal disregard for the American constitution. What language had been used to describe the conscriptions of one had to, in his book, be used to lay bare the machinations of the other. Wright was not alone in drawing such moral equivalencies. Others felt the same, among whom Whitman stands out, a man and a poet Wright quoted probably more than any other, even Emerson. As Mumford said of Whitman, he, too, "saw the kings of iron and oil and cotton supplant not merely the older ones who ruled by divine right but the new one elected quadrennially by the people."[42] The link between old slavery and the new version is complex and fraught with uneasy interpretations. And yet Wright believed we should contend with it.

Was he right? Was Wright correct in drawing a straight line between the oppressions of industrial work and those exercised by the white planters on enslaved Black people? The quick and most obvious answer is no, and we should critique him for doing so, if indeed my reading of his language is correct. As awful as factory work was, and also the office, it could not compare with the way enslaved Black people were denied their human rights. And yet the story is not without lineage, before and after the Civil War. Before the Civil War it was not uncommon to compare hardship suffered in the mills with that suffered by enslaved Black people on the plantation, driving the point home that industrial work was indeed that terrible, even if, in reality, it wasn't. One newspaper in 1845 referred to mill workers as "white slaves of capital." It was a quick and efficient way to strike a nerve and try to effect change. After the Civil War, the equivalency would take an interesting, if inverted, trajectory, in this case using the very laws that were established to protect Americans against themselves. Written with the best intention to protect the civil rights of people, the Fourteenth Amendment used words that were vague enough that they could be interpreted to mean more than people but any entity that could enjoy the fruits of freedom, including corporations. "It didn't take long," tell us the authors of *The 1619 Project*, "for corporate attorneys to realize that the Fourteenth Amendment could help strengthen business interest too."[43] They go on to quote an 1866 US Supreme Court decision that agreed that "the Fourteenth Amendment applied to corporations as well as to people." In a 1902 decision, the Supreme Court invoked the Fourteenth Amendment to strike down "attempts to end child labor and establish minimum wage." What started as a legal attempt to continue the legacy of the Emancipation Proclamation was inverted to serve opposite ends. The matter may not exonerate Wright for so hastily drawing a parallel between two very different forms of economic heartlessness, but it does give his angle perspective.

In the end, and in examining the corpus of Wright's intellectual production, it is difficult to conclude that Wright actually believed in the equivalency between chattel Black slavery and that exercised at the office or the factory. In all likelihood, what he sought in words associated with slavery was a rhetorical tool with which to bind Americans in a fight against a common enemy, namely work under capitalism. In that, he was not unlike George Washington, who used the term "slavery" as a metaphor with which to unite colonists in their struggle against the British, under whom they had suffered equally. Even as Bostonians may have shared little in common with those in South Carolina, ideologically and spiritually, they could agree on the degree to which the British had limited them economically. To drive the oppression home, Washington relied on the rhetoric of slavery, saying at one point that "those from whom we have a right to seek protection are endeavoring by every piece of Art and despotism to fix the shackles of Slavery upon us." And this from a man who himself had benefited from the forced labor "of more than 120 human beings." It was precisely because Washington "so well understood the degradation of actual slavery," and how universally reviled the practice was, "that the metaphor of slavery held so much power to consolidate [the] disparate interests" of those who had come to define the emerging nation.[44]

But to continue with Broadacre City and the continued rhetoric of slavery and work, the ground there is not merely property but land "emancipated from the lucky lot," the word "emancipation" being a term by then and now inextricably linked with the Emancipation Proclamation and the freeing of enslaved Black people. Back in the city, property was evaluated and priced based on location and proximity to desirable contexts. If you bought early and the neighborhood around became gentrified, raising the value of your lot, you could consider yourself "lucky." The "lucky lot" was an accident of the times, subject to the fluctuations of a market outside your realm of control. No such limitation and anxiety grip the value of land in Broadacre, given that it doesn't belong to anyone and isn't subject to commercial whims. It is "emancipated." And so along those lines, Wright sought to reverse the awful conditions that befell modern life in the city. Just as Emerson had attacked the practice of slavery with all his might, describing it as "the greatest calamity in the universe," so would Wright do the same in his own fight against modern work, seeking to put it back on par with spiritual calling. No more mindless employment. "No, employment is not enough!" he declared. "What a man wants in democracy is not so much employment as freedom to work at what he believed in, what he likes to work with and work for."[45]

This was not the first or last time that Wright would insist that work be tied to a spiritual calling or in other ways be associated with religious duty. As the twentieth century opened and it was clear that the Industrial Revolution had dealt work a bad blow, for reasons already mentioned, he felt it important that he and other architects consider the problem and look for solutions. At the Larkin Building in Buffalo, designed and built around 1906, he did not so much make the workplace happier as press upon us, and of course those who worked there, the need to see in the office a kind of church. As Jack Quinan notes, both Wright and the executives of the company, "sincerely believed in the virtue of work."[46] Both "were men of strong, if varied, religious convictions." Interestingly, both were also followers of Emerson, clear in the fact that "quotations from Emerson appeared with some frequency in the Larkin staff publication *Ourselves*."[47] The building has been described as "cliff-like" and akin to a monumental work of religious architecture. At its center a five-story atrium is cut out of the main mass, introducing light from above and an unmistakable sense that what work is being done on the ground is blessed with divine supervision. A famous photo of the atrium shows a preacher giving a sermon in the space during lunchtime, presumably reminding the congregation of workers that what they are doing is nothing short of God's work. Another picture of the same space shows women resigned as if to a contract between God and the task at hand, which, however dreary it may be, remains work that teaches discipline and good ethical behavior. Even the furniture is of no ordinary design but kept the worker forever, or at least during the course of the day, connected with her work. Chair and desk are tied at the hip, along a swivel and in such a way where every time the worker wished to leave and, say, go to the bathroom, it took an act of bodily contor-

FIG. 26. Swivel chairs at the Larkin Building, Buffalo, New York, 1906. Demolished 1958. Copyright © 2022 Frank Lloyd Wright Foundation, Scottsdale, AZ. All rights reserved. The Frank Lloyd Wright Foundation Archives (The Museum of Modern Art | Avery Architectural & Fine Arts Library, Columbia University, New York)

tion to rotate, twist, and get up (fig. 26). Wright wasn't so much interested in brightening the spirit of work as he was making sure that we keep vigil over its purpose and role in our lives.

More or less Wright would bring a similar approach to the design of the "Grand Workroom" at the Johnson Wax Headquarters. Now thirty years after the Larkin, the problem of work was less a matter of exploitation and moral degradation and more one associated with potential spiritual emptiness. "Mere employment" Wright called it, where the worker was important only insofar that a person finished a task and then went home. That they possessed interests and ideals, ambitions and aspirations, did not matter. Wright would solve the issue by placing the worker in a kind of cathedral, a room of soaring height topped by a halo of indirect light. And just as the structure of the cathedral was of no ordinary design but carved to imbue space with lightness and elegance, so the columns at this Grand Workroom at Johnson Wax. They, too, rise with grace and tiptoe around space like a ballerina. Unlike other midcentury modern offices, such as the Lever House Building in New York, or the Seagram, also in New York, fully glazed and visually open to the outside, this one insists on drawing views in and focused on the inside. The worker may look up and partake in the visual delight of the space, where everything was designed to blend and unify, but that person may not view scenes across the street. This was truly a space meant to fuse body and work, soul and performance. Bending over and poring over one's work is in effect an act of meditation, uplifting the worth of man and strengthening the bond between him or her and their fellow community of workers.

Be it at the Larkin or the Johnson Wax Headquarters, or pretty much every other building Wright designed, the architect begged to know what constitutes good and meaningful work. The matter for him required stepping back and refraining from work so that we can contemplate its exigencies. In many ways he was asking us to be aristocrats, not of blood line, but of those who, being secure in their own mind and body, know when to engage and when to retreat. In fact, when asked about the underpinning of democracy, Wright "replied that it is the highest form of aristocracy the world has ever seen."[48] The two systems of thought may seem at odds and indeed as forms of government they are, but not so much as traits with which to shape and define character. Seen this way they are interdependent, each playing a key role in the honest and complete fulfilment of the other.

Land and Democracy as the Highest Form of Aristocracy

Which of course begs the question, who is the aristocrat and why might that person be needed in a democracy or at work? Emerson again provides several helpful insights. Through him, we realize that chief among the aristocrat's traits is the ability to see beyond the self, that while that self must by necessity care for its own station and place in life, its role is not first and foremost limited to the person behind it; it also must recognize the place of others in society. It may possess bodily beauty, but its real magnificence lies in its ability to know where it stands, including being in the presence of "objects . . . truly . . . superior to [it]self." What good would democracy be if all its members voted based solely on self-interest alone? Wouldn't that result in a kind of aimless and random body politic, each unto their own, incapable of developing shared values?

Other attributes of the aristocrat include the possession of a kind of aura in whose presence the negative become positive, the sad happy, the insecure secure. Rather than bringing people down, that person lifts them up, releasing inner vision and potential. No sooner does the aristocrat arrive in place than they draw "all men around [them], all sorts of men." What deficiency they may have felt had corrupted them, now "fades away." The supposedly stupid now "discover that they were not stupid." Even "the coldest" of hearts find that they are drawn "to their neighbors by interest . . . in things" that previously they had deemed of no shared value. The aristocrat is fundamentally not petty, understanding that not all conflicts are born equal and certainly do not merit similar responses or any response at all. It is beneath the aristocrat to tell a truth "with bad intention," knowing that "it beats all the lies you can invent," to mention a saying by Blake that Wright admired and occasionally quoted. Indeed, the aristocrat is high-minded and honorable precisely because they are able to place the interest of others above their own. Democracies thrive in their presence.

They may seem absent, but they are not, only temporarily gone from view. The aristocrat appears and disappears with care, casting greater philosophic and spiritual influence in their absence than in their presence. Not unlike a priest who guides just as much by their presence as their absence, so the aristocrat, too, quiets down a place and creates peace by the invisible trail they leave behind. Between their manner and behavior "in the house and in the field" they resemble "men at rest." In that they are descendants of a long lineage of class of individuals who initially, and through various acts of domination of enemy property and people, came to stand above them. What belonged to the opponent was now theirs, including property and labor, now appropriated to advance and promote their own clan and culture. Over the centuries, Veblen tells us in his study of the leisure class, matters changed only in degree but not in kind. In our "pecuniary" age of the last two hundred years, the aristocrat looked for different forms of differentiation from the crowd. No longer in a position to simply physically coerce his or her counterpart, they sought to separate themselves through property, walling themselves off and making clear their position of superiority. In due course the barrier became too oppressive, not for the oppressed but the oppressor themselves. What concrete walls they put up to separate themselves from the riffraff ultimately became acts of self-imprisonment. Who needs that?

A better way had to be invented, and it came in the form of leisure and the active decision to step away from work as an expression of higher status. Those who could afford to loaf and travel had clearly triumphed over the need to engage in menial tasks, or any tasks for that matter, to make a living. "Abstention from labour," says Veblen, "is the convenient evidence of wealth and is therefore the conventional mark of social standing." No longer merely about money alone, wealth becomes a goal to which one aspires to achieve a moral higher ground in the world. "According to well established laws of human nature," adds Veblen, "prescription presently seizes upon this conventional evidence of wealth and fixes it in men's habits of thought as something that is in itself substantially meritorious and ennobling; while productive labour at the same time and by a like process becomes in double sense intrinsically unworthy. Prescription ends by making labour not only disreputable in the eyes of the community, but morally impossible to the noble, freeborn man, and incompatible with worthy life."[49]

To refrain from work is to devote quality time to other morally deficient aspects of the community, serving as its priest or consultant to professional boards, city council, and the like. This is how Wright put it in a response to a question about the meaning of Broadacre City: "This Broadacre city model means just that. It shows too how to end the now senseless travel to and fro of our present wasteful and wasting situation. Waste of time and life in here, in Broadacre City, ended in favor of a better use of life to understand ourselves and to cultivate leisure in the enjoyment of our own nature."

The modern city was awful on several accounts, not least the way it sent the individual running back and forth in a tizzy trying to keep up, wasting precious time better spent developing a mind, an identity, and ultimately a useful and accurate response to community. Wright's leisure, in this sense, is not for the whiling of the day but for the return to the self, the cultivation of "our own nature," and for restoring a democratic capacity lost in the shuffle of the industrial city. Again, Mumford's comments from his *Golden Day* are instructive. In it he says of Thoreau, himself a country aristocrat of sort, that he went to the country less to escape the city and more to return to it refined, cultivated, and more civilized. "One returned to nature," he says, "in order to become in a deeper sense, more cultivated and civilized, not in order to return to crudities that men had already discarded."[50]

Indeed, the question is, what should the aristocrat do in his or her free time? They could engage in "conspicuous consumption" to further impress upon the public their financial superiority to the crowd. Or they could use that time to work on cultivating a stable and balanced personality, able to weigh with emotional detachment the good and the bad. Which is what Wright would like that person to do: transcend commercial culture and see what is best for the collective. This is not necessarily the same aristocrat who has arrived upon their status through inheritance but one who has managed to manufacture the same air through reflection. They need not, in other words, be rich in money but rich in inner balance. We need not look beyond Wright himself for an example, whose departure from Chicago and the urban crowd, while riddled with questions of infidelity, was at base a move made to restore in himself the capacity for democratic practices. He had been in the city for twenty years and had developed a reputation for being an architect of a certain kind, excellent but also controversial and whose voice, while deep and philosophical, could also be ungracious. He could, on the one hand, endorse collective work, admitting at one point to the need for "heart to heart" connections with fellow architects, but then turn around, on the other, and call them "'weeds' who choked of the promise of the new American Architecture."[51] Matters came to a head when he entered into a romantic relation with the wife of a wealthy and notable client, giving the press further fodder to drag him down and amplify his already tainted reputation. What capacity for democratic action he could muster at that point was already too mired with anger to be responsible or useful. He needed distance again to recoup his aristocratic stamina and return triumphant to his work, to the city. The idea was never to leave the city behind but to bring it along with him, master it inside so that he could contribute to it on the outside. It is easy in fact to be in the city and follow city rules, and in the country and adhere to rural views, but it is he, the aristocrat and the great stabilizer of democracy, who could be in one and advocate for the other and vice versa. Or as Emerson put it in "Self-Reliance": "It is easy in the world to live after the world's opinion; it is easy in solitude to live after our own; but the great man is he who in the midst of the crowd keeps with perfect sweetness the independence of solitude."

There is more than a hint that when finally the people do reappear in Broadacre City, they are of a certain kind, rich in vision but poor in money, even if only metaphorically. In several places and as Wright was struggling to imagine the residents of Broadacre, their character and behavior patterns, he mentions the poor. He is concerned with the economically depressed, but he is not sure that reversing course is the right way to go, making the poor rich and sending them on their way. He likes the idea of the poor, otherwise the same city problems will likely creep up again, including dynamics of exploitation and alienation. "We are all parasites," he says, "but it is not true to say that the poor are poor because the rich are rich."[52] The poor are poor because they follow a different world order, bias values that retain a measure of balance between living and meaning, production and consumption, mental and physical activity. Of course, there are the abjectly poor, who can barely eat let alone keep a roof over their heads. We should care for those and help them out, which Wright will try to do elsewhere in Broadacre City, but for now the poor he is concerned about are those who will help him ensure a critical degree of connectivity between people, and people and the built environment. They are the people who will build a society not to outgain but to sustain themselves, differentiate between important and superfluous concerns. Poverty in this case is not a hindrance but a source of freedom, necessary for citizens of a democracy to feel and sense clearly. In Wright's words, "poverty of the spirit is thus built into our own free country."[53]

Again, Wright's poor need not be actually poor but poor as in devoid of wasteful excess. They must follow Emerson's words when he says that "the great depend on their heart, not their purse. Genius and virtue, like diamonds, are best plain set, set in lead, set in poverty."[54] They are likely to receive scorn and ridicule from society, especially educated society. But go on they must. And yet for what? Emerson's answer is: "to find consolation in exercising the highest functions of human nature." Which is what? Which is to "raise [themselves] from private considerations and breath and live on public and illustrious thoughts." In that they become "the world's eye and the world's heart. They resist vulgar prosperity that retrogrades ever to barbarism, by preserving and communicating heroic sentiments, noble biographies, melodious verse, and the conclusions of history."

Veblen said that cities are made for the poor, namely that it is for them that sidewalks and roads, parks and plazas, are made. Not out of the goodness of heart of those who build and govern those cities but out of necessity, to make sure that those who feed the means of production do so with efficiency and obedience. They must get there on time, day after day, to keep up and make ends meet. And yet they don't have the means to do so without public help, amenities that will allow them to circumvent their meager provisions and remain functional and out of trouble. They need the help of public transportation, access to basic nearby shopping, plazas, and parks for recreational relief during afterhours and on weekends. In the Marxist lexicon they need to keep those who control the means of production happy, or at least prove to them that they can return to the same workplace and keep the machinery of production going and their managers satisfied. The same is not the case for the rich. Yes, they may benefit from the same infrastructure built for the poor, but by and large they can do without it. What obstacles in space and time they may face they can transcend by various technological acquisitions; the car, the plane, the boat to name only three.

The same goes for obstacles in weather and climate change, triumphing over heat and cold, rain and snow, either through bodily migration or, again, technological adaptations. And not only that but they can double and triple their presence by hiring people who could accomplish their supervisory role on their behalf, allowing them to do their job better than they could have done it themselves. Whether we call those "clones" of the self or just managers, it does not matter; the point remains that the rich don't even have to move to accomplish their tasks and multiply their wealth. They can in fact stay home and in so doing develop a different side of their power, one reminiscent of Jeremy Bentham's "Panopticon." An instrument of imbalance between the visible and the invisible, the concept of the panopticon was conceived to solve the problem of surveillance in prisons. How might the one jailer supervise the movement of so many jailed under his vigil? Well, you lift him up and hide him behind blinds, making him omnipresent and his presence powerful precisely because it is unsure. Not knowing whether he is there or not and given the punitive measures legislated against the prisoner should he or she transgress, the latter stays put. How poetic and how well used by the rich against the poor when they make their movement unpredictable. Anytime, the boss can show up and raise hell, fire and order employees around, should they seem out of place to him. And so the employees keep their nose to the grind.

Wright's views on work had been formed from an early age, probably as early as his time on his uncle James's farm, when he was but ten or eleven. That office and farm work had to be connected was a matter of course by the time he was a teenager. But what that may have meant in physical form remained an open-ended question. Ebenezer Howard and his Garden City provided suggestions, but they were too diagrammatic to be practical or useful. A more tangible proposal was needed, and it wouldn't emerge until Henry Ford and Thomas Edison converged on a small town in northwest Alabama in 1921 and announced plans to merge nature with industry and build a huge city. In it they intended to build many factories, supplying America's demands for post–World War I needs but also homes and other facilities Americans desired to live a happy and prosperous life. Power would be supplied in the form of electricity, clean and renewable and generated from damming the nearby Tennessee River. All is well, but what is important for our purposes here is the added vision of work that Ford brought to the table. Predicated on the cheap supply of cars, now available to regular middle-class Americans, it stretched the prospects and meaning of work. Now that Americans didn't have to live right next to their work, they could move closer to the countryside, indeed in connection to farms and fewer sidewalks and congested built environments. They could in fact split their time between factory and farm work, renting what they needed in terms of farm equipment to till, cultivate, and harvest the land, when those times came around, and as such live a healthy and independent life. Wright loved Ford's scheme, calling it "the best thing that I have heard of."[55] The empty fields in Broadacre City, mentioned earlier, may very well be without people because those who had worked in them are now working in the factories nearby, soon to return to work in the fields again. The greatness of Ford's big idea did not lie in the factories per se but in the "revolutionary new way of structuring society," Thomas Hager tells us in *Electric City*, a book about "Muscle Shoals" that bears the name of Ford's city. Rather than seeing in Americans bifurcated personalities, either factory laborers or farmworkers, they would be both, separated only by season and not professional specialization. According to one article mentioned in *Electric City*, "Ford would have the factory and the farm working hand in glove."[56]

The Removal of Sidewalks

Sidewalks in Broadacre City exist but in limited quantity and in fact in only one of the perspectives drawn of the city. They are crowded out by tilled fields, small farms, and roadside markets, among a few other functions. Their elimination is interesting in that by doing so Wright flips the narrative of the poor on its head, insisting that we think of them less as an isolated group of disenfranchised people who must walk and ride the bus to get where they need to go and more as an integrated component of the modern city. There are no or few sidewalks not because Wright wants to wipe out their means of circulation but precisely because he wants to eradicate any signs of differentiation between rich and poor. Also, by removing the sidewalks he forces walking onto the road, sharing space with the car and thus lessening its hegemonic rule over civil infrastructure. Wright loved cars, but more so he loved making sure power does not eddy around any one feature lest it suffocate the potential of the weak to rise and stand on their feet. To that end, it would be good to note that Broadacre City was formed in direct response to the Wall Street Crash of 1929, to which several key cultural and economic players contributed—not least the auto industry. By 1920 the car had already become part of the American unconscious, a piece of equipment the American had to have to get ahead. Car registration in that year topped eight million, an increase from under a half million ten years before. What General Motors did or did not do meant the rise or demise of the stock market. No sooner did Ford announce the closure of a plant in 1927, for instance, than the market pulled back, causing a recession in the "federal reserve index of industrial production."[57] A year later, when John Raskob, the director of General Motors, announced on his way to Europe that his company's stocks should be evaluated at a price higher than the current rate at that time, he "sent the market into a boiling fury," which in turn "set off a burst of trading elsewhere in the list."[58] It is not for nothing that the cars Wright introduced in Broadacre City look nothing like those produced by General Motors. Part bicycle, part dragonfly, they roll in defiance of commercial practice, reducing capacity to one, maybe two individuals per vehicle. Indeed, they may not be cars at all but repositories of past icons, both lamenting their passage by the same technology that made the car possible and also celebrating their potential return as ornaments with which to grace and advance a new way of living. Zero in on the back wheel of one of these vehicles (fig. 24), for instance, and it is hard not to see in it the work of the Secessionists, whose unmistakable metal filigree graces many a public building in Vienna and elsewhere in Europe.

The Usonian Home

Just as the car played a part in the economic crash, so did the house. Off and beyond the fields, there it lies on its own one-acre of land, large enough to sustain a family of four or five but not so large that it sinks its owner into debt. It, too, like the car, was a response to the Wall Street Crash of 1929, namely, in this case, excess speculation in housing and easy money. "One thing in the twenties that should have been visible is the inordinate desire to get rich quickly and with a minimum of physical effort," says John Kenneth Galbraith in his book on the Depression. Florida was one prominent site on which to do that. Because of its good weather and up-to-date transportation system, it represented an attractive draw for northerners. "On that indispensable element of fact men and women had proceeded to build a world of speculative make belief," Galbraith continues.[59] Making things worse was the fact that weather in Florida was and remains prone to violent eruptions which, if not planned for, can wipe out neighborhoods wholesale. Which of course it did, devastating the speculative market across the state.

Wright's Broadacre homes would rise in response, not only to provide for the middle class and those hit hard by the crash, but more fundamentally to rebuild in those who will come to occupy them a renewed appreciation for place and construction. Left to the market, the American home had become little more than a cardboard feature of the real estate market, meaningless and forever cycled between buyers and sellers. No economy would likely survive for too long under these conditions. The key lay in empowering the Americans to build their own homes. "And then what house for the poor man?" he asks in *When Democracy Builds*. "Where and how may he [the American] himself go to work to build it with his family?"[60] Wright had been steeped in this philosophy going all the way back to the time when he designed and built his own home in Oak Park, Chicago, but even before that watching his uncle Thomas build structures for his clan, including Wright's aunts. The famous Hillside Home School he built for them was in many ways just an ordinary structure, but given the familial ties with which it rose, it soon became more than a matter of walls and functions but a beacon of intellectual strength and passion. The school remains standing today.

And yet it was one thing to advocate for seasoned designers and builders to build their own home and something altogether different for the ordinary American to do so. Wright had to simplify the game and package architecture in such a way as to make it easy to ship and assemble, not, say, unlike a premanufactured piece of furniture which comes precut and stuffed inside a box. All Americans needed to do is open the box and follow the instructions. Wright had experimented with premanufactured structures as early as the second decade of the twentieth century, with what he called the "American System Redi-Cut," perhaps borrowing from a trend already popular and underway by Sears, Roebuck and Company. "From 1908 to 1940, Chicago-based Sears sold between 70,000 to 75,000 homes," offering anything from Craftsman to Cape Cods, "which were sent via train car and set up as far afield as Florida, California, and even Alaska."[61] But it wasn't until the 1930s that Wright sat down to systematically design homes that would potentially arrive as a "kit of parts" ready to be assembled by the owner. His first real success was the Jacobs House in Madison, Wisconsin, conceived on the promise that it was a kit of parts that could be configured in an infinite number of ways to suit the needs of a particular site and client. Shortly after the completion of the house, Wright struck it big when the editors of *Architectural Forum* in 1938 decided to devote their magazine's January issue to his ideas and demonstrations of the virtues and possibilities of the Usonian home. *Life* magazine would soon do the same, publishing "renderings and plans for eight small houses—four modern and four in traditional styles, for families with incomes of 2,000–10,000 a year."[62] The publications worked to bring Wright a slew of work the same year and with it the incentive to now and in good faith "develop the Usonian house as a kit of parts," later to be classified by shape and layout as follows: "polliwog or L, Diagonal, Hexagonal, In line and Raised Usonian."[63]

All along, Wright's aim was never to merely remedy a functional or even economic problem but to restore to the American self-confidence and skill. In empowering Americans to build their own homes, he was also opening before them the space with which to "release" a potential they did not quite realize they had. In Wright's words, they "would be earning the natural increase [themselves]—[their] ability to do so increased not merely because [they are] employed but because [their] own initiative had been set free to employ [themselves] to the greater advantage of other men like [themselves]."[64] In that, Wright was following John Dewey's advice in *Individuality and Democracy*, mentioned earlier, advocating for public engagement less as an exercise in free choice and more as the means with which to discover the potential in oneself. The word "initiative" is telling, not unlike "release," Dewey's favorite in explaining human potential, in that it suggests that the purpose of manual labor, besides getting things built, is to set in motion that which had become dormant inside. Under capitalism most of our needs are met by gadgetry, quick push-button techniques that kill the desire to get up and do something. Machines are useful but also powerful in the way they program our habits, training our behavior to crave them, slowly but surely. Soon we find that we can't do without them and that what had been a mere tool is now an instrument of control, reversing the order of hierarchy between man and machine. Worse is the impact of the machine on the boss, who, rather than using the machine to open opportunities for those who labor under it, "becomes more and more like the tool he uses," cold, calculating, and oppressive.[65]

Before too long we all turn into zombies, walking and talking but dead to the world. We buy gadgetry less to ease the day but more to keep up with the neighbor or the general standard imposed on us by those who control the "means of production." Washing machines and ice boxes seem particularly sinister to Wright. "When we got the machine going and got science going like we have it going so that the very streets crawl with it, even out into the tenth mile beyond the center of the city, and when gadgetry is at it everywhere—the oven, the washing machine and especially the ice box, not to mention the deep freeze—what have we?"

We have a society of individuals gripped by herd mentality, incapable of innovative thinking and creating. Which is not what the early 1930s needed, a time when more than anything else society sought resourceful minds to turn hardship into opportunity. The matter was something on the magnitude of a constitutional crisis, requiring all hands on deck to empower human imagination and "release our native resources," Wright would say. Only through "fruitful activities"—activities, that is, that developed and nurtured self-reliance—could Americans shake off the shackles of industrial slavery and "create nobler longings." Beside the spaces necessary for cooking, sleeping, and living, Wright in his Usonian homes included a room or two for training and developing new skills. This was no separate garage space or storage-like shack in the back of the house but an extension of it, made clear by the way the roof "continu[ed] in a straight line over the . . . bedrooms and [toward] a woodworking shop and study."[66] This is how Alvin Rosenbaum described the Jacobs House, arguably the most famous Usonian home produced, telling the story of a seamless feedback loop between living and working, keeping the American resilient and resourceful.

Wright practiced what he preached. Even as early as his first years in Chicago, he did not merely advocate building your own home, but he actually took out a loan and built his own. How he did that at such a young age remains baffling. The conviction continued when he returned to Spring Green to build his second home and later Fellowship. Much has already been said about the ambitious extent of the project, but it bears repeating that it was only in a limited scope that the house and supporting functions were meant as a place to stay; more so, it was a work intended to remain forever in process and in progress, a living philosophy of what it means to live life through work and vice versa. Even today, work continues on-site, at both locations, Taliesin and Taliesin West, in preservation and maintenance but in other ways as well. In a conversation I had with the preservationist on-site at Taliesin, he mentioned, without a hint of exaggeration, that he could live another two lives and still not see his work on the house finished.

Work on the Farm

Work was also central to the philosophy of the Fellowship that Wright, along with his wife Olgivanna, started in 1932. Indeed, Wright hardly knew how to teach without it. And not just construction work but work as related to milking cows, tending to the fields, fixing toilets, and the like. There was no point teaching architecture without first teaching character and creativity. Or so Wright believed. There was always going to be time enough for the Fellowship to learn architecture, especially when commissions finally returned after the Depression in the 1930s, but in the meantime there was plenty to do on the farm and around the house. Indeed, as one of the apprentices later recalled: "construction was paralleled by intensive farm and garden work, a necessity in those days of financial hardship. . . . The dairy supplied whole milk for thirty apprentices and cottage cheese, yogurt and cream to be whipped or churned into butter. The chickens scratching in the sunny barnyard produced healthy eggs and animals browsing in the meadows furnished beef and pork that we smoked for ham and bacon."[67]

No lesser figure than Jesus was Wright's model; to be as ethical, clear, and as humble as he. Jesus's success was no accident but a direct expression of his ability to demonstrate to people that despite his rise he was unashamed to do simple and even menial work. "Now I think that applies to milking," Wright pointed out in this vein.

> I think it applies to the garden, it applies to anything at all that you do, whatever it is that you are doing. And I think once that element is in it there is a certain nobility in whatever you do. . . . That is why I think the man that cleans the drain—the man that shovels manure from behind the cows—the man that does that work with senses in of it—he is growing, and he is a man and he is doing a man's work. And when he hasn't got that, he is some kind or degree of a slave.[68]

Of the many virtues of down-to-earth work for Wright was the attempt to stave off the dehumanizing impact of excess machinery. We may like mechanical tools for the way they help us cut work in half and achieve refined aesthetics, but we may also remain skeptical of their manner of severing ties to vernacular roots and communal connections. In that, he was picking up on a similar concern expressed by the people of *Erewhon*, mentioned earlier, to which he attributed his use of the term "Usonia." Erewhonians were not so concerned by the machine itself as by the speed and acceleration with which machinery had developed elsewhere. They were neither luddites nor ignorant of the benefits that machines were likely to bring to daily life, only worried about their rapid proliferation. "Do not let me be misunderstood," cautions one of the residents in a dialogue with the narrator. Neither he nor his comrades live "in fear of any actually existing machine." They know that "there is probably no known machine which is more than a prototype of future mechanical life."[69] They know that "the present machines are to the future as the early saurian is to man." Indeed, they are not stupid, but they are careful and want to make sure that what machines they do introduce have the effect of easing pain—yes—but also of slowing down the explosion of further machinery.

The Blessings of the Higher Eye

None of this would be possible without the blessings of a higher power. For Wright, democracy needed more than voters and critics, more than proponents and opponents. It needed a third party, an eye in the sky, keeping vigil over undertakings below. What interactions were taking place on the ground had to come together with justice and equity. What good would a democracy be if much of what went on in its name took place behind doors, in backrooms, corrupt and ugly? No legal system can find and correct all misdeeds. There has to be a silent agreement between members of society, namely that despite what may or may not happen on the surface, the ground under which their constitution was formed is solid and worth sacrificing for.

Broadacre City represents a call for a paradigm shift in the way we live happy and functional lives. To make it possible, though, more than two or three people must be on board. The whole of society has to be on the same page. Should differences exist, and they are likely to exist, they cannot override the basic belief system of the community. Constant visual reminders are key to this venture, such as icons, banners, sayings, and the like—making sure that no one veers off message. Wright included them throughout his work, in homes, churches, and office buildings alike, including his first home and studio in Oak Park. There and at the outset of the house, we see an inglenook, a confession booth of sorts, housing two benches and a fireplace, which like a confessional can be closed by a curtain, drawn, as figure 27 shows, from opposite ends. In it and above the fireplace, Wright has carved a quote that reads: "Truth is Life. Good friends, around these hearth stones, speak no evil

FIG. 27. Inglenook in Wright's Oak Park home and studio, a confession booth–like room located at the front of the home and meant to offer a moment of mental and spiritual resolution before occupying the rest of the house. 1889 onward. Photograph courtesy of James Caulfield.

word of any creature." No one can police or enforce such sentiments; they can only emerge and catch traction from within and between self and one's God. It is a private matter, and the best we can do is protect it from prying eyes. He would do something similar at the Larkin Building, famously inscribing in the railing walls of the atrium spiritual messages, urging employees to think of their work as a form of higher calling.[70]

No such words were etched in Broadacre, not least because the city was never quite realized, at least not fully. And yet it needed the blessing of a higher power, nonetheless, to protect it from physical despoliation and moral erosion. Wright tells as much when he includes at the outset of his *Living City* a passage from the sixteenth-century devout scientist Paracelsus, quoting him as saying that "man must realize the presence of the highest in his own right," but then again cautioning against "mere opinions and creeds," because they are "the product of ignorance." Paracelsus was an influential scientist, contributing critical findings to the study and science of optics, but never as an end in itself, always in relation to spiritual guidance. How and in what form this spiritual guidance appeared in Broadacre is, of course, unsure, but we can safely say that it is evident in the eye in the sky through which we have been studying the city all along. Or that which sat and peered over the city from the flying saucers above, weaving in and out of sight and independent of the law of the land below.

And yet Wright never quite left spiritual guidance hanging in midair like that, vague and without human corollary. Consider his and Richard Bock's *Flower in the Crannied Wall*, a midsized statue of a woman whose countenance reflects introspection and care for the people under her gaze (fig. 28). Based on a poem by Alfred Tennyson, she first appeared at the Dana-Thomas House in Springfield, Illinois; a second version is located at Taliesin. The poem goes like this:

> Flower in the crannied wall,
> I pluck you out of the crannies,
> I hold you here, root and all, in my hand,
> Little flower—but if I could understand
> What you are, root and all, and all in all,
> I should know what God and man is.

God and man: this was the mainstay of Wright's struggle against existence, namely, how to keep one in view of the other. The sculpture of the woman is relatively small, only a few feet tall, but she might as well be a hundred or even a thousand. Her head is downcast at an angle that suggests she is way up, looking down from a mountaintop. She is neither happy nor sad but sim-

FIG. 28. *Flower in the Crannied Wall* sculpture. First appeared at the Dana-Thomas House in Springfield, Illinois. Photo by author.

ply keeping vigil, her gaze constant and resigned. She is keeping evil out and the circulation of people and spirit nicely under surveillance.

She would soon reappear in a different guise at the Midway Garden, in Chicago, a festive center where the local community could come to socialize and enjoy events such as weddings and summer concerts. There, she would become taller, more slender and more geometric, at one point carrying a cube as if ready to launch it on those who may have veered off message or lost their moral grounding, a sense of higher purpose. There, too, she came in essentially three forms, a "Spindle," a "Sprite," and the third a kind of hybrid carrying the cube mentioned above.[71] The Spindle looked askance and carried a slightly crazed look; the Sprite was straighter and swept by a deeply religious gaze, downcast and serious. Of the former, Wright confirms that in her "we do sense a certain psychic quality."[72] Where the first warns, the second prays, together recognizing man's inevitable weakness and the cycle of sin and redemption. Man will always veer off track, but so long there is a mechanism by which he realizes his mistakes and the ability to make a U-turn, self-correction will happen. No civil law can match that, and even if it did, it would result in joyless living. Better to leave moral judgment to a higher vigil, an eye in the sky under whose guidance man, and Americans specifically in this case, will find the trust needed to sustain thoughtful existence. Neither Spindle nor Sprite referred to anything specific, say a myth or national icon, only a source deep inside Wright's religious mind. Religious, not in the sense of monotheism but in that of believing in principles and finding a way to stay true to them. Had Broadacre City been built, it is likely that Spindles would have lined critical corners of the city, to bless and to keep out the evil eye.

In the end, Wright's city is a meditation on life in the emerging modern metropolis. In it, Wright asked us to pray over things on which we have come to rely, but which in doing so we may have also ruined. Things like the earth, air, each other, and work. But also inanimate objects like cars, boats, and clothes, all of which must be considered as part of a singular ecosystem that must be balanced, lest we lose the future itself. And so, with Wright we may close our eyes here and look inside toward the distant horizon.

5

BLACK & BLUE
Mental and Physical Furniture

> The influence of the senses has in most men overpowered the mind to that
> degree that the walls of time and space have come to look insurmountable.
> —R. W. EMERSON, "The Over-Soul"

At one point in his essay "Literature," Emerson speaks of "mental furniture." The context is British culture and the style of literature it consumed, namely Gothic. Much as a decorator may place a chair here and a table there, to steer attention toward a certain view and shape an identity, so will culture, if steeped in a certain literature, soon assume its style. "For two centuries," says Emerson, "England was philosophic, religious, poetic," its "mental furniture larger [in] scale," than any age before.[1]

Wright turned the metaphor around and made it a reality, using actual furniture to shape an eventual mental one. Furniture may not seem much, today mass-produced and assembled in a matter of minutes, but not for Wright. Placed in a certain way, he wagered, it could activate a link otherwise dormant, perhaps memories long lost to the demands of the day. Who knows, it might block traffic and as such require a circuitous route to the next space over. If so, it could result in a complex and thickened understanding of the world, or at least of the context in which one lives. Make that a daily occurrence and the impact can be lasting. Add weight, namely heavy furniture, and soon the effect could turn into a matter of mental reconstruction, a struggle toward a higher and more meaningful existence. "As soon as the soul sees any object," says Emerson, "it stops before that object." An impasse ensues, requiring thinking, introspection, and, ultimately, a decision. Where should the "soul" go next? Left or right? If left then what? If right the same? What if the left demands a view of the garden, the right a view of the neighbor? Should the soul prioritize one over the other? Back and forth the questions swirl, and with them moral and ethical consequences. By the time it arrives at a decision, it will have grown stronger, more aware of the world out front. Wright knew about all this early on, often offsetting light against heavy furniture, mobile against immobile. Walk around the Darwin Martin House, especially the famous living room (fig. 29), and you will see them in play, the two engaged in a dance of opposites vying for resolution inside the American mind. Neither one alone is sufficient, but together they yield a balanced intellectual repose. If the first seeks to lock the viewer in a certain self-evident and stable perspective, the second shakes that perspective loose. No reality is unchangeable. Everything is subject to interpretation.

And yet Wright went further, often setting up furniture to fashion a kind of obstacle course with which to prevent easy and facile movement through space. No viewer under his watch, or resident, or visitor, shall take reality for granted but must remain awake to its changes and evolutions. All must

FIG. 29. Martin House reception room, Buffalo, New York, 1905, photographed 2022. Courtesy Frank Lloyd Wright's Martin House, Buffalo, New York.

remain intellectually engaged. The world he created for them was different from the one elsewhere, and they took note. Jonathan Lipman calls it consecrated, sacred in the way it took disparate forces and unified them under a singular visual regime. "Wright placed an obstacle in one's path at the point of entry into a room," he said in his essay "Consecrated Space: Wright's Public Buildings," "further separating the room from its environment."[2] And yet, once separated, the obstacle course could not stop but continued well into the interior, ensuring the continued and complete cycle of unity between space and mind. What good would it be if after all the effort to provide his audience with art and design, no one paid attention or stopped to contemplate, a possibility he knew was likely for Americans? These were the people, he said, prone to devolving from "barbarism to degeneracy," completely capable of missing out on great cultural developments unfolding right before their eyes. Better to prevent that with the help of furniture. Stop here, go there, sit, look up, and then walk—altogether and in the meantime building a kind of gestalt between subject and object, mind and material things, each anticipating and completing the intent of the other. To be in a Wright room is to complete an otherwise incomplete whole, adding value to an otherwise spiritually inadequate concrete reality.

No one spoke of furniture in this way better than Edith Wharton, who came out of the same era as Wright, between 1862 and 1937, and who was similarly troubled by the way Americans were beginning to fill their houses with derivative furniture and trite decorative objects. "Bric a Brac," she called them, or, to use a uniquely American lexicon, "knick-knacks." There was nothing wrong with Americans wanting to make their rooms "look pretty," she said, but overstuffing houses with "useless trifles" "diminishes the dignity of a good room." Having had neither the training nor the eye for aesthetics, Americans just kept stuffing their interiors. If only they knew better, they could have saved themselves a lot of headaches and money. "It is surprising to note," Wharton lamented, "how the removal of an accumulation of knick-knacks will free the architectural lines and restore the furniture to its rightful relation with the walls." It was in many ways just that simple in her eyes, the solution being a matter of less is more. "There is a sense," said Wharton scholar Lisa Stephenson, "in which works of art may be said to endure by virtue of what is left out of them. And it is this "tact of omission" that characterizes the master hand."[3]

So troubled was Wharton that she wrote a book about the subject with the architect Ogden Codman. Titled *The Decoration of Houses*, it was intended to educate, not unlike Catharine Beecher before her, her audience about the issues they should think about before furnishing their houses. In it she places a lot of emphasis on proportions and cautions that no matter the finishes and the colors, a room that is badly proportioned will remain ugly and feel awkward. And yet good proportions alone won't cut it; furniture must be commensurately scaled to the room to make those proportions stand out and be felt. For those who find in "house furnishing" a "mystery," the answer for Wharton lay in the "fitness of proportion." Indeed, the livability of the room was for her predicated on "the arrangement of furniture."[4]

Nowhere is this better played out than in *The House of Mirth*, one of Wharton's more central novels and for which she won the Pulitzer Prize, the first woman to do so. There, interestingly, furniture plays a triangulated role between the physical environment in which it sits and the individuals who come to occupy that environment and use that furniture. Occupying a middle space between the two, it serves as a tool with which to calibrate a relation between them. As rooms grow, individuals shrink, or the other way around, with furniture serving as the visual index by which to understand that change.

The House of Mirth is the story of one Lily Bart, a beautiful young lady, aged twenty-nine, caught between freedom and the lack thereof. On the one hand, she is free because her parents had died earlier in life, leaving her to construct her own identity independent of familial control; on the other, she is unfree because she is now reliant on an aunt, Mrs. Peniston, who took her in and who monitors the flow of her income. She has no other choice but to work with her aunt, heeding her words and ways of going about life. Which Lily finds limiting and stifling, not least because it belongs to an old world of staid mannerisms. Mrs. Peniston's "grandmother had been a Van Alstyne," the narrator tells us. She belonged to "the well fed and industrious stock of early New York," which found expression in "the glacial neatness of Mrs. Peniston's drawing room." Indeed, Lily finds her aunt frozen in time, which wouldn't be so bad it if hadn't also begun to rub off and impact Lily's chances at exploring the world, including finding the right partner. Lily tries to change her aunt, "to bring her into active relations with life," but to no avail. The matter is so stubborn "it was like tugging at a piece of furniture screwed to the floor." If only she could "do over [her] aunt's drawing room [she] know[s] [she] should be a better woman." If only she could do what Gertrude Farish, a rival of sorts, is able to do, namely "arrange furniture just as one likes," she should emerge on the other side happier, more fulfilled. Mind and matter are here conflated, furniture at once a source of laying out space but also in so doing spelling out the making of a certain mental construct. To move one is to agitate the other, back and forth, until a position of repose is achieved, or so Wharton and by inference Wright had hoped for. The ability to move tables and chairs around is synonymous with what gives license to charting new and adventurous paths.

Heavy furniture for Lily just did not work, or so Wharton's story suggests. Whether her aunt's furniture was actually heavy or metaphorically so, she found it hard to move. It was obstructive and as such oppressive, keeping her from dreaming and evolving as a person. Wright picked up where Lily left off, though in his case he welcomed heavy furniture instead of shunning it, finding in it a useful psychological tool, and effective. A heavy table or couch is one that is going nowhere, assertive in the way it lands and lays claim on space and thus a special view of room and surroundings. Try lifting any of Wright's furniture, especially his early pieces, and you risk breaking your back, immediately pinned back down to the ground. So heavy it was, in fact, "somebody suggested that the only way they could deal with [it] is to motorize [it]," Wright said. A lighter version wouldn't do, not least because it would be too prone to being shifted and moved, which wouldn't be so bad had Americans been steeped in the art of composition and so could be trusted to rearrange rooms while still keeping the integrity of the architecture intact. But they were not, and knowing that, Wright preempted the problem by making it as difficult as possible for his clients to rearrange furniture.

More on rearranging furniture later, but for now it is important to note that Wright's furniture is as rooted to the ground as plants are rooted to the soil, growing from the seed out, so to speak, specific to time, space, and cultural identity, as plants are to soil chemistry and biology. To remove it, or pull it out as the metaphor may suggest, is to undergo the pain and suffering of uprootedness, the process of yanking an entity out of its locale and placing it elsewhere. Wright's furniture was heavy precisely because furniture came and still does with the opposite premise, namely that unlike a building it is light and movable. Placing it and using in a way counter to its premise, more like a building and less a flighty chair, makes Wright's furniture less actual and more mental, in effect materializing consciousness and making it visible. Much like a counterweight is applied to balance and stabilize an object on the other side, so does Wright's heavy furniture: it operates as a counterforce with which to stimulate awareness of an otherwise hidden psychology.

Wright's furniture insisted on the local, tying awareness to the context at hand. To lift it is also to disturb a part of one's inner self, letting it be known that while displacement is possible, it cannot take place without a commensurate mental rearrangement. We need only look at the modernists working in parallel to Wright to appreciate his determination, indeed, his frustration with the way society and the modernists in particular had capitulated to the speed and pace of the time, now in the late nineteenth century and early twentieth century. Rather than critiquing the influence of the machine and the factory, the modernists, Wright believed, were merely exemplifying them, placing a mirror instead of a judge to alter their deleterious impact. The results were emaciated and elemental expressions, boxes with hole cutouts to let in light and air and few other basic needs, but no architecture with which to lift the human spirit. Wright hated it and called it "a cultural dilator, fit for fascism, intolerable to democracy." It was no more than "an old bare box, stripped bare."[5] The remedy was "organic architecture," evolved from the inside out. Like a plant it grew from the soil up, slowly but surely coming into its own, including an expression reflective of its own genetic code, so to speak. Nothing is imported or foreign but an outgrowth of the problem itself. "Organic architecture is essential structure of the timeless sort," Wright said. "It is no less the structure of whatever is music, poetry, or painting, or whatever else man's interior sensibilities may thrive upon when disciplined from within by the appropriate organic ideal."[6] Among other things, organic architecture spoke to a perfect synthesis between two opposing forces, gravity imposed on architecture by place, program, and geography, on the one hand, and final expression, on the other. In that, it resembled John Ruskin's argument on behalf of Gothic architecture, namely that it was not a style per se to

FIG. 30. Taliesin's inner court and main entrance, Spring Green, Wisconsin, 1911. Photo by author.

be chosen as if from a catalog but a perfect expression of nature's resolutions: "Now, I wish the reader especially to observe that we have arrived at these forms of perfect Gothic tracery without the smallest reference to any practice of any school, or to any law of authority whatever. They are forms having essentially nothing to do with Goths or Greeks. They are eternal forms, based on laws of gravity and cohesion; and no better, nor any others so good, will ever be invented, so long as the present laws of gravity and cohesion subsist."[7]

Nowhere is organic architecture, the resolution of gravity and cohesion, better experienced, and indeed felt, than at Wright's two Taliesins, East and West. There, structures not so much rise as heave up through the ground as if like a plant pushing up through the soil in early spring (fig. 30).

Mental Furniture and Freud

Wright never spoke of Sigmund Freud or the other way around, but the two shared a keen if quiet interest in the relation between architecture and mind. Freud often spoke of the mind as having a kind of architecture, of walls and doors, hallways and rooms, through whose encounter and movement the mind navigated a balance between interior consciousness and exterior reality. Central to his study was the play between the id, the ego, and the super-ego but also the conscious and the unconscious, each contained in a kind of compartment whose porosity determined how much of one reality seeped into the other. "He imagined the unconscious," says Sophia Psarra, "as an interior with an entrance hall, where mental impulses jostle one another like separate individuals," and the unconscious as "a drawing room." Between the two there lay a threshold "in which a watchman examines the different mental impulses" and "act[s] as a censor," admitting that which pleases and editing that which "displease[es]."[8] Where furniture was placed in these interiors mattered greatly, giving the self the tools to remain intellectually and socially functional. Arranged properly and the self has a good chance to maintain a healthy relation with the world. Improperly arranged and things are likely to lead to pathologies of difficult and even dangerous consequences. To protect against or correct a negative slide, it only made sense to find a way to enter the mind and scan its interior, rearrange furniture, so to speak, and stabilize that which had become unstable. Freud did that by modeling his own practice on the same principle, famously dividing it into three compartments and using furniture to analyze and theorize and ultimately help his patients overcome certain insecurities.[9]

Of central importance to us is the examination room. The other two rooms were the waiting room and study. It was in the examination room that Freud's famous couch and chair found their first appearance, the couch serving as the surface on which patients relaxed and let their mind go; the chair, as the seat on which the examiner sat and listened. Both were shoved against the wall, leaving the center of the room free of obstacles and open to movement. In all this, the mind found its equivalent, the room serving as the container and skull of the mind, the couch its subconscious, the chair the conscious. The three had to collaborate before any solution could meaningfully emerge. What Freud was in effect doing was lending his patients the tools with which to go on and conduct their own therapy independent of him and well after the therapy session was over. In one way or another they had to recognize that within them lies the answer, that by allowing the subconscious to open up and speak, the conscious to sit back and listen patiently, the self would realize what is at stake and go on to self-correct. Mental blockage was the problem, and should patients be able to root it out, very much like a plumber may do with a clogged pipe, they will be able to triumph over stifling mental hang-ups.

What Freud sought to conflate between examination and mental rooms, Wright would repeat in his own approach to architecture and interiors, but, you could say, in reverse. Rather than clearing the room of furniture, he filled it with chairs and tables. He wagered that should he stop the Americans in their track, he could get them to perk up and take note, awakening, much like Freud had sought in his own patients, long-buried fears, sentiments, and generally inhibitions piled up over the years. Industrial capitalism, among other related forces examined throughout this book, had made Americans acquiesce and succumb to a herd mentality. Like sheep they moved without knowing why or where. Having been flogged repeatedly, so to speak, they became resigned to the message and direction they were being asked to follow. Anything else seemed needless and futile after a while. To change course and in effect restore to Americans self-confidence, not to mention the desire to fight for creative justice again, Wright had to find a way to stop the mindless march and, in a way, force the herd to face its flogger all over again. The subjugated must face the subjugator, or, in Freudian terms, the conscious the unconscious.

It was not for nothing that Wright insisted that his furniture come with his architecture. You don't design the house and then bring in the furniture; the two go hand in hand. Where the work of walls and windows leave off, the place of sofas, chairs, and hassocks comes in, extending the slow but methodical therapy he sought to exercise on the American mind. "Always there is something in the mind when these things are done," Wright said in this light and continued, "I tried to make my clients see that furniture and furnishings that were not built in as integral features of the building should be designed as attributes of whatever furniture was built in and should be seen as a minor part of the building itself even if detached or kept aside to be employed only on occasion."[10]

In some ways Wright was doing little more than rehashing the principles of Gesamtkunstwerk, or "Total Work of Art," first proposed by the philosopher Karl Friedrich Eusebius Trahndorff in the early nineteenth century, and later adopted and popularized by European artists and architects. Which is true, but his version was still different, characterized by the peculiarly Emersonian mention of mental furniture, heard at the outset of the chapter, namely that the part and the whole for Wright were a matter less concerned with achieving aesthetic unity and visual harmony and more with administering a mental corrective. If for Charles Rennie Mackintosh in Glasgow, one of the champions of Gesamtkunstwerk, art and the whole were knit to weave a special spiritual relation between flesh and stone, or more precisely wood, "in which the whole was very much more important than the sum of the individual parts," for Wright the same was true but specifically to point out the degree to which Americans had to refurbish long-lost creative priorities.

Between the layout of a room and that of the mind there was continuity for Wright, the two braided in a mutual campaign to strengthen and indeed correct each other's constitution. To move a piece of furniture in one environment was to move a corollary one in the next. Or, better yet, bang against a knobby and heavy piece of wood and get hurt, an armchair or a protruding desktop, flashing a commensurate awakening in the mind. Wright knew of the effect from direct experience, himself a victim of his own pointy furniture. "I have been black and blue in some spot, somewhere, all my life from too intimate contact with my own early furniture."[11]

Not all realizations can be achieved through passive lifting. Some require active pushback, a kind of pushing and shoving and elbowing whose purpose is to create enough discomfort, even pain, to shake loose calcified perspectives. Furniture, of course, does not get up and push, or shove, but it can be designed to cause pain, inciting violence against the body, breaking its passive movement through space. No sooner does one enter a Wright space than that person finds themselves encountering the aggressive pointing of a table or a chair. The thing is so massive it creates a physical but ultimately a mental and emotional eddy all unto itself, drawing the person in as if by magnetism. Note the built-in sofas around the fireplace at the Barnsdall Home, also called the Hollyhock House, in Los Angeles (fig. 31). They are gigantic and rise in a manner akin to a battleship headed for war. To bang against them is to bang against one's own existence, as Wright himself must have done when he admitted that he has "been banged black and blue on the leg somewhere all my life from [my own] furniture." It is not for nothing that the Barnsdall Home looks like an Egyptian tomb, complete with Egyptian corbelled walls and concrete doors, floors that step down, seemingly into the grave, and up,

FIG. 31. Built-in couch at the Hollyhock House, Los Angeles, California, 1921. Note the prow-like end of the couch seemingly ready to do battle with the enemy out in the open seas. Photograph courtesy of Mark Hertzberg.

as if forever teetering between life and the afterlife. Wright often spoke of his need to see in architecture a total work of art, making it clear in this case that between the furniture and the walls there is but a singular message, namely that what the furniture taketh in body, having now attacked and destroyed it, figuratively speaking, the house will bury and then resurrect in soul. We shall all return wiser the second time around, or so Wright hoped.

The Barnsdall Home is orthogonal, but not all Wright's work is that way. Quite a few of his homes are diagonal, fashioned along 30/60 angles or hexagons reflecting either natural abstractions or patterns found in nature. The Hanna House in Palo Alto, California, is a good example, as is the Robert Berger residence in San Anselmo, California—the first following a beehive pattern, the latter a 120/60 angular order. "The sixty degree triangular module, in which the plan is based," says Judith Dunham of the Berger house in her book *Details of Frank Lloyd Wright*, "recurs on many scales: in the lights set into the living room soffit, in the diamond matrix scored on the concrete floor, in the overall shape of the terrace outside the living area."[12] And more, including the table that juts out of the wall separating the dining room from the bedroom and whose one edge points like an arrow at anyone, as it were, ready to do battle (fig. 32). It is truly a remarkable gesture, unabashed in its suggestive capacity to inflict pain. Watch out.

Ivan Ilych, in Tolstoy's short novel *The Death of Ivan Ilych,* did not quite watch out and was dinged by a "step ladder" while rearranging the décor of his newfound house. He was a man of great repute, a public prosecutor who had garnered the support and admiration of his community but who had also

FIG. 32. Built-in dining table at the Robert Berger House, San Anselmo, California, 1957. Photograph courtesy of Scot Zimmerman.

at one point become disenchanted and resentful. He had been "expecting to be offered the post of presiding judge in the University town, [when] someone else came to the front and obtained the appointment instead." The incident irritated the man to no end. "It was then that it became evident on the one hand that his salary was insufficient," for he and his family, "and not only this but that what was for him the greatest and most cruel injustice appeared to others a quite ordinary occurrence." He felt awful but soon bounced back when he finally found a job worthy of his name and talent again. To celebrate he went out and found a new "delightful house, just the thing that he and his wife had dreamt of." "Spacious" and "lofty," it was just the right vessel through which he could channel his new energy and feel alive again. The place needed some work, and so he picked up hammer and nail and went to work renovating. It didn't matter that he did not possess prior knowledge in design and decoration; he still found in the task enough leeway to take it up on a whim. He "chose the wallpapers, supplemented the furniture and supervised the upholstering." So much did he enjoy the work that it became all-consuming, replacing in importance duties back at the office. But alas the matter would bring about his slow but sure demise. One day, when "mounting a step ladder to show the upholsterer" how to hang the drapery, "he made a false step and slipped . . . and only knocked his side against the knob of the window frame." The incident would prove fatal, the ding triggering something, a tumor perhaps, that would metastasize into something so painful no painkiller could relieve it. Nor the right furniture, his bed in particular amplifying the discomfort and broadcasting in cries and moans the agony inside.

Ilych finally dies but not before serving as Wright's stand-in for the man and the mind Wright was trying to correct all along. In finding his second wind and in effect regaining his self-worth, Ilych transgresses. He finds a house and refurbishes it but less to make the interior of his home more beautiful and more to keep up with the Joneses. He decorates in earnest to make a difference but ends up copying what the middle class does when it tries to look rich. And so, while he thought his work was unique, "in reality it was what is usually seen in the houses of people of moderate means who want to appear rich, and therefore succeed only in resembling others like themselves," the narrator of the story tells us. The look is familiar, featuring the usual "damasks, dark wood, plants, rugs, and dull and polished bronzes—all the things people of a certain class have in order to resemble other people of that class." Wright called the practice "mummery," a blend of mimicry and death, or death by imitation. The features that appeared on the Queen Anne homes near Oak Park, where he lived, baffled him. Where did "the murderous corner tower serving as bay-window" come from? he wondered. The more he walked and looked about, the more he found the houses of his time "senseless" and "comfortless." And not just in Oak Park but everywhere. "Those who lived in this ambitious Eastlake mimicry called Queen Anne were blissfully unaware of any serious losses or self-inflicted insults."[13] And yet aware they had to become, Ilych by way of banging against the very offensive interior he had aped from the upper class and Wright's clients by Wright's own careful manipulation of furniture design.

Having become seriously ill, Ilych falls victim to the making of his own undoing, sitting and leaning and generally relying on the very furniture he acquired to turn his life around but which also caused his downfall. The bed won't do as it increases the feeling of pain on his side. He has to switch to the sofa instead, previously the symbol and object of artificial social reintegration but which here is turned into a tool of mental awakening. The same with the armchair, previously a lavish expression of status, now the seat of bodily disintegration. So badly did his body fall apart that he feared looking at it, but simply "drew on a dressing gown, wrapped himself in a plaid, and sat down in the armchair to take his tea."[14] Indeed, none of his acquired furniture was right or comfortable anymore, all proving equally pretentious and damning of the soul. If there was a position that brought him comfort, it was that which was provided by one of his servants, a youth of modest education, named Gerasim, kind and tolerant. So generous, in fact, that he didn't mind holding his boss's leg high and over his shoulder. It was the only position at which Ilych felt little or no pain, tellingly independent of material contact but also false humanity. Gerasim is nothing but innocence personified, devoid of deception and double entendre. As death nears, Ilych becomes acutely aware of the deceptions that had led up to this point, including those fomented by members of his own household, specifically his wife, who seems, accurately or not, to be merely interested in her own financial survival.

On Furniture and Pain

In her book *The Body in Pain,* Elaine Scarry examines torture techniques employed by various political regimes to coerce prisoners to talk and give up information. Of one, she describes the way furniture is used to inflict pain. An otherwise simple and seemingly innocent object of comfort, furniture here is used to cause bodily damage and suffering. The method is particularly effective precisely because it relies on reverse logic, not only to cause harm but to work that harm into the memory and psychology of the victim. What had been trusted as a source of unconditional pleasure and relaxation is here used against those aims, deconstructing normal reliance on everyday things, important to the functioning and advancement of everyday life. Unsettling established norms is critical to a world in need of constant moral and technical renovation, but to do so on daily basis and with daily objects is to unsettle the very ground on which existence depends. What makes the matter particularly sinister with furniture is that the latter stays behind. A gun, a bat, or knife can be retrieved or stashed elsewhere, but less so with furniture. Furniture must be left behind for the victim to keep using—to do ordinary but important things such as sitting, eating, and sleeping—and in so doing revisiting the awful pain inflicted earlier, as if nothing had happened, indeed normalizing it. What had been an aberration of the human condition now becomes the new normal, the expected regime by which to live a life.

Different regimes use different techniques, of course, but all at one point or another rely on furniture or the absence of which to deliver their blows. Speaking of torture techniques used in the Philippines during the martial law era under Ferdinand Marcos, Scarry mentions the degree to which that regime used structures to assimilate the process of torture. There, rooms and their furnishings were converted into weapons, including chairs used to tie men and women, but also cots, filing cabinets, beds. Other descriptions involve chairs pressed against hands to crush them, and heads "repeatedly banged on the edges of a refrigerator door" or "repeatedly pounded against the edges of a filing cabinet," to inflict pain but also to create a reminder of it well after the physical torture had taken place.

Day and night the chair works its terrible residual magic on the psyche of the prisoner, bringing that person to their knees, even when there is no one around. In one story, Scarry recounts the aftereffects of a memory of a finger crushed by a chair. The prisoner had looked at the chair a million times without so much as giving the object a second thought. Now, however, the mere sight of the chair triggered terror, a resurgence of pain all over again. Nothing was to be trusted anymore, including doors and windows and the like. Of the door in particular, Scarry reminds us that "Solzhenitsyn describes how in Russia guards were trained to slam the door in as jarring a way as possible or to close it in equally unnerving silence." The two were played against each other, the loud against the quiet, until the mere looking at the door caused nerves to rattle. Over time, the jailor became unnecessary, his return now nicely and efficiently replaced but the simple look at the door.

In focusing on the role that furniture plays in acts of torture, Scarry makes available another key point, namely the degree to which architecture eliminates self, at least as a conscious image in those who come to rely on it. It is because of the provision and assembly of its walls and floor, windows and doors, that we are able to take up projects, work on tasks, design, sleep, remain healthy, and so on. So ubiquitous is shelter that we take it for granted, at one point becoming a mere extension of our body, or an echo version of it. "There is nothing contradictory about the fact that the shelter is at once so graphic an image of the body and so emphatic an instance of civilization," says Scarry. It is "only because it is the first can it be the second." Indeed,

> It is only when the body is comfortable, when it has ceased to be an obsessive object of perception and concern, that consciousness develops other objects, that for any individual the external world comes into being and begins to grow. Both in the details of its outer structure and in its furniture the room accommodates and thereby eliminates from human attention the human body: the simple triad of floor, chair and bed makes spatially and therefore steadily visible the collection of postures and positions the body moves in and out, objectifies the three locations within the body that most frequently hold the body's weight, objectifies its need continually to shift within itself the locus of its weight, objectifies, finally, its need to become forgetful of its weight, to move weightlessly into a larger mindfulness.[15]

Architecture, in other words, undermines its own memory. By being reliable and remaining functional day in day out, it eliminates the need to think twice about it. Once underway it become just there, even forgettable. Which is good lest we get bogged down worrying about it and can't function anymore. But also not so great in the sense that we may stop appreciating its value, technical and cultural. Wright understood the former but was troubled by the possibility of the latter and did what he could to remind Americans of the importance of architecture, in this case through furniture. Note on this point the tall-backed dining chairs he designed early on for clients but also for his own house at Oak Park (fig. 33), placing them around tables so as to form "rooms within rooms," to use his words. Just in case Americans forgot what architecture means as they sat down to eat, and the fact that what makes architecture great, among other things, is the integrity of the room, especially if it was designed by him, here was a reminder.

Seated in these chairs, Americans became synonymous with the walls that enclosed them, stout and responsible for the very support of the structure above, and by inference the household and the larger society beyond. They had to be as studded, as careful and keen as the exterior walls, steeped in the knowledge of light, ornament, material, and everything else that exterior walls admitted in creating the room they were in. That meant sitting up well, eating with elegance, and recognizing the bounty in front of you. It meant using the right language and using eye contact that unified those seated. Wright made no secret of the way he found Americans graceless in the way they ate and generally used space, who, not unlike Grim Silas in Nathaniel Hawthorne's classic *The Blithedale Romance,* "behave less like civilized Christians than the worst kind of an ogre." Wright's sentiments were made all the more vivid in the wake of his travels to Japan and seeing how the people of that country moved through and occupied interiors. Of the rituals he observed there, he was most envious of their tea ceremony, revealing the degree to which they were willing to go the extra mile to train their focus and confirm their commitment to simplicity and beauty. "All cultured women, rich or poor," he wrote in awe in his *Autobiography,* "must learn to properly perform the tea ceremony according to cultural rules laid down by the celebrated master-esthete Rikkyu." Americans did not match up very well, not least because they "have not the spirit of it nor could [they] stand it—very

FIG. 33. Dining chairs and table at Frank Lloyd Wright's home and studio, Oak Park, Illinois, 1889. The chairs and their backs rise so high as to form a room within a room surrounding the table. The two end chairs are missing from the picture, but their presence would have made the effect even more pronounced. Courtesy Frank Lloyd Wright Trust, Chicago. Photographer: Tim Long.

long." Instead, they, like Grim Silas again, "pour it out and gulp it down with no more sense of its exquisiteness than if it were a decoction of catnip." It is not so much the serving and drinking of the tea that is important of course, but the reverence the Japanese paid to keeping things clean, including reducing waste to a minimum: "Such reverent concentration as this tea ceremonial carries the ideal of "be clean" to such heights and lengths too, as weary us of the more direct West." Might furniture change that, forcing a certain discipline unto Americans to approach and engage something as simple and yet critical as eating and uniting with each other. Wright believed so.

The Pain of Furniture

On several occasions, the pain that Wright's furniture caused was more than a matter of concept but an integrated feature of the logic of his designs. Like a self-reciprocating motor, his chairs often tipped to correct an otherwise lazy posture, forcing the redistribution of body weight. Sit without thought as to what you are doing and you could risk flying backward. Wright hated sitting anyway, finding in it a naturally offensive posture and way of appearing in space. "I don't know why that when nature decided that man was to stand up on his two legs and be straight that he had to find a place to back up to, and fold up on," he puzzled at one point in the company of his students at the Fellowship. Sitting caused the human to slouch and before too long bunch up in a shrivel. How ugly, he thought. "It's kind of in itself an indignity, isn't it?" he puzzled. "He's only charming and respectable when he is standing; when he's seated he isn't much to look at."[16]

A remedy had to be engineered so that the very act of sitting could trigger an equal but opposite reaction from the sitter, self-correcting that which had been destabilized by sitting. Unless conscious and aware of the changes wrought by sitting, and, by philosophical inference, reality itself, the sitter could, in this case, risk flipping and getting hurt. Which is exactly what happened on a few occasions, most famously at the Johnson Wax Headquarters, where three-legged chairs were designed so as to force awareness of posture and balance (fig. 34). This was no ordinary workplace but one whose owners were religious and believed in work as a kind of calling, blessed by a higher power. Arriving to work was akin to arriving at a religious center, something like a "cathedral," in Wright's words, where what one did was meaningful precisely because it had been conducted in the spirit of meditation and prayer. To lose sight of that purpose would in effect amount to losing the building itself, an otherwise artificial construct of brick and stone. What good would the elegant and eternally graceful "Lily Pad" columns, discussed in chapter 2, amount to if the worker working next to them isn't commensurately spiritually stout on the inside? There the three-legged chair kept them upright, always aware of the need to keep body and world calibrated to the message at hand. On more than one occasion, workers capsized, and when the matter stopped being funny, the chairs finally had to be altered. "Eventually the

FIG. 34. Originally a three-legged design, the Great Workroom chair at the Johnson Wax Headquarters has since been redesigned to feature four legs, as seen in the photo. Photograph courtesy of Mark Hertzberg.

chairs had to be converted to four-legged models," Paul Goldberger tells us in a 1987 *New York Times* article, "after workers complained that the chairs tipped over continually."[17] By then, presumably, Wright didn't need the lopsided chairs anymore, his message having already become burned into the ideals of the place, reminiscent of Scarry's point earlier regarding the use and residual impact of chairs on political prisoners.

In another tipping episode, Wright recalls getting a taste of his own medicine, this time flipping on a chair while showing off a former client's house in New York. "I was hoist by my own petard in the house down in New York City," he tells us. To demonstrate the virtues of integrated living, he had sat on one of the chairs, but no sooner did he do so than he found himself going "over backward. Up in the air." Cornelia Berndston, one of the apprentices in the 1950s, did the same on the same tour, she, too, doing a "back somersault" of her own.[18]

Back in 1905 and in the wake of Wright's completion of the Martin House in Buffalo, Wright received an interesting, if funny rebuke from Martin, a lifelong supporter and loyal client. Wright had spent much time and mental effort designing the dining chairs for the house, to accomplish what he had done at his own house back in Oak Park. Naturally he wanted to be fairly reimbursed, which Martin does but not before letting him know that his designs didn't work and wouldn't do. The dining chair would have to be redesigned: "Yesterday afternoon a lady of more than ordinary intelligence, sat down in the chair to try it and nearly tipped over. We do not want chairs that will cause even one percent of our guests to wildly clutch the air and ejaculate as this design would certainly do."[19]

Wright's chairs, of course, were nothing like those that Scarry discussed in *The Body in Pain*. The first were household items of comfort and décor, the latter, objects with which to interrogate political prisoners. But the two did share a similar corrective purpose, powerful and indeed effective precisely because of the ease with which they could be "flipped" into weapons of mental coercion. Seemingly innocuous in one sense, they appealed to their users' sense of comfort and trust, but only to flip at a moment's notice and draw out otherwise inhibited or repressed feelings.

Lest all this talk about body and mind, furniture and thought, sound too far-fetched, it was brought up later in the twentieth century in response to back pain and generally long and sedentary work at the office. Was the problem centered in the body or the chair? Was the body just badly suited for sitting, as Wright had said, or had the right design for a chair remained elusive to the world of chair designers and manufacturers? Galen Cranz, the author of *The Chair*, at first thought it was the former but later realized that it was the latter and in her search for an answer found out that besides designing the perfect chair, the solution also entailed understanding the role the mind plays in making the mental adjustments required to change the way we think of sitting habits and posture. She calls this, using found research, "somatics" and says that "over the last twenty years an integrated body-mind perspective has emerged from the field of inquiry and practice termed somatics, that differs from osteopathy, chiropractic, and physical therapy in its focus on the relationship between body and intellectual thought, cultural belief, individual feeling and will."[20]

She goes on to point out that what all this meant and still does is that understanding and using furniture properly must necessarily require education.

After so many years of passive sitting, we had come to take simple features of everyday life practice for granted, at the expense of our health and happiness and, for Wright and America, the vital intellectual engagement with ideas. As it turned out, the notion of the "reminder" is key to letting furniture and architecture serve us well.

Wright and Freud

For Wright as it was for Freud, the difficulty of reversing repressed feelings included the importance of carryover, namely the need to continue the lessons imparted onto patient and client well beyond the meeting sessions had ended. After all, what good would it be if after all the work they had exercised inside the office vanished right after? If the intention of architect and doctor was to change a culture and not merely earn a living, their impact had to last beyond the four walls and the hour or so spent at the outset or even once a week. Not unlike the banging of the door in the torture situation mentioned earlier, Wright and Freud had to outlast the temporariness of the moment.

To that end, Freud wagered that should he conduct his examination in such a way so as to make himself invisible, the patient could in effect take what he or she learned during that session and apply it to oneself later on, independent of Freud. Examination sessions are only an hour or so long, and yet the psyche is a matter that goes on at all hours. An hour or two a week weren't going to cut it unless their effects can be so designed so as to extend their influence at all hours, even into sleep, where dreams can take over and reveal important information. And yet how might Freud become invisible, even while he is in the same room as the patient? The answer lay in the arrangement of furniture. Where he placed his chair, next to or around the patient's couch, mattered greatly. Placing it on the side of the couch wouldn't do, as that would put Freud in view of the patient. A better location is behind the couch, where the patient could hear the examiner but not see him, privileging voice and even smell over sight. What sight the patient did see had to be of something else, in this case a cabinet full of miniature sculptures, serving as totems of some symbolic purpose, precisely not humans but nonhierarchical figures meant as stand-ins of memories key to the success of mental correction. Rather than absorbing attention they deferred it to secondary projections in the room, namely Freud's soothing voice and aromatic cigar. This was in effect less about an examination between patient and examiner and more between patient and him or herself. It is less likely that a patient will change if he or she is told what to do by a figure of authority than if the same person were to realize the need to do so on their own, or so Freud believed.

Though not an examination room per se, Wright's office in Oak Park, Chicago, was so choreographed as to allow Wright the ability to puppeteer a complex nexus of mental loops between him and clients. What he sought to sell, after all, was not a market product first and foremost, but a life of meaning. Which naturally meant giving up few comforts in favor of others, or no comforts at all, but a life driven by solid principles, almost monk-like and ascetic. Before they could buy his product, clients had to first understand what he was selling, requiring a kind of mental immersion into a world unlike their own, perhaps dreamlike and wondrous. Here they had to relinquish association with the past and take stock, and indeed, enjoy new realities. And just as Freud had arranged his interior furnishing to induce a kind of alternate world of free thinking, so Wright would shift and manipulate the furniture of his own office to invite his clients to release mental shackles. The process required just as much admission as acquisition, the need to confess to certain sins of the past, so to speak, to induce clients to gravitate and adhere to critical realizations. Something akin to a chapel or a church was needed, a consecrated space where clients could put their heads down and come to terms with their own trespasses before going on. Wright considered himself prone to the same sins as his clients, the same likely weaknesses that led them to feelings of envy and lust. Recall the inglenook in his own home, introduced toward the end of the previous chapter. An alcove featuring the requisite wooden bench, curtain, and a spiritual saying, it resembled the confessional box of a church. As bombastic as Wright was, he was also unafraid at times to admit to his weaknesses, perhaps most stunningly when he confessed a greater sense of fatherly association with his buildings than with his children. Again when he wrote to his mother after he left Chicago for Europe, he admitted to his prodigal transgressions.[21] In a similar vein, in their book *The Fellowship*, Roger Friedland and Harold Zellman liken the built-in furniture Wright designed for his clients to a church's "wooden pews" and quoted

Wright as saying that they were in "complete harmony, nothing to arrange, nothing to disturb."[22]

To that end we may recall a story told by a woman who lived in not one but two Wright houses. She describes going through a two-step emotional connection, first of rebellion, "an anger at any dwelling-place that presumes to dictate how its occupants live, followed by a kind of religious submission." She goes on to explain that her transformation was in large part due to the realization that "because a Wright house does not allow for many extraneous possessions, it enforces humility." And then adds that "the stripping of accoutrements resulted in a stripping of self or self-hood."[23]

Wright's office was not unlike Freud's. It, too, had three essential rooms, a central waiting room flanked by two others, a drafting room to the left and a library to the right. We may liken it to an asymmetrical cross, a central axis of arrival and waiting, followed by a cross axial line whose polar ends are defined by the opposite functions of intellectual thinking and manual performance. Throughout, everything lived under the aura of spiritual light, including the way furniture absorbed and reflected light, serving as altar space and source of attention. Friedland and Zellman again compare the office to religious spaces, the drafting room to a "cathedral," and the library to a "baptistery," both "flooded with sunlight from [their] high clerestory windows." These were interiors with which to impress upon clients certain deep values but also rooms small and intimate enough that they could double as confessional boxes. It was here that Wright the preacher and amateur psychologist could draw out tired associations from his clients and replace them with ones more aligned with the American project explored throughout this book. He had wanted to do just that, "to play the role of preacher," in his words, and this was his opportunity. Indeed, "if great architecture in the old sense no longer exists," he declared, then it will be incumbent upon the architect to translate "the homes of the people" into "sermons of stones."

And not only with furniture did Wright's office resemble that of Freud's but also in the role and placements of objects. Just as Freud relied on totems of past deities to draw attention away from him and anything tangible for the moment, so did Wright. He, too, placed objects of beauty and symbolic importance throughout his office to deflect attention away from faux stylistic concerns and onto seats of deep meaning and heritage. Even in his early days with Cecil Corwin he had been cognizant of the need to keep the eye on the prize, so to speak, making sure that it is the likes of native cultures, not spectacular Beaux-Arts eye candy, that should capture his client's attention. This was shortly after he and Corwin had left their respective offices and were ready to start on their own, sharing a modest two- or three-room office. In it, Wright tells us, "there was a large flat oak chest of drawers each side of the door with some Hermon MacNeil's Indian statuettes standing on them."[24] These figures could have easily been ones of Greek and Roman poets, philosophers, and politicians, but no, they had to be of something much more rooted to the earth. Later and back at his studio and office in Oak Park, the octagonal library, or "baptistery," doubled as a kind of gallery or a "museum/ laboratory . . . filled with beautiful objects intended to inspire and instruct," but also indoctrinate.[25] "Windowless at eye level," tells us the Wright scholar Jonathan Lipman, the library "seems to have also been used for the indoctrination of clients by the eloquent Wright."[26]

The return to furniture was another way that Wright kept his influence on clients, family, and friends intact well after his first encounter at the office. Like a Houdini, he would appear and disappear back in the space of his clients' homes, rearranging furniture, sometimes to restore original layouts, other times to alter the feel of the décor, now that his clients had lived in it for a while. Sometimes the effect was truly magical, turning a donkey into a horse, or a hat into a rabbit. On one occasion Wright would return to the home of a reliable patron and benefactor, the Darwin Martin House in Buffalo, New York, not to correct a misplaced chair and sofa but this time to shuffle things around completely. Perhaps the effect of seeing the house done and occupied gave Wright a different perspective on the potential and ethic of the project. Who knows, but either way he tackled the change with gusto. As David Hanks says: "Wright's compulsion to rearrange furniture and objects, was . . . transferred to the interiors that he had designed for clients. On subsequent visits to the Darwin Martin House, Wright would rearrange the furniture differently from the plan he had specified on first designing the house. Although a definite furniture arrangement plan was frequently part of the designing of the house, Wright made subsequent changes when possible, always attempting to make his arrangements closer to the artistic idea, which was in a perpetual state of development."[27]

On a slightly different note but still a clear illustration of the degree to which Wright felt furniture was instrumental to shaping the American mind, Maginel, Wright's sister, tells the following interesting story: Wright was in New York working on the Guggenheim, stationed at the Plaza hotel, and Maginel had come to visit. The room was beautiful, but Wright still found a chair not quite placed right. The windows were closed, keeping the sound of outside traffic soft. Suddenly Wright walked askance and "with a gentle kick shifted an armchair a few degrees to one side." Dissatisfied, he "kicked it back to its original position." Maginel chuckles and can't help reflecting on her brother's idiosyncrasy: "I had seen him do this in my own house many times, and in my daughter's." In fact, "once, when he was staying in the house of friends, they'd been away for a few days and when they returned they found their furniture completely rearranged, without invitation or explanation."[28]

The Electric Chair

The narrator of "The Fall of the House of Usher," Wright's favorite Poe story, may not have rearranged furniture while visiting his old boyhood friend, but he, too, found in the interior of the house the sign of his counterpart's mental disorder. The two went together, on the one hand "the gloomy furniture of the room," on the other, "the inexplicable vagaries of madness." Roderick Usher had asked his friend to come visit because he wanted company to help ease his anguish. The narrator complies. Usher's sister had fallen ill and was about to die, leaving the brother deeply conflicted and sad. There is more than a hint that Usher's melancholy was the product of a life lived without exposure to diverse social discourse, perhaps limited to a dark incestuous relation. As such it had suffered great instability, even a kind of madness. The effect was one not unlike that of a storm, constantly breaking on Usher's mind and threatening its rational constitution. Something had to happen to remedy the situation, say, opening the equivalent of mental windows to release pressure and restore a modicum of fresh air. Having entered his guest's room at one point in the story, Usher "hurried to one of the casements, and threw it freely open to the storm." A gust of wind blew in, causing "frequent and violent alterations" to the interior, presumably tossing this and that "terrestrial object" about. Usher had to be seated and calmed down, assured that what he had been experiencing was nothing more than "merely electrical phenomenon not uncommon."

Poe's "The Fall of the House of Usher" was first published in 1839, around the same time that Emerson's *Nature* came out, a time, that is, of shared cultural agreement that America had fallen behind. It may have been sufficiently fine on the outside, but it was terribly distraught on the inside. For cure, it had to be exhumed, turned upside down, its internal furniture moved around. The effort required something like a tempest with a force powerful enough it can blow open "casement" windows to create "frequent and violent alterations." Wright would follow suit, he, too, returning to former clients and blowing open their interiors and rearranging their furniture and, in effect, their mental electrical wiring. The understanding of the brain as an electrical phenomenon had yet to be fully fleshed out by the time of Poe and Wright, but enough had been done in that field to give the two authors the license to invoke it in their work. "During the latter half of the nineteenth century," says Craig Brandon, author of *The Electric Chair,* "many major hospitals had departments of electrotherapy that used electricity to treat paralysis, rheumatism, gout, arthritis, and sciatica." But also "insanity, hysteria, skin diseases, drunkenness, opium poisoning and nervous exhaustion."[29]

No doubt Poe and Wright knew that to change the mind, it was necessary to also change the electrical infrastructure with which it processes information, the so-called wiring of the brain. What that might look like was anyone's guess, but Poe came close when he drew a visual likening between the crackling in the sky and that in the mind, both the product of an "electrical phenomenon not uncommon." Usher's mental anguish was the result of internal electrical excitement, not unlike that formed when clouds collide, generated in this case not by gusts of wind but by cultural and familial conflicts. Of which there were many in the nineteenth century, now that people were converging on a singular spot, moving from rural to urban settings and becoming both the source and victim of social frictions. "The psychological foundation upon which the metropolitan individuality is erected," Georg Simmel writes in his essay "The Metropolis and Mental Life," "is the intensification of emotional life due to the swift and continuous shift of external internal stimuli."[30] In the wake of modern cultural misalignments, difficulties wrought by a barrage of industrial demands, it was the mind that had to absorb the blow, resulting in mental and electrical misfiring. To solve the problem, it seemed only rational to do so at the electrical level, in one way or another, matching in the physical world that which went on, and still does, inside the brain.

There is more than a likeness between the electric chair, conceived and designed to euthanize people, and those designed by Wright, if not from the start of his career then by the first decade of the twentieth century. Both were made out of oak, and both had tall backs, made of either horizontal or vertical spindles. Both were designed in relation to domestic settings, namely the belief that to correct the mind one must start with the home, namely the home as the basis of cultural formation and transformation. To explain, we can start with Thomas Edison's invention of the light bulb in 1879, leading "directly to the use of electric lighting in homes." What had been a place limited to certain functions, such as eating and sleeping, now could be used to advance other functions, such as performing professional and school work. Night and day blended, at times switching places and allowing functions that used to be conducted during the day to now be conducted during the night and vice versa. What had been the realm of dreams now became the realm of real action, naturally resulting in a kind of mental disorientation. "This development had a direct impact on the invention of the electric chair," says Craig Brandon, fusing domestic flares with those sparked by electric currents.[31] Interestingly electrocution did not start with the chair at all but simply with a desire to terminate the lives of criminals in as humane a manner as possible. The prior practice of hanging people in the gallows had been deemed "savage" and "uncivilized"—by politicians, clergymen, and ordinary civilians alike—and a better and more dignified approach was deemed necessary. For a while the solution entailed no more than the criminal standing in a small wooden cabin box and receiving electricity at high voltage between head and feet. But that resulted in the criminal falling to the ground in a heap of flesh and bones, which was not dignified. No matter how awful the criminal and their crime, the body deserved a modicum of respect. Might a table with straps serving as both ties and electrodes prove a remedy? Perhaps, but that would be too reminiscent of a body in a coffin, already dead and beyond the capacity to serve its purpose as example and message for mental reformation. The execution of prisoners was and remains only to a limited extent about

justice; it was and remains intended to be more of a message for future criminals, deterring thoughts of ill intent from ever maturing.

How about an oak chair? That seemed more like it, strong and reminiscent of the furniture produced by the Arts and Crafts movement. It not only
retained, more or less, the posture of the deceased criminal but also honored
it by giving it a backdrop by now well associated with the dignity of work
and the idea that life is a "total work of art." One description of the electric
chair referred to it as looking akin to a "modern device." "In 1889, New York's
Electrical Execution Law, the first of its kind in the world, went into effect,"
it said. For it, "Edwin R. Davis, the Auburn Prison electrician, was commissioned to design an electric chair." "Closely resembling the modern device,
[it] was fitted with two electrodes, which were composed of metal disks held
together with rubber and covered with a damp sponge. The electrodes were
to be applied to the criminal's head and back."[32] Another description said that
the chair was large and had "a high back and comfortable seat." It also came
with "a footrest, which may or may not be used." At the top "an adjustable bar
of wood projects from the back over the head of the occupant."[33]

In one fell swoop electrocution became about more than one thing, at
once a simple matter of domestic furniture, an oak chair with a straight-up
backing, and a devastating tool with which to ensure moral alignment. Just as
John Ruskin had preferred his "mahogany heavy chairs" to fluffy "gilded up-
holstery," to keep his mind trained on truth and authenticity, so the electric
chair conflated domesticity with cultural awakening. Good behavior started
at home, in such activity as sitting and eating a meal, in being aware and
building in one's mental construct the proper electrical wirings. At a time
when political and social pressures were every day converging on the individual, demanding new and complex responses, it was more than a matter of
metaphor that Americans needed rewiring. What had been morally possible
twenty years prior, around the turn of the century, now became legally infea-
sible, even impossible.

The nineteenth century was a time of rapid urbanization. Between 1790
and 1890, the number of people living in urban areas in the United States
went from 5 percent to 35 percent, and by the 1920s, more people lived in
the inner city than in the country. The story is familiar, attributed largely to
advances in technology, transportation, construction, and generally a world

in which the lure of urban jobs outweighed the thankless work back on the farm. Hope and drive were high and yet were soon dashed once the migrant arrived and the realization set in that the center was not all it was cracked up to be but quite the opposite: dirty and dangerous. Or so thought the recently arrived Lithuanians when they landed in Chicago in Sinclair's novel *The Jungle*. No sooner did their train come to a stop than they looked out of the window and saw "they were on a street which seemed to run for ever, mile after mile," lined with row upon row "of wretched little two-story frame buildings." Farther down, as they walked the town, "here and there" there were "railroad crossings with a tangle of switches, and locomotives puffing and rattling freight cars filing by." The most awful was the sight of the "great factory, a dingy building with innumerable windows," from whose chimneys smoke belched, "darkening the air above and making filthy the earth beneath."

The Metropolis and Mental Life

Indeed, the city was no easy place to be but a cacophonous environment constantly demanding full attention from those converging on it. Not for a minute could a resident afford to doze off without also risking being hit by a streetcar or a vendor carrying goods across town. Or stepping in a puddle and ruining one's dress. Or, on a slightly different note, but more importantly, relaxing for a day and letting their competition ruin their chances at a job. Everyone had to be on high alert, now actively engaged in a Darwinian struggle to be among the fittest just to survive. The fight was not without its impact on the mental interior of the individual. "With every crossing of the street," writes Georg Simmel in "The Metropolis and Mental Life," "with the tempo and multiplicity of economic, occupational and social life– [the metropolis] creates in the sensory foundations of mental life . . . a deep contrast with the slower, more habitual, more smoothly flowing rhythm of the sensory-mental phase of small town and rural existence."[34] Whereas in the village the individual had been valued for their subjective contribution to the community, in the city they are only a number. What worth they do bring to the table is a function of their ability to enter into a contract between seller and buyer, employer and employee. For their skill they shall earn a certain dollar, and for their dollar a certain purchase. If in the country "all intimate emotional relations between persons are founded in their individuality," in the city they are "reckoned with like a number, like an element which is in itself indifferent." Further, in this urban center "only the objective measurable achievement is of interest."

No individual with half a beating heart could withstand such cold and calculated treatment. They'd have to find a way out, restore at least a modicum of subjectivity to their relationship with the world. In that, they rediscover their dualistic nature all over again, or perhaps for the first time, namely that they have an interior and an exterior and that though they may not have needed to distinguish and mobilize them before in the village, they do need to do so now in the city. Indeed, the fact that we have always had two sides should not come as a surprise, only now they must be resurrected and reinforced to serve a specially divided and contradictory modern world. "The whole of history of society," tells us Simmel in an essay titled "Fashion," "is reflected in the striking conflicts, the compromises, slowly won and quickly lost, between socialistic adaptation to society and individual departure from its demands."

Throughout his work Simmel renders the relationship between the city and the individual inverse; the bigger and more alien the city becomes, the smaller and more distant becomes the individual. Something has to give, and it is the psyche that has to take the brunt of the blow, constantly trying to find a way to repress feelings and desires deemed unsuitable for public life. Sooner or later pathologies begin to make themselves visible in the form of anxieties and disorders which, if not addressed, can manifest themselves in obstacles to living a happy and healthy life. Professional and social relations suffer and with them a meaningful coexistence with family and friends.

Better to start the new rewiring at home, in the safe confines of one's private space first, before going out and exploring the new world alone. Better to sit up and take note and "look like something," to quote Wright. Indeed, Wright would design his chairs to compensate for the lack of physical and mental structure with which Americans had found themselves by the end of the nineteenth century, so that even when they reclined, "seated in that chair [they looked] graceful in spite of [themselves]."

The sleight of hand, conflating domestic furniture with mental furniture, home with criminal reformation, did not go unnoticed, not least by the mas-

---

ter of magic himself, Harry Houdini, who after one of his shows had come upon an exhibit in which the electric chair was on display. Being a connoisseur of clever acts of death and disappearance, but also technology, he purchased the chair and put it in his home, less as a functional piece of furniture and more an index of mental transformation, symbolic of the method and aim of his own profession. It wasn't for naught that the electric chair was known as the "seat of consciousness."

The first electric chair was designed to have three legs, two in the back and one in the front, and this to support a ledge where the legs of the condemned could be gathered and strapped. Whether Wright based his later-three legged chairs on that design is unknown, but the resemblance is interesting. Just as the electric chair had demanded from Americans participation in a world of increased complexity, so Wright's three-legged chairs insisted that Americans enter into an active relation with the environment in which they were a part. Of particular note is the "Swivel Armchair" at the Larkin. Not only was it three-legged, but it was also equipped with a requisite electrocution material feature, a metal backrest made up, in the words of one museum exhibit, of "perforated brown steel."

No actual electricity passed through this chair, of course, but a different kind certainly did, namely a current whose purpose was, in Wright's words, an "emphatic outstanding protest against the tide of meaningless elaboration sweeping the United States." This "furniture was all made of steel and magnesite built into place—even the desks and chairs we made with the building." The Larkin, which we encountered in a previous chapter, was a mail order company whose vision of success was steeped in a blend of Emersonian spirituality and fiscal responsibility. Work was no ordinary task but a method by which the individual could demonstrate commitment to a higher purpose. Even when not underway, work was still part of one's devotion to life and community. Just because the worker may have left her desk did not mean that that person was not working, in this case on matters of character and alignment with the social, professional, and spiritual responsibility of the company. Of particular note in this light is a piece of furniture, also previously mentioned, in which the chair and the desk are attached at the hip, so to speak, the chair hung in the air and pivoted to one side of the desk through a structural swivel (see figure 26, page 189). No sooner did the worker swing out and, say, go to the bathroom, then her place (they were all women) on the chair was "automatically folded back" and her memory retained.

It might be difficult and indeed strange to speak of the electric chair in terms of comfort and human justice, but in fact it was in these terms that the device was conceived. Prior hangings in the gallows had been determined to be inhumane, often ending in gruesome strangulations lasting minutes. Electricity was deemed humane by comparison, in that it was believed (based on tests on animals) that it could eliminate life instantaneously. That that did not happen was tragic and horrible. But the belief remained that electricity zapped through the body was the swiftest and most just way to accomplish what the ending of a life was intended for, namely the destruction of one form of consciousness in favor of the construction or reformation of many others. Wright did not hook up his chairs to electrical outlets, but he did seek in his furniture a way to straighten the backs of Americans and end their apathy.

Conclusion

Mental furniture and actual furniture occupy two very different realities, and yet Wright conflated them, insisting that whereas the latter is material and the former is not, the two are interrelated. To throw furniture around and set up a path is to shape a view and direction that, if maintained, could effect a certain commensurate consciousness in the mind. Change that direction perennially and you could effect a slow but sure transformation of the same. Change the layout every day and we may see a certain lack of orientation in the self, or perhaps a propensity toward randomness. No such control and ease of manipulation can happen through the architecture of walls and windows alone; those are just too cumbersome and slow to impact psychological transformation. A better way is through furniture, which can go in either direction, heavy and slow, or on wheels and fast. Wright employed both, for different effects and for different clients and cultures, sometimes to impress upon us and his audience the need for place, other times for motion and instability.

We may liken it to dual paths in the city, A and B. Path A offers exposure to homelessness, path B to opulence and wealth. You are interested in pointing out the debilitating effects of homelessness to a local politician so you choose path A, presumably not merely to make the politician feel bad but also to reveal the source of the problem. Driving randomly across town won't do, necessarily diluting the effects of the problem. A more poignant plan would be necessary, narrowing driving options to certain paths, perhaps ones that implicate the business community or the local government. Add to that the need to make homelessness a national problem and that path may all of a sudden need to take a detour across local national monuments, including local federal structures from whose policies the problem may have emanated.

And so, Wright went about organizing furniture to achieve those kinds of ends, often relying on the method of contraction and expansion, mentioned earlier in the book and for which he was always famous, to get where he wanted. And because furniture is low and does not go all the way up to ceiling, it could compress and expand space in ways that are far more complex than just walls and doors, doing for one part of the body what it cannot do for the other and vice versa, making sitting and standing, bending and moving more than what they seem, but a complex component of the dynamic of being in place. Between dining and lounging there is a difference of posture, and then again between bathing and reading, which, when played against each other, turn the self into a synthesis of opposites, rich and diverse. Going through Wright's buildings and specifically his homes, it is hard not to feel directed, turned this way and then that, first to see the tree but then the kitchen, the planter and then the bedroom, the table and then the bench, and so on, all eventually resolved into a singular space of mental formation.

6

THE GUGGENHEIM &
THE PHYSICS OF
CONTINUITY

The natural world may be conceived of as a system of concentric circles,
and we now and then detect in nature slight dislocations which apprise
us that this surface on which we now stand is not fixed but sliding.
—R. W. EMERSON, "Circles"

N arratives on the Guggenheim often start with the letter from Hilla Rebay to Wright in 1943 inviting him to come to New York and talk about
a new building design for nonobjective art. The tone is strangely casual, as if the two had been friends for a long time. "Could you ever come to
New York and discuss with me a building for our collection of non-objective
paintings?" she opened. Rebay was of course the painter and baroness especially handpicked by the industrialist Solomon Guggenheim to lead the effort
toward finding a home for his six to eight hundred paintings collected in this
genre. Rebay and Solomon had known each other since the late 1920s, when
Solomon's wife purchased paintings from the artist. Why Rebay thought
Wright would know much about nonobjective art is not clear, but what is
certain is that she wanted a daring architect, "a fighter and a lover of space,"
and thought Wright would be the one who could achieve those aims. She had
consulted with European architects about the project, even asking László
Moholy-Nagy, the Hungarian and onetime faculty member at the Bauhaus,
to draw up a list of potential architects. Which he did and which included the
likes of Le Corbusier, Walter Gropius, Marcel Breuer, and Richard Neutra, all

of whom were European and unsuitable for a place and a time in which the choice of who built where was of utmost importance. It was a time of war, 1943, and scarcely anyone was building anything except maybe public housing for veteran soldiers and their families. The architect who would design the Guggenheim had to be carefully considered, preferably an American and preferably a maverick and a visionary.

Wright did not know anything about nonobjective art, nor did he care much for European art in general, at one point calling it degenerate. Picasso and Duchamp he particularly thought twisted.[1] His allegiances to art were almost altogether drawn toward Asian and particularly Japanese art. And yet he took the commission to design the Guggenheim anyway—for economic reasons for sure but also those that had to do, no doubt, with a clear overlap between his mission in life and that articulated by the priests of nonobjective art. Both emanated from a desire to restore to man a spiritual purpose. "Non-objectivity is the religion of the future," Rebay had written in a catalog on nonobjective art, as well as that "non-objective paintings are prophets of spiritual life."[2] Wright said more or less the same thing, at one point indicating that art "isn't something up here at all," pointing at his head, "but an expression of inner experience." And then adding that "to be a real master of these subjective objectives, you have to live them and it takes many years of conscientious abnegation, subordination, to really get into that interior life of the spirit."[3]

Wright's response to the call for "a temple of spirit," to use Rebay's words again, was to design a spiral, an ancient form steeped in spiritual symbolism. He had previously tested it with projects such as the "Automobile Objective" in Maryland and the V. C. Morris store in San Francisco, but he hadn't quite manifested it at the scale of a whole museum. This was his opportunity to do so, and as we know, the rest was history. The question is, what does it mean? What was Wright thinking when he not only proposed the spiral but inverted it upside down, the top now heavier than the bottom instead of the other way around, as traditional ziggurats had come down to us throughout history? He would come to call the result "an optimistic ziggurat," presumably in reference to the way, among other things, it defied gravity. The spiral was much ridiculed in its day and since, some calling it a "washing machine," others a "windup toy" and so on, all rightfully so and for the good reason that anything this loud and different inevitably results in an image larger than the content it seeks to contain, a surplus visual value that naturally overwhelms our interest and indeed our ability to reach beyond what we see. And yet this chapter seeks to do just that, to reach beyond the image and see in the spiral a meaning and a purpose beyond the form. It will piece together data from Wright and others, including the creators of nonobjective art, and propose a reading, among other readings, of the spiral as an instrument of science, ridding man of his deterministic side in favor of something much deeper than that, so deep, in fact, that the mind has nothing to do with it. In this world and in this experiment, there is nothing to determine, only something to realize. For too long man had been forced to manufacture constructs less because they reflect a core belief and more because they help him navigate moral and ethical standards set by others. Try to violate those expectations and the risks could be great, even fatal. Better keep the facade of propriety going, which, while built on deception, staves off disaster. Indeed, man had assembled a whole educational system based on this mind-set, namely, to teach him how to design and build this facade, becoming in effect the master of deception. It was time to reverse course, to "divest [man] of the conditioning [he has] received instead of the enlightenment which should have been [his.]"[4] Wright's version of the Enlightenment doesn't belong to the late eighteenth century but lies at the core of man's being, for no "books" or "scientific theories" will ever save him unless he is able to aim beyond the surface and reach down for the truth within himself. "[H]e who is not true himself will not see the truth as it is taught by nature," says Paracelsus, quoted by Wright at the outset of *The Living City,* the architect's third and last book on Broadacre City, the subject of chapter 4 of this book. The question was how to probe that deep.

Toward a Belief in Atomic Energy

The answer for Wright lay, in part, in physics, which may sound strange given his repeated attacks on science throughout his life. In *When Democracy Builds,* for instance, the second of the three books on Broadacre City, he accuses science of "forestall[ing] a genuine culture of our own," calling it arrogant. Emerson had taught him well, arguing against the reduction of life and ideas to narrow facts. In focusing too much on minutiae science, Emerson believed, one loses perspective on what drives humanity forward, fuels its passions, and compels it to look for meanings. "It is not so pertinent to man to know all the individuals of the animal kingdom," he writes in *Nature,* "as it is to know whence and whereto is this tyrannizing unity in his constitution, which evermore separates and classifies things, endeavoring to reduce the most diverse to one form."[5] Science is a hindrance precisely because it seeks answers in methods premised on division and compartment, and that can't be good. No, Emerson won't go there. "I cannot greatly honor minuteness in details, so long as there is no hint to explain the relation between things and thoughts; no ray of *metaphysics* of conchology, of botany, of the arts, to show the relation of the forms of flowers, shells, animals, architecture, to the mind, and build science upon ideas."[6]

Science was fine so long it was built on ideas and not the other way around, which, if so, could stifle and co-opt thought. Indeed, Emerson remained tenacious in his vigil against letting science run the show and reduce the world to the narrow pursuits of empirical truths, not because these truths were bad or inaccurate but because they inevitably lacked the means with which to see the world in a complex way. They were two-dimensional and void of, in his words, "sufficient humanity." And yet to say that Emerson disliked science or in any way campaigned against it would be to speak untruths. He in fact often relied on it to explain a message and make clear the extent to which its trajectory was important and self-evident. Here he is explaining the importance of the Civil War, which while awful and tragic was necessary because it broke loose the old and unjust order in favor of a new and more equitable one. It "passes the power of all chemical solvents," he says, "breaking up the old adhesions and allowing the atoms of society to take a new order."[7] In "Farming," an essay that Wright cut-and-pasted and added to the end of his *Living City,* Emerson makes the farmer, whom he treasures, synonymous with science: "He takes the pace of seasons, plants and chemistry." Just like nature, the farmer "never hurries [but] atom by atom, little by little [he] achieves [his] work."[8]

And so, just as it would be wrong to render Emerson's relation with science in binary terms, so it would be a mistake to limit Wright's appreciation of life and ideas to the arts alone. He, too, was damning about science but only to insist that we shouldn't rule by that order alone. Between 1945 and

1946 he went from blaming science for creating a cold and soulless life to singing its virtues and crediting it with contributing to "a new expansion of human life on earth." Standing in front of a group of Unitarians, ready to sell them his ideas for a new church in Madison, Wisconsin, he gave atomic science the highest appraisal, calling it a "liberat[or]." "Universal Atomic power looms ahead of all present day institutions to render them all obsolete," he said right off the bat. "Looms not so much [as] a danger as an expansion of human life on earth." He implored his audience to accept the new age: "The church must accept atomic energy as the new power of construction."[9] So convinced was Wright of this new turn of events in physics that he was basically ready to anoint it the new religion of the age. The church members in attendance neither asked for nor were particularly interested in hearing about nuclear science, but here they were being schooled on recent development in world events. No doubt, the fact that two atomic bombs had just been dropped to end a devastating war must have contributed to Wright's decision to speak with enthusiasm about atomic energy, but doing so to a group of religious people was also surely an effort to conflate and unite two forms of disparate powers: science and religion. He was determined to spiritualize what had otherwise come down to us to mean utter destruction, indeed, to channel it toward a constructive and transformative end. In chapter 3 on the sublime, we saw what Wright may have meant by all that, there proposing nuclear power as the energy with which to propel elevators up his "mile high" skyscraper. The idea may have seemed crazy to many, and still does, but Wright wasn't kidding, going so far as to commission the Otis Elevator company to help him study the suggestion and turn it into a reality.

Did Wright's meeting with Einstein effect his change of view? He had first met the genius scientist at La Miniatura in Pasadena, the house he had designed for Alice Millard, and then again later that year in 1931 at the Chicago train station.[10] It is hard to know, for subsequent communications between the two seemed to dwell less on physics per se and more on housing and quality-of-life issues. He did make clear mention of the scientist in *The Natural House,* now looking back at his past work from an aged perspective. Reflecting on how modernity, including advances in science, was breaking loose from old shackles, he reminds us that "architects were no longer tied to Greek space but were free to enter into the space of Einstein."[11] We also do know that Wright was enamored by the physicist, as was Le Corbusier and other architects, repeatedly inviting him and his wife to join him and Olgivanna for a stay at Taliesin, presumably to discuss the intersection of physics and architecture. Either way, what is clear is that Wright from thereon seemed to wish to buy into science in a way he hadn't before. No doubt one of the reasons had to do with the philosophic nature of particle science itself, including those who championed it such as Einstein but also Heisenberg, Niels Bohr, and others of the early twentieth century. It, and they, probed so far down into the human it seemed only inevitable that questions about the nature of existence should surface and demand investigation.

One passage from Wright's oeuvre exemplifies both his enthusiasm and his struggle. It appears at the outset of *The Living City*. He is ready to give science the benefit of the doubt but then again not accept it wholesale. His fidelity still lies in art and religion. Might the two or three seemingly disparate forces of life enter into a mutually beneficial set of support systems? Which should take precedent over which? Science or art? What is the hierarchy between the two? And so here he is: "Salvation depends upon the realization that with science carried far enough and deep enough, we will find great art to be the sure significance of all that science can ever know of life and see that art and religion are valid prophecy of everything science may ever live to convey."[12] This is one heck of a braided sentence, bringing together science, art, and religion, each vying for more room than the next, each unwilling to relinquish too much ground lest the other take over and control the union. But the sentence does make science the first thread in the braid; if only it could be carried far and deep enough, it would reveal what we have always known about art and religion, namely that they are the sole cause of man's purpose and happiness on earth. We need science to probe that far not because it will change the world but simply to validate what we had imagined but could not prove. This way hopefully not a handful of people but an entire population will come along. Once there, "we will find that philosophy to be the science of man from within the man himself."[13]

There was always something quasi-scientific about Wright's organic architecture anyway, always at pains to shed the superfluous in favor of the self-evident and the inner. All those ornaments architects added to their buildings, all the copying and pasting, the incessant clinging to classical forms—all that had to go in favor of solutions that emanate from the depth of things, their very atomic composition. No American architect will ever be able to expand American civilization, Wright said, unless he applies himself "according to his inner vision to develop the integral beauty derived only from self-culture."[14] Only then will "the democratic spirit of man" be realized, his "confusion of communal life" be lifted and give way to "a creative civilization of the ground."[15] It was time to put man in a blender, or, more aptly, a "washing machine," as some had called the Guggenheim spiral, and push the button.

The Physics of the Spiral

It is through that lens that this chapter will proceed, looking at the ramp and the spiral not so much as forms but as an apparatus of centrifuge, turning and spinning and generally inducing man to suspend one form of power in lieu of another, the conscious in lieu of the unself-conscious, the rational over the reflexive. Of Emerson's work, the chapter will rely on two of his essays, "Circles" and "Experience," both of which anticipate the need to understand man at a level well below the surface. Long before the likes of Einstein, Heisenberg, and Bohr were debating the science of quantum mechanics, Emerson was hinting that there was such a thing, not in those terms, of course, but clearly evocative of their role in mining the depths of the human soul. In "Circles" he tells us that "the life of man is a self-evolving circle, which from a ring imperceptibly small, rushes on all sides outwards to new and larger circles, and that without end."[16] Man may remain confined to any one of those circles, but should he be "quick and strong," he can "burst over that boundary on all sides and expand another orbit on the great deep." With enough energy man can have the capacity to not only walk between circles but "burst," namely jump, leapfrog, and transcend the space in between, soon realizing that the surface on which all this is happening isn't "fixed but sliding."

Where "Experience" will prove useful is in describing the role that time plays in understanding the spiral. Wright had described it as belonging "to the science of continuity," which is a term peculiarly central to the lexicon of work by Henri Bergson and his effort to describe time as continuous, not separated and distinguished by segments. We do not hold images from the past in distinct containers and pull them out at will but do so with everything else that came before and after. Bergson was an avid reader of Emerson and relied on the sage for insights into the flow of time. Words such as "man is a stream whose source is hidden" must have resonated with him, and he turned them into ideas in books such as *Matter and Memory* and *Duration and Simultaneity*. More on that later in this chapter. But before getting too far into the physics of the ramp, let us go back and look at nonobjective art. What were its aims and to what extent was it the "religion of the future," produced, to quote Rebay, by "the prophets of spiritual life"?

Nonobjective Art

For a long time, art could only be appreciated in terms associated with moral questions. It told stories about good and evil, right and wrong, David and Goliath, demanding that we take sides and chart a moral life accordingly. Persons fell and rose under the weight of monarchies, but also of religious orders and oppressive ideological regimes. Gravity bore down on the human with a ton of force, at times crushing him or her completely. Some held on for dear life; others turned away with shame and disgust. Light and dark were played against each other to either point out or hide unspeakable transgressions. Transgress like that, objective art warned, and you, the observer, shall suffer similar destiny. Nothing could the observer do without also being followed by a wagging finger, warning of consequences and of things to come should he follow a wayward path. Do this, don't do that. How stressful. No wonder the Victorians hid behind thick curtains and closed their doors.

Impressionism and cubism tried to lighten things up, remaining attached to moral questions but in ways that made it clear that those questions were much hazier than ever before, less determined by sharp distinctions in either politics or religion. But attached they still were, still testing human judgment even if the world against which those decisions were made had become looser and indeterminate. Nonobjective art ventured further, cutting the umbilical cord once and for all, dissolving the link between cause and effect, object and reason. For its authors the human had become too rationalized, so guarded that nothing remained but psychological armor. What spirit the previous human had cultivated, the modern world now tamped down or, worse, castrated. In his politically charged novel *It Can't Happen Here,* Sinclair Lewis describes the effect as one of having created in the citizen, in this case the American citizen, a "pious façade," and a resignation to the idea that all he can do is playact. His main character, Doremus Jessup, cannot find solace in "having lost his old deep pride in being an American." He must sit back and enjoy the show or what Lewis likens to "a stage revival of an equally lovely and familiar Elizabethan play."

To restore man to himself, his rational side had to be decommissioned in favor of something that was unself-conscious, automatic. Where objective art insisted that we see our plight in the image of those represented, non-objective art wiped that away. It asked that we see the image for what it is, independent of moral judgment. Shapes came with neither rule nor order but were simply shapes, neither beginning nor ending but merely floating as circles and triangles, on the left or right of the canvas. The same with lines; they, too, could start and stop any moment, intersect, interrupt or violate any other line, and no one would be better or worse for it. Everything just coasted, as if on a puff of cloud, slowly migrating from one section of the canvas to the next. In the words of Peter Selz: "lines, shapes colors, planes etc.," all hung in there "without reference to anything outside the canvass."[17]

Not even nature was allowed in, for it, too, had become too implicated in modern man's struggle toward progress and meaning. "The observer of today," said Kandinsky, considered the father of nonobjective art and a friend of Rebay, "is seldom capable of feeling [deep] emotions. He seeks in a work of art a mere imitation of nature which can serve some definite purpose or a presentment of nature according to certain convention or some inner feeling expressed in terms of natural forms."[18] Indeed, by the mid-nineteenth century, man had fully co-opted nature to serve his productive and spiritual needs, in effect replacing God as the link to a higher order. No, nature could no longer be relied on to play the role of a neutral agent. It had to stay out of the picture, better replaced by abstract compositions of lines and circles, arcs and triangles, but also color and light, altogether less faithful to rational arguments than to self-evident phenomena like math and physics, electrons and photons.

Specifically, what the nonobjective artists were after was the suspension of gravity, or at least the altering of its course. For too long it had pinned the individual down to laws he or she neither knew nor agreed with but simply followed. "Our minds," said Kandinsky, "which are even now only just awakening after years of materialism, are infected with the despair of unbelief, of lack of purpose and ideal." The nightmare "had turned the life of the universe into an evil, useless game, hold[ing] the awakening soul still in its grip." In the first decade of the twentieth century, at around the same time that Kandinsky and his nonobjective colleagues were exploring gravity, scientists were doing the same in physics. Not since Newton in the seventeenth century had gravity been examined as a contributor to physical laws and the way they shape movement and relational realities. But even Newton had to throw his arms up and accept gravity as a given, a black box of sorts that we knew impacted existence but did not know how or why. Albert Einstein changed that, insisting that gravity, while constant and invisible, can be measured and examined. The task required delving into a realm well beyond what the eye can see, even with the best and most powerful ocular equipment. And yet this was worthwhile, not least because it could help us understand ourselves at the molecular level.

Even before Kandinsky and "before Arthur Dove, who ventured into abstraction not long after Kandinsky, and who was followed in short order by Robert Delaunay, Frantisek Kupka, and Francis Picabia,"[19] there was Hilma af Klint, the Swedish artist of Wright's age, born in 1862 and dying in 1944. Before Kandinsky she had lit the world on fire when she proposed a link between consciousness and cosmic order. She had studied at Stockholm's Royal Academy of Fine Arts but soon took an interest in theosophy and Rosicrucianism. By the first decade of the twentieth century she was fully immersed in nonobjective art, drawing on exploration in physics and biology to explore her own interest in mind expansion and reality. She was particularly drawn to the theory of evolution and the atom, as forms of vital energy whose locomotion naturally and inevitably led to higher realms of spirituality. Of a series she painted in 1907, she said that they "were painted directly through me, without any preliminary drawings and with great force" and that she "had no idea what the paintings were supposed to depict" or whether they were guided by "the High Lords of the Mysteries" but knew only "that . . . they [the Mysteries] were always standing by my side." Might there be a side of her that lay beyond the ability of the conscious mind to grasp? she wondered. As one scholar said of her work, it had "cosmic aura" and, much like "a revelation of spirit," had its essence "beyond the visible world." In one series, called the *Primordial Chaos*, af Klint explored the creation of the physical world, at first unified but soon spiraling out of control and forming male and female energies. "These works are full of spirals of energy and sparks of creation of symbols of fertility and rebirth," says Efi Michalarou.[20] Af Klint, who had imagined her work exhibited in "a spiral temple," finally got her wish in October 2018, when the Guggenheim put up a show of her work titled *Hilma af Klint: Paintings for the Future*, featuring, among other series, a series on the atom, curious and interesting for our purposes in this chapter.[21]

Whether Kandinsky knew of af Klint or not is uncertain, but he, too, was affected by the discovery of the atom and, more specifically, "the division" of it. He had been a lawyer, and like all lawyers won or lost cases based on the ability to make clear and sound rational distinctions. Between one step and the next there had to be linear analysis, one step making the next clear and necessary. The "collapse of the atom" would alter his direction. "The collapse of the atom was equated in my soul with the collapse of the whole world," he said at one point in his *Reminiscences*. "Suddenly, the strongest walls crumbled. Everything became uncertain, precarious and insubstantial." It was shortly thereafter, around 1909, that he started creating paintings whose content would emerge "chiefly unconscious[ly], and in which there would "suddenly [arise] expressions of events of an inner character, hence impressions of 'internal nature.'"[22] The worlds of physics, art, and spirituality seemed to converge on a singular spot, and it was the likes of Kandinsky and af Klint who felt the need to use their skill and sensitivity to develop it into an art form.

Besides mass and distance, Einstein added acceleration to his explorations, namely that to measure and understand gravity, it was necessary to subject mass to a change of speed. A man seated inside, say, a cargo compartment moving at constant speed feels neither motion nor gravity and might as well be stationary. But accelerate the car and the same man will feel his body push back against the seat. Tilt that compartment ninety degrees and shoot it up like a rocket and the impact of gravity will be felt, no longer an abstract given but one that has measure and quality. Pressed against the seat, the body deforms, temporarily shrinking in size and acquiring a shape different from that of its normative and stationary condition. The difference would result in nothing less than Einstein's transformative theory of general relativity and a new understanding of space as fabric and warp.

In his *Elegant Universe*, Brian Greene explains the theory using an example familiar to most of us from visits to amusement parks over the years, a ride called the "Tornado." Cylindrical in form and usually made of thick Plexiglas, it spins at high speed, causing those lined around its interior cylindrical wall to push out and get plastered against that wall, demonstrating the power and operations of centripetal forces. Rather than a rocket shooting up into space, this example, which apparently resembles the same apparatus Einstein used to come up with his own findings, works with circular rather than linear velocity. Greene asks two fictional individuals to jump into the ride. He names one Slim, the other Jim, placing the first at the perimeter, the second at the center. He then asks "Slim and Jim, who are currently enjoying a spin on the Tornado, to take few measurements for us" with the intention of comparing them with those taken when the ride was not moving. He tosses "one of our rulers to Slim, who sets out to measure the circumference of the ride, and another to Jim, who sets out to measure the radius." Because of the spin of the ride and the way Slim is measuring along the circumference and against the direction at which the ride is moving, the ruler contracts. Which makes it smaller. A shorter ruler results in a longer circumference measurement. The change, however, does not translate to Jim and his measurement of the radius. His "ruler is not pointing along the instantaneous direction of the motion" and as such remains the same as before. Between measurements taken under spin and those taken under no spin, there is a discrepancy, resulting in warped space between the two. "Just as the warped or curved mirror in an amusement park fun-house distort the normal spatial relationships of your reflection," explains Greene, so will the difference between the two measurements "also be distorted."

Warped space describes the change gravity assumed when it went from Newton to Einstein. If under Newton gravity was given and largely outside man's capacity to scrutinize, under Einstein it would become rather elastic and complicit in man's quest for change and self-determination. The spin ride did not just make possible the tenets of gravity; it also pointed out that in doing so the direction of gravity had changed, from the vertical to the horizontal. Spin the ride at high speed, in fact, and you could do away with

FIG. 35. *Composition VIII*, by Vasily Kandinsky, 1923, Solomon R. Guggenheim Museum, New York. The Solomon R. Guggenheim Foundation / Art Resource, NY.

the floor altogether. Indeed, at high speed Slim, in the example above, could pick himself up and walk on the walls of the ride, as if suspended in midair and without a single care in the world. Ask him to open and close his eyes and report on what he sees, now looking down on the spokes of the wheel, and he may very well register random lines and objects suspended in midair. The image in all likelihood will resemble Kandinsky's *Composition VIII*, a permanent part of the Guggenheim collection, which, as a set of geometric non sequiturs engulfed in a yellowish haze, itself resembles either the workings of outer space or the inner mind, or both (fig. 35). At that speed, the brain simply can't register reality as cause and effect, only sensation, or, in Kandinsky's terms, pure "emotion."

By the early 1920s, the general theory of relativity and its new and powerful assessment of gravity began to give rise to theories about the formation of the earth and the beginning of life. Now that gravity was understood less as this passive glue with which the universe was held and more the active force critical to the shaping of everything, including who we are, it was believed that it could be used to trace back the origins of time. Among the first to take interest was the Jesuit priest Georges Lemaitre, who, according to Brian Greene in *Until the of End of Time*, "used Einstein's newly minted description of gravity to develop the radical idea of a cosmos that began with a bang and has been expanding ever since."[23] Gravity did not just cause contraction as it had traditionally been thought to do under Newton; it also caused expansion. "According to the general theory of relativity," Greene tells us, "the gravitational force can be repulsive." He adds that, "according to Einstein's equations, big clumsy things like stars and planets exert the usual attractive version of gravity, but there are exotic situations in which the gravitational force can drive things apart."[24] As the original rock shrunk under intense heat and finally blew up, it sent rock debris scattering all around the universe. Around "some fourteen billion years ago," Greene continues, "the entire observable universe was compressed into a stupendously hot, incredibly dense nugget, which then rapidly expanded." He gives the process a name, calling it an "entropic two step," first pulling in and then pushing out, back and forth, again and again. Much like a mother who sends her child to school at the outset of the day but only to yearn for her at the end, so is the universe in constant gravitational cycles of push and pull.

The Guggenheim's spiral is no different, on the one hand, pulling the individual inward to look at the void just inside the ramp, along with the art across the way, but on the other, pushing him or her outward and toward the art hung on the outer wall. To know that this tension is true, we need only look at the latter wall, splayed and pushed out and hanging for dear life, lest it might fly away, as it were (fig. 36). Indeed, if it weren't for the ramp floor to which it is attached, this outer wall would conceptually depart the scene. Having been subjected to intense centripetal gravitational forces, it had nowhere to go but obey the laws of physics, ready to break away and fly out, not unlike the forces that triggered the big bang. Wright had a different explanation, which we will address later in the chapter, but for now it would be good to note that thinking of the ramp and the spiral in cosmic terms had been on Wright's mind for some time, at least since the 1920s, when he first tested them in the design for the so called "Automobile Objective," considered by many to be the predecessor of the Guggenheim.

FIG. 36. Exterior of the Solomon R. Guggenheim Museum, New York, 1959. Note the outer walls of the spiral; they slant as they curve up and down. Photograph courtesy of Mark Hertzberg.

Commissioned by a wealthy businessman named Gordon Strong in 1924, the "Automobile Objective" was "to serve as an objective for short motor trips on the part of residents of the vicinity," in this case, Washington, DC, and Baltimore, the site being located between the two on Sugarloaf Mountain in Maryland. There is much to tell about the project, but for our purposes here what is important is the fact that it, like the Guggenheim, was defined by a spiral ramp, not for people but for cars. Even more prescient for us is that within the void of the ramp Wright inserted a planetarium, making it clear that the emphasis we as a society were going to place on motion and cars had to be informed or at least framed through the lens of new and emerging investigations into modern gravity and the big bang theory. In the words of one scholar, the planetarium "made the project a kind of cosmic center, both metaphorically and literally. Like all domes, the planetarium suggested the vault of the sky, and it created an actual representation of the heavens."[25] Where prior to Einstein, talk about and interest in the planet and the cosmos had been either nonexistent or limited to a narrow cadre of physicists, now it became the source of public fascination, and a deep-seated query into who we are and where we came from. What new inventions we were contemplating, Wright insisted that we do so with an eye and a sense for the larger picture.

In another setting, this time closer to the development of atomic energy and the atomic bomb in 1945, we see Wright invoking the science and dynamic of the big bang to explain the rebooting of American living. The city had become at once exploitative and self-destructive, and it was only a matter of time before it exploded. Just like the nugget that Greene talked about above, the city had become intensely hot, made so not least literally by open furnace factories, but also, socially and economically, by a "rent" system, to use Wright's term, that allowed the financial class to sap the energy of the labor sector. The complaint is familiar by now, but Wright uses it to explain the need for the return to the countryside and the emergence of Broadacre City. Centripetal forces must give way to centrifugal, centralization to expansion. In Wright's words, the city had "[wound] space up tighter and tighter," which like a "centripetal device revolving at increasing speed" had become "terrible beyond control" resulting in a "centrifugal [force] ending all by dispersal or explosion."[26] Indeed, Broadacre is not just any other agrarian place but one on whose soil consciousness was born for the first time, to follow Wright's thinking, in this big bang reaction to the city. Anything before was mere matter, a nugget without feeling for pain or happiness, only particles bouncing around and finally exploding. The title of Wright's first book on Broadacre, *The Disappearing City*, is telling—disappearing precisely because the city blew up and the only remnant we have of it is that which can be explored and examined through history and science.

Man in Wheelchair

In the early stages of the design for the Guggenheim and in his excitement for the ideas swirling in his head, Wright writes to Rebay to explain that the museum "should be one extended expansive well-proportioned floor space from bottom to top—a wheel chair going around and up and down, *throughout*."[27] Wright can't contain himself, nor can he wait to put things down on paper, which is understandable, given the prominence and location of the project. But "wheel chair"? Why a wheelchair, a reference normally invoked in relation to accessibility, and not in matters of early artistic conceptions? What did Wright have in mind?

Wright, of course, did not mention the wheelchair to draw attention to a certain group of occupants. That wouldn't happen until much later in the century, culminating in the passage of a major building code, the ADA, in 1989, that would make access into and out of buildings by people of disability a matter of law. Instead, Wright proposed the prosthetic as a means with which to drive home the theory of continuity and the need to kick from underneath Americans the legs that had for too long determined where they went and how they experienced the world. More on the theory of continuity later, but for now it is critical to note, through Wright, that Americans, as we've seen throughout, had become so beholden to forces outside themselves that they did not know who they were anymore. Were they still human, animals, robots? They certainly did not have say in much. It was time to return them to their senses, based less in rational thinking and more in particles lying, or, more accurately, spinning, deep inside their human body. If legs are guided by the mind and its system of cognitive hierarchies, structured around fears and notions of self-interest, telling the legs what to do and where to go, particles answer to no such diktats but to rules and operations central to the laws of physics and chemistry. To set them in motion, something other than the ordinary had to happen, something to push and pull at them on their own terms and less on ours. Particles do not respond to our desire to pick them up like we pick up soccer balls, or scoop them or in any way cradle them. But they do respond to forced gravity, which when kicked into gear through spin can be amplified to trigger motion and separation at the nuclear level. In the lab, the experiment would be handled through centrifuge and through machines by that name, which, according to one manufacturer, is a "device that is used for the separation of fluids, gas or liquid, based on density." It works by "by spinning a vessel containing material at high speed [creating] a centrifugal force [that] pushes heavier materials to the outside of the vessel."[28] In architecture something of the same has to happen to separate man the particle from man the overzealous and self-conscious thinker, which Wright achieves by letting the floor of the Guggenheim slip and then turn.

A flat floor won't do, not least because gravity has no reason to spike and effect change at that level. Keep the floor flat in fact and the wheelchair remains a conversation about human disability at the social, political, and, indeed, moral level. But tilt it and the wheelchair will inevitably go flying, the person in it now needing to contend with forces that are decidedly less social and political and more gravitational. Turn the floor in a circle and matters become that much more precarious, even dangerous. What had been rational and measured gives way to automatic and reflexive reactions, resembling those examined at the particles level than, say, those experienced between citizens in civic discourse. The time traveler in H. G. Wells's classic novel *The Time Machine* can vouch for that, he, too, at one point realizing that he had become less a block of self-consciousness and more a bunch of atoms. Having sent himself flying across time at high speed, he found himself at one point feeling "attenuated," slowly but surely "slipping like vapour through interstices and intervening substances." The faster he went, the more molecular he became, now able to jam himself, like "atoms[,] into such intimate contact with . . . obstacles that a profound chemical reaction [could] result and blow" everything up, including his machine, "into the [great] unknown." If only Wright could send Americans at speed down the spiral ramp, with the help of the wheelchair, he might, just might, force them to relinquish ties with material obsessions and reach a state of pure existence.

Wright's gripe with the critics of the Guggenheim, including Rebay, is legendary, all of whom insisted that the curved and sloping walls on the exterior of the spiral were simply impractical as background against which to display art. And of course they were right. How exactly should a curator hang a flat piece of canvas on a wall that does not only curve but splays out? The problem seemed obvious and, to those trying to argue against it, exacerbating. And yet Wright insisted on keeping it, not least to consummate the experiment he started when he sat Americans in a wheelchair and sent them rolling and spinning down the spiraling ramp. There, again, he had wanted to denude them of their conscious power in lieu of one which lies at the core of their being, untrammeled by social judgment and political correctness. A power, in fact, so pure it predates them, and even though they possess it, they know neither where nor whence it came. To connect the two, Americans and their inner core, a special architecture had to be set up, loyal less to the rules of composition and space and more to equipment found in labs, such as centrifuges, as mentioned above, decoupling particles from each other. Those who cynically called the Guggenheim a "washing machine" weren't too far off, in this case separating not water from cloth but Americans from their social consciousness. And so having been spun, the spiral ramp at the Guggenheim must now splay out, not because the architect wants them to but because the laws of gravity, of push and pull, demand that they do. And with that the exclusion of art as well. Indeed, art is too heavy, too representational, and thus too associated with moral baggage, which once under the spell of spin gravity has to be pushed out. To conduct the experiment properly, to get to the bottom of man's core, all aspects of human representation must cease, at least for the duration of the experiment. Let the critics say what they want, the matter is out of anyone's hand, including Wright's. The walls of the spiral must push out.

Wright's ramp is an apparatus not unlike that which Karen Barad talks about when she invokes the work of Niels Bohr in her book *Meeting the Universe Halfway*. "The lesson that Bohr takes from quantum physics is very deep and profound," she says. "There aren't little things wandering aimlessly in the void that possess the complete set of properties that Newtonian physics assumes," she adds. "Rather, there is something fundamental about the nature of measurement interactions such that, given a particular measuring apparatus, certain properties become determinate, while others are specifically excluded."[29] That the design of the Guggenheim ramp must exclude art and all matters representational, in other words, is not an indictment of Wright, but a matter of commitment to a particular experiment and a particular moment in history. Once underway the experiment cannot be stopped, nor its design changed, lest the integrity of its results be compromised. When Wright writes Rebay to reprimand her for being spineless in her incapacity to stay the course in the face of pushback against the spiral, he does not so much defend the design of the ramp as lament her willingness to cut and indeed abort the experiment underway: "Surely you have not failed so completely to grasp the essential idea with which you were so completely delighted when presented to you as you now pretend."[30] Just as you can't run an experiment meant for the microscope with a telescope, so you can't do the same at the

Guggenheim with straight walls when they should be splayed. The results would just not be true. Rather, they'd be compromised.

The ramp warps as it slips and curves from one level to the next, marking the difference in measurement, as we saw, between premodern and modern gravity, the first under stationary circumstance, the next, speed and acceleration. So far so good, and yet not much happens until the man, or woman, in the wheelchair travels full circle and finds his or her opposite on the other side, now one level down. The warp of the ramp becomes his/her warp, now internalized by them as the difference between the two sides of their interior, the conscious and the unself-conscious, or the moral and the particle. It is here that they realize that they are a bifurcated self, on the one hand a viewer seeing art in the round and in panorama, on the other, buried in the weeds and viewing art up close. Back and forth in a downward cycle of self and self-affirmation. What one part of the self may suffer from reading art too closely, the other corrects by insisting on seeing the same piece of art from a distance. "A characteristic experience of the museum," says Stan Allen in his account of the Guggenheim, "is the pleasure of an unexpected and often unfamiliar new vista of a work just seen, from across the void."[31] Indeed, as the two selves spin about each other, they not only keep vigil and protect, they also see what the other cannot see alone. They see an "unfamiliar new vista," namely potential which when captured can keep the two parts of the self healthy and forever engaged in the act of self-renewal. The idea is not to unite the selves but to keep them forever active and aware, for no matter how narrow the spiral gets, its opposite sides getting closer and closer to each other, it can never close. Zeno's paradox of "finite size" already told us so: so long we can divide entities in half, they can never come to naught.

Barad is again instructive here. At one point she points out Bohr's query into the problem of intention. Seemingly self-evident and straightforward, intentions for Bohr were anything but. In our normative use of the word, we tend to think of intentions as prepackaged thoughts, held up somewhere in the mind, to be discharged whenever decisions are at stake. But do we really know where they come from, the nature of their structure and so on? Doesn't the matter require an intention of its own, taking time away from daily concerns and examining what our intentions are? Yes, says Barad through Bohr;

it requires an "attempt to observe your own thoughts," namely the "intentions concerning the thing you're thinking about." Indeed, she continues, "we can then deduce that there is a reciprocal or complementary relationship between thinking about something and knowing your intentions." Standing on the ramp at the Guggenheim and looking down across the void you first see what you are about to see, in few moments, but from a bigger picture, a wider frame. From that height and angle the art you will encounter shortly is seen through the lens of a wider spectrum of artworks, perhaps even blended by the very fluidity and continuity of the ramp. Nothing is about one thing from that perspective, but about a diverse many things. Up close things are different, more personal and more demanding of our attention and judgment. There the art must speak to us and we back to it, each claiming a degree of sovereignty over the other. If it hadn't been for our bifurcated self having watched over us, our intentions would be of a certain kind, perhaps stymied, premature, and narrow. But given the observer-observed duality set in motion before us, we are likely to vet and mine the source of our intentionality.

Barad talks about performance, namely that for her "reality" is neither established by objective science nor by subjective interpretation but by performing that which we seek to understand. Which means that to understand intentionality we'd have to perform the dance, so to speak, necessary that would allow us to unpack its dynamics. The spiral at the Guggenheim enacts that performance or more accurately puts us on a conveyor belt with which we can do that on our own. Unique and of interest is the fact that the ramp does not spiral once but over the course of six floors, making it evident that the observer and the observed in us do not play out their reciprocity once but several times. Which means that by the third or fourth go-around their roles may very well travel in reverse, the observed anticipating the observer's vigil and providing its own corrective measure in reply. Even as the man in the wheelchair may be heading down the spiral, an eddy of sorts forms inside his head, say about halfway down the ramp, complicating matters, and making his self-awareness just a matter of forward movement as backward. Indeed, it is entirely possible that consciousness does not begin to form until that eddy begins its counterflow in the opposite direction, upward and in defiance of Newtonian classical gravity.

Pauli's Spin Psychology

Spin physics and psychology found an interesting intersection in Wolfgang Pauli, the Austria physicist who in the 1920s sought to adapt studies of atoms to those of psychic energy. Electrons he had determined operated dualistically, spinning about each other and keeping each other and the life of the atom tight and intact. That the spinning was less geometric than it was mathematical did not matter; what did matter was Pauli's conception of it as a kind of dance between two people. What one dancer does drives the other to move equally back in the other direction, until a kind of mutual magnetic bond arises between the two. Pauli's spin equation says as much, which, in the words Chris Hardy, "states that the spins of a pair of particles must always be complementary; thus if one rotates to the right, the other rotates to the left."[32]

Might discoveries at the atomic level explain development swirling inside the mind? Might theories in quantum mechanics help us grapple with mental leaps, in dreams, thoughts, and meditation? Pauli would come to collaborate with Carl Jung, the psychoanalytic giant of the time, on these matters, starting by examining his own dreams and understanding of himself. Pauli's first goal was "to get a dialogue with his own self, via his anima," triggering what Jung called "the individuation process—the progressive harmonization between one's ego and one's self." Just as the electron was self-driven by its opposite, so the self, under this theory, had to bifurcate itself into two just so that it could ultimately become whole again, each side serving in a kind of supervisory role to monitor the flow and progress of the other. Between the two there is "oscillation," back and forth, switching roles and keeping the dynamic of hierarchies in balance. Contraction and expansion, recalling Greene's description of the big bang, is how Hardy, the author of *The Cosmic DNA*, puts it. "The dream of the contracting and expanding space," he tells us, "begins with Pauli's anima, starting to oscillate."[33] Which is quite baffling, not least because "material physics properties and soul qualities" occupy two different realms and as such are calibrated against two different forms of measurements. And yet here was Pauli exploring a synthesis of the two, believing that "through oscillation, the anima influences the very geometry and dynamics of space." The process "is non-linear, triggering a 'bifurcation' and the emergence of a novel global organization."[34]

On Vertigo

Back on earth, we may look to Alfred Hitchcock's *Vertigo* for clarity. There the filmmaker takes us on a spin theory of his own, not unlike Pauli's, looking at the nature of man as a bifurcated self. Every character in the movie has an opposite, including Scottie, the leading man, played by James Stewart, who suffers from vertigo. His division is marked by time spent under the spell of vertigo, on the one hand, and that outside vertigo, on the other. There is more than a hint, however, that his vertigo is the product of deceptions inflicted upon him by double-faced people, be it friends, family, or clients. In having to deal with this slippery situation he loses orientation and can't quite figure out here from there, near from far. To correct matters and indeed to triumph over his physiological deficiency, he has to monitor the flow of those with whom he is enmeshed and expose them for what they are. They are at odds with themselves and in being so they have caused damage and destruction to him, and others.

Beside Scottie there is Madeleine, played by Kim Novak. An old friend of Scottie hires him to follow her, on the premise that she is his wife, and monitor her behavior. She exhibits extreme deviancy of her own, an affliction that draws her away from the present moment and unto a different and distant one. The problem is a sham, orchestrated by the friend as part of an elaborate scheme to kill his actual wife. If he could only set things up so that the wife appears to have committed suicide, he could get off scot-free. He needs a witness to see her drop from, say, a high spot atop a tall building, confirming that her death was an act of suicide and not one inflicted by a hideous murderer. He's got just the right person in mind. Scottie is afraid of heights and can only go up so far. What if he sends him up a tower with the supposed wife but only to have him stop halfway and let the supposed wife go on to her demise? Long story short, this is what he does, concocting a clever scheme of seduction and deception to get what he wants. Having seduced and romantically implicated Scottie, the doppelganger proceeds to fake a suicide on the premise that she can't live with herself, now attached to two partners. And so she drags Scottie up a religious steeple to do just that. Scottie chases her but again he can only ascend so far before dizziness sets in. She continues up, but waiting on the top platform is the friend holding the dead wife, whom he throws off the ledge once the fake wife arrives up there. A third of the way down Scottie can only watch the fall take place, through a window alongside the stairs. Between his vertigo and the devastating tragedy, he blacks out.

A medical source describes a person with vertigo as one who has experienced "a sense of spinning and dizziness." Another suggests it is a function of a perceptual lag between vision and the capacity of the brain to comprehend unfamiliar visual fields, leading to a kind of feeling in which the floor seems to be slipping away or falling down. To triumph over that, you'd have to return to the same spot and repeat the visual process again and again. To a concern by a house buyer that the house she is about to buy and which she likes gives her vertigo, a doctor insists that she will get used to it, so long she keeps at it. "Yes you should get used to it," he says, "but there may be certain places in the house you won't be able to focus on for long or you will get a little dizzy."[35] And sure thing, in the movie, Scottie does not triumph over his vertigo until he returns to the spot of the problem and faces it, as it were, square in the face. Interestingly, he doesn't do it alone but by exploiting the very instrument of desire that excited his phobia in the first place. It is the same seductress who had played the role of the fake wife. Having died as the fake wife, she now returns ready to love and be loved all over again, authentically and without masquerade, as herself. No entity triumphs over its weakness unless it comes around full circle, meets its opposite side, and wrestles it down.

The Guggenheim does not cure vertigo but induces it, destabilizing the very ground on which Americans had walked and taken things for granted, including gravity and their place on this earth. No sooner do they arrive at the Guggenheim than the ground underneath them begins to open and turn. What flat land they may have come from is here dropped, slipped, and spun, forcing travel in circles and down a ramp. By the time they go around two or three times they are already dizzy, wherewithal marginalized and now begging for rest, or at least the desire to lie down. Consciousness begins to give way to a lack thereof, designed specifically to reboot the mind. Of help is the low parapet rail, so low that people generally can't stomach to come close. "Afraid of heights?" asks a *New York Times* article. "Don't lean over the 36-inch-tall parapet [at the Guggenheim]—an extraordinarily low barrier that is certainly not up to contemporary building codes—and peer down into the 96-foot atrium beneath the rotunda."[36] You might just lose balance and fall.

Vertigo is one way Kandinsky explains the aims of nonobjective art, with the idea being this: that art should be designed so as to be capable of inducing wooziness, thereby drawing the mind away from one kind of allegiance and to another, from objective to nonobjective spiritual feelings. Kandinsky is particularly fond of the work of the poet Maeterlinck, whose "principal technical weapon" lies in the way he uses words. Not the words themselves but the way he uses them. Of note is the use of repetition, repeating words "twice, three times, or even more frequently, according to the need of the poem," resulting in the intensification of not only "inner harmony" but also the "spiritual properties of the word itself."[37] Further, "frequent repetition deprives the word of its original external meaning," making it less an entity corresponding to a material thing and more a string plucked to trigger a certain vibration with the inner soul. "Even a familiar word like 'hair,'" adds Kandinsky, "if used in a certain way can intensify an atmosphere of sorrow or despair."[38] Spin vertigo and poetic repetition together, round and round the Guggenheim ramp, as it were, and what you might get is something akin to the whirling dervish, who since the thirteenth century has whirled his body in "repetitive circles" in an attempt to abandon his "nafs," or ego, in favor of a more perfect version of himself. He wears a hat made of camel hair and a skirt akin to a white gown which when spun resembles a sphere or a planet. Indeed, when whirling with a group of other whirling dervishes, which is the tradition in the Sufi world of whirling dervishes, he and his cohorts symbolize the cosmos and the "solar System orbiting the sun," as one author tells us, a reminder of the story of the big bang all over again.

On Continuity

In explaining the ramp, Wright referred to it as corresponding to the "science of continuity," a term more loaded than it sounds and one central to the study of time and to notions of "Duration" and "Simultaneity." Bergson made ample use of it in explaining the extent to which there are neither distinct pasts nor distinct presents, but a continuation between the two. Our memories of past events are not the product of thoughts packaged and stored for use later on but very much part of an ongoing process of becoming. "The capital error of associationism," he says in *Matter and Memory*, "is that it substitutes for this continuity of becoming, which is the living reality, a discontinuous multiplicity of elements, inert and juxtaposed."[39] Life is not discontinuous but continuous, in other words, not a set of isolated encounters experienced over time but events that accumulate and nest inside our psychic system. We are who we are precisely because we learn and grow through each moment, each containing, "by reason of its origin, something of what precedes," that moment but "also of what follows." Each moment is thus "impure," a mixture of past and present connections and overlaps. Emerson likens the flow to skating, insisting that we "live amid surfaces and the true art of life is to skate well on them."[40] Live each moment to the fullest, enriched as it were by all the moments that had come before it, and the rest will take care of itself. From there you will see that "five minutes [spent well] today," will be worth just "as much to [you] as five minutes [spent] in the next millennium."[41]

What this meant for Emerson and Wright is a critical opening of oneself to experiences and encounters. Instead of the hierarchies that modernity imposed on us, between boss and bossed, architect and engineer, rich and poor, let us dive headlong into all that comes our way. We are at once plumbers and designers, farmers and factory managers. Even when we may not know the subject, or station in life, let us be open to learning about them. The consequences are far and wide and go beyond professional or economic boundaries. They can impact how we care for each other, spread social justice, and ultimately make the world a better place. "Men live in their fancy," Emerson laments, "like drunkards whose hands are too soft and tremulous for successful labor." Let us have respect for the hour and less for social status: "Without any shadow of doubt, amidst this vertigo of shows and politics, I settle myself ever the firmer in the creed that we should not postpone and refer and wish, but do broad justice where we are, by whomever we deal with, accepting our actual companions and circumstances, however humble or odious, as the mystic officials to whom the universe has delegated as its whole pleasure for us."[42]

In Wright's world, the destruction of barriers would find expression in all sorts of endeavors, most notably perhaps in the way he fashioned education at the Fellowship. First formed in the 1930s in response to the Wall Street Crash of 1929, when architecture commissions had come to a halt, it pried open the architectural curriculum, which, having followed the Beaux-Arts model in Paris for a while, had stifled notions of vision and creativity. No architect could become whole and beneficial that way. Wright had a better idea. To him what mattered more than the skill of design and drawing was character. It was character that gave the skill of design and drawing discipline and meaning. Limit architectural learning to the studio and you'd doom the architect to a narrow vision of life, Wright thought, skilled in the art of understanding standards perhaps, but not so much in expanding the potential of man. To correct the problem, Wright would include in his educational program the building of structures but also milking cows and fixing equipment. "Taliesin," said Wright in his first promotional circular, "aims to develop a well-correlated human being, [currently] lacking in modern education." Nothing was too low or too high for him—all work was honorable if it served the betterment of both self and humanity. To Wright, no "shovel, hoe, or axe" was too menial to carry and use; it was, rather, the source of education in the round, including empathy and sympathy.

Hurtling down the ramp, the man in the wheelchair has no other choice but to break down all these barriers. Between the wheels on his chair and the ramp there is a conspiracy, to lead him down the continuity path and subject him to an experience in which time is no longer compartmentalized but ongoing, nested in him in the form of joys, values, and capacities that defy definition. He is all of a sudden a collection of particles, just like the next person over, no better no worse, capable of anything so long he is willing to take the time and the energy to do those things.

Wright was famous for saying, when asked about his favorite building, that it was "the next one," taking pleasure in the idea that even his own work does not constitute compartmentalized memories but a self-erasing force whose virtue is onward movement. Past projects, however good they are, are only good insofar that they make possible "the next one." They may accumulate and add up, nest and glom on to each other, but not one is so good that it becomes an end in itself. "Everything is good on the highway," says Emerson, not least because by traveling on it at high speed you create turbulence, stirring up air that would otherwise remain stagnant. And that is never healthy. Indeed, "every good quality is noxious if unmixed," adds the sage of Concord. Hybrids are better, more capable of adapting to change, than purebreds.

Car Crash

To better understand why, let's stay on the highway and entertain a car crash. Indeed, let's say a bunch of cars are traveling at normal speed heading to a place of routine destination. Every day they travel this route expecting more or less the same thing, the same traffic, the same turns, and so on. But on this day, something different is underway. New road work is ahead, slowing traffic to a crawl. One driver simply does not see the slowed cars in time and has to slam his brakes to slow down enough so that he doesn't crash into those ahead. Unfortunately, the change is too sudden for the cars behind, resulting in a multicar chain accident, say, five total, each slamming into the one before. What a mess, but for our purposes a productive one. Continuity is what we want to learn from it, each car now acting it out for our intellectual consumption. Swept by continuity, all cars exceed their physical limitations and enter into each other's territory. Neither the Buick nor the Audi is the same anymore, each altered to the point where it cannot be recognized, at least temporarily. Once and for all the "type" is gone, or what Emerson calls "usages." "All good conversation, manners and action," he says, "come from a spontaneity which forgets usages and makes the moment great."[43] Much like the cars which lost their identity when they slammed into each other, so the moment becomes great when not held back by specific plans and expectations. In the case of the cars, the opportunity opens itself up for a new car to emerge, not unlike that in the real world when two companies merge or, better yet, when necessity pushes engineers to think outside the box and turn aircraft into cars or one car into a more efficient version of the previous one.

This is no joke but part and parcel of civilization's greatest attributes. Witness, for instance, the history of transformations of airplanes into cars throughout the twentieth century, for civilian purposes but also those for testing the limits of transportation. The development started before World War I, but "it was between the two world wars where we find the first ex-

FIG. 37. *Inopportune: Stage One,* by Cai Guo-Qiang, 2004. Eight cars and sequenced multi-channel light tubes. Collection of the artist. Installation view of exhibition copy at Solomon R. Guggenheim Museum, New York, 2008. Photo by Hiro Ihara, courtesy Cai Studio.

amples of a car and aeronautical engines being smashed together," says a 2019 *Carbuzz* article on the subject. Of the results, the so-called Sun Beam is probably the most famous, a car powered by two aircraft engines capable of speeds, for the first time in history, exceeding 200 mph: "The engines were a pair of sunbeam Matabele 22.4 litre aircraft engines previously used in powerboats." So hybridized was the result that the car looked nothing like any other before it, meriting a nickname of its own: "the slug," at once car and fuselage.

Of the shows that have appeared at the Guggenheim over the years, the one by Cai Guo-Qiang in 2008 titled *Cai Guo-Qiang: I Want to Believe* is perhaps the most opportune for us. The main installation not only picks up where the car crash above left off but does so in a way that echoes the spiral of the ramp. Rather than a linear crash between several cars, it captures the impact of a single car having just been blown up by a bomb. In other, more tunnel-like, galleries, the installation had been positioned horizontally, but at the Guggenheim it tumbles vertically and inside the void of the spiral (fig. 37). Depending on the installation, eight or nine Ford Tauruses twist and turn and altogether appear as if swept up by a vortex or a tornado. Interestingly, the first and last cars in the installation remain on the ground, at the top and bottom of the ramp, suggesting "the start and the end of the bombing motion." What this suggests is that the car as a type, or any type for that matter, need not undergo permanent change for change to be effective and lasting, only that that change should take place perennially and trigger new perspectives. The car in Cai's installation returns to its original state of being but not before "firework rods" come shooting "out of the car's windows [which] change hues almost in the same manner that fireworks do."[44] No fireworks accompany the damage accrued by the BMW in the car crash metaphor mentioned earlier, but it, too, ultimately goes back to its original look and function, but also not before teaching those involved a thing or two about the car and everything that contributed to the cause of the accident. It is not so much then that the "type" must be destroyed as turned and revised and as such adapted to new and emerging conditions.

At a different show and place from the Guggenheim, Cai complements the installation with a video (titled *Illusion*) and puts it on a loop so that no sooner does the effect of the bomb come to a stop than the whole process is played out all over again. When asked about the notion of circularity in the video, Cai explained that "just like the cars in the main gallery," where the last car "lands back on its four wheels, safely undamaged, unharmed," so does the video; it, too, "repeats, going right back to the very first car, suggesting that it's just one car" that is involved. "This continuous loop suggests that something might or might not have happened," that what we are seeing in front of us might just be an "illusion."[45] What this suggests is that continuity is powerful precisely because it hides that which it has affected; namely that even while it causes change, that change is nowhere to be seen.[46]

The Wall as Easel

The reason Wright gave in defense of the slanting walls of the Guggenheim, in lieu of the one offered earlier in this chapter, is that they simulate the easel set up by artists back in studio, specifically tilted at 97 degrees to allow for a manageable visual relation between art and artist. How interesting, demanding that we erase all and any superficial divides between artist and world, home and museum. Wright, of course, practiced what he preached, turning his own home into at once an art gallery and a place to sleep and entertain. Look at any of the walls in Taliesin and before long you'll see an almost perfect merging between art and structure, art usually covering the entire wall and becoming synonymous with it and vice versa (fig. 38).

Indeed, there is no need for the museum, not least because art should be anywhere and everywhere, at home, down the street, on the sidewalk. Once you hold it back, restrain it behind enclosed walls, it become the purview of the elite, limited in scope and capacity to change the world. Museums are the very opposite of continuous; they are discontinuous and suffocate that which by nature needs to breath to survive, including the way we access and understand civilizations. Rather than the dead things that museums make them out to be, past civilizations need to live through us. We need to see them as active and forever in dynamic relations with those who come after them and through time.

The sooner we get rid of museums, the better—healthier—society will be. They have distorted our understanding of culture and made it seem that it is in institutions like them that man is born, indeed validated. "You may

FIG. 38. Japanese screens in the living room at Taliesin, demonstrating the extent to which Wright fused art and architecture. Photo by author.

have heard it said concerning something, some man or his conduct," Wright lamented in "The Eternal," an essay and a talk he shared with the Fellowship, that he, this man, is only great when he has become a "A museum piece?" Unfortunately, this is "what we Americans are calling our culture." "Visit our museums [and] what you see there has been described by education as the "accumulated riches of the human race." But what you see there is [also] no longer living, because the civilizations to which all belonged have failed to apprehend and adjust themselves. To the law of change, that applied to their own time, place and man."

Wright in the same essay differentiates between major and minor traditions. The minor tradition is what we cling to in fear of the new and the unknown, but the major is the one that deals with the eternal "law of change," that conveyor just underneath our feet that keeps us moving and "always in a state of becoming." Minor tradition would be wise to operate in sync with the major tradition, lest it destroy human potential. Indeed, "it is clear enough that there is no minor tradition that dares ignore this great tradition, this tradition with a capital 'T.' We see in [it] the very principle of growth itself and therefor elemental to Nature." Wright then adds that "if you observe the great major Tradition, you will soon wish to become aware of might well be a better tomorrow than our today and to try to find what it is that will keep you as a being continually alive, alert and conscious: let's say creative."

The Guggenheim's ramp along with its slanted walls are an assembly put together to both destroy the museum and explain why it is necessary to do so. If, on the one hand, the museum had become associated, indeed bogged down, with minor traditions, with shows, say, of a specific genre and artist, the ramp is there to erode that through the lens of constant change. Put differently and through the metaphor of the car crash earlier, if the minor tradition is the car type, the major is the crash itself, mangling that which had been set by time and culture. Whoever is on the ramp has to be on a conceptual wheelchair, constantly moving and at a speed significantly faster and more constant than the jittery legs of the human. And should the human stand up and leave the wheelchair behind, there is at least the parapet railing to correct the transgression, designed in this case to specifically remove from view the legs in favor of the upper body alone. The body must not be held back by the slow and tentative movement of walking; it must appear as if gliding at all costs, even, indeed, when it is walking, smooth and continuous. Peter Blake puts it this way: "Wright had felt for some years prior to the Johnson Wax Building that the only way truly to experience space in motion was to let people 'glide' effortlessly through the space so conceived."[47]

When asked by the permitting body how many floors the Guggenheim contained, Wright said "one." Naturally this confused the officials, who demanded that Wright give them a different answer, perhaps as determined by the number of stops the elevator made while on its way to the top of the ramp. But Wright was right in the sense that the ramp did not stop nor did it differentiate between one floor and the next; it simply flowed. "Here for the first time," Wright said, "architecture appears plastic one floor flowing into another."[48] Wright was not doing this to be glib or annoying but to provoke us, including the building officials, to think deeply about the structure and meaning of the industrial city, the degree to which it had divided society between rich and poor, power and powerlessness. "Instead of the usual superimposition of stratified layers, cutting and butting into each other by way of post and beam construction," he said, the ramp would promote visual and physical continuity.

Stan Allen, in his essay on the Guggenheim, describes the ramp as being inserted "into the laminal flow of the urban grid and works to de-stratify the space of the city."[49] It takes the division between streets and sidewalks, roads and highways, and unifies them into a singular continuum up the ramp, ruffling old and established policed and hierarchical norms associated with the modern metropolis. Right-angled turns, and their requisite stop signs and traffic lights, are like mental blocks whose effect on the psyche, intentional or not, is to gum up free and creative mobility. More than one modern writer and urban planner had commented on that, including Franz Kafka, most famously in *The Trial* when he has the main character, Joseph K, teleport, from one corner of the city to another, just to triumph over the various barriers and delays caused by urban traffic. Better to smooth those wrinkles out and pave the way for a new ramp between conscious and unconscious thought. The question, of course, is how does one get on that ramp? Given the incommensurate ratio between it and the rest of the established city, something other than an arrow sign leading to it must compel attraction. According to *North by Northwest*, the classic movie by Hitchcock, filmed and produced in 1959, the year of Wright's death, the answer lies in trickery, tricking Americans onto one path when another is the more correct or factual. False news is what ultimately leads to correct news, even if everything in between is fraught with intentional misreading, lies, and deceptions.

That we know the movie involves Wright is evident by the fact that the end centers around a house which, though not by him, was very much designed to reflect his philosophy and architectural grammar. Wright had in fact been contacted to design the house, but he asked too much in fees, so the filmmakers dropped him. An in-house team of designers did the job instead, coming close to emulating the master's aesthetics but not all the way. The open space, limestone walls, and extensive use of glass, even the cantilever outside the house reflecting somewhat the premise and character of Fallingwater, are all features culled from Wright's oeuvre and with good fidelity. But the references go beyond that and cover more than one area of Wright's philosophy and work. So much so that it is not too much to say that the entire movie is about Wright, traveling over familiar terrain central to his project, including at one point a nod to Broadacre City. For those familiar with the movie, that part is indexed by the famous crop duster scene, in this case flying over fields, much like the "Aerators" in Broadacre, to surveil the lay of the land and, in the movie, to kill the main character, played by Cary Grant.

The story, one of mistaken identity involving searching for one suspect but chasing another, rumbles toward the open and continuous landscape. It starts in New York, the hometown of the Guggenheim, but soon moves out into the open, first toward the suburbs and then beyond, first by way of the car, then the train, and finally back to the car. Cycles of return in fact are key to its premise, a reference back to the Guggenheim, including an important one back to the city, critically Chicago, Wright's town and, more importantly, one that claimed and perhaps still claims the envious reputation of being America's architectural center of gravity. It should come as no surprise by now that Wright championed the countryside and believed that the modern city that America finally settled on, claiming it reflect the nation's philosophy and aspiration, had to be siphoned through the lens of agrarian values and scenes. New York, from which the story of the movie decamps, is not so much a terrible place empirically as it is one that is "diseased," to use Wright's term, precisely because it has not been conceptually and theoretically flushed out by the underpinning of the American project, dependent to a great extent on the open expanse. In fact, the one visible connection it has with the countryside, namely Central Park, is totally artificial and much closer to England in principle than to this side of the Atlantic. Nor has it been meaningfully informed by other American cities, large and small, which like Chicago can shed a more authentic view of how to build a city and remain true to first principles.

It is not clear why the mistaken identity had to happen in the movie, but that is not important. What is important, is the resignation that Americans were too derailed by capitalism to reason with. They were either in hot pursuit of more wealth, or they were merely trying to survive in a world that is perpetually trying to sink them down. Either way, they had lost their mental capacity to understand what is best for them or, for that matter, what is beautiful. To set them back on track, they had to be tricked back in that position, including Wright himself, whose arrogance and high note of contempt had soured the country on him. Only his most hard-nosed followers were buying his sermons; the rest were looking the other way, to other modernists. A new person, man or woman, had to speak for him, tone down the rhetoric and appear in public in a way that was graceful and elegant. Cary Grant in the movie was that person: tall, handsome, and well-spoken. He is mistaken for a man by the name of George Kaplan, a stand-in for Wright and on whose behalf he was going to consummate what Wright could not in person. At one point in the movie, he comes face to face with clothes that belong to Kaplan aka Wright, and in putting the pair of pants against his body he realizes that they were at least four to six inches too short. Wright was only five foot eight inches tall, matching the height at which the pants hung. In replacing Wright as his spokesman, Grant also replaced his physique and this for a good reason; namely that in good part Wright's cantankerous behavior against the world was the product of a deep-seated insecurity about his height, made evident by the way he lowered the height of his ceilings and compressed his audience to follow that order. A taller and better-looking Grant, who by profession is an advertising agent, has none of these hang-ups and is therefore able to deliver Wright's message in a way that is less angry or distorted. He does in fact remain calm and collected throughout the movie, even when chased and attacked by thugs.

In his attempt to escape the clutches of evil, Cary Grant finds himself on a train, the "Twentieth Century Limited," limited precisely because it is no match for the car. Wright, as we saw in chapter 4 and in the three books he wrote on Broadacre City, wanted, in fact, to kill it. On the train, going full steam toward Chicago and the countryside, Grant meets an attractive woman. She has been inserted precisely to advance the locomotion of the trick and keep it going until it is time to end it. She seduces Grant but only as a practical means to continue the plot. She is part and parcel of the trick and as such on the wrong side of the good, at least initially. Ultimately, she switches sides, not least because she finds herself falling in love with Grant but also because she was complicit in a scheme that was nothing but evil. Having tricked Americans onto a path they had no desire to be on, but which in the movie is good for them, a whole lot of twists and turns ensue, luckily only long enough for the final good to be restored and brought back into circulation. What had been an evil knot between Grant and the seductress is now unwound and retied in the form of a genuine love affair between the two. Fake happiness yields to an authentic one.

What trick did Wright play on Americans to get them off the streets of New York and onto the ramp? The answer must lie in the image of the spiral itself, beguiling in its form and, more important, its capacity to defy gravity. Where other historic spirals and Wright's own "Automobile Objective" were all bottom heavy, wider at the ground and narrower at the top, this one is the other way around, puzzling many a viewer as to how the structure was conceived and structured in the first place. Particularly confusing was the separation between the coils, involving an air gap that made the spiral seem buoyant and as if held in place by some invisible thread from above. The whole thing looked and felt different from anything else seen in architecture, so much so that there was no ready-made language to describe it. A new one had to be invented, some referring to it, as we have heard, as a "washing machine," others as a "windup toy," and still others as a "slinky." The name-calling was just as much an effort to understand the form as to ridicule it, the latter out of fear of the unknown and a creation that could, if allowed, wipe away the entire history of architecture. So strange was and remains the spiral that it sent out an explosion of messages, a "floating chain of signifieds," to quote Barthes in his classic study on images, whose source and content no one knew but which had to be tamped down and brought under control. "Hence in every society," says Barthes, "various techniques are developed intended to fix the floating chain of signifieds in such a way as to counter the terror of uncertain signs, [and] the linguistic message (name-calling, in this case) is one of these techniques."[50] To reduce the Guggenheim to household items on par with appliances and playthings is to domesticate its image and make it part of a cultural mainstream, ready to be consumed at any time. There is good reason to believe that Wright went along, in fact relishing the name-calling himself and contributing a name of his own, an "optimistic ziggurat," presumably in reference to turning the ancient form upside down and "optimistically" hoping it would stick.[51] On another occasion he would refer to it, apropos of his fascination with drawing our attention to his obsession with atomic energy, as a coil that was so indestructible it could outlast an atomic blast. "When the first atomic bomb lands in New York it will not be destroyed," he said. "It may be blown a few miles into the air, but when it comes down it will bounce."[52] This wasn't necessarily name-calling per se, but it was an attempt to reduce the spiral to a cartoon, cutting right through the layers of linguistic layers separating public from the regular Americans. Washing machine or windup toy, it did not matter; his point was, let the critics and the general public have their way, so long the trick is successful and Americans are led out of the city and onto the highway, toward the open landscape.

Photography and Continuity

Of the tactics designed to compel mass consumption, photography may be the most clever. It can take an object larger than life and reduce it to fit into a wallet or a photo album, ready to be pulled out at a moment's notice and used to demonstrate superior mobility over worlds known and unknown, but also control over the unfamiliar and potentially dangerous. Susan Sontag's classic study *On Photography* is instructive, saying at one point that a "photograph is not only like its subject, an homage to the subject [but] a part of an extension of that subject; and a potent means of acquiring it, of gaining control over it."[53] To photograph the Eiffel Tower and the Statue of Liberty, two of the most photographed structures in the world, is to level the ground between photographer and monument, monumentalizing the self and domesticating the monument. According to a map by sightmap.com, "tracking the number of photos taken in a given location and tagged through Google's Panoramio," the Guggenheim is the most photographed building in the world, right on cue with Wright's wishes and intentions. Now that he was approaching the end of life, he was particularly intent on distributing his message far and wide, not out of megalomania, although some might argue that, but out of a deep-seated belief that it was time to get the nation off the urban grid and onto the ramp and toward the open landscape. Whatever trick had to be played to prompt that derailment he was ready to play it, including creating an image with which to shock the nation and compel multiplication. So unusual was the spiral it was hard not to be attracted to it, like a moth to a flame, and snap a picture of it, immediately, without thinking and intellectualizing the process. This was how Wright was going to get to the heart and soul of Americans, to cut through the layers of rationalization and aim for the visceral. "You've got to see fast, to see quick," he said to a class of photography students, "and often times that's the best way of seeing."[54]

To snap a picture quickly is to do so prematurely, before its content has had the time to incubate and, in the case of the Guggenheim, to become part of the national and cultural unconscious. It is necessarily unfinished, and yet handed over to the public nonetheless, precisely so that the public can finish it. The upside-down spiral was and will forever be unfinished in that it defied and continues to defy gravity and had to be corrected, turned around, and put right side up—mentally, culturally, and conceptually. No critic, fan, or commentator has said what he or she has had to say about the building without also noting the challenge it posed to the laws of physics. Wright had given us spirals before, always right side up, including in his initial proposals for the Guggenheim, but not now, at the completion of the museum and at the end of his life. The contrast is striking and no doubt played out by Wright to precisely compel Americans to photograph the spiral, quickly and impulsively. He wanted them to take it home and grapple with it, right the wrong, and in so doing join him in advancing his campaign against the industrial city, and toward an exodus from the center to the edge. Susan Sontag used the word "control," specifying that once snapped, a photograph allows those who own it control of its message and the belief that they have a say in its distribution and consumption. "The photographic exploration and duplication of the world fragments," she says, "continues and feeds the pieces into an interminable dossier, thereby providing possibilities of control that could not even be dreamed of under earlier systems of recording information."[55] To create a form that could and would "feed" an "interminable dossier," is exactly what Wright started and indeed wished with the Guggenheim, giving Americans at least the illusion that they could join him in taking control of America's collective national destiny. Things had gone wrong, and no right was going to take place until the entire country was on board. Up until that happens, the Guggenheim will continue to do its duty unabated. Up until then it will continue to be the most photographed building in the world.

NOTES

Preface

1. Ralph Waldo Emerson, "Circles," in *Ralph Waldo Emerson: Selected Essays*, ed. Larzer Ziff (New York: Penguin, 1982), 237.

2. Ralph Waldo Emerson, "The Over-Soul," ibid., 208.

3. John Lloyd Wright, *My Father Who Is on Earth*, ed. Narciso G. Menocal (Carbondale: Southern Illinois University Press, 1994), 71.

4. Ken Johnson, "The Flaws in Frank Lloyd Wright's Design for Living: The Portland Museum Shows Downside of the Architect's Indoor Vision," *Boston Globe*, August 26, 2007.

Introduction

1. Randall Fuller, *Emerson's Ghosts: Literature, Politics, and the Making of Americanists* (New York: Oxford University Press, 2007), 7, italics in original.

2. Louis Sullivan, *Democracy: A Man-Search* (Detroit, MI: Wayne State University Press, 1961), 83.

3. Quote found in introduction to Edward O'Donnell, *Henry George and the Crisis of Inequality: Progress and Poverty in the Gilded Age* (New York: Columbia University Press, 2015), xx.

4. Jenkin Lloyd Jones, "The Word of the Spirit to the Nation," in *The Word of the Spirit: To the Nation, City, Church, Home and Individual* (Chicago: Unity, 1894), 12.

5. Anecdote experienced by author while on a tour of Kentuck Knob, one of Wright's houses in central Pennsylvania.

6. Frank Lloyd Wright, *When Democracy Builds* (Chicago: University of Chicago Press, 1945), 17.

7. Elaine Hedges, introduction to *Democracy: A Man Search*, by Louis H. Sullivan (Detroit, MI: Wayne State University Press, 1961), ix.

8. Frank Lloyd Wright, *An Autobiography* (New York: Duell, Sloan and Pearce, 1943), 71.

9. Theodore Dreiser, *Sister Carrie* (1900; New York: Norton, 1991), 12.

10. Randall Fuller, *Emerson's Ghosts: Literature, Politics, and the Making of Americanists* (New York: Oxford University Press, 2007), 16.

---

11. Wright, *An Autobiography*, 26.

12. Maginel Wright Barney, *The Valley of the God-Almighty Joneses*, with Tom Burke (New York: Appleton-Century, 1965), 53–54.

13. "The American Scholar," a talk by Frank Lloyd Wright to the Taliesin Fellowship, September 2, 1951, Reel 25, Box 1, Folder 28, The Frank Lloyd Wright Foundation Archives (The Museum of Modern Art | Avery Architectural & Fine Arts Library, Columbia University, New York).

14. Ibid.

15. Ralph Waldo Emerson, *The Journals and Miscellaneous Notebooks of Ralph Waldo Emerson*, vol. 4: *1832–1834*, ed. Alfred R. Ferguson (Cambridge, MA: Belknap Press of Harvard University Press, 1964), 27.

16. Martin Kevorkian, *Writing beyond Prophecy: Emerson, Hawthorne, and Melville after the American Renaissance* (Baton Rouge: Louisiana State University Press, 2013), 10.

17. It is common to think of Wright as a hater of cities, not least because he often referred to them using less than complimentary terms, but the reality is far more complex, which this book seeks to unpack.

18. Frank Lloyd Wright, *The Living City* (New York: Mentor, 1958), 47.

19. Ibid.

20. John Lloyd Wright, *My Father Who Is on Earth* (Carbondale: Southern Illinois University Press, 1994), 131.

21. Ralph Waldo Emerson, "Editor's Address," in *The Complete Works of Ralph Waldo Emerson*, vol. 11: *Miscellanies* (Boston: Houghton Mifflin, [1903–4]), 385.

22. T. C. Archer, "On the Probable Influence Which the Centennial Exhibition Will Have on the Progress of Art in America," *Art Journal* 39 (1877): 7.

23. James F. O'Gorman, *Three American Architects: Richardson, Sullivan, and Wright 1865–1915* (Chicago: University of Chicago Press, 1992), 13.

24. Bernard Michael Boyle, "Architectural Practice in America, 1865–1965—Ideal and Reality," in *The Architect*, ed. Spiro Kostof (New York: Oxford University Press, 1977), 310.

25. Mario Manieri-Elia, "Toward the Imperial City: Daniel Burnham and the City Beautiful Movement," in Giorgio Ciucci et al., *The American City: From the Civil War to the New Deal* (New York: Granada, 1980), 20.

26. Ralph Waldo Emerson, *Nature*, in *Ralph Waldo Emerson: Selected Essays*, ed. Larzer Ziff (New York: Penguin, 1985), 35.

27. Emerson, "Editor's Address," 11:385.

28. Cornel West, *The American Evasion of Philosophy: A Genealogy of Pragmatism* (Madison: University of Wisconsin Press, 1989), 27.

29. Ibid.

30. Andrew Murphy, *Prodigal Nation: Moral Decline and Divine Punishment from New England to 9/11* (New York: Oxford University Press, 2009), 54.

31. Boardman quoted ibid., 58.

32. Washington, quoted in Ron Chernow, *Alexander Hamilton* (New York: Penguin, 2004), 213.

33. James Madison, quoted ibid., 214.

34. Frederick Douglass, *Narrative of the Life of Frederick Douglass, An American Slave,* ed. John Stauffer (New York: Penguin Random House, 2014), 52.

35. Ralph Waldo Emerson, "The Fugitive Slave Law," in *The Complete Works of Ralph Waldo Emerson,* vol. 11: *Miscellanies,* 186.

36. Eduardo Cadava, *The Climates of History* (Stanford, CA: Stanford University Press, 1997), 26.

37. Murphy, *Prodigal Nation,* 53.

38. Henry Adams, "The Education of Henry Adams," in *Novels, Mont Saint Michel, The Education* (New York: Viking, 1983), 760.

39. Ralph Waldo Emerson, "Emancipation Proclamation," in *The Complete Works of Ralph Waldo Emerson,* vol. 11: *Miscellanies,* 321.

40. Jenkin Lloyd Jones, "The Cause of the Toiler: A Labor Day Sermon," Unity Library, no. 20, 1892.

41. Wright, *When Democracy Builds,* 38.

42. Upton Sinclair, *The Jungle* (New York: Penguin Classics, 2006), 4.

43. Wright, *When Democracy Builds,* 95–96, my emphasis.

44. https://livinghistoryfarm.org/farminginthe30s/water_11.html.

45. Jennifer Gray, "Reading Broadacre," *Frank Lloyd Wright Quarterly* (Winter 2018).

46. Giorgio Ciucci, "The City in Agrarian Ideology and Frank Lloyd Wright: Origins and Development of Broadacre City," in Ciucci et al., *The American City,* 301.

47. Ralph Waldo Emerson, "Farming," in *Society and Solitude* (New York: Houghton Mifflin, 1870), 116.

48. Sophia Forster, "Peculiar Faculty and Peculiar Institution: Ralph Waldo Emerson on Labor and Slavery," *ESQ: A Journal of the American Renaissance* 60, no. 1 (2014): 53, my emphasis.

49. Wright, *When Democracy Builds,* 91.

50. C. R. Ashbee, "Frank Lloyd Wright: A Study and an Appreciation," in *Frank Lloyd Wright: The Early Work,* ed. Edgar Kaufman Jr. (New York: Horizon, 1968). See also Kenneth Frampton's *Modern Architecture: A Critical History.*

51. Frank Lloyd Wright, "F. L. Wright on Slavery," 1957, MSS 2401.570, The Frank Lloyd Wright Foundation Archives (The Museum of Modern Art | Avery Architectural & Fine Arts Library, Columbia University, New York).

52. Frank Lloyd Wright, "In the Cause of Architecture: Purely Personal" (1928), in *Frank Lloyd Wright on Architecture: Selected Writings, 1894–1940,* ed. Frederick Gutheim (New York: Grosset and Dunlap, 1941), 131.

53. Wright, *An Autobiography,* 83.

54. Ibid.

55. Louis Sullivan, *Kindergarten Chats and Other Writings* (New York: Dover, 1979), 32.

56. See Elaine Hedges's introduction to Sullivan's *Democracy,* where she goes over a short list of books found in Sullivan's library, spanning a wide spectrum of subjects, from philosophy to sociology to medicine and more.

57. David Hertz, *Angels of Reality: Emersonian Unfoldings in Wright, Stevens, and Ives* (Carbondale: Southern Illinois University Press, 1993), 47.

58. John Michael Desmond, "A Clearing in the Woods: Self & City in Frank Lloyd Wright's Organic Communities" (PhD diss., MIT, 1996), 612.

59. Frank Lloyd Wright, *Truth against the World: Frank Lloyd Wright Speaks for an Organic Architecture*, ed. Patrick J. Meehan (New York: John Wiley and Sons, 1987), 28.

60. Emerson, *Selected Essays*, 36.

61. Grant Hildebrand, *The Wright Space: Pattern and Meaning in Frank Lloyd Wright's Houses* (Seattle: University of Washington Press, 1991), 35.

62. Narciso Menocal tells us that the reading of "The Arts and Crafts of the Machine" at the Hull House was not the first but the third (see Menocal, "Frank Lloyd Wright as the Anti Victor Hugo," in *American Public Architecture: European Roots and Native Expressions*, 139–50).

63. Ralph Waldo Emerson, "Thoughts on Modern Literature," in *The Complete Works of Ralph Waldo Emerson*, vol 12: *Natural History of Intellect, and Other Papers* (Boston: Houghton Mifflin, [1903–4]), 319.

64. Frank Lloyd Wright, *Frank Lloyd Wright: Writings and Buildings*, ed. Edgar Kaufmann and Ben Raeburn (New York: Meridian, 1970), 70.

65. Emerson, *Selected Essays*, 269.

66. Wright, *An Autobiography*, 162.

67. Emerson, *Selected Essays*, 194, italics in original.

68. Ibid., 184.

69. Wright, *An Autobiography*, 17.

70. Ibid., 16.

71. In his book *The Urbanism of Frank Lloyd Wright*, Levine nicely and immediately debunks the myth that Wright hated the city and notes that, in fact, he returned to it to complement and complete *The Living City*.

72. Emerson, *Selected Essays*, 181.

73. Frank Lloyd Wright and Lewis Mumford, *Frank Lloyd Wright and Lewis Mumford: Thirty Years of Correspondence*, ed. Robert Wojtowicz and Bruce Brooks Pfeiffer (New York: Princeton Architectural Press, 2001), 121.

74. Barney, *The Valley of the God-Almighty Joneses*, 10.

75. Wright and Mumford, *Thirty Years of Correspondence*, 79.

76. Ibid., 147.

77. Ralph Waldo Emerson, *The Portable Emerson*, ed. Mark Van Doren (1946; New York: Penguin, 1977), 115.

78. Wright, *An Autobiography*, 26.

79. Emerson, *The Portable Emerson*, 115.

80. Frank Lloyd Wright, "Planning Man's Physical Environment" (speech at Princeton University Bicentennial Conference), Reel 268, Box 6, Folder 6, 1947, The Frank Lloyd Wright Foundation Archives (The Museum of Modern Art | Avery Architectural & Fine Arts Library, Columbia University, New York).

81. Wright, *An Autobiography*, 150.

82. John Dewey, "Individuality in Our Day," in *John Dewey: The Political Writings*, ed. Debra A. Morris and Ian Shapiro (Indianapolis, IN: Hackett, 1993), 87.

83. Sacvan Bercovitch, *The American Jeremiad* (Madison: University of Wisconsin Press, 1978), 5.

84. Emerson, "Circles," in *Selected Essays*, 236.

85. Frank Lloyd Wright, "To Interview a Prophet," 193–, MSS 2401.128, The Frank Lloyd Wright Foundation Archives (The Museum of Modern Art | Avery Architectural & Fine Arts Library, Columbia University, New York).

86. Richard Chase, "The Classic Literature: Art and Idea," in *Paths of American Thought*, ed. Arthur M. Schlesinger Jr. and Morton White (Boston: Houghton Mifflin, 1963), 53.

87. Scott Gartner, "The Shining Brow: Frank Lloyd Wright and the Welsh Bardic Tradition," in *Wright Studies*, vol. 1: *Taliesin 1911–1914*, ed. Narciso Menocal (Carbondale: Southern Illinois University Press, 1992), 30.

88. Ibid., 28.

89. Wright, "To Interview a Prophet."

90. J. J. Polívka to *San Francisco News*, ca. 1950, Box 1, Folder 5, MS 48, Polívka (J. J.) Papers, 1945–1959, University Archives, University at Buffalo, State University of New York.

91. Ibid.

92. See Brian Greene, *Until the End of Time: Mind, Matter, and Our Search for Meaning in an Evolving Universe* (New York: Knopf, 2020).

1. Of Prophets, Heroes & Poets

1. Richard Hofstadter, quoted in Randall Fuller, *Emerson's Ghosts: Literature, Politics, and the Making of Americanists* (New York: Oxford University Press, 2007), 10.

2. Martin Kevorkian, *Writing beyond Prophecy: Emerson, Hawthorne, and Melville after the American Renaissance* (Baton Rouge: Louisiana State University, 2013), 32.

3. Emerson, quoted in F. O. Matthiessen, *American Renaissance: Art and Expression in the Age of Emerson and Whitman* (New York: Oxford University Press, 1941), 6.

4. Ibid., italics in original.

5. Joseph Campbell, *The Hero with a Thousand Faces*, 3rd ed. (Novato, CA: New World Library, 2008), 23.

6. Glyn Iliffe, *Return to Ithaca* (self-published), 29.

7. Campbell, *The Hero with a Thousand Faces*, 30.

8. Olgivanna Lloyd Wright, *Frank Lloyd Wright: His Life, His Work, His Words* (New York: Horizon, 1966), 11.

9. Frank Lloyd Wright, "American Architecture," 1937, MSS 2401.372, The Frank Lloyd Wright Foundation Archives (The Museum of Modern Art | Avery Architectural & Fine Arts Library, Columbia University, New York).

10. Meryle Secrest, *Frank Lloyd Wright: A Biography* (New York: Harper Perennial, 1993), 50.

11. This is the Druid motto that the Lloyd Joneses, Wright's maternal side of the family, wore on their sleeve throughout their lives but particularly in the process of immigrating to the United States and weathering the trials and tribulations of a difficult journey.

12. John Garraty, ed., *Labor and Capital in the Gilded Age: Testimony Taken by the Senate Committee upon the Relations between Labor and Capital—1883* (Boston: Little, Brown, 1968), vii.

13. Ibid.

14. Ibid., viii.

15. Secrest, *Wright: A Biography*, 69.

16. Ralph Waldo Emerson, *Ralph Waldo Emerson: Selected Essays*, ed. Larzer Ziff (New York: Penguin, 1985), 89.

17. Ibid.

18. Secrest, *Wright: A Biography*, 40.

19. Thomas Carlyle, *Carlyle; on Heroes and Hero Worship and the Heroic in History*, ed. Archibald MacMechan (Boston: Ginn, 1901), 51.

20. Ibid., 63, italics in original.

21. Emerson, *Selected Essays*, 183.

22. Ibid., 153.

23. Jackson Lears, *Rebirth of a Nation: The Making of Modern America, 1877–1920* (New York: Harper Perennial, 2010), 142.

24. Frank Lloyd Wright, *An Autobiography* (New York: Duell, Sloan and Pearce, 1943), 65.

25. Lear, *Rebirth of a Nation*, 142.

26. Wright, *An Autobiography*, 67.

27. Ibid., 70.

28. Wright, *An Autobiography*, 103.

29. Robert Twombly, *Louis Sullivan: His Life and Work* (Chicago: University of Chicago Press, 1987), 210.

30. Wright, *An Autobiography*, 113.

31. Frank Lloyd Wright, "Organic Architecture Looks at Modern Architecture," 1952, MSS 2401.30, The Frank Lloyd Wright Foundation Archives (The Museum of Modern Art | Avery Architectural & Fine Arts Library, Columbia University, New York).

32. Wright, *An Autobiography*, 34.

33. Donald Johnson, *Frank Lloyd Wright: The Early Years: Progressivism: Aesthetics: Cities* (New York: Routledge, 2017), 15.

34. Frank Lloyd Wright, *Frank Lloyd Wright: Writings and Buildings*, ed. Edgar Kaufmann and Ben Raeburn (New York: Meridian, 1970), 68.

35. Johnson, *The Early Years*, 11.

36. Louis Sullivan, *Kindergarten Chats and Other Writings* (New York: Dover, 1979), 64.

37. Wright, "Organic Architecture Looks at Modern Architecture."

38. Herbert Muschamp, *Man about Town: Frank Lloyd Wright in New York City* (Cambridge, MA: MIT Press, 1983), 93.

39. Sullivan, *Kindergarten Chats*, 67.

40. Wright, *An Autobiography*, 162.

41. Sullivan, *Kindergarten Chats*, 90.

42. Ralph Waldo Emerson, "Society and Solitude," in *Society and Solitude* (New York: Houghton Mifflin, 1870), 13.

43. Ibid., 11.

44. Sullivan, *Kindergarten Chats*, 114.

45. Emerson, *Selected Essays*, 93.

46. John Dewey, "Individuality, Equality, Superiority," in *John Dewey: The Political Writings*, ed. Debra Morris and Ian Shapiro (Indianapolis, IN: Hackett, 1993), 78.

47. Ibid., 79.

48. Henry David Thoreau, *Walden, or Life in the Woods, and On the Duty of Civil Disobedience* (New York: Harper and Row, 1965), 45.

49. Olaf Hansen, *Aesthetic Individualism and Practical Intellect: American Allegory in Emerson, Thoreau, Adams, and James* (Princeton, NJ: Princeton University Press, 1990), 126.

50. Thoreau, *Walden*, 66.

51. Bruce Brooks Pfeiffer, "Frank Lloyd Wright, Taliesin West," special issue, *Global Architecture Traveler* (2002): 24.

52. Thoreau, *Walden*, 85.

53. Ibid., 65.

54. Wright, *Taliesin*, no. 1, 1936, MSS 2401.525, The Frank Lloyd Wright Foundation Archives (The Museum of Modern Art | Avery Architectural & Fine Arts Library, Columbia University, New York).

55. Wright, *Taliesin*, 36.

56. Henry Russell Hitchcock, *In the Nature of Materials, 1887–1941: The Buildings of Frank Lloyd Wright*, 2nd ed. (New York: Da Capo, 1975), 65.

57. Karsten Harries, *The Ethical Function of Architecture* (Cambridge, MA: MIT Press, 1998), 33.

58. Ibid., 32.

59. Owen Jones, *The Grammar of Ornament: A Visual Reference of Form and Colour in Architecture and the Decorative Arts* (1856; Princeton, NJ: Princeton University Press, 2001), 31.

60. Ibid., 32.

61. F. O. Matthiessen, *American Renaissance: Art and Expression in the Age of Emerson and Whitman* (New York: Oxford University Press, 1968), 172.

62. Wright, *An Autobiography*, 106.

63. See Kenneth Frampton, *Studies in Tectonic Culture*. There, and in his chapter on Wright, he goes over the influence of German intellectuals on the midcentury Chicago architectural market.

64. Gottfried Semper, *The Four Elements of Architecture and Other Writings* (Cambridge, UK: Cambridge University Press, 1851), 103.

65. Hitchcock, *In the Nature of Materials*, 65.

66. Frank Lloyd Wright, "Ode to the Liar," 1938, MSS 2401.410, The Frank Lloyd Wright

Foundation Archives (The Museum of Modern Art | Avery Architectural & Fine Arts Library, Columbia University, New York).

67. Wright, "American Architecture."

68. Emerson, quoted in Matthiessen's *American Renaissance*, 6.

69. Emerson, *Selected Essays*, 270.

70. Matthiessen, *American Renaissance*, 8.

71. Emerson, *Selected Essays*, 270.

72. Sigmund Freud, *The Interpretations of Dreams*, trans. James Strachey, 3rd ed. (New York: Discus, 1967), 269.

73. Melanie Klein, *Envy and Gratitude and Other Works, 1946–1963* (London: Vintage, 1997), loc. 748, Kindle.

74. Wright, *An Autobiography*, 49.

75. John Lloyd Wright, *My Father Who Is on Earth* (Carbondale: Southern Illinois University Press, 1994), 28.

76. Secrest, *Wright: A Biography*, 188.

77. Ibid.

78. Christina Wieland, *The Undead Mother: Psychoanalytic Explorations of Masculinity, Femininity, and Matricide* (New York: Routledge, 2018), 53.

79. Ibid., 54.

80. Wright, *An Autobiography*, 88.

81. Secrest, *Wright: A Biography*, 203.

82. Frank Lloyd Wright, "Conversation with Hugh Downs," 1953, Reel 298, Box 6, Folder 19, The Frank Lloyd Wright Foundation Archives (The Museum of Modern Art | Avery Architectural & Fine Arts Library, Columbia University, New York).

83. Wright, *An Autobiography*, 11.

84. Ibid., 173.

85. J. L. Wright, *My Father Who Is on Earth*, 72.

2. On the Brink of Fear: The Sublime in Wright's Work

1. Edmund Burke, *Edmund Burke: A Philosophical Enquiry into the Origin of Our Ideas of the Sublime and Beautiful*, ed. Paul Guyer (New York: Oxford University Press, 2015), 34.

2. Ibid., 33.

3. Mary Arensberg, ed., *The American Sublime* (Albany: State University of New York Press, 1986), 5.

4. Jefferson, quoted in David Nye, *American Technological Sublime* (Cambridge, MA: MIT Press, 1994), 20.

5. Ibid., 22.

6. Bryan Jay Wolf, *Romantic Re-Vision: Culture and Consciousness in Nineteenth-Century American Painting and Literature* (Chicago: University of Chicago Press, 1982), 178.

7. Ralph Waldo Emerson, *Ralph Waldo Emerson: Selected Essays,* ed. Larzer Ziff (New York: Penguin, 1983), 38.

8. Ibid.

9. Emerson, "Self-Reliance," in *Selected Essays,* 176.

10. Reyner Banham, *The Architecture of the Well-Tempered Environment,* 2nd ed. (London: Architectural Press, 1984), 91.

11. Michael Osman, "American System-Built Houses," in *Frank Lloyd Wright: Unpacking the Archives,* ed. Barry Bergdoll and Jennifer Gray (New York: MOMA, n.d.), 154.

12. Quote found in Bruce Brooks Pfeiffer, "Usonian Homes," special issue of *Global Architecture Traveler,* no. 5 (2002): 36.

13. Pfeiffer, quoted ibid., 14.

14. Matthew Skjonsberg, "Do It Yourself: Usonian Automatic System," in *Unpacking the Archives,* ed. Bergdoll and Gray, 158.

15. Ibid., 161.

16. Norbert Wiener, "Men, Machines, and the World About," in *The American Intellectual Tradition,* vol. 2: *1865 to the Present,* 7th ed., ed. David Hollinger and Charles Capper (New York: Oxford University Press, 2016), 376.

17. Frank Lloyd Wright, *The Future of Architecture* (New York: New American Library, 1970), 83.

18. Ibid.

19. Donald Francis Roy, "Hooverville: A Study of a Community of Homeless Men in Seattle" (master's thesis, University of Washington, Seattle, 1935), 56.

20. Frank Lloyd Wright, *The Natural House* (New York: Horizon, 1954), 85.

21. Henry George, *Progress and Poverty* (New York: Doubleday, 2019), 396.

22. Frank Lloyd Wright, "American Architecture," 1937, MSS 2401.372, The Frank Lloyd Wright Foundation Archives (The Museum of Modern Art | Avery Architectural & Fine Arts Library, Columbia University, New York).

23. For further analysis, see chapter 4, where I take a deep dive into the question of land and the various philosophical sources Wright looked into to sustain his Usonian proposal.

24. Frank Lloyd Wright, *When Democracy Builds* (Chicago: University of Chicago Press, 1945), 93.

25. Frank Lloyd Wright, "From an Architect's Point of View," 1957, MSS 2401.222A, The Frank Lloyd Wright Foundation Archives (The Museum of Modern Art | Avery Architectural & Fine Arts Library, Columbia University, New York).

26. Frank Lloyd Wright, "Broadacre City Matter," MSS 2401.175, The Frank Lloyd Wright Foundation Archives (Museum of Modern Art | Avery Architectural & Fine Arts Library, Columbia University, New York).

27. Frank Lloyd Wright, "The Line between the Curious and the Beautiful," 193–, MSS 2401.088, The Frank Lloyd Wright Foundation Archives (The Museum of Modern Art | Avery Architectural & Fine Arts Library, Columbia University, New York).

28. Frank Lloyd Wright, quoted in *Frank Lloyd Wright on Architecture: Selected Writings, 1894–1940,* ed. Frederick Gutheim (New York: Grosset and Dunlap, 1941), 192.

29. John Howe, quoted in Donald Hoffman, *Frank Lloyd Wright's Fallingwater: The House and Its History,* 2nd. rev. ed. (New York: Dover, 1993), 12.

30. Edgar Kaufmann, quoted ibid.

31. Ibid., 13.

32. Ibid., 26.

33. Quotes from the engineers' reply, ibid., 28.

34. Ibid., 31.

35. Ibid., 44.

36. Frank Lloyd Wright, "Dinner Talk at Hull House," 1939, MSS 2401.235, The Frank Lloyd Wright Foundation Archives (The Museum of Modern Art | Avery Architectural & Fine Arts Library, Columbia University, New York).

37. Hoffman, *Fallingwater,* 54.

38. Frank Lloyd Wright, "Man Is Not a Parasite," 1952, MSS 2404.003A, The Frank Lloyd Wright Foundation Archives (The Museum of Modern Art | Avery Architectural & Fine Arts Library, Columbia University, New York).

39. Jonathan Lipman, *Frank Lloyd Wright and the Johnson Wax Buildings* (New York: Rizzoli, 1991), 7.

40. Ibid., 51.

41. Ibid., 65.

42. Immanuel Kant, *Critique of Judgement,* trans. Werner S. Pluhar (1790; Indianapolis: Hackett, 1987), loc. 3806, Kindle.

43. Frank Lloyd Wright, "Skyscraping," 1935, MSS 2401.152, The Frank Lloyd Wright Foundation Archives (The Museum of Modern Art | Avery Architectural & Fine Arts Library, Columbia University, New York).

44. Manfredo Tafuri, "The Disenchanted Mountain: The Skyscraper and the City," in Giorgio Ciucci et al., *The American City: From the Civil War to the New Deal* (New York: Granada, 1980), 390.

45. Here it has to be noted that this was not the first time that Wright had proposed and worked with the taproot idea, most famously using it as the main structural *parti* for the Johnson Wax research tower in the late 1940s.

46. Burke, *A Philosophical Enquiry,* 59.

47. Frank Lloyd Wright, "The Illinois," 1956, MSS 2401.366, The Frank Lloyd Wright Foundation Archives (The Museum of Modern Art | Avery Architectural & Fine Arts Library, Columbia University, New York).

48. O. J. Doyle, district manager, Otis elevator, to Wright, October 13, 1956, 0050a01-04, The Frank Lloyd Wright Foundation Archives (The Museum of Modern Art | Avery Architectural & Fine Arts Library, Columbia University, New York).

49. Nye, *American Technological Sublime,* 227.

50. Peter Bacon Hales, "Imagining the Atomic Age," https://www.webpages.uidaho.edu/AmSt301_hart/Fifties/Chapter%205.pdf, 103.

51. Richard E. Engler, *Atomic Power in Space: A History,* report prepared for US Department of Energy, 1987.

52. Nye, *American Technological Sublime,* 231.

53. Frank Lloyd Wright, *Letters to Clients: Frank Lloyd Wright,* ed. Bruce Brooks Pfeiffer (Fresno: California State University Press, 1986), 251, italics in original.

54. Merrill Bush, quoted in Paul Boyer, *By the Bomb's Early Light: American Thought and Culture at the Dawn of the Atomic Age* (Chapel Hill: University of North Carolina Press, 1994), 29.

55. Nye, *American Technological Sublime,* 234.

56. Robert Hotz, "Sputnik in the Sky," *Aviation Week & Space Technology,* October 14, 1957, 21.

57. Burke, *A Philosophical Enquiry,* 53.

58. J. J. Polívka "What's It Like to Work with Wright," ca. 1948, Box 1, Folder 7, MS 48, Polívka (J. J.) Papers, 1945–1959, University Archives, University at Buffalo, State University of New York.

3. Designing for a New Ocular Regime

1. Many have examined Emerson's "transparent eyeball," some seeing in it a concept, some a metaphor, some both, but all agreeing, in one way or another, that it is a place where contradictory concepts can come and dwell, thereafter blending and sparking new and generative ideas. For one scholar it speaks to "the special function of the eye" as having the ability to process "basic information of the present and also integrate more complicated data (or 'omens') for the future." See Robert Tindol, "Emerson's Transparent Eyeball as a Conceptual Blend," *Orbis Litterarum* 76, no. 1 (2021), https://onlinelibrary.wiley.com/doi/full/10.1111/oli.12280.

2. Ralph Waldo Emerson, *Ralph Waldo Emerson, Selected Essays,* ed. Larzer Ziff (New York: Penguin Classics, 1983), 38.

3. Lewis Mumford, *The Golden Day: A Study in American Literature and Culture* (New York: Beacon, 1957), 7.

4. A. R. Hall, *The Scientific Revolution, 1500–1800: The Formation of the Modern Scientific Attitude* (Boston: Beacon, 1956), 36.

5. Emerson, *Nature,* in *Selected Essays,* 38.

6. A. Mark Smith, *From Sight to Light: The Passage from Ancient to Modern Optics* (Chicago: University of Chicago Press, 2015), 27.

7. Ibid., 29.

8. Ibid., 384.

9. Emerson, *Selected Essays,* 39.

10. Smith, *From Sight to Light,* 81.

11. Frank Lloyd Wright, "Query (Myself)," 1938, MSS 2401.221, The Frank Lloyd Wright Foundation Archives (The Museum of Modern Art | Avery Architectural & Fine Arts Library, Columbia University, New York).

12. Emerson, *Selected Essays*, 183.

13. Frank Lloyd Wright, *Frank Lloyd Wright on Architecture: Selected Writings, 1894–1940,* ed. Frederick Gutheim (New York: Grosset and Dunlap, 1941), 127.

14. Baudelaire, quoted in Marshall Berman, *All That Is Solid Melts into Air: The Experience of Modernity* (New York: Penguin, 1988), 135.

15. Thomas A. Heinz, *Frank Lloyd Wright's Stained Glass & Lightscreens* (Salt Lake City, UT: Gibbs Smith, 2000), Kindle, loc. 529.

16. Smith, *From Sight to Light,* 86.

17. See Frank Lloyd Wright, "A Reading of William Blake," Box 4, Folder 12, The Frank Lloyd Wright Foundation Archives (The Museum of Modern Art | Avery Architectural & Fine Arts Library, Columbia University, New York).

18. Heinz, *Stained Glass and Lightscreens,* loc. 181, Kindle.

19. Frank Lloyd Wright, *Frank Lloyd Wright: Writings and Buildings,* ed. Edgar Kaufmann and Ben Raeburn (New York: Meridian, 1970), 78.

20. Alan Taylor, quoted in Jay Koziarz, "Restoration Done Wright: A Look inside Unity Temple," June 7, 2017, https://chicago.curbed.com/2017/6/7/15751444/frank-lloyd-wright-architecture-unity-temple-restoraton.

21. Joseph Siry, *Unity Temple: Frank Lloyd Wright and Architecture for Liberal Religion* (New York: Cambridge University Press, 1996), 95.

22. Ibid.

23. Kathleen Raine, *William Blake* (1970; rpr., London: Thames and Hudson, 2000), 76.

24. Hall, *The Scientific Revolution,* 173.

25. Karen Barad, *Meeting the Universe Halfway: Quantum Physics and the Entanglement of Matter and Meaning* (Durham, NC: Duke University Press, 2007), 107.

26. Ibid., 119.

27. Anthony Bunt, "Blake's 'ANCIENT OF DAYS': The Symbolism of the Compasses," *Journal of the Warburg Institute* 2, no. 1 (July 1938): 53–63, 56.

28. Northrop Frye, *Fearful Symmetry: A Study of William Blake* (Princeton, NJ: Princeton University Press, 1974), 213.

29. Frank Lloyd Wright, "The Line between the Curious and the Beautiful," 193–, MSS 2401.088, The Frank Lloyd Wright Foundation Archives (The Museum of Modern Art | Avery Architectural & Fine Arts Library, Columbia University, New York).

30. Leopold Damrosch, *Symbol and Truth in Blake's Myth* (Princeton, NJ: Princeton University Press, 2014), 14.

31. Frank Lloyd Wright, "To Interview a Prophet," 193–, MSS 2401.128, The Frank Lloyd Wright Foundation Archives (The Museum of Modern Art | Avery Architectural & Fine Arts Library, Columbia University, New York).

32. Frank Lloyd Wright, *An Autobiography* (New York: Duell, Sloan and Pearce, 1943), 123.

33. Ibid., 126.

34. The memory would inspire the last section of Wright's iconic "The Arts and Crafts of the Machine." It starts by admonishing the reader to go up a tall building of choice in the city and look around: "Be gently lifted at nightfall to the top of great down-town office building, and you may see how in the image of material man . . . is this thing we call a city."

35. Gaston Bachelard, *The Psychoanalysis of Fire,* trans. Alan C. M. Ross (Boston: Beacon, 1964), 11.

36. *The Arabian Nights: Tales of 1001 Nights,* vol. 3: *Nights,* 719–1001, trans. Malcolm Lyons, with Ursula Lyons (New York: Penguin, 2010), 746.

37. Ibid., 747.

38. Roger Friedland and Harold Zellman, *The Fellowship: The Untold Story of Frank Lloyd Wright and the Taliesin Fellowship* (New York: HarperCollins, 2007), loc. 4467, Kindle.

39. Wright, *An Autobiography,* 15.

40. Eduardo Galeano, *The Memory of Fire Trilogy: "Genesis," "Faces and Masks," and "Century of the Wind,"* trans. Cedric Belfrage (New York: Open Road, 2014), loc. 1950, Kindle.

41. Bachelard, *The Psychoanalysis of Fire,* 14.

42. Franklin Toker, *Fallingwater Rising: Frank Lloyd Wright, E. J. Kaufmann, and America's Most Extraordinary House* (New York: Knopf, 2003), loc. 6091, Kindle.

43. Ibid., loc. 7286, Kindle.

44. Ibid., loc. 2722, Kindle.

45. Olivier Darrigol, *A History of Optics: From Greek Antiquity to the Nineteenth Century* (New York: Oxford University Press, 2012), 3.

46. Wright, *An Autobiography,* 3.

47. Sylvia Lavin, "Open the Box: Richard Neutra and the Psychology of the Domestic Environment," *Assemblage,* no. 40 (December 1999): 11.

48. Vivian Hopkins, *Spires of Form: A Study of Emerson's Aesthetic Theory* (New York: Russell and Russel, 1965), 83.

49. Wright, *An Autobiography,* 162.

50. Frank Lloyd Wright, *The Future of Architecture* (New York: New American Library, 1970), 155.

51. Richard Etlin, *Frank Lloyd Wright and Le Corbusier: The Romantic Legacy* (Manchester, UK: Manchester University Press, 1994), 39.

52. Wright, *Selected Writings,* 179.

53. Frank Lloyd Wright, "Organic Architecture," 193–, MSS 2401.187, The Frank Lloyd Wright Foundation Archives (The Museum of Modern Art | Avery Architectural & Fine Arts Library, Columbia University, New York).

54. Thomas Mical, ed., *Surrealism and Architecture* (London: Routledge, 2005), 2.

55. Denis Hollier, *Against Architecture: The Writing of Georges Bataille,* trans. Betsy Wing (Cambridge, MA: MIT Press, 1989), x.

56. See Michel Foucault, "Of Other Spaces, Utopias and Heterotopias," in Neil Leach, ed., *Rethinking Architecture: A Reader in Cultural Theory* (London: Routledge, 1997), 350–55.

57. Le Corbusier, *Oeuvre complète*, vol. 1, *1910–1929*, as found here: http://www.fonda tionlecorbusier.fr/corbuweb/morpheus.aspx?sysId=13&IrisObjectId=5061&sysLanguage =en-en.

58. Ibid.

59. Wright, *Future of Architecture*, 144.

60. Jonathan Crary, *Techniques of the Observer: On Vision and Modernity in the Twentieth Century* (Cambridge, MA: MIT Press, 2001), 42.

61. Ibid., 43.

62. Ibid., 48.

63. Wright, *Future of Architecture*, 117.

64. Ibid., 245.

65. W. G. Sebald, *Vertigo*, trans. Michael Hulse (New York: New Directions, 2000), 17, e-book.

66. Judit Pieldner, "Narrative Discourse, Memory and the Experience of Travel in W. G. Sebald's *Vertigo*," *ActA Universitatis Sapientiae, Philologica* 8, no. 1 (2016): 67–78.

67. Ada Louise Huxtable, *Frank Lloyd Wright: A Life* (New York: Penguin, 2008), loc. 861, Kindle.

68. Jerome Klinkowitz, *Frank Lloyd Wright and His Manner of Thought* (Madison: University of Wisconsin Press, 1914), x.

69. For an in-depth examination of the Progressive Era in Chicago, including a thorough discussion of its contributors, see Jennifer Louise Gray's doctoral dissertation, "Ready for Experiment: Dwight Perkins and Progressive Architecture in Chicago, 1893–1918" (Columbia University, 2011).

4. The Loss of Perspective in Broadacre City

1. Thomas Lemke, *Foucault's Analysis of Modern Governmentality: A Critique of Political Reason*, trans. Erik Butler (London: Verso, 2019), 165.

2. Frank Lloyd Wright, *The Disappearing City* (New York: W. F. Payson, 1932), 21.

3. Ibid., 22.

4. Ibid., 30.

5. Ibid.

6. Ibid., 16.

7. Leo Marx starts his now-iconic *Machine in the Garden* with an analysis of the impact of the locomotive, or the "iron horse," on the countryside, using, among other texts, Irving's "The Legend of Sleepy Hollow."

8. The history of immigration in the nineteenth century is riddled with policies and stories about a preference for white Europeans over other racial groups, especially the Chinese (see Carl Bon Tempo and Hasia Diner, *Immigration: An American History* [New Haven, CT: Yale University Press, 2022]).

9. Ibid., 10.

10. Wright, "Organic Architecture Looks at Modern Architecture," 1950, MSS 2401.305, The Frank Lloyd Wright Foundation Archives (The Museum of Modern Art | Avery Architectural & Fine Arts Library, Columbia University, New York).

11. Wright, "Planning Man's Physical Environment," 1947, Reel 268, Box 6, Folder 6, The Frank Lloyd Wright Foundation Archives (The Museum of Modern Art | Avery Architectural & Fine Arts Library, Columbia University, New York).

12. Quote found in Leo Marx, *The Machine in the Garden: Technology and the Pastoral Ideal in America* (New York: Oxford University Press, 1967), 13.

13. Frank Lloyd Wright, *The Living City* (New York: Horizon, 1958), 38.

14. Octavius Brooks Frothingham, *Transcendentalism in New England: A History* (New York: Harper Torchbooks, 1959), 24.

15. Ralph Waldo Emerson, "Farming," in *Society and Solitude* (Boston: Houghton, Mifflin, 1897), 114.

16. Samuel Butler, *Erewhon, or Over the Range* (Digireads, 2004), 105.

17. Donna Haraway, *Staying with the Trouble: Making Kin in the Chthulucene* (Durham, NC: Duke University Press, 2016), 61.

18. Emerson, "Farming," 115.

19. John Dewey, *John Dewey: The Political Writing*, ed. D. Morris and Ian Shapiro (New York: Hackett, 1993), 87.

20. Henry David Thoreau, "Walking," in *Henry David Thoreau: The Natural History Essays* (Salt Lake City, UT: Peregrine Smith, 1980), 104.

21. Frank Lloyd Wright, *When Democracy Builds* (Chicago: University of Chicago Press, 1945), 94.

22. G. D. H. Cole, quoted in Jean-Jacques Rousseau, *The Social Contract & Discourses*, trans. and introd. Cole (1920; repr., Helvoirt, Netherlands: Heritage, 2019), loc. 89, Kindle.

23. Wright, *When Democracy Builds*, 85.

24. Ibid., 108.

25. Lionel March, "Broadacre City: Intellectual Sources," in *Frank Lloyd Wright: The Phoenix Papers*, vol. 1 (Tempe: Arizona State University), 92–93.

26. Ibid., 92.

27. www.ourdocuments.gov.

28. Lewis Mumford, *The Golden Day: A Study in American Literature and Culture* (Boston: Beacon, 1957), 56.

29. Scott Pratt, *Native Pragmatism: Rethinking the Roots of American Philosophy* (Bloomington: Indiana University Press, 2002), 165.

30. Ibid., 166.

31. Emerson, "Farming," 127.

32. Rousseau, *The Social Contract*, loc. 1718, Kindle.

33. Ibid., loc. 1708.

34. Thorstein Veblen, *The Theory of the Leisure Class* (New York: Dover, 1994), 9.

35. Wright, *When Democracy Builds*, 18.

36. Louis Sullivan, *Democracy: A Man-Search* (Detroit, MI: Wayne State University Press, 1961), 30.

37. Ibid., 28, italics in original.

38. Ibid., 30.

39. Frank Lloyd Wright, *Truth against the World: Frank Lloyd Wright Speaks for an Organic Architecture,* ed. Patrick Meehan (New York: John Wiley and Sons, 1987), 311.

40. Wright, *When Democracy Builds,* 90.

41. Ibid., 97.

42. Mumford, *The Golden Day,* 61.

43. Nikole Hannah-Jones, Caitlin Roper, Ilena Silverman, and Jake Silverstein, eds., *The 1619 Project: A New Origin Story* (New York: New York Times Company, 2021), 172.

44. Ibid., 13.

45. Wright, *When Democracy Builds,* 97.

46. Jack Quinan, *Frank Lloyd Wright's Larkin Building: Myth and Fact* (Chicago: University of Chicago Press, 2006), 100.

47. Ibid., 102.

48. Frank Lloyd Wright, "Aristocracy & Democracy / Our Civilization today / Architecture Must Lead Culture," Reel 67, Box 2, Folder 18, 1953, The Frank Lloyd Wright Foundation Archives (The Museum of Modern Art | Avery Architectural & Fine Arts Library, Columbia University, New York).

49. Veblen, *The Theory of the Leisure Class,* 14.

50. Mumford, *The Golden Day,* 57.

51. Cheryl Robertson, *Frank Lloyd Wright and George Mann Niedecken: Prairie School Collaborators* (Milwaukee, WI: Milwaukee Art Museum, 1999), 14.

52. Wright, *When Democracy Builds,* 84.

53. Ibid.

54. Ralph Waldo Emerson, "Domestic Life," in *The Complete Works of Ralph Waldo Emerson,* vol. 7: *Society and Solitude* (Boston: Houghton, Mifflin, [1903–4]), 115.

55. Thomas Hager, *Electric City: The Lost History of Ford and Edison's American Utopia* (New York: Abrams, 2021), 175.

56. Ibid., 170.

57. John Kenneth Galbraith, *The Great Crash, 1929* (Boston: Houghton Mifflin Harcourt, 2009), 8.

58. Ibid., 13.

59. Ibid., 3.

60. Wright, *When Democracy Builds,* 85.

61. https://www.curbed.com/2018/10/16/17984616/sears-catalog-home-kit-mail-order-prefab-housing.

62. Alvin Rosenbaum, *Usonia: Frank Lloyd Wright Design for America* (New York: Wiley, 1993), 150.

63. Ibid., 151.

64. Wright, *When Democracy Builds,* 91.

65. Frank Lloyd Wright, "Aristocracy and Democracy" and "Talks," 1953, Reel 67, Box 2, Folder 18, The Frank Lloyd Wright Foundation Archives (The Museum of Modern Art | Avery Architectural & Fine Arts Library, Columbia University, New York)

66. Rosenbaum, *Usonia,* 149.

67. Cornelia Brierly, *Tales of Taliesin* (Tempe: Arizona State University, 1999), 10.

68. Frank Lloyd Wright, "Values of Life at Taliesin," in "Talks," 1952, Reel 46, Box 1, Folder 45, The Frank Lloyd Wright Foundation Archives (The Museum of Modern Art | Avery Architectural & Fine Arts Library, Columbia University, New York).

69. Butler, *Erewhon, or Over the Range,* 202.

70. See Quinan, *Frank Lloyd Wright's Larkin Building: Myth and Fact.*

71. See Paul Kruty, *Frank Lloyd Wright and the Midway Gardens* (Champaign: University of Illinois Press, 1998).

72. Quote found ibid., 197.

5. Black & Blue: Mental and Physical Furniture

1. R. W. Emerson, "English Traits: Literature," in *The Complete Works of Ralph Waldo Emerson,* vol. 5 (Boston: Houghton, Mifflin, [1903–4]), 236.

2. Jonathan Lipman, "Consecrated Space: Wright's Public Buildings," in *On and by Frank Lloyd Wright: A Primer of Architectural Principles,* ed. Robert McCarter (New York: Phaidon, 2005), 266.

3. Lisa Stephenson, "Decorating Fiction: Edith Wharton's Literary Architecture," *University of Toronto Quarterly* 79, no. 4 (Fall 2010).

4. Edith Wharton and Ogden Codman, *The Decoration of Houses* (New York: Charles Scribner and Sons, 1917), 19.

5. Frank Lloyd Wright, "Organic Architecture," 1956, Reel 160, Box 4, Folder 19, The Frank Lloyd Wright Foundation Archives (The Museum of Modern Art | Avery Architectural & Fine Arts Library, Columbia University, New York).

6. Frank Lloyd Wright, *When Democracy Builds* (Chicago: University of Chicago Press, 1945), 56.

7. John Ruskin, *The Stones of Venice,* vol. 1 (London: George Allen, 1874), 209.

8. Sophia Psarra, "The Scholar-Collector as a Site of Production: Spatial and Imaginative Intersections in Soane's and Freud's Spaces and Private Collection," in *The Production Sites of Architecture,* ed. Psarra (London: Routledge, 2019), loc. 9, Kindle.

9. See also Ro Spankie's book *Sigmund Freud's Desk: An Anecdoted Guide* (London: Freud Museum, 2017).

10. Frank Lloyd Wright, *An Autobiography* (New York: Duell, Sloan and Pearce, 1943), 145.

11. Ibid.

12. Judith Dunham, *Details of Frank Lloyd Wright: The California Work, 1909–1974* (London: Thames Hudson, 1999), 98.

13. Wright, *An Autobiography*, 80.

14. Leo Tolstoy, *The Death of Ivan Ilych*, trans. Louise and Aylmer Maude (Seven Treasures, 2009), loc. 45, Kindle.

15. Elaine Scarry, *The Body in Pain: The Making and Unmaking of the World* (New York: Oxford University Press, 1985), 39.

16. Frank Lloyd Wright, "Furniture Design for Industry," 1954, Reel 93, Box 2, Folder 43, The Frank Lloyd Wright Foundation Archives (The Museum of Modern Art | Avery Architectural & Fine Arts Library, Columbia University, New York).

17. Paul Goldberger, "Wright's Vision of the Civilized Workplace," *New York Times*, November 1, 1987.

18. Frank Lloyd Wright, "Re-Recording of Ben Raeburn's Questions," 1954, Reel 97, Box 3, Folder 2, The Frank Lloyd Wright Foundation Archives (The Museum of Modern Art | Avery Architectural & Fine Arts Library, Columbia University, New York).

19. Quote found in Cheryl Robertson, *Frank Lloyd Wright and George Mann Niedecken: Prairie School Collaborators* (Milwaukee, WI: Milwaukee Art Museum, 1999), 24.

20. Galen Cranz, *The Chair: Rethinking Culture, Body and Design* (New York: Norton, 1998), 120.

21. See the end of chapter 1 in this book.

22. Roger Friedland and Harold Zellman, *The Fellowship: The Untold Story of Frank Lloyd Wright and the Taliesin Fellowship* (New York: Harper Perennial, 2007), loc. 523, Kindle.

23. Ken Johnson, "The Flaws in Frank Lloyd Wright's Design for Living: The Portland Museum Shows Downside of the Architect's Indoor Vision," *Boston Globe*, August 26, 2007.

24. Wright, *An Autobiography*, 123.

25. Lipman, "Consecrated Space," 266.

26. Ibid., 266, 267.

27. David Hanks, *The Decorative Design of Frank Lloyd Wright* (New York: Dutton, 1985), 19.

28. Maginel Wright Barney, *The Valley of the God-Almighty Joneses*, with Tom Burke (New York: Appleton-Century, 1965), 12.

29. Craig Brandon, *The Electric Chair: An Unnatural American History* (Jefferson, NC: McFarland, 2009), loc. 314, Kindle.

30. Georg Simmel, "The Metropolis and Mental Life," In *Georg Simmel: On Individuality and Social Forms*, ed. Donald N. Levine (Chicago: University of Chicago Press, 1971), 325.

31. Brandon, *The Electric Chair*, loc. 343, Kindle.

32. History.com editors, "First Execution by Electric Chair," https://www.history.com/this-day-in-history/first-execution-by-electric-chair.

33. Brandon, *The Electric Chair*, loc. 2490, Kindle.

34. Simmel, "The Metropolis and Mental Life," 325.

6. The Guggenheim and the Physics of Continuity

1. Frank Lloyd Wright, "Art, Man and Culture," 1952, edited 1960, Reel 37, Box 1, Folder 39, The Frank Lloyd Wright Foundation Archives (The Museum of Modern Art | Avery Architectural & Fine Arts Library, Columbia University, New York).

2. Hilla Rebay, quoted in Brendan Gill, *Many Masks: A Life of Frank Lloyd Wright* (New York: Da Capo, 1988), 433.

3. Frank Lloyd Wright, "Corner Window," 1952, Reel 2, Box 1, Folder 7, The Frank Lloyd Wright Foundation Archives (The Museum of Modern Art | Avery Architectural & Fine Arts Library, Columbia University, New York).

4. Frank Lloyd Wright, "American Architecture," 1937, MSS 2401.372, The Frank Lloyd Wright Foundation Archives (The Museum of Modern Art | Avery Architectural & Fine Arts Library, Columbia University, New York).

5. Ralph Waldo Emerson, *Nature*, in *Ralph Waldo Emerson: Selected Essays,* ed. Larzer Ziff (New York: Penguin, 1983), 75.

6. Ibid.

7. Eduardo Cadava, *Emerson and the Climates of History* (Stanford, CA: Stanford University Press, 1997), 43.

8. Ralph Waldo Emerson, "Farming," in *Society and Solitude* (New York: Houghton Mifflin, 1870), 114.

9. Frank Lloyd Wright, *Letters to Clients: Frank Lloyd Wright,* ed. Bruce Brooks Pfeiffer (Fresno: California State University Press, 1986), 251.

10. Milton Cameron, "Albert Einstein, Frank Lloyd Wright, Le Corbusier, and the Future of the American," Institute for Advanced Study, 1914.

11. Frank Lloyd Wright, *The Natural House* (New York: Horizon, 1954), 21.

12. Frank Lloyd Wright, *The Living City* (New York: Mentor, 1958), xii.

13. Wright, *When Democracy Builds* (Chicago: University of Chicago Press, 1945), 34.

14. Wright, "American Architecture."

15. Wright, *The Living City,* 27.

16. Emerson, *Selected Essays,* 227.

17. Peter Selz, "The Aesthetic Theories of Wassily Kandinsky and Their Relationship to the Origin of Non-Objective Paintings," *Art Bulletin* 39, no. 2 (1957): 127–36.

18. Wassily Kandinsky, *Concerning the Spiritual in Art,* trans. M. T. H. Sadler (New York: Dover, 1977), 15.

19. Sanford Schwartz, "Hilma af Klint at the Guggenheim," *Raritan* 38, no. 4 (2019): 80.

20. Efi Michalarou, "Art-Presentation: Hilma af Klint-Artist, Researcher, Medium," Dream-Idea- Machine, http://www.dreamideamachine.com/.

21. For a thorough examination of af Klint's art and philosophy of spiritualism, see "Hilma af Klint: The Art of Seeing the Invisible," a series of essays assembled in tandem with a major show of her work at the Moderna Museet in Stockholm in 2013 titled *Hilma af Klint: A Pioneer of Abstraction.*

22. Quotes found in William R. Everdell's *The First Moderns: Profiles in the Origins of Twentieth-Century Thought* (Chicago: University of Chicago Press, 1997), a book of great scope that should be consulted for a wider discussion on the diverse forces that constituted Kandinsky's milieu and that shaped the artist's ideas. Interestingly, the author does not mention Hilma af Klint, but that is probably because she only recently, and before *The First Moderns* was published, came of age in the world of scholarship and the discourse on nonobjective art.

23. Brian Greene, *Until the End of Time* (New York: Knopf, 2020), 51.

24. Ibid., 52.

25. Mark Reinberger, "Architecture in Motion: The Gordon Strong Automobile Objective," *Frank Lloyd Wright Quarterly* 29, no. 4 (2019).

26. Wright, *The Living City,* 34.

27. Gill, *Many Masks,* 437, italics in original.

28. biocompare.com.

29. Karen Barad, *Meeting the Universe Halfway: Quantum Physics and the Entanglement of Matter and Meaning* (Durham, NC: Duke University Press, 2007), 19.

30. Gill, *Many Masks,* 438.

31. Stan Allen, *Practice: Architecture, Technique + Representation* (New York: Routledge, 2000), 129.

32. Chris H. Hardy, *Cosmic DNA at the Origin: A Hyperdimension before the Big Bang: The Infinite Spiral Staircase Theory* (self-published, 2015), 83.

33. Ibid., 90.

34. Ibid., 91.

35. https://www.brownstoner.com/forum-archive/2008/01/vertigo-from-sl/.

36. https://www.architecturaldigest.com/story/you-didnt-know-new-york-city-guggenheim-museum.

37. Kandinsky, *Concerning the Spiritual in Art,* 26.

38. Ibid.

39. Henri Bergson, *Matter and Memory,* trans. Nancy Margaret Palmer and Paul Palmer (New York: Macmillan, 1929), 171.

40. Emerson, *Selected Essays,* 294.

41. Ibid., 295.

42. Ibid.

43. Ibid., 299.

44. https://publicdelivery.org/cai-guo-qiang-inopportune/.

45. "Spirituality, Chaos and "Inopportune,'" interview with Cai Guo Qiang, https://art21.org/read/cai-guo-qiang-spirituality-chaos-and-inopportune/.

46. https://publicdelivery.org/cai-guo-qiang-inopportune/.

47. Peter Blake, quoted in Allen, *Practice,* 123.

48. Ibid.

49. Allen, *Practice,* 121.

50. Roland Barthes, *Image-Music-Text* (London: Hill and Wang, 1978), 39.

---

51. Gill, *Many Masks,* 437.

52. Allen, *Practice,* 129.

53. Susan Sontag, *On Photography* (New York: Noonday, 1989), 155.

54. Frank Lloyd Wright, "Talk to Photo Journalism Class at the University of Wisconsin," 1953, Reel 261, Box 6, Folder 20, The Frank Lloyd Wright Foundation Archives (The Museum of Modern Art | Avery Architectural & Fine Arts Library, Columbia University, New York).

55. Sontag, *On Photography,* 156.

BIBLIOGRAPHY

Adams, Henry. *Novels, Mont Saint Michel, The Education.* New York: Viking, 1983.

Aguar, Charles E., and Berdeana Aguar. *Wrightscapes: Frank Lloyd Wright's Landscape Designs.* New York: McGraw-Hill, 2002.

Allen, Gay Wilson. *Waldo Emerson.* New York: Penguin, 1982.

Allen, Stan. *Practice: Architecture, Technique + Representation.* New York: Routledge, 2000.

American Public Architecture: European Roots and Native Expressions. Edited by Craig Zabel and Susan Munshower. Papers in Art History from the Pennsylvania State University, vol. 5. State College: Pennsylvania State University, 2002.

The Arabian Nights: Tales of 1001 Nights. Vol 3: *Nights, 719–1001.* Translated by Malcolm Lyons, with Ursula Lyons. New York: Penguin, 2010.

Arensberg, Mary, ed. *The American Sublime.* Albany: State University of New York Press, 1986.

Bachelard, Gaston. *The Psychoanalysis of Fire.* Translated by Alan C. M. Ross. Boston: Beacon, 1964.

Banham, Reyner. *The Architecture of the Well-Tempered Environment.* 2nd ed. London: Architectural Press, 1984.

Barad, Karen. *Meeting the Universe Halfway: Quantum Physics and the Entanglement of Matter and Meaning.* Durham, NC: Duke University Press, 2007.

Barney, Maginel Wright. *The Valley of the God-Almighty Joneses.* With Tom Burke. New York: Appleton-Century, 1965.

Barolsky, Paul. *Walter Pater's Renaissance.* University Park: Pennsylvania State University Press, 1987.

Barthes, Roland. *Image, Music, Text.* New York: Hill and Wang, 1977.

Bercovitch, Sacvan. *The American Jeremiad.* Madison: University of Wisconsin Press, 1978.

———. *The Puritan Origins of the American Self.* New Haven, CT: Yale University Press, 2011.

Bergdoll, Barry, and Jennifer Gray, eds. *Frank Lloyd Wright: Unpacking the Archive.* New York: Museum of Modern Art, n.d.

Berman, Marshall. *All That Is Solid Melts into Air: The Experience of Modernity.* New York: Penguin, 1988.

Blake, William. *The Portable Blake.* Edited by Alfred Kazin. New York: Viking, 1946.

Bloom, Harold. *The Anatomy of Influence.* New Haven, CT: Yale University Press, 2011.

———. *The Daemon Knows: Literary Greatness and the American Sublime.* New York: Random House, 2015.

Boyer, Paul. *By the Bomb's Early Light: American Thought and Culture at the Dawn of the Atomic Age.* Chapel Hill: University of North Carolina Press, 1994.

———. *Urban Masses and Moral Order in America, 1820–1920.* Cambridge, MA: Harvard University Press, 1978.

Brand, Dana. *The Spectator and the City in Nineteenth-Century American Literature.* New York: Cambridge University Press, 1991.

Brandon, Craig. *The Electric Chair: An Unnatural American History.* Jefferson, NC: McFarland, 2009. Kindle.

Bronowski, Jacob. *William Blake and the Age of Revolution.* London: Faber and Faber, 2008.

Burke, Edmund. *Edmund Burke: A Philosophical Enquiry into the Origin of Our Ideas of the Sublime and Beautiful.* Edited by Paul Guyer. New York: Oxford University Press, 2015.

Burkholder, Robert E., and Joel Myerson. *Critical Essays on Ralph Waldo Emerson.* Boston: G. K. Hall, 1983.

Butler, Samuel. *Erewhon, or Over the Range.* Digireads, 2004.

Cadava, Eduardo. *Emerson and the Climates of History.* Stanford, CA: Stanford University Press, 1997.

Campbell, Joseph. *The Hero with a Thousand Faces.* 3rd ed. Novato, CA: New World Library, 2008.

Carlyle, Thomas. *Carlyle; on Heroes, Hero Worship and the Heroic in History.* Edited by Archibald MacMechan. Boston: Ginn, 1901.

Chernow, Ron. *Alexander Hamilton.* New York: Penguin, 2005.

Cheyfitz, Eric. *The Transparent Sexual Politics in the Language of Emerson.* Baltimore, MD: Johns Hopkins University Press, 1981.

Ciucci, Giorgio, et al. *The American City: From the Civil War to the New Deal.* New York: Granada, 1980.

Conn, Steven, and Max Page, eds. *Building the Nation: Americans Write about Their Architecture, Their Cities, and Their Landscape.* Philadelphia: University of Pennsylvania Press, 2003.

Craig, Theresa. *Edith Wharton: A House Full of Rooms, Architecture, Interiors, and Gardens.* New York: Monacelli, 1996.

Cranz, Galen. *The Chair: Rethinking Culture, Body, and Design.* New York: Norton, 1998.

Crary, Jonathan. *Techniques of the Observer: On Vision and Modernity in the Nineteenth Century.* Cambridge, MA: MIT Press, 2001.

Cronon, William. *Nature's Metropolis: Chicago and the Great West.* New York: Norton, 1991.

Cullen, Jim. *The American Dream: A Short History of an Idea That Shaped a Nation.* New York: Oxford University Press, 2003.

Cunliffe, Marcus, ed. *American Literature to 1900.* Rev. ed. London: Sphere Reference, 1986.

Damrosch, Leopold. *Symbol and Truth in Blake's Myth.* Princeton, NJ: Princeton University Press, 2014.

Daniels, Roger. *Coming to America: A History of Immigration and Ethnicity in American Life.* 2nd ed. New York: Harper Perennial, 1990.

Darrigol, Olivier. *A History of Optics: From Greek Antiquity to the Nineteenth Century.* New York: Oxford University Press, 2012.

De Long, David G., ed. *Frank Lloyd Wright and the Living City.* Weil am Rhein: Vitra Design Museum, 1998.

Dewey, John. *The Essential Dewey.* Vol. 2: *Ethics, Logic, Psychology.* Edited by Larry A. Hickman and Thomas M. Alexander. Bloomingdale: Indiana University Press, 1998.

———. *John Dewey: The Political Writings.* Edited by Debra Morris and Ian Shapiro. Indianapolis, IN: Hackett, 1993.

Desmond, John Michael. "A Clearing in the Woods: Self & City in Frank Lloyd Wright's Organic Communities." PhD diss., MIT, 1996.

Dorman, Robert L. *A Word for Nature: Four Pioneering Environmental Advocates, 1845–1913.* Chapel Hill: University of North Carolina Press, 1998.

Douglass, Frederick. *Narrative of the Life of Frederick Douglass, an American Slave.* Edited by John Stauffer. New York: Library of America, 2014.

Dreiser, Theodore. *Sister Carrie.* 1900. New York: Norton, 1991.

Dunham, Judith. *Details of Frank Lloyd Wright: The California Work, 1909–1974.* London: Thames Hudson, 1999.

Elliott, Emory, ed. *Puritan Influences in American Literature.* Urbana: University of Illinois Press, 1979.

Emerson, Ralph Waldo. *The Complete Works of Ralph Waldo Emerson.* Boston: Houghton, Mifflin, [1903–4].

———. *Essays and English Traits*. Edited by Charles Eliot. Danbury, CT: Grolier Enterprises, 1991.

———. *The Journals and Miscellaneous Notebooks of Ralph Waldo Emerson*. Vol. 4: *1832–1834*. Edited by Alfred R. Ferguson. Cambridge, MA: Belknap Press of Harvard University Press, 1964.

———. *The Portable Emerson*. Edited by Mark Van Doren. 1946; New York: Penguin, 1977.

———. *Ralph Waldo Emerson: Selected Essays*. Edited by Larzer Ziff. New York: Penguin, 1982.

———. *Society and Solitude*. Boston: Houghton, Mifflin, 1870.

Etlin, Richard. *Frank Lloyd Wright and Le Corbusier: The Romantic Legacy*. Manchester, UK: Manchester University Press, 1994.

Everdell, William R. *The First Moderns: Profiles in the Origins of Twentieth-Century Thought*. Chicago: University of Chicago Press, 1997.

Fant, Åke. *Hilma Af Klint: Occult Painter and Abstract Pioneer*. Translated by Ruth Urbom. Stockholm: Bokförlaget Stolpe, 2021.

Filler, Martin. *Makers of Modern Architecture*. Vol. 2: *From Le Corbusier to Rem Koolhaas*. New York: New York Review of Books, 2013.

Fishkin, Shelley Fisher. *Writing America: Literary Landmarks from Walden Pond to Wounded Knee*. New Brunswick, NJ: Rutgers University Press, 2017.

Foucault, Michel. "Of Other Spaces, Utopias and Heterotopias." In *Rethinking Architecture: A Reader in Cultural Theory*, edited by Neil Leach. London: Routledge, 1997.

Frampton, Kenneth. *Modern Architecture: A Critical History*. 5th ed. New York: Thames and Hudson, 2020.

———. *Studies in Tectonic Culture: The Poetics of Construction in Nineteenth and Twentieth Century Architecture*. Edited by John Cava. 1995. Reprint, Cambridge, MA: MIT Press, 2001.

———. *Wright's Writings: Reflections on Culture and Politics, 1894–1959*. New York: Columbia Books on Architecture and the City, n.d.

Freud, Sigmund. *The Interpretation of Dreams*. Translated by James Strachey. 3rd ed. New York: Discus, 1967.

Friedland, Roger, and Harold Zellman. *The Fellowship: The Untold Story of Frank Lloyd Wright and the Taliesin Fellowship*. New York: Harper Perennial, 2007. Kindle.

Frothingham, Octavius Brooks. *Transcendentalism in New England: A History*. New York: Harper Torchbooks, 1959.

Fuller, Randall. *Emerson's Ghosts: Literature, Politics and the Making of Americanists*. New York: Oxford University Press, 2007.

Galbraith, John Kenneth. *The Great Crash, 1929*. Boston: Houghton Mifflin Harcourt, 2009.

Galeano, Eduardo. *The Memory of Fire Trilogy: "Genesis," "Faces and Masks," and "Century of the Wind."* Translated by Cedric Belfrage. New York: Open Road, 2014.

Galvin, Anthony. *Old Sparky: The Electric Chair and the History of the Death Penalty.* New York: Carrel, 2015.

Garraty, John, ed. *Labor and Capital in the Gilded Age: Testimony Taken by the Senate Committee upon the Relations between Labor and Capital—1883.* Boston: Little, Brown, 1968.

Geduld, Harry M., ed. *The Definitive Time Machine: A Critical Edition of H. G. Wells's Scientific Romance.* Bloomington: Indiana University Press, 1987.

George, Henry. *Progress and Poverty.* 1879. New York: Doubleday, 2019.

Gere, Charlotte. *The House Beautiful: Oscar Wilde and the Aesthetic Interior.* London: Lund Humphries, 2000.

Gill, Brendan. *Many Masks: A Life of Frank Lloyd Wright.* New York: Da Capo, 1988.

Graber, Marjorie, and Rebecca Walkowitz. *One Nation under God? Religion and American Culture.* New York: Routledge, 1999.

Greene, Brian. *The Elegant Universe: Superstrings, Hidden Dimensions, and the Quest for the Ultimate Theory.* New York: Norton, 2003.

———. *Until the End of Time: Mind, Matter, and Our Search for Meaning in an Evolving Universe.* New York: Knopf, 2020.

Hager, Thomas. *Electric City: The Lost History of Ford and Edison's American Utopia.* New York: Abrams, 2021.

Hall, A. R. *The Scientific Revolution, 1500–1800: The Formation of the Modern Scientific Attitude.* Boston: Beacon, 1956.

Hanks, David, *The Decorative Design of Frank Lloyd Wright.* New York: Dutton, 1985.

Hannah-Jones, Nikole, Caitlin Roper, Ilena Silverman, and Jake Silverstein, eds. *The 1619 Project: A New Origin Story.* New York: One World, 2021.

Hansen, Olaf. *Aesthetic Individualism and Practical Intellect: American Allegory in Emerson, Thoreau, Adams, and James.* Princeton, NJ: Princeton University Press, 1990.

Haraway, Donna. *Staying with the Trouble: Making Kin the Chthulucene.* Durham, NC: Duke University Press, 2016.

Hardy, Chris. *Cosmic DNA at the Origin: A Hyperdimension before the Big Bang: The Infinite Spiral Staircase Theory.* Self-published, 2015.

Harries, Karsten, *The Ethical Function of Architecture.* Cambridge, MA: MIT Press, 1998.

Hawthorne, Nathaniel. *The Blithedale Romance.* New York: Penguin Classics, 1986.

———. *Selected Tales and Sketches.* Edited by Michael Colacurcio. New York: Penguin, 1987.

Heinz, Thomas A. *Frank Lloyd Wright's Stained Glass & Lightscreens*. Salt Lake City, UT: Gibbs Smith, 2000. Kindle.

Helm, Bertrand. *Time and Reality in American Philosophy*. Amherst: University of Massachusetts Press, 1985.

Hendrickson, Paul. *Plagued by Fire: The Dreams and Figures of Frank Lloyd Wright*. New York: Knopf, 2019.

Herberger, Gary, ed. *Frank Lloyd Wright: The Phoenix Papers*. Vol. 1: *Broadacre City*. Tempe: Arizona State University, College of Architecture and Environmental Design, 1991.

Hertz, David Michael. *Angels of Reality: Emersonian Unfoldings in Wright, Stevens, and Ives*. Carbondale: Southern Illinois University Press, 1993.

Hildebrand, Grant. *The Wright Space: Pattern and Meaning in Frank Lloyd Wright's Houses*. Seattle: University of Washington Press, 1991.

Hitchcock, Henry Russell. *In the Nature of Materials, 1887–1941: The Buildings of Frank Lloyd Wright*. 2nd ed. New York: Da Capo, 1975.

Hoffmann, Donald. *Frank Lloyd's Wright's Fallingwater: The House and Its History*. 2nd rev. ed. New York: Dover, 1993.

Hofstadter, Richard *Anti-Intellectualism in American Life*. New York: Vintage, 1963.

Hollier, Denis. *Against Architecture: The Writings of Georges Bataille*. Translated by Betsy Wing. Cambridge, MA: MIT Press, 1989.

Hollinger, David A., and Charles Capper, eds. *The American Intellectual Tradition*. Vol. 2: *1865 to the Present*. 7th ed. New York: Oxford University Press, 2016.

Hopkins, Vivian. *Spires of Form: A Study of Emerson's Aesthetic Theory*. New York: Russel and Russel, 1965.

Huxtable, Ada Louise. *Frank Lloyd Wright: A Life*. New York: Penguin, 2008. Kindle.

Johnson, Donald. *Frank Lloyd Wright: The Early Years: Progressivism: Aesthetics: Cities*. New York: Routledge, 2017.

Jones, Owen. *The Grammar of Ornament: A Visual Reference of Form and Colour in Architecture and the Decorative Arts*. 1856. Princeton, NJ: Princeton University Press, 2016.

Kandinsky, Wassily. *Concerning the Spiritual in Art*. New York: Dover, 1977.

Kant, Immanuel. *Critique of Judgement*. Translated by Werner S. Pluhar. 1790. Indianapolis, IN: Hackett, 1987. Kindle.

Kaufman, Edgar, ed. *Frank Lloyd Wright: The Early Work*. New York: Horizon, 1968.

Kazin, Michael. *American Dreamers: How the Left Changed a Nation*. New York: Knopf, 2011.

Kevorkian, Martin. *Writing beyond Prophecy: Emerson, Hawthorne, and Melville after the America Renaissance*. Baton Rouge: Louisiana State University Press, 2013.

Klein, Melanie. *Envy and Gratitude and Other Works, 1946–1963*. London: Vintage, 1997. Kindle.

Klinkowitz, Jerome. *Frank Lloyd Wright and His Manner of Thought*. Madison: University of Wisconsin Press, 2014.

Kostof, Spiro, ed. *The Architect*. New York: Oxford University Press, 1977.

Krauss, Rosalind. *The Optical Unconscious*. Cambridge, MA: MIT Press, 1993.

Lears, Jackson. *Rebirth of a Nation: The Making of Modern America, 1877–1920*. New York: Harper Perennial, 2010.

Lemke, Thomas. *Foucault's Analysis of Modern Governmentality: A Critique of Political Reason*. Translated by Erik Butler. New York: Verso, 2019.

Levine, Neil. *The Architecture of Frank Lloyd Wright*. Princeton, NJ: Princeton University Press, 1996.

Lewis, Sinclair. *It Can't Happen Here*. 1935. New York: Signet Classics, 2014.

Lipman, Jonathan. *Frank Lloyd Wright and the Johnson Wax Buildings*. New York: Rizzoli, 1991.

Lopez, Michael. *Emerson and Power: Creative Antagonism in the Nineteenth Century*. DeKalb: Northern Illinois University Press, 1996.

Lyotard, Jean-Francois. *Lessons on the Analytic of the Sublime*. Translated by Elizabeth Rottenberg. Stanford, CA: Stanford University Press, 1994.

Mahoney, Patrick. *Frank Lloyd Wright's Scholarly Clients: William and Mary Heath*. Buffalo: State University of New York Press, 2015.

Makdisi, Saree. *Reading William Blake*. Cambridge: Cambridge University Press, 2015.

Marx, Leo. *The Machine in the Garden: Technology and the Pastoral Ideal in America*. New York: Oxford University Press, 1967.

Matthiessen, F. O. *American Renaissance: Art and Expression in the Age of Emerson and Whitman*. London: Oxford University Press, 1941.

McCarter, Robert, ed. *On and by Frank Lloyd Wright: A Primer of Architectural Principles*. New York: Phaidon, 2005.

McCrea, Ron. *Building Taliesin: Frank Lloyd Wright's Home of Love and Loss*. Madison: Wisconsin Historical Society Press, E-book, 2013.

Meehan, Patrick J., ed. *Frank Lloyd Wright Remembered*. Washington, DC: Preservation Press, 1991.

Menand, Louis. *The Metaphysical Club: A Story of Ideas in America*. New York: Farrar, Straus and Giroux, 2002.

Menocal, Narciso G., ed. *Taliesin, 1911–1914*. Carbondale: Southern Illinois University Press, 1992.

Mitchell, Stephen A., and Margaret J. Black. *Freud and Beyond: A History of Modern Psychoanalytic Thought*. New York: Basic, 1995.

Mumford, Lewis. *The Golden Day: A Study in American Literature and Culture.* Boston: Beacon, 1957.

Murphy, Andrew. *Prodigal Nation: Moral Decline and Divine Punishment from New England to 9/11.* New York: Oxford University Press, 2009.

Muschamp, Herbert. *Man about Town: Frank Lloyd Wright in New York City.* Cambridge, MA: MIT Press, 1983.

Newfield, Christopher. *The Emerson Effect: Individualism and Submission in America.* Chicago: University of Chicago Press, 1996.

Nye, David E. *American Technological Sublime.* Cambridge, MA: MIT Press, 1994.

O'Donnell, Edward. *Henry George and the Crisis of Inequality: Progress and Poverty in the Gilded Age.* New York: Columbia University Press, 2015.

O'Gorman, James F. *Three American Architects: Richardson, Sullivan, and Wright, 1865–1915.* Chicago: University of Chicago Press, 1992.

Packer, Barbara. *The Transcendentalists.* Athens: University of Georgia Press, 2007.

Poe, Edgar Allan. *The Fall of the House of Usher and Other Tales.* Digireads, 2013.

Porter, Carolyn. *Seeing and Being: The Plight of the Participant Observer in Emerson, James, Adams, and Faulkner.* Middletown, CT: Wesleyan University Press, 1981.

Pratt, Scott L. *Native Pragmatism: Rethinking the Roots of American Philosophy.* Bloomington: Indiana University Press, 2002.

Psarra, Sophia, ed. *The Production Sites of Architecture.* London: Routledge, 2019. Kindle.

Quinan, Jack. *Frank Lloyd Wright's Larkin Building: Myth and Fact.* Chicago: University of Chicago Press, 2006.

Raine, Kathleen. *William Blake.* 1970. Reprint, London: Thames and Hudson, 2000.

Reynolds, David. *Beneath the American Renaissance: The Subversive Imagination in the Age of Emerson and Melville.* New York: Knopf, 1988.

Richardson, Robert D., Jr. *Emerson: The Mind on Fire.* Berkeley: University of California Press, 1995.

Robertson, Cheryl, *Frank Lloyd Wright and George Mann Niedecken: Prairie School Collaborators.* Milwaukee, WI: Milwaukee Art Museum, 1999.

Rorty, Richard. *Contingency, Irony, and Solidarity.* New York: Cambridge University Press, 1989.

Rosenbaum, Alvin. *Usonia: Frank Lloyd Wright Design for America.* New York: Wiley, 1993

Rousseau, Jean-Jacques. *The Social Contract & Discourses.* Translated and introduced by G. D. H. Cole. 1920; reprint, Helvoirt, Netherlands: Heritage, 2019. Kindle.

Roy, Donald Francis. "Hooverville: A Study of a Community of Homeless Men in Seattle." Master's thesis, University of Washington, Seattle, 1935.

Scarry, Elaine. *The Body in Pain: The Making and Unmaking of the World.* New York: Oxford University Press, 1985.

Schlesinger, Arthur M., Jr., and Morton White, eds. *Paths of American Thought.* Boston: Houghton Mifflin, 1963.

Sebald, W. G. *Vertigo.* Translated by Michael Hulse. New York: New Directions, 2000. E-book.

Secrest, Meryle. *Frank Lloyd Wright: A Biography.* New York: Harper Perennial, 1993.

Semper, Gottfried. *The Four Elements of Architecture and Other Writings.* Cambridge, UK: Cambridge University Press, 1851.

Siry, Joseph. *Unity Temple: Frank Lloyd Wright and Architecture for Liberal Religion.* New York: Cambridge University Press, 1996.

Slovic, Scott. *Seeking Awareness in American Nature Writing: Henry Thoreau, Annie Dillard, Edward Abbey, Wendell Berry, Barry Lopez.* Salt Lake City: University of Utah Press, 1992.

Smith, A. Mark. *From Sight to Light: The Passage from Ancient to Modern Optics.* Chicago: University of Chicago Press, 2015.

Sontag, Susan. *On Photography.* New York: Noonday, 1989.

Steinbeck, John. *America and Americans.* New York: Viking, 1966.

Sullivan, Louis. *Democracy: A Man Search.* Detroit, MI: Wayne State University Press, 1961.

———. *Kindergarten Chats and Other Writings.* New York: Dover, 1979.

Tandt, Christopher Den. *The Urban Sublime in American Literary Naturalism.* Champaign: University of Illinois Press, 1998.

Thoreau, Henry David. *Henry David Thoreau: The Natural History Essays.* Edited by Robert Sattelmeyer. Salt Lake City, UT: Peregrine Smith, 1980.

———. *"Walden, or Life in the Woods," and "On the Duty of Civil Disobedience."* New York: Harper and Row, 1965.

Toker, Franklin. *Fallingwater Rising: Frank Lloyd Wright, E. J. Kaufmann, and America's Most Extraordinary House.* New York: Knopf, 2003. Kindle.

Tolstoy, Leo. *The Death of Ivan Ilych.* Translated by Louise and Aylmer Maude. Seven Treasures, 2009. Kindle.

Twombly, Robert. *Louis Sullivan: His Life and Work.* Chicago: University of Chicago Press, 1987.

Uechi, Naomi Tanabe. *Evolving Transcendentalism in Literature and Architecture: Frank Furness, Louis Sullivan, and Frank Lloyd Wright.* Newcastle upon Tyne, UK: Cambridge Scholars Publishing, 2013.

Veblen, Thorstein. *The Engineers and the Price System.* New York: Viking, 1934.

———. *The Theory of the Leisure Class.* New York: Dover, 1994.

Versluis, Arthur. *The Esoteric Origins of the American Renaissance.* New York: Oxford University Press, 2001.

Von Frank, Albert. *The Trials of Anthony Burns: Freedom and Slavery in Emerson's Boston.* Cambridge, MA: Harvard University Press, 1998.

West, Cornel. *The American Evasion of Philosophy: A Genealogy of Pragmatism.* Madison: University of Wisconsin Press, 1989.

Wharton, Edith. *The House of Mirth.* Garden City, NY: International Collection Library, n.d.

Wharton, Edith, and Ogden Codman Jr. *The Decoration of Houses.* New York: Charles Scribner's Sons, 1917.

Wieland, Christina. *The Undead Mother: Psychoanalytic Explorations of Masculinity, Femininity, and Matricide.* London: Routledge, 2018.

Wolf, Bryan Jay. *Romantic Re-Vision: Culture and Consciousness in Nineteenth-Century American Painting and Literature.* Chicago: University of Chicago Press, 1982.

Wright, Frank Lloyd. *An Autobiography.* New York: Duell, Sloan and Pearce, 1943.

———. *The Disappearing City.* New York: W. F. Payson, 1932.

———. *Frank Lloyd Wright: Writings and Buildings.* Edited by Edgar Kaufmann and Ben Raeburn. New York: Meridian, 1970.

———. *Frank Lloyd Wright on Architecture: Selected Writings, 1894–1940.* Edited by Frederick Gutheim. New York: Grosset and Dunlap, 1941.

———. *The Future of Architecture.* New York: New American Library, 1970.

———. *Genius and the Mobocracy.* New York: Duell, Sloan and Pearce, 1949.

———. *Letters to Clients: Frank Lloyd Wright.* Edited by Bruce Brooks Pfeiffer. Fresno: California State University Press, 1986.

———. *The Living City.* New York: Horizon, 1958.

———. *The Natural House.* New York: Horizon, 1954.

———. *Truth against the World: Frank Lloyd Wright Speaks for an Organic Architecture.* Edited by Patrick Meehan. New York: John Wiley and Sons, 1987.

———. *When Democracy Builds.* Chicago: University of Chicago Press, 1945.

Wright, Frank Lloyd, and Lewis Mumford. *Frank Lloyd Wright and Lewis Mumford: Thirty Years of Correspondence.* Edited by Bruce Brooks Pfeiffer and Robert Wojtowicz. New York: Princeton Architectural Press, 2001.

Wright, John Lloyd. *My Father Who Is on Earth.* Carbondale: Southern Illinois University Press, 1994.

Wright, Olgivanna Lloyd. *Frank Lloyd Wright: His Life, His Work, His Words.* New York: Horizon, 1966.

———. *The Roots of Life.* New York: Horizon, 1963.

INDEX